Unorthodox Beauty

SRLT

NORTHWESTERN UNIVERSITY PRESS

Studies in Russian Literature and Theory

Unorthodox Beauty

Russian Modernism and Its New Religious Aesthetic

Martha M. F. Kelly

NORTHWESTERN UNIVERSITY PRESS / EVANSTON, ILLINOIS

Northwestern University Press
www.nupress.northwestern.edu

Printed in the United States of America

10 9 8 7 6 5 4 3 2 1

Library of Congress Cataloging-in-Publication Data

Names: Kelly, Martha M. F., author.
Title: Unorthodox beauty : Russian modernism and its new religious aesthetic / Martha M. F. Kelly.
Other titles: Studies in Russian literature and theory.
Description: Evanston, Illinois : Northwestern University Press, 2016.
Series: Northwestern University Press studies in Russian literature and theory
Identifiers: LCCN 2015034894 | ISBN 9780810132399 (cloth : alk. paper) | ISBN 9780810132382 (pbk. : alk. paper)
Subjects: LCSH: Russian poetry—20th century—History and criticism. | Religion in literature. | Modernism (Literature)—Russia (Federation)
Classification: LCC PG3065.R4 K45 2016 | DDC 891.71/3093823—dc23 LC record available at http://lccn.loc.gov/2015034894

To my parents

Contents

Illustrations

Acknowledgments

When I walked into a Russian Orthodox cathedral for the first time in St. Petersburg in September 1996, I had no idea that my notions of church were about to change, along with so much else. In the intervening years, though I have not converted to Orthodoxy, I have undergone a kind of intellectual conversion. As I have deepened and focused my study of Russian literature and culture, the Orthodox tradition has become for me a kind of node, an eloquent intersection of social, political, artistic, and religious threads that connect my own interests and concerns with ongoing themes pervading Russian cultural life. In the course of writing a whole book on Russian modernism and Russian Orthodoxy, I have developed and revised my own understanding of what roles poetry and religion can play in modern life—both separately and together.

I have relied on many people as I have pushed forward in my explorations. The first priest of this project was my advisor, Gregory Freidin, who had the wherewithal to grasp why I would study religious appropriations in these writers rather than the usual suspects; he has shown a sustained and gracious interest in this book. Gabriella Safran, Monika Greenleaf, Lazar Fleishman, Oksana Bulgakowa, and Viktor Zhivov also helped me tremendously in the project's dissertation stage to ask good questions and raise the stakes of my inquiries. They provided me not only through their comments but also through their diverse and engrossing courses an ever richer understanding of Russia's cultural context. The interdisciplinary Orthodoxy Reading Group at Stanford (including my co-organizer Tom Roberts) helped establish my project in a broader conversation and introduced me to relevant historiographical, religious-philosophical, and theological works.

Many people have helped this project evolve at different stages. Sibelan Forrester deserves special thanks for her amalgam of insightful criticism and cheerleading. Other generous readers of portions of the manuscript include Joanna Eleftheriou, Natasha Ermolaev, Maria Khotimsky, Judith Kornblatt, Ol'ga Raevsky-Hughes, Ol'ga Sedakova, Irina Shevelenko, Elise Wirtschafter, and many of my colleagues in the German and Russian Studies

Department at the University of Missouri, including Roger Cook, Stefani Engelstein, Sean Franzel, Sean Ireton, Tim Langen, and Brad Prager. Conversations with George Pahomov, Scott Kenworthy, and with members of the Association for the Study of Eastern Christianity strengthened my sense of Russian Orthodox culture and history. My colleague Gennady Barabtarlo gave me generous assistance in navigating liturgical books and was quick with helpful answers to questions about the minutiae of Russian Orthodox tradition. All these scholars deserve much credit for strengths in this book; responsibility for its remaining flaws resides with the author.

Several organizations have supported my project, sometimes with funding and sometimes in other ways: at Stanford, the Center for Russian, East European and Eurasian Studies and the Division of Literatures, Cultures and Languages; at the University of Missouri, the Research Board, the Research Council, the Arts and Humanities Small Grants program and Special Collections; at the University of Illinois, Urbana-Champaign, the Summer Research Lab on Russia, East Europe and Eurasia Fellowship, Special Collections and the incredible Slavic Reference Service; in Russia, staff of the Russian State Archive of Literature and Art (RGALI) (Moscow); Natalia Kraineva in the Archives of the Russian National Library (St. Petersburg); and Natal'ia Petrovna Pakshchina at the Anna Akhmatova Museum at the House on the Fontanka (St. Petersburg).

Material from two chapters appeared in earlier publications, in somewhat modified form. Part of chapter 1 appeared as "Aleksandr Blok's Other Body" (*The Russian Review* 70 [January 2012], 38–55), and part of chapter 4 appeared as "Social Transformation as Transdisfiguration in Pasternak's *Doctor Zhivago*" (*Russian History* 40, no. 1 [2013], 68–89). I thank the editors of *The Russian Review*, published by Wiley Periodicals, and *Russian History*, published by Brill, for allowing me to reprint this material.

I owe personal debts of gratitude to a number of people: my family, who have been unfailingly supportive in all my work on this book, and many friends, including Ali, Allison, Bonny, Charis, Kyla, Lena, Slava and Ksenia, Mindi and David, Nadya, Zhenya and Dina, Netta, Rose and Sean, Sara, Sylvia, and Valerie. And my dear Gabriel: everything is better with you, even finishing a book manuscript.

Note on Spelling and Abbreviations

I have used Library of Congress transliterations, except in the case of commonly used proper names, such as Dostoevsky and Merezhkovsky. In these cases I have used the familiar spelling. To transliterate Church Slavonic from liturgical texts, I have also used the Library of Congress system ("Church Slavic Romanization").

For sources that I use frequently in the work I have used in-text citations instead of endnotes, employing abbreviations to indicate the relevant volumes. A list of these abbreviations follows.

Abbreviations

AASS Akhmatova, Anna. *Sobranie sochinenii v shesti tomakh*. Moscow: Ellis Lak, 1998.

ABPSS Blok, Aleksandr. *Polnoe sobranie sochinenii i pisem v dvadtsati tomakh*. Moscow: Nauka, 1997.

ABSS Blok, Aleksandr. *Sobranie sochineniia v vos'mi tomakh*. Moscow, Leningrad: Gosudarstvennoe izdatel'stvo khudozhestvennoi literatury, 1962.

APLB Pyman, Avril. *The Life of Alexander Blok*. Vol. 1: *The Distant Thunder, 1880–1908*. New York: Oxford University Press, 1979. And Vol. 2: *The Release of Harmony, 1908–1921*. New York: Oxford University Press, 1980.

BBP Barnes, Christopher. *Boris Pasternak: A Literary Biography. Vol. 2: 1928–1960*. New York: Cambridge University Press, 1998.

DZh Pasternak, Boris. *Doktor Zhivago*, in *Sobranie sochinenii v piati tomakh*, vol. 3. Moscow: Khudozhestvennaia literatura, 1990.

FBP Fleishman, Lazar. *Boris Pasternak: The Poet and His Politics*. Cambridge, Mass.: Harvard University Press, 1990.

FM *The Festal Menaion*. Trans. Mother Mary and Archimandrite Kallistos Ware. London: Faber and Faber, 1977.

LT *The Lenten Triodion*. Trans. Mother Mary and Archimandrite Kallistos Ware. Boston: Faber and Faber, 1978.

M *Minię* (Menaion). Kiev: Kievan Cave Lavra Press, 1893. Reprinted Moscow: Pravilo very, 1996. 12 vols. The Menaion is divided into twelve volumes designated by month of the year. The month given following "M" indicates the particular volume in which the given citation can be found.

MBMK	Malmstad, John E., and Nikolay Bogomolov. *Mikhail Kuzmin: A Life in Art*. Cambridge, Mass.: Harvard University Press, 1999.
MIIE	Mondzain, Marie-José. *Image, Icon, Economy: The Byzantine Origins of the Contemporary Imaginary*. Trans. Rico Franses. Stanford, Calif.: Stanford University Press, 2005.
MKP	Kuzmin, M. A. *Proza*. 3 vols. Ed. Vladimir Markov. Berkeley, Calif.: Berkeley Slavic Specialties, 1984.
MKSS	Kuzmin, M. A. *Sobranie stikhov*. 3 vols. Ed. John E. Malmstad and Vladimir Markov. Munich: Wilhelm Fink Verlag, 1977–78.
MTSS	Tsvetaeva, Marina. *Sobranie sochinenii v semi tomakh*. Moscow: Ellis Lak, 1994.
NBDR	Berdyaev, Nicolas. *Dream and Reality: An Essay in Autobiography*. Trans. Katharine Lampert. London: Geoffrey Bles, 1950.
NBSP	Berdiaev, Nikolai. *Samopoznanie (Opyt filosofskoi avtobiografii)*. Paris: YMCA, 1949.
PBG	Akhmatova, Anna. *"Ia ne takoi tebia kogda-to znala . . .": Anna Akhmatova: Poema bez Geroia, Proza o Poeme. Nabroski baletnogo libretto: Materialy k tvorcheskoi istorii*. Ed. N. I. Kraineva. St. Petersburg: Mir, 2009.
RGALI-MK	Rossiisskii Gosudarstvennyi Arkhiv Literatury i Iskusstva (Russian State Archive of Literature and Art). Fond. 232. Kuzmin Mikhail Alekseevich, op. 1.
SSVSS	Solovyov, Vladimir. *Sobranie sochinenii V. S. Solov'eva*. 12 vols. Brussels: Foyer Oriental Chrétien, 1966.
TP	*Trīōd' postnaę* (Lenten Triodion). Moscow: Moscow Patriarch Press, 1992.
TTs	*Trīōd' tsvětnaę* (Flowery Triodion). Moscow: Izdanie Moskovskoi patriarkhii, 1992.

Unorthodox Beauty

Introduction

> The basic theme of Russian thought at the beginning of the twentieth century is the theme of the divine in the cosmos, of cosmic divine transfiguration, of the energies of the Creator in creation. It is the theme of the divine in man, of the creative vocation of man and the meaning of culture. It is an eschatological theme of the philosophy of history.
>
> —Nikolai Berdiaev, *The Russian Idea*

AT THE CENTURY'S very turn, Rainer Maria Rilke made a pilgrimage to Russia. The first fruits of his journey appear in his early and luminous *Book of Hours* (*Das Stundenbuch*, 1905).[1] In the section "The Book of Monkish Life" ("Das Buch vom mönchischen Leben," 1899), the reader witnesses the inner experience of a monk and icon-painter, Apostol, as he prays before an iconostasis. For Apostol the wall of icons figures as the perceived wall between the believer and God:

> The wall is built from your images.
>
> And your images stand in front of you like names,
> And when the light in me flares forth
> by which my deepest self knows you,
> the radiance is squandered on their frames.
>
> And my senses, which quickly flag,
> are homeless and depart from you.[2]

(Aus deinen Bildern ist sie aufgebaut. // Und deine Bilder stehn vor dir wie Namen. / Und wenn einmal das Licht in mir entbrennt, / mit welchem meine Tiefe dich erkennt, / vergeudet sichs als Glanz auf ihren Rahmen. // Und meine Sinne, welche schnell erlahmen, / sind ohne Heimat und von dir getrennt.)[3]

In these lines the poet seeks to dissolve barriers to knowing; he hopes for sense to lead to transcendence. If we read this poem through the lens of priest and symbolist Pavel Florensky's *Iconostasis* (1922), Apostol experiences a momentary resolution to the tension he knows between Eastern and Western European art, between tradition and innovation, between spirit and flesh. For Florensky post-Renaissance Western art comprises "aesthetic delusion," blocking the viewer from a spiritual reality beyond by its emphasis on mimesis, or on mechanically reproducing the appearance of earthly reality.[4] Eastern European art, represented by the icon, however, "*speaks* . . . the Name of God"—that is, because its form "accords to its essential symbolism," it serves as a conduit for the viewer to ascend to God.[5]

This conducive power of the icon seems reflected in Rilke's poem. In Apostol a light by which the monk knows God flares up, called forth by the icons. In the radiance "squandered" on the icons' frames we find, in fact, an image not of wasted energies but of excess luminosity from light meeting light: when the monk's inner light meets the gilt of the icons—their "sent light"—evoking the moment of knowledge, of meeting with God. The wall, like God's name, stands not as barrier but as gateway. Indeed, Rilke, who immersed himself for periods in the study of icon traditions, emphasizes in his many depictions of icons in this volume the use and symbolism of gilt, which represents the divine presence and the divine energies that can penetrate and transform the human person, body and soul, uniting her with God. In such a reading of Rilke's poem the deepest, most inaccessible part of the person unites with God through the medium of the icon that he contemplates. Rilke endows this poem, however, with certain ramifications for this union, which Florensky's theological aesthetics set forth with such certainty. While the icon wall seems to call to the prayer's inmost self, the refracting action of the frames suggests at least a partial (if not a total) frustration of the monk's efforts to pierce the divide. Even if we see, between the lines, a fleeting connection, the senses cannot sustain it. Artistic form, then, both mediates and obscures the experience of union.

In many ways this poem captures the intended look of Russian modernism—a look *through* and a look *beyond*, and at once a look *inward*. Rilke's poem projects the hope that through physical sense, through the body, the individual might come to know in its essence something beyond himself—even if only in a flash of insight. The dumb frames, like names, seem to channel this union and recede behind it—but only for a moment, after which they rear up again as the senses slacken. But if a window opens to let the senses connect with what lies beyond, the individual also returns to his "depths," or his deepest being (*meine Tiefe*).

Rilke knowingly accesses the icon tradition, which proposes the believer's immediate access to the holy presence through crafted earthly media.

Icons, which had enjoyed a rediscovery at the end of the nineteenth century, denote a specifically Russian spirituality and also an alternative narrative for Western modernity. If God can be known through matter and not mind, we have sidestepped Descartes. Rilke's poem cannily echoes Russian modernism in its evocation of an exceptional relation between beauty, sense, and knowledge.

While Russian modernists hastened toward a cosmopolitan worldview, embracing many aspects of European modernism, they had their own word to say; we hear it most clearly in their evocations of Russian Orthodoxy. In Russian modernism we find in tension with fragmentation and fracture a sustained quest for integrality. In this period Russia's artists imagine Russia as able to withstand the fragmentation of self and society conceptualized in the discourse of modernity. While they envision a struggle rather than a fait accompli, they anchor their hopes in the peculiarities of Orthodox Christianity. In this, the dominant Russian religious tradition, they often see a connection with Russia's unsecularized masses; they also see a non-dualist worldview, according to which things can be directly known through both sense and sign, and the intelligible and sensible realms converge. Russian modernism was a religious movement of a unique kind. It brought together Orthodoxy and the ideas of the Slavophiles and other Russian religious philosophers with Nietzsche and with elements of many religious traditions to posit a new aesthetics based on the unity of spirit and matter. This book shows how four prominent modernist poets—Aleksandr Blok, Mikhail Kuzmin, Anna Akhmatova, and Boris Pasternak—pursue such unity. In their work we find related models for a new pursuit of religion in late modernity.

In what follows I will describe Russian modernism as an artistic and cultural movement starting somewhere around 1893—when Dmitry Merezhkovsky first published his groundbreaking critical essay, "On the Reasons for the Decline and the New Currents in Contemporary Russian Literature"—and ending somewhere around 1930, with the inception of the first Five-Year Plan (1928–1933) and the lead-up to the First Soviet Writer's Congress in 1934.[6] From a theoretical standpoint, my understanding of modernism as an international phenomenon accords closely with Astradur Eysteinsson's model, in which modernist art (especially literature) neither functions autonomously from everyday practical and political affairs, nor, conversely, reflects an existential disruption that modernity somehow incurs. Eysteinsson views modernism, rather, as "an attempt to *interrupt* the modernity that we live."[7] Russian modernism especially accords with this model, in its conscious attempts to speak a new word into the modern world.

From a cultural standpoint, I view Russian modernism as a series of responses to—above all—Friedrich Nietzsche and Vladimir Solovyov, two philosophers whose mystical leanings and elevation of the aesthetic had tremendous resonance in Russia. In *The Revolution of Moral Consciousness* Edith Clowes outlines how Nietzsche's critique of positivism, mystical attitude, and emphasis on the aesthetic helped inspire a new art and new social perspectives in Russia.[8] Perhaps even more important were Solovyov's mystical poetry and his religious-philosophical works that modeled and described how artists could sublimate and channel the erotic into art that would transfigure the world. The influence of these figures was manifested in modernists' privileging of the aesthetic over the utilitarian, in their forays into mystical experience and mystical art, in their creation of many kinds of rituals, both secular and unorthodoxly religious. The phenomenon of *zhiznetvorchestvo*—life-creation—as Irina Paperno, Joan Delaney Grossman, and others have described it, perfectly encapsulates the concrete applications of these thinkers' ideas, in concert with other influences.[9] In the life-creating current of Russian modernism artists reflected their lives rather directly in their art and also crafted their own lives into works of art. They sought new ways to live out gender and sex according to their heady theories.[10] Some artists experimented with mystical erotic triangles in intriguingly literal interpretations of Solovyov's ideas. The figures of commedia dell'arte came to stand as emblems of this kind of modernism, with its all-encompassing role-playing and theatricality—but modernist culture often lacked the playfulness of this stage tradition, seeing in its life-art the key to personal and national fulfillment.[11] As Paperno suggests, modernism itself planted the seeds of Soviet aesthetics in the 1920s and 1930s, in its insistence that art could construct new worlds.[12]

But Nietzsche, Solovyov, *zhiznetvorchestvo*, and commedia dell'arte are just the beginning of the story. Alongside all these philosophical and literary developments came a growing interest on the part of the Russian intelligentsia and artistic elite in Russia's religious past. This interest expressed itself in many areas. Key realist writers such as Tolstoy and Dostoevsky had not simply depicted religious (and especially Orthodox) settings, but they had themselves both made visits to influential *startsy*, or "elders," men known for their wisdom and spiritual authority. This ancient tradition had seen a massive resurgence in Russian in the nineteenth century especially.[13] Beyond the realm of letters, though, artists gathered at an estate called Abramtsevo, outside Moscow, sought to create a new Russian visual art for a new Russian culture.[14] Supported and inspired by the wealthy Savva Mamontov, painters such as Vasily Polenov, Ilya Repin, Victor Vasnetsov, Mikhail Nesterov, and Mikhail Vrubel' turned not only to Russian historical, folk, and religious themes, but also to historical models, including the Byzantine icon tradition and Russian church architecture. (See figure i.) They would even receive commissions to decorate church interiors with lavish religious scenes. (See figure ii.) These

Figure i. Page from *World of Art* (*Mir iskusstva*) journal (nos. 10–11, 1903) with reproduction of *Weeping at the Grave* by Mikhail Vrubel' and graphic by Stepan Iaremich.
Courtesy of the Division of Special Collections, Archives, and Rare Books, University of Missouri.

and other groundbreaking forays into Russia's archaeology and aesthetics were featured and echoed in modernist journals, such as *World of Art* (*Mir iskusstva*), which brought images of and essays on art from around the world together with lavishly illustrated pieces on Russian art and architecture, not infrequently of a religious nature. We find, for instance, a feature in 1904 on the patriarch's sacristy, its historic collection of ornate and valuable ritual objects (pictured in figures iii and iv).[15] The immensely productive and influential explorations of the Abramtsevo circle were paralleled and aided by unprecedented study of the Russian icon beginning in about the 1880s. With the renewed interest in the icon came an intense interest in restoring icons, and in 1913, the Exhibition of Old Russian Art in Moscow brought to the public an astounding collection of these icons with newly revealed features.[16] Nikolai Punin, an art critic and later husband to Akhmatova, wrote of the exhibition as "a revelation to us all! Has not a new artistic consciousness begun in Russia?"[17] Other modernists—Merezhkovsky, Valery Briusov, and Viacheslav

Figure ii. Page from *World of Art* (*Mir iskusstva*) journal (no. 12, 1904) with photograph of Mikhail Nesterov's murals in the Alexander Nevsky Church in Abastumani, Georgia.
Courtesy of the Division of Special Collections, Archives, and Rare Books, University of Missouri.

Ivanov among them—reinvigorated legends of Moscow as the Third Rome and imagined ways that Russia could bridge Western antiquity and Eastern spirituality to render a more integral modernity.[18]

"HOLY FLESH": THE RELIGIOUS-PHILOSOPHICAL MEETINGS

In the autumn of 1901, the first Religious-Philosophical Meeting—without which this story cannot be told—took place. Organized by members of the intelligentsia in hopes of establishing dialogue with representatives of the Russian Orthodox clergy, the meetings were held regularly from 1901 to 1903 and served—for a few years, at least—as one of the only forums in which intelligentsia and clergy alike could freely address social, cultural, and political topics in a public setting.[19] The meetings were initiated and sus-

Figure iii. Page from *World of Art* (*Mir iskusstva*) journal (no. 10, 1904) with title page of article, "The Patriarch's Sacristy." Illustration by Viktor Zamirailo surrounding a photograph of the Epigonation (*Palitsa*) of Metropolitan Photios of Constantinople.
Courtesy of the Division of Special Collections, Archives, and Rare Books, University of Missouri.

tained largely by the efforts of Zinaida Gippius and Dmitry Merezhkovsky, through whose circle of influence much of Russian modernism initially passed. Indeed, Merezhkovsky's 1893 essay "On the Reasons for the Decline and on the New Directions of Contemporary Russian Literature" served as a milestone on the road that much of the Russian intelligentsia traveled from populism to the "religious renaissance."[20] The essay presents the Russian educated classes as cut off from life by the abstracted and artificial modes of knowledge inherited from European philosophy, and it calls the intelligentsia to turn to the faith of the projected Russian people in order to re-infuse themselves with life—and to draw more ably the people into a truly enlightened modernity. In the essay, Merezkovsky asserts,

> Lest we [the intelligentsia] perish in abstraction, in emptiness, in faithlessness, we must protect our blood link with the source of all power and all

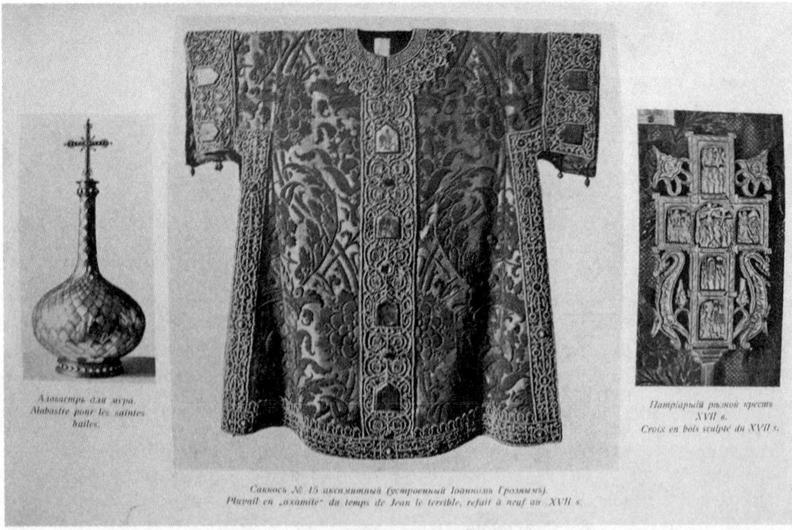

Figure iv. Page from *World of Art* (*Mir iskusstva*) journal (no. 10, 1904) with photographs of objects in the patriarch's sacristy, including a liturgical vestment dating from the time of Ivan IV.
Courtesy of the Division of Special Collections, Archives, and Rare Books, University of Missouri.

> faith—with the people [*s narodom*]. . . . Only by returning to God can we return to our people, to our great Christian people. There is no other path. And of course then we will not be ashamed of beauty, or of Pushkin, of poetry or of European culture, of statistics or of political economy, for the people have greater need of this even than we, or rather, they *will* have greater need of it.[21]

In some senses the essay follows a discourse of degeneracy common throughout Europe (and indeed, its main theoreticians were well known in Russia), but its call to turn to Orthodoxy, to the people's religion, has a unique ring to it, compared to its European counterparts. This note resounded throughout the Religious-Philosophical Meetings and, moreover, informed the work of Silver Age artists, whether in sympathy or not.

Other scholars have told the story of this group (although a great deal remains to be explored), but for the purposes of this study, its key interest lies in the practical dialogue these meetings forged between the intelligentsia and the Orthodox Church.[22] The meetings lasted only two years (although similar meetings were held later), and the influence of Gippius and Merezhkovsky—with their attempts at starting their own, bizarre church—secured an ambiguous legacy (as adduced, for instance, by Andrey Bely's memoirs).[23] But hundreds of educated Russians flocked to these meetings, including Blok and Bely, for here the intelligentsia could discuss their knowledge and sense of Orthodoxy in an effort to understand what common ground they could discover or cultivate with the spiritual tradition that lay right under their noses. The transcripts of these meetings (published in the journal *A New Way* [*Novyi put'*]) demonstrate in particular a desire on the part of the intelligentsia to know how Orthodoxy might figure in everyday life and, moreover, to envision how their work and gifts might transform the role of Orthodox spirituality in culture. For Merezhkovsky and others, the Orthodox Church upheld only an ideal pertaining to life beyond the grave (*zagrobnyi ideal*), "without the embodiment of truth," and the intelligentsia had the resources—indeed, was called—to "bring back to life the dead and deadly letter, imbuing it with the real content of life."[24] That is, the intelligentsia was to translate Orthodoxy into terms relevant for life—through applying to it the scientific disciplines, but also through creating artistic and cultural forms—models, or embodiments, of truth and meaning.

In the end the meetings came to a standstill due to the apparent lack of success in finding a common language between clergy and intelligentsia; yet ultimately their concerns could be addressed not through talk but only through sustained effort.[25] What transcripts of these meetings cannot tell is the way that artists increasingly thereafter fostered their own visions of a Russian religious art, and how some of Russia's intelligentsia (not to say its artists) became the center of an international renewal of Orthodox Christianity and a new instilling of its theology with forms accessible to the modern person.[26] The paper with which Valentin Ternavtsev opened the meetings—"The Great Task Facing the Russian Church" foresees, in a sense, this trajectory. An "intelligent" and teacher at the theological academy, he emphasizes the self-sacrificing service that he believes the intelligentsia had rendered Russia's people throughout the centuries, fighting for social and political reforms on their behalf; and he suggests that their service now must be focused on a renewal of culture by means of religion. In his words, "*The rebirth of Russia can take place—on a religious basis*" (*na religioznoi pochve*; italics in the original).[27] Orthodox Christianity lacked a form palpable to society, embroiled as it was in questions of the "spirit"; the intelligentsia, on the other hand, "accepted and taught the 'Copernican heaven,' murderously shut over mankind." While Ternavtsev includes here an implicit critique of the intelligentsia, he also notes that their focus on the earth spurred the group to social action, forcing them "to view the earth as the single refuge of our existence and human society as the single arena of every action, every sacrificial deed" (*podvig*).[28] Increasingly, conversations between these two groups would become bogged down in questions of doctrine and confessionality. But the topics that fascinated and drew the representatives of the intelligentsia—church history, delineations of physical and mystical love, rearticulations of ancient Christian texts—found their way into their writing and art. In *The Russian Idea*, Nikolai Berdiaev writes of these meetings that

> everything said by the representatives of secular culture presumed the possibility of a new religious consciousness, of a new epoch in Christianity. This was hard for the hierarchs of the Church, even for the most enlightened. For the representatives of the clergy, Christianity had long since become everyday prose, but those who sought a new Christianity wished it to be poetry.[29]

VLADIMIR SOLOVYOV AND ART'S NEW BODY

Without question the most important figure to stimulate this quest for a new, poetic Christianity was Vladimir Solovyov. Russia's greatest religious philosopher and also a poet, Solovyov aimed to reinvigorate Western philosophical traditions with religious approaches adapted particularly from Orthodoxy. For Solovyov beauty is paramount, and therefore art plays a special role in his project. A number of his works influenced the discussions leading up to the Religious-Philosophical Meetings. Notably in "Beauty in Nature" (1889) the philosopher writes that beauty would save the world (*Krasota spaset mir*) (*SSVSS*, 6:33).[30] Here the philosopher demonstratively borrowed from art itself, taking as epigraph Dostoevsky's hopeful prescription for a human race in which "everyone has a limp of some kind."[31] Dostoevsky, Solovyov, and their Silver Age successors in Russia saw modern society as a body divested of its original beauty, a body fragmented, even dissected.[32] Solovyov's thesis, "The Crisis of Western Philosophy," suggested that modern models of knowing bore the blame. A focus on individual and empirical knowledge rendered a world teeming with "material, mechanical phenomena . . . the monstrous phantom of the dead external reality of material separateness" (*SSVSS*, 1:150).[33] Analytic thought, with its principle of "decomposition" into parts, could not reintegrate this world (which, it seems, took a wrong turn in medieval scholasticism), but only a philosophical thought with the "character of *religion*" (*SSVSS*, 1:101, 29, 118).[34]

In this work and his *Lectures on Godmanhood*, Solovyov presents a "positive dialectic," as Richard Gustafson calls it, by which the achievements of Western philosophy must undergo a synthesis with the Christian truth preserved in Eastern Orthodoxy in order to create a truly Christian culture and, through it, universal harmony.[35] Solovyov sometimes proves more sanguine about Western philosophy than Slavophile predecessors such as Aleksei Khomiakov and Ivan Kireevsky; but like them he emphasizes that primarily the *narod*, the (unmodernized and largely uneducated) people, has preserved a capacity for unity thanks especially to its preservation of religious faith. At the heart of *narod* culture, for Solovyov and Slavophiles alike, dwells Russian Orthodoxy. The philosopher centers his vision of the renewed flesh on Eastern Christian notions of *theosis*, as Gustafson persuasively shows.[36] *Theosis*, or deification—literally, divinizing the human being or making them more like God—is a central term in Eastern Christianity, not least in Russian Orthodoxy, and is used to describe the spiritual path as that tradition understands it.

Indeed, we find clear references to and reflections of *theosis* and the Transfiguration in Solovyov's poetry. Solovyov's poetic works, though relatively slim and often overlooked, in fact constitute an important part of his contribution to Russian modernist aesthetics. Judith Kornblatt has shown how the philosopher's poems encapsulate many of the concerns of his other work, especially "the incomprehensible interpenetration of the divine and the material."[37] We find the direct lineage of Solovyov's poems not least in the work of Aleksandr Blok, whose seminal early volume *Verses on the Most Beautiful Lady* emerged partly in response to a volume of Solovyov's poems (*APLB*, 1:69). In terms of Transfiguration/*theosis* tradition, consider two brief examples from Solovyov's poetry. In an 1886 poem the poetic voice testifies, "In mid-day rays by such burning languor / Grace descended from the shining heavens" ("Zemlia-vladychitsa! K tebe chelo sklonil ia . . . ," *SSVSS*, 12:22). Here we find the image of divine grace, or divine energies—the divine action in the world—as rays of light descending from heaven, a key image in *theosis* theology, as well as in Transfiguration icons. In another poem inspired by the philosopher-poet's encounter with Sophia in Cairo we read, "And in the rays of the rising day / The soul lit up with a quiet light" ("Vsia v lazuri segodnia iavilas' . . . ," *SSVSS*, 12:12). On one hand, casting the vision of the beloved in the language of light is typical enough, not least for romantic thought. And indeed, as Gustafson and others have pointed out, Schelling was very influential for Solovyov. On the other hand, Gustafson also points out that Schelling was drawing on early patristic theology, much as Solovyov was—and it is in patristic theology that one finds the fundamental articulations of *theosis*.[38] We find a great deal of language and imagery drawn from *theosis* tradition in Solovyov's prose, too.[39]

Merezhkovsky sees in Solovyov's work an approach to bringing about social justice with new tools—not with the tools of positivism and rationalism alone. Viewing Solovyov as emblematic of new movements in Russian literature and thought, he writes that here, "social justice once more emerges . . . as a boundless and divine ideal, as a sacred reserve [*sviatynia*], as inspiration, in the aureole of beauty and poetry."[40] Indeed, for Merezhkovsky, Solovyov, and many others, the new body and its new world would emerge at the intersection of religion, beauty, and social engagement. Not only did Solovyov base his own body of philosophical work on mystical visions of the Beautiful Lady, Sophia, but he also built key works on literary fundaments. More than decoration, poetry in essays such as "Beauty in Nature" (1889) and "The Universal Meaning of Art" (1890) seeks to revitalize philosophy from within, to endow moribund discourse with effective beauty (*SSVS*, 6:33–74, 75–92).[41] (We can see Pavel Florensky's artistic *Pillar and Ground of Truth*, a theology in epistolary form, as seeking to achieve a similar renovation of non-aesthetic discourse through aesthetic method.)[42]

For key readers of Solovyov, however, it was not the philosophers who would restore modernity, but the artists. In his 1908 essay "Two Elements in Contemporary Symbolism" Viacheslav Ivanov summarizes Solovyov's call to artists as he understands it from "Three Meetings" and even quotes Solovyov on this point in his "Three Speeches in Memory of Dostoevsky":

> Vladimir Solovyov posits the theurgical task as the highest task of art. By the theurgical task of the artist, he means a world-transfiguring revelation of supernatural reality and the emancipation of true beauty out from beneath the coarse coverings of matter. Solovyov spoke in this sense in his speeches on Dostoevsky: "artists and poets must once again become high priests and prophets, but now in another, even more important and sublime sense: not only will they be possessed by the religious idea but they themselves will possess it and consciously govern its earthly incarnations."[43]

The term "theurgy" finds relatively common use among the symbolists especially, and here Ivanov outlines what I will refer to as the "sophianic task" that not a few Russian modernists adapt. For Ivanov the task that Solovyov sets forth for artists—the theurgic task—is to incarnate in their works of beauty the eternal beauty that can transfigure the world. His description of emancipating beauty "out from beneath the coarse coverings of matter" speaks eloquently to the ways Ivanov and his peers would embrace the material world (bodies, earth, cultural rites and realia, artistic media of all kinds) as providing conduits for eternal realities.[44]

Solovyov's revitalization of philosophy with literary elements and his call for theurgy epitomize his broader project, and the project the present study will explore—that is, the "sophianic task" Ivanov describes and consciously tries, with many others, to body out. In choosing the term "sophianic" instead of the more commonly used term "theurgic" I wish to emphasize the engagement with matter and not only spirit that Solovyov intends in the Sophia figure. Religion in the Silver Age has often been viewed through the lens of Solovyov's work, and especially his visions of Sophia. Solovyov plays a major role in the periods under discussion. A central goal of the present study, however, is to show that each writer responds not merely to

Solovyov, but to a larger impulse in their epoch that Solovyov's work represents. In service of this key aim I will draw especially on Paul Valliere's characterization of sophiological thought (not only Solovyov's, but also Sergei Bulgakov's) as offering a "conceptual representation of the dialogue between the Orthodox theological tradition and modern liberal civilization."[45] The sophianic impulse as I will present it here, then, is an impulse to unite: earthly and heavenly, human and divine, flesh and spirit, secular and sacred. As Oliver Smith comments in his study on Solovyov, Sophia represented or even demonstrated to the philosopher and poet "the consonance between the spiritual and material realms" and, as such, remained a "constant backdrop to his thinking."[46] At the same time, as Judith Kornblatt points out in her work on Solovyov's sophian writings, even within the work of this one religious philosopher diverse Sophias emerge.[47] Our task in this study, then, is not to apply a monolithic reading of Solovyov or of Sophia across modernist poetic works but rather to understand how poets adapted Orthodox traditions—as they encountered them—to craft a new religious aesthetic for a new world.

It is important to emphasize from the outset, moreover, that the authors I treat here come at the sophianic task from divergent angles—a fact that can hardly surprise us. In fact, the authors' divergent approaches to this task will comprise the central drama of this book. Blok and Pasternak hew relatively closely to a Solovyovian model, even as they adapt it to their own purposes. For both of these writers the beauty of the universal feminine element draws humanity toward transfiguration into its divinized self. Kuzmin, however, transcribes this task into differently gendered terms and at the same time shifts the focus from Sophia as the transfigurational object of desire to Sophia as an emblem of embodiment of the divine element. He seems to draw, notably, more on the Gnostic sophian texts themselves than on Solovyov's renditions of them. Akhmatova, meanwhile, presents a more refracted relationship to the sophianic project. Her poetry indisputably advances a project to adapt Orthodox tradition and liturgical culture to a modern context—therefore echoing Valliere's discussion of "sophiological" thought. But for her, as with Marina Tsvetaeva, whom we will discuss briefly, the role of the feminine element and especially the female body plays a much more problematic role. The writings of both these women poets display a keen consciousness of the implications of embodiment—on a literal and metaphoric level—and of the ways sophianic discourse extends and relies on the association of woman with flesh. In this sense they engage with the "sophianic task" by way of critique, yet still essaying the possible relations between spirit and flesh. In the very act of complicating and critiquing sophianic discourse and offering alternative revisions of Orthodox culture, they confirm the importance of the sophianic project as one to which modernist writers felt compelled to respond. Akhmatova's *Poem without a Hero* represents the most direct critique we will explore of modernism's sophianic project—and canonizes this project by placing it at the very center of the work's dark revaluation of Russian modernism.

MODERNISM AND THE NON-RATIONAL

The penchant toward poetry in Solovyov's philosophy emblematizes the fin-de-siècle move away from empirical modes toward non-rational modes of knowing the world.[48] "If 'thought,' i.e., any rational cognition, is a 'lie,' then one must cherish all extrarational forms of apprehending the world," wrote Valery Briusov in 1910.[49] French poets such as Baudelaire, whose work and poetics Briusov did so much to promote in Russia, oozed with the "extrarational." Consider, for instance, Baudelaire's "Le Poison" from *Fleurs du mal* (1857).[50] Here, wine, opium, sex, dream, "la volupté" (sensuousness) engender and dominate the poetic landscape and the poet's reality. Across the West literature and art witness a move away from realism and toward the realm of sensation, dream, intuition, imagination, fantasy, mysticism, ritual, and spirituality. The French symbolists flesh out this focus on sensuality and intuition through the intoxicating confusion of sense and the senses, as when Mallarmé exclaims "Hosanna on the lute and in the censers, / Our Lady, hosanna of our limbo garden bed!"[51] In English letters, Poe heralds a shift toward mystery and the fantastical, while Yeats echoes in "The Celtic Element in Literature" (1898) and in his poetry the rising interest in primitive religion and ritual exemplified in J. G. Frazer's *Golden Bough*. The English aestheticism and decadence movements also rejected many of the tenets of a utilitarian worldview, insisting that art holds its own.[52] German aestheticist poets such as Rilke and Stefan George express "an unfulfilled longing at the heart of modernity that seeks to establish an immediate, unalienated, and nonsignifying contact among everything in the world," according to Carsten Strathausen.[53] For them, aesthetic experience serves as "a sort of religious epiphany that allegedly spiritualizes and redeems external reality from the inside out."[54] Across Europe and the West modernism responds to realist and positivist modes and proposes its own ways of knowing.

At the same time, there is something special about Russian modernism. That is to say, Russian modernists consciously distinguished their art from that of their European counterparts. Specifically, they identified the modernist turn to alternate modes of knowledge as nothing more or less than a manifestation of ancient Russian tradition, via Byzantine iconophilia. As Strathausen points out, even Rilke's poetry quickly begins to exhibit a tension between transcendence and the impossibility of immanence. Certainly this same tension often characterizes Russian modernism. Yet for Rilke and other Western modernists, the tension arises from creeping doubt that art can offer the transcendence and/or communality once credited to religion; whereas for Russian modernists, the tension arises from doubt that a turn to religious tradition comes in time. Consider, for instance, Mallarmé's poem "Windows" ("Les Fenêtres"), which associates religion (and its "horrific holy oils") with "the impure vomit of Inanity"—that is, with the earthly, from which one desperately tries to escape into the eternal and infinite, the blue.[55] By contrast Merezhkovsky and Solovyov and the modernists who reflect or extend the concerns they express see in established religion (of a Russian variety, in any case) a potential window into eternity.

Such Russian exceptionality bears closely on two concerns. First, Russian artists are keen to demonstrate Russia's significance among European nations, and they do so by pointing to a religious tradition that seems to obviate key modern philosophical problems by its emphasis on the unity of flesh and spirit, sense and transcendence—seen especially in the sensuality and materiality of its ritual and its icons. Second, Russian artists express a concern for national unity in their attempt to return to Russian Orthodoxy specifically as a means to bringing together peasants and Westernized (rather secularized) elite. On one hand, the modernists are echoing nineteenth-century Slavophile ideas about Russia's character and role in history; on the other hand, the cosmopolitanism intrinsic to their work and thought establishes a more complex and refracted relationship with Orthodoxy.

CONSTRUCTIVE APPROPRIATIONS

This study explores Russia's relation to modernity through its poetry, and especially modernist poetry concerned with religious tradition. Likewise it presents Russian modernism as one instance of what Dilip Parameshwar Gaonkar and others have described as "alternative modernities"—modernities deeply contingent on unique cultural circumstances.[56] In Russia's case modernism often takes on the aspect of a neo-religious model of modernity.

Solovyov echoed a model poetically expressed in Tiutchev's "These poor villages . . ." ("Eti bednye selen'ia"), that posed Russia as a nation in which most citizens dwelt in a pre-modern state, still living by the rhythms of land, liturgy, and folk ritual.[57] Russia's primary religious tradition—Orthodox Christianity—had circumvented modernity, maintaining a practically medieval hold over the peasant population. Largely unaffected by secularization and scientific authority, according to this model, Orthodox culture represented an opportunity to try again, to use the experience of Western history to recast Western culture. (The work of Aleksei Khomiakov presents a paradigm for the contrast of the "organic" and vibrant Christian East with the analytic West.)[58] This time, for Solovyov and those who followed his cue, the luminaries of this project could bring together the humanities and all forms of scientific disciplines with religious practice, uniting all spheres of experience and culture. Poetry represented an ideal place where the legacy of the Western humanities could meet ritual and insight, of a Russian variety. Through such means one could restore the fractured body of modern society.

With Zinaida Gippius and Dmitry Merezhkovsky leading the charge, some Russian modernist artists began to forge an unlikely union with Russian Orthodox tradition. Seeking to endow modern culture with a "holy flesh" (*sviataia plot'*), they began to adapt Eastern Christian aesthetic forms to their own ends.[59] Such a union seemed unlikely not for any unprecedented nature (consider, for instance, the eighteenth-century Russian ode), but for its strange bedfellows. Dostoevsky and Solovyov had already identified the Christianity preserved by the Russian people as the source of modernity's salvation; but surely they did not envision invocations of Orthodoxy by decadents, cabaret artists, and occultists.

Yet perhaps they did. And perhaps, anyway, Russian modernists were not as severed from Orthodox tradition as much scholarship implies. Most Russian modernists were hardly practicing Orthodox Christians, or "*tserkovnye*"; nevertheless, they grew up in an Orthodox culture and could not have failed to recognize the most central emblems of the Orthodox Church, its most prominent feast and fast days, its key iconic images. Indeed, the rich and ancient liturgy, its sounds, gestures, and pictures, constituted a tremendous poetic resource. In Silver Age poetry we find a profound attention to and innovative use of Orthodox culture and liturgical tradition. Poets such as Blok, Kuzmin, Akhmatova, and Pasternak in no way limit Orthodox echoes to filtered versions of Solovyov's Sophia. In their work, as with many of their peers, we meet icons and Easter, monks and baptisms, incense and annunciations. We also meet higher-level structural similarities—adapted narratives, calendrical series, space and time models, even models of knowledge. In much of their work Silver Age writers evince knowledge of Orthodox culture in its details and in larger, uniting elements.

This work, though, tells a story not of filial imitation, or even influence, but of foolhardy and breathtaking appropriation. The poets discussed here seek to meld a new religious reality, built from the mixed materials of Orthodox and literary traditions. They were engaged in a religious project, which has been described in broadly divergent ways as a "religious renaissance."[60] I address, then, two inextricable questions about the Silver Age project. How do we understand the rich and abundant uses of Orthodox tradition in the seemingly unlikely context of modernism? (Although modernism is marked by broad interest in religious traditions, scholars have generally treated Orthodoxy as devoid of interest for modernists, except in its negation.) And what might the Silver Age religious project tell us about religion in the context of modernity?

NEW RELIGIOUS MODELS

Above all, the poetry examined here demonstrates an attempt to create a new religious model of perceiving and engaging with the world and the other. Registering neither simply a protest against modernity nor a retreat into pure aesthetic space, these artists present an alternative modernity depicted as a new, spiritual age. Merezhkovsky and others make good use of Joachim of Fiore's notion of a third and final spiritual age; and Hegel's teleology resounds.[61] But neither of these schemas sufficiently conveys the nature of these poets' collective and individual visions. In the worlds that they create, humans access eternal truth, noumenal essence, through participation in the beauty and form of the artistic text. Art becomes the new *litourgos*—the common labor—by which humans encounter, and are transformed by, the sacred.

In her study on religion in modernity, Danièle Hervieu-Léger underscores the tremendous growth of new religious forms (especially NRMs, New Religious Movements) in the twentieth century, which she describes as the "reconstruction of religious belief" in the face of modernity. Revising models such as those of Weber and Durkheim, which projected the inevitable decline of religion in modern societies, she outlines the advent of a more "dispersed" model of religion.[62] According to Hervieu-Léger, religious actors increasingly locate and create religious dimensions in diverse facets of their day-to-day lives, with decreasing concern for established and institutionalized religious forms and dogmas. In doing so, they find recourse to tradition as "an ethico-cultural heritage, a fund of memory and a reservoir of signs at the disposal of individuals."[63] Processing tradition, they create unprecedented forms of religious practice. The key marker, for Hervieu-Léger, that distinguishes religion from individual spirituality is a group's self-legitimization, or establishment of authority, on the basis of past tradition (even as reconstructed, reimagined and simply imagined).

Hervieu-Léger's working definition helps formulate the Russian modernist project for it provides a way of understanding its religious—rather than anti-religious—nature. Russian modernists exemplify both the modern move away from institutionalized religion and the establishment of new religious possibilities. As the following chapters illustrate abundantly, modernist poets articulate in religious terms even the most seemingly un-Orthodox facets of earthly life, such as in Mikhail Kuzmin's lyrical depictions of homosexual love in a liturgical key. Further, their religious articulations manifest an ongoing reprocessing of established religious, and especially Orthodox, symbols and meaning systems. Finally, these poets legitimize and extend their religious task through reference to a special commission of Russian religious tradition, and, concomitantly, Russian culture as a whole, in modernity.

As with any longstanding religious tradition, to speak of "Orthodoxy" is in certain senses to speak heuristically. Just as we can speak of multiple modernities, we can also speak of multiple Orthodoxies, as even a glance at twentieth-century controversies within the Eastern Orthodox tradition will remind us.[64] In this work I use the singular term "Orthodoxy" to indicate the belief these modernist poets had that they were drawing on and revising a coherent national religious tradition (even as they simultaneously drew on sectarian and occult movements). As artists they approached this Orthodoxy via its sensual elements—its ritual texts, its icons, gestures, implements, song. To access and adapt liturgical traditions was, for them, to access and change Orthodoxy. Of all four modernists treated here Kuzmin seems to have engaged the most intently in theological study, playing out as a young writer the struggles between official Orthodoxy and Old Belief, but even he comes to a more unified view of Eastern Christian tradition, as we will see. What interested Russian modernists most was less defining old orthodoxies than creating, as in Hervieu-Léger's model, new unorthodox religious art.

THE FLESH TRANSFIGURED

Hervieu-Léger's approach, meanwhile, falls short at a key point in this study: the new religion she describes does not necessarily rely on recourse to the sacred, as the vehicle of humanity's accessing truth or a transcendent signifying presence. She offers instead a way of describing how the individual reaches through the fragmentation of modernity to establish meaning and connection for herself via created religious genealogies. Yet the Russian modernist religious vision insists specifically on art's capacity to reveal the noumena, the eternal essence at the heart of reality. In this aspect Hervieu-Léger's work reflects an understanding of religion that is closely bound up with Western Christian models.[65]

As current research shows, the Russian situation looks rather different. Philosophical, linguistic, and literary works demonstrate a unique tendency toward faith in the possibility of sense to access immediate truth about the world.[66] Such a difference between East and West corresponds to a central theological difference in models of salvation. Across the multiple "Orthodoxies" we have indicated, we find a common understanding of salvation that resides in the notion of *theosis*, or deification.[67] This approach stands distinct from Western Christian models especially in its emphasis of the restoration—indeed, divinization—of the body along with the soul. Although Orthodox Christianity as a historical entity provides many examples of the negation of fleshliness, Russia's artists in this period became fascinated with images of the transfigured body and its implications for the redemption of materiality. Just as in icon tradition the holy presence manifests itself in and through earthly materials, poetry was to weave the transfigured fabric of a new being. Through this new body, one could participate directly in the sacred, not needing further mediation. Observers of the Silver Age have noted the importance for the period of this feature in Orthodoxy. Irene Masing-Delic has written of the Silver Age "salvation myth," according to which artists and thinkers projected the "gradual transformation of matter into spirit"—although Masing-Delic emphasizes immortality, above all, rather than the specific ways artists borrowed concrete images of transfigured flesh from the Orthodox liturgy to picture this matter—my project.[68] And no less an observer than Nikolai Zernov, who wrote the epoch-defining *Russian Religious Renaissance of the Twentieth Century*, states of Orthodoxy, as modernists (including himself) saw it:

> The fundamental conviction of the Russian religious mind is the recognition of the potential holiness of matter, the unity and sacredness of the entire creation, and man's call to participate in the divine plan for its ultimate transfiguration. These ideas can be grouped under the name of Hagia Sophia, Holy Wisdom, the vision of which has never faded out in the long evolution of Russian Christianity.[69]

ORTHODOXY AND UNORTHODOXIES

In my study I follow the story of four poets who contemplated the world's remaking as the fruit of a new religious art. Their work betrays their knowledge and use of many elements of Orthodox tradition, even though none of them was religious in a traditional way. Where would they have gone to find these elements? How would they have come up with the kinds of religious realia, figuration, and metaphysics so evident in their work? While these poets' versions of the Orthodox-inspired aesthetic vary, and while they draw on varying elements of Orthodoxy, we can say of them as a group that they drew on elements vividly present within the Orthodox liturgical cycle, which centers on the creation and re-creation of the world. From biographical materials as well as from their writings, we know that all of them spent time in churches and were attentive to Church feasts; moreover, they could not have escaped the ways that liturgical images, texts and the liturgical calendar flowed out into and shaped public discourse.

Here I will use the term "liturgy" both in its proper sense as the celebration of the Holy Eucharist, or communion, and in its secondary sense to indicate the entire yearly cycle of worship services particular to the Orthodox Church, including the ritual traditions and rhythms that supplement the verbal texts.[70] The millennium-old liturgy figures vividly the transformation of the world from its fallen state into a glorious New Creation and shapes time, for its participants, according to this narrative—and the liturgy's larger patterns and associations were not lost on Russia's artists. These poets—Aleksandr Blok, Mikhail Kuzmin, Anna Akhmatova, and Boris Pasternak—knew the liturgy well enough to transgress its boundaries, but also well enough each to craft his or her own adaptation of the salvation theology the liturgy implies. Their accounts differ as much as did their own natures and as the historical events which shaped them. They were all children, of course, of a worldview in many ways foreign to the official Orthodoxy they knew—that of European culture, its Enlightenment and ensuing romantic response. With this heritage came an education that seemed fated to separate them from both the *narod* and God, or from any hope of knowing either as native or continuous with their own experience. They also inherited a keen sense of historical crisis, of the decline of the civilized world, and a concomitant search for new ways of seeing. Suddenly the "Russian religious renaissance" blossomed, and many influential Russians of the educated classes (in part, taking Solovyov's cue) began to cast Western philosophy as an orthodoxy against which they should revolt. The gathering of poetry into this endeavor epitomized the new conviction (shared by many Western European contemporaries) that art could foster a more viable way to truth than the positive sciences and other modes of a limping modernity. The search for a new, religious poetry, moreover, epitomized Russia's distinct way, vis-à-vis Western Europe, of addressing the discourse of degeneracy in religious terms.[71] Indeed, Russia's Christianity early on and to the present has endowed art and beauty with a role more essential than in (at least modern) Western Christianity.

Russian modernism was awash with creative appropriations of Christianity. In music Igor Stravinsky adapted religious and even liturgical forms, as in his *Wedding* (*Svadebka*).[72] Aleksandr Scriabin sought to generate a Solyovovian "total unity" by turning theater into liturgy, as in his work on the *Mysterium*.[73] Sergei Diaghilev sought to produce a ballet representing the Orthodox liturgy as a *gesamtkunstwerk*.[74] Russian modernist and avant-garde painting was revolutionized by the study of Byzantine icons and its peculiar perspective, its flattening out of surfaces, its emphasis on pattern and ornamentation.[75] This influence makes itself felt in Natalia Goncharova's *Evan-*

gelists (1911), larger-than-life panels of the four Gospel writers. It emerges in Kuzmin Petrov-Vodkin's *Mother of God Mercy for Evil Hearts* (*Bogomater' Umilenie zlykh serdets*, 1914–15) and in Kazimir Malevich's *Peasants in Church* (1909–10). Andrew Spira writes at length about the "spiritual implications" of Malevich's adaptations of icon aesthetics, and Alexei Kurbanovsky about Malevich's "new theology."[76] Spira sees in pieces such as *Painterly Realism: Boy with Knapsack—Color Masses in the Fourth Dimension* (1915), for instance, the representation of an iconic sense of supreme presence—art that "intuit[s] the infinite, without attempting to induce it artificially through strategic effort."[77] Camilla Gray connects the representations of planes in infinite space in Malevich's suprematist works—*Black Square* but also works like *Sensation of a Mystical Wave Coming from the Earth* (1917)—with the symbolist aesthetics of Andrei Bely. Both Gray and Spira point out strong elements of icon tradition in the works of Vladimir Tatlin.[78] The mystical worlds of *zaum*, the "transrational" language created by poets Velimir Khlebnikov and Aleksei Kruchenykh, resonate in certain ways with these visual projects, as in their reengagement with Slavonic roots and ritual chant. If we consider poetry alone, we find many more representative figures than can fit satisfactorily into one study. Viacheslav Ivanov springs immediately to mind as one who wrote erudite religious poetry and tirelessly researched ancient religious traditions, framing them as precursors to Christianity. He inspired many of his contemporaries with his attempts to create new rituals for modern life.[79] Vladimir Mayakovsky is generous with the Christ images he bestows on his poetic personae, as in his "A Few Words about Myself" ("Neskol'ko slov obo mne samom," 1913). Zinaida Gippius and Dmitry Merezhkovsky work to bring about a synthesis of paganism and Christianity and create new and unorthodox liturgical rites.[80] Nikolai Kliuev brings to life in his poetry Old Russian culture and many of its elements of Orthodoxy and Old Belief.[81] Osip Mandelstam contemplates the mysteries of grace and prophetic charisma.[82]

The artists I have selected, then, are not isolated in their experimentation with Orthodoxy, and this study could include numerous others. A central reason I have chosen these poets and excluded someone such as Viacheslav Ivanov is that I want to show how even poets not normally considered to be religious thinkers or even particularly religious artists build their work around the kind of project Ivanov articulates so keenly. A more important factor, however, in my choice of subjects relates to how their lives and works intertwine around one another, and I believe this aspect speaks especially to the shared nature of their endeavor—that is, it enables us to speak at all of a "religious project" or "religious movement." The extended conversation we find among the works of these particular poets exemplifies the larger conversation of the period. I begin with Blok, whom Akhmatova and Pasternak both present, in the works I discuss here, as a founding father of the movement, buoyed up by his readings of Solovyov. I move to Kuzmin, who wrote the preface for Akhmatova's first volume of poetry (*Vecher*, 1914), and whom Akhmatova excoriates as almost a kind of anti-Christ in *Poem without a Hero*. Akhmatova and Pasternak emerge as rival interpreters of and rival heirs to these other poets and as rival interpreters of the modernist period in general in their late works that I discuss here. In a sense, then, I allow Akhmatova's and Pasternak's evaluations of the Silver Age to speak to my own choice of authors—with Blok as their failed hero and, for Akhmatova, at least, Kuzmin as a far darker embodiment of the Silver Age impulse. Even along these lines, though, Marina Tsvetaeva and Osip Mandelstam could very fruitfully speak into this discussion. Pasternak reprocessed Tsvetaeva's idiosyncratic religious mythologies in his later work, including, notably, in *Doctor Zhivago*—using her as a model for his earthy Sophia, Lara.[83] And Mandelstam's life and poetry form an important subtext in *Poem without a Hero*. I have, therefore, accorded these two poets their own brief passages since one book cannot afford the space all of these poets deserve. It is important to note, though, that in speaking of all these poets, I refer to larger conversations that they all shared, and I offer substantial contextualizing discussions of Silver Age religious thought of the period—addressing figures such as Viacheslav Ivanov, Vasily Rozanov, Pavel Florensky, and Nikolai Berdiaev.

The poets gathered here fall into two groups: those whose work falls easily within the chronological parameters of modernism (Blok and Kuzmin) and those who emerged as modernists in the Silver Age but are writing about the modernist period retrospectively (Akhmatova and Pasternak). In this sense my project works in two complementary portions: the modernist project as it was developing and the modernist project as it was reinvoked, critiqued, extended in the Soviet mid-century. In fact, I read Akmatova and Pasternak as some of the first to identify the modernist religious project, while bending it to their own purposes. In their late works Akhmatova and Pasternak give us a framework for understanding the epoch in which they matured as artists, and both of their respective frameworks bear religious delineations. Taking my cue from them, I offer yet one more way to delimit and describe what we call modernism.

This story begins with the young Aleksandr Blok, that self-proclaimed starry-eyed lover of Sophia, who appeared to the world as the first incarnation of Solovyov's artist. A child of privilege, Blok believed he could, through Orthodoxy and inspiration, make art that would forge a meeting place between the everyday world and the world beyond, one he imagined along both Platonic and Solovyovian lines.[84] In 1901 Blok began to compose his *Verses on the Most Beautiful Lady* (*Stikhi o Prekrasnoi Dame*). In this volume Blok strives to envision a new, apocalyptic body that can achieve union with (knowledge of) the world's essence, the Beautiful Lady. He frames this embodiment as an overcoming of the Kantian divide between noumena and phenomena—a divide, however, to which his vision frequently, wittingly, and tragically succumbs. Blok's belief in this project largely erodes by around 1905, but it never entirely recedes; and the foundational nature of his early volume for Russian modernism—even as a vision against which to rebel—cannot be overstated. For this reason I will restrict myself primarily to a discussion of this model volume rather than surveying Blok's oeuvre. We might see *Verses on the Most Beautiful Lady* as the most earnest and perhaps the foundational adaptation of Solovyov's Sophia, as Blok understood her (mostly through Solovyov's poetry).

The story continues with the maverick poet, composer, and born scholar Mikhail Kuzmin, who charmed Petersburg with his *Alexandrian Songs* after the disappointment of the 1905 Revolution, offering up his songs in the aesthetic retreat of Viacheslav Ivanov's "Tower" and World of Art circles. Kuzmin's art built thereafter a religious vision of a world at once endearingly mortal and capable of bodying out the eternal. True to homosexuality as the "defining fact of Kuzmin's life and art,"[85] the poet responds to Blok's legacy by replacing the cosmic Sophia as lyrical addressee with domestic and intimate images of the contemplative monk, who, with his angelic guide, quietly climbs the ladder of perfection toward mystical unity with the eternal, with Love. His poetry offers both a revised asceticism and the writing of sensual experience into a liturgy of the body. Throughout his work, Kuzmin posits poetry as instilling a ritual-bound, gradual, and bodily transformation that contrasts with the sudden, apocalyptic version that the early Blok desired. While Kuzmin's Sophia often appears in re-gendered manifestations, the poet still maintains a basic faithfulness to and optimism about the sophianic task of unifying flesh and spirit through artistic practice.

From Kuzmin we move beyond modernism proper to its aftermath and to critical artistic representations of modernism. Anna Akhmatova has written one of the most important literary evaluations of this period in her *Poem without a Hero*. Early on Kuzmin's protégée, Akhmatova voiced her strongest response to this dialogue decades later, bringing the story back to spectral life. As one who witnessed the "Real Twentieth Century," as she called it—that is, Russia from 1914 and far beyond—Akhmatova presented herself as compelled to evaluate the aspirations and actions of the Silver Age (*PBG*, 884). Her late long poem *Poem without a Hero* examines the underside of the fabric of new flesh, presenting negatively modernism's desire to incarnate the eternal in human forms. We find in this work a rejection of the sophianic idea that art can bring about a new world, but we also find Akhmatova's replacement of the sophianic vision with another, equally religious one. Specifically, Akhmatova definitively replaces Sophia with Mary,

Mother of God. This move allows her to sustain a vision of a new age that will come while suggesting that the artist can only await it. The poem presents at once the impossibility and ever-suspended potential of fleshing out fundamental truth. Such a poetry depicts the more tragic aspects of the sophianic process, even while sustaining a hope that "still sings in the distance," sings of resurrection and transformation (*AASS*, 3:22).

Boris Pasternak offers, next to young Blok, the most direct transpositions of Solovyovian-sophianic topoi, in his late novel-with-poetic-cycle *Doctor Zhivago*. Moreover, in the novel he vividly connects Solovyovian themes—of erotic love that inspires world-building art—with strongly drawn references to liturgical culture. In a corrective recapitulation of the modernist project, Pasternak brings images of Sophia directly together with images of the Feast of the Transfiguration, that feast that celebrates the possibility of a "holy flesh" par excellence. The highly conscious nature of this recapitulation becomes evident on the novel's meta-aesthetic plane, where Pasternak distinctly figures the process by which the artist can render the eternal in transitory, earthly forms. Whereas the later Akhmatova profoundly suspects art that presumes to present the eternal, Pasternak suggests that art only ever presents the eternal, although its particular form must ever adapt to new circumstances. Pasternak's novel constitutes, in many ways, a sanguine summing up of the Silver Age religious project, for in it the author provides a model of how life proceeds precisely by inspired, unorthodox adaptations of cultural forms.

In my epilogue I consider briefly how the contemporary poet Ol'ga Sedakova reimagines Russian Orthodoxy. Though an heir of the Silver Age, Sedakova draws Orthodox tradition into an encounter with different cultural circumstances from those of her predecessors. The conceptualization of Orthodoxy in her work reflects, on a broader scale, a refashioning of Russia's self-imagination, and of poetry within that nexus, over the last decades.

One important note should be added here, regarding how accessible the liturgical language of Church Slavonic would have been to the authors gathered here. Sedakova is the easiest to address in this regard since one of her most important scholarly projects has been to put together a dictionary for Russian speakers seeking to understand the Church-Slavic of the services.[86] With Kuzmin and Pasternak, who copied out many passages of liturgical services, we can at least say that while their understanding may not have been perfect, nevertheless they were at least relatively comfortable with the basic language of the services, enough to copy down and interact with it. The evidence for Blok and Akhmatova is somewhat less direct. Akhmatova quotes the liturgy in *Requiem* and writes explicitly about the Great Canon (see appendix). But in addition, all four of these writers use images and types of images found throughout the liturgy and use them in not merely biblical but specifically liturgical configurations—that is, in ways that access traditional interpretations of biblical images that have made their way into the liturgical texts which, as Alexander Schmemann and others show, offer a central form of theology.[87] For example, in the canons—the central hymns—for each feast, Noah's ark floating across the flood waters with a remnant of humanity and the animal world is presented in parallel to the prophet Jonah in the belly of the whale, harboring the message of God's salvation (see appendix). Liturgical texts also find parallel images in Mary's womb that holds Christ, the promised Messiah, and in Jesus's own tomb that will release the ultimate salvific force. Many more images are drawn into this constellation over the course of the liturgical year. While some or all of these images can be found dispersed across various icons, it is precisely in the texts for the services that they occur over and over again in repetitive clusters. These writers do refer directly and indirectly to icons, but the specific ways they connect images in their poems (and prose) suggest special attention to liturgical texts that order the religious imagination. All of these writers certainly attended services at one point or another (some rather regularly). And so it seems that, whatever their relative degree of understanding of Church Slavonic, they gleaned enough—perhaps in conjunction with icons seen—to reappropriate elements of the liturgical imagination. These artists engage liturgical culture in other ways, too, and I will address more of them chapter by chapter.

SUPERSEDING OLD ORTHODOXIES

Berdiaev and his peers do not overstate the novelty of their project to create a "new Christianity," and yet their literary and intellectual predecessors used Orthodox traditions to their own ends well before the "religious renaissance." After all, a central tenet for Slavophile writers and thinkers lay in an identification of the spiritual capacities of Russia with its primary religious tradition, Orthodoxy. The Slavophiles saw in Russian Orthodoxy the true heir to the living tradition of the Church, a history, as Aleksei Khomiakov writes, "no longer intelligible to the schism."[88] Khomiakov's poetry of the 1850s offers a paradigmatic example of Slavophile poetry, grounded as it is in a vision of Russia as a holy nation. Consider, for instance, his "Russia" (1854), in which the poet calls out, "Arise, my native country, / For the cause of your brothers! God is calling you."[89] Orthodox culture finds ample expression, though, outside Slavophile circles, too. Unsurprisingly, Pushkin's poetry has undergone the most extensive examination to date in regard to its use of Orthodox traditions and forms.[90] Aleksei Tolstoy and Fyodor Tiutchev also rank among those poets most cited in reference to the use of Orthodox Christian motifs.[91] Tolstoy's long poem *John of Damascus* (*Ioann Damaskin*) represents a rich verse experiment in transposing liturgical texts, by translation and paraphrase, into modern poetic form. Meanwhile, most critical discussion of religion in nineteenth-century literature focuses on prose writers—most notably Dostoevsky, but also Tolstoy, Gogol, Leskov, and others.[92] As in Joseph Frank's tomes on Dostoevsky, the most successful discussions of nineteenth-century fiction and religion often link realism's "tendentsioznost'," its dedication to messages geared toward social and political reform, with Orthodoxy's emphasis on sacrificial and merciful love as a basis for social life.[93] Such an approach, though, obviously falls short if applied to poetry (except perhaps for Nekrasov's), and can more subtly limit our readings of realist prose in connection with religion and ritual. A recent work by Tatiana Koshchemchuk, *Russian Poetry in the Context of Orthodox Culture* (*Russkaia poeziia v kontekste pravoslavnoi kul'tury*), aims to rectify a significant gap in scholarship, but the volume (which focuses on the nineteenth century) comprises more a meditation on broadly religious themes that the author, despite her impressive knowledge of Orthodox thought and tradition, fails to anchor in aesthetic and poetic terms.[94]

Such a far-reaching religious-literary project as found in modernism had not been seen in Russia since the eighteenth century, when Russian poets grounded key genres in religious poetry. Marcus Levitt has recently written of an "Enlightenment Orthodoxy" that sought a cultural synthesis of Russian religious tradition and "the new demands of Russian culture (secular, national, Enlightenment)."[95] One has only to think of the endless number of Psalms that poets such as Lomonosov and Derzhavin set in modern Russian poetic form—as a part of the very process of establishing that form.[96] Their panegyric and religious odes, too, as Harsha Ram has shown, appropriated religious symbols to shore up the legitimacy of the modern Russian state.[97] Their poetry drew on scriptural and theological tradition to establish a modern moralism, as in Derzhavin's "To Rulers and Judges."[98] This poem echoes numerous scriptural passages, from Psalm 82:2 and 9:19 to Isaiah 64:6 and James 1:27; but ultimately the poem moves beyond biblical forms and enters the discourse of enlightened monarchy. It also weds ascetic and enlightenment discourses of virtue, as we see especially in the reference to passion—"But you are passionate as I" ("No vy, kak ia podobno, strastny"). Poetry in this period also channels Masonic mysticism and the concern for universal brotherhood, as in Kheraskov's long poem "Vladimir."[99] As Ruth Coates points out, religion in eighteenth-century Russia is used not primarily to distinguish Russia from the West, but rather to trace and project its status as an enlightened (namely, Western) nation. (The emergence of satire as a central mode attests to the increasingly modern, secular framing of virtues and vices.) Consequently Christianity at times appears in the new literature in its most universalizing and cosmopolitan forms, as deism or Freemasonry, especially.[100] But whereas these earlier poets geared their use of religious tradition toward entering modernity, Russia's twentieth-century poets were using religion to construct an alternative modernity.

Modernism's transpositions of Orthodox forms comprise but one wave of creative engagement with Russia's primary religious tradition. Religion's cultural dynamism ensures that each generation finds its own encounter with and expression of a given tradition. As a whole, though, modernism's transpositions of Orthodoxy stand in distinction from previous borrowings in their bold-faced redefinition of Russia's primary religion and, concomitantly, of Russian culture. Thanks in part to Nicholas II's 1905 *Ukaz* promoting religious tolerance, but also to a desire to make modernity and Orthodoxy meet, Russian modernists envisioned something like a Reformation. With Merezhkovsky known as the Russian Luther, modernism—represented here by key poets—tried to unite a religion of presence with an essentialist aesthetic. Religion was to bear its fruits in the here and now, and the here and now was to attain eternal, ideal dimensions.

NOT BY RIGHT TEACHING ALONE

In *Modern Russian Theology* Paul Valliere describes the development of a theology that would bring Orthodox dogma into conversation with Western philosophical thought. He aims to highlight the legacy of the "Russian school" of theology (in which he includes Aleksandr Bukharev, Solovyov, and Sergei Bulgakov), whose contributions have often been marginalized in modern theological discussions of Orthodoxy. Valliere writes,

> The theology of the Russian school grew out of the need to relate the Orthodox faith to what is usually called a modern or free society, that is to say, a society consisting of relatively autonomous, unharmonized spheres of activity operating outside the tutelage of church or state. . . . The Russian school . . . dealt with contemporary problems all the time because its overarching concern was to promote the engagement of Orthodox believers with the modern world in all sectors—politics, society, economy, education, science, the arts and so on.[101]

In many ways Valliere's work offers a necessary companion to the present study, highlighting as it does the key concerns of this period for secular and religious thinkers alike. One has only to think of the stated mission of the Religious-Philosophical Meetings to give "flesh" to a church tradition too much concerned with the "spirit"—to translate Orthodoxy into modernity, thereby shoring up Russian culture and securing Russia's future.

This book's subject is the attempt by the Russian intelligentsia to lay bare—and reconstruct—the foundations of their culture, and to do so in part by means of shoring up the religious consciousness of their society. As they imagined it, Russia's stability and prosperity would flow out of a revised Orthodoxy, uniting them with the mythologized *narod*. By extension, Russia would offer the West a new path through modernity. It is not difficult to argue that priests and theologians bore such a mission; to show that even modernist "revelers" and "fornicators" (as Akhmatova once called her generation) bore this aim underscores the urgency the educated classes felt in locating the pulse of the people and reviving what they saw as the crippled body of their nation.[102]

Alexander Schmemann has written that in its liturgy, one finds the essence of the Orthodox Church, for the Church's worship "embraces, expresses, inspires and defines the whole Church, her whole essential nature, her whole life. 'The Christian religion is not only a doctrine . . . it is a public action or deed.'"[103] In the liturgy (especially if one includes the icon) one also finds the primary source for literary engagements with Orthodoxy, even the most unorthodox. It is important to emphasize, however, that these poets engage with the liturgy in a holistic way, in line with how Schmemann describes it. That is, he speaks of it as comprising the whole of the Church's worship and life. It is tempting to think of liturgy as primarily text, but in fact liturgical texts themselves constitute merely part of a pattern that generates a whole culture. Therefore I will speak of "liturgical culture" in my study, meaning cultural norms that emerge out of the ways worshipping communities deploy and incorporate liturgical texts. Along these lines the parallels I will draw between Orthodoxy and modernist writing focus less on borrowed language and more on how poets adapt certain aspects of liturgical culture: ritualism and ritual practice, religious themes played out in calendrical seasons, cosmic aspirations to build a world reflecting God's order, use of biblical models to picture new ways of being in the world. I have included an appendix on the liturgical cycle at the end of this study to give a sense of the structure, relation, and coherence of the Church's services and to indicate what repeating and prominent elements one might be likely to pick up even from exposure merely to the central feasts.

This study looks to the liturgy as an artistic resource, as a poet might see it. Art, though, often stands as a means of individual religious expression, as well as a constructive and normative articulation of a community's belief and practice. Focusing on this constructive dimension of art for religious culture, I work with an array of secondary sources that address cultural understandings of Orthodox meaning systems so as better to conceptualize the religious significance of poetic examples. I draw from theology, but also cultural, art, and religious history, as well as sociology. The last decade and a half in particular has witnessed a burgeoning of historiographical interest in religion in Russia, richly opening out our picture of Russian culture. (Patrick Michelson and Judith Kornblatt have referred to this phenomenon as a "religious turn" in the historiography of Russia.)[104] Such works address the "terrific religious mobilization" around the turn of the twentieth century (Mark Steinberg and Heather Coleman),[105] the cultural significance of Orthodoxy in this period (Vera Shevzov, Nadiezda Kizenko, Scott Kenworthy),[106] the practice and regulation of Orthodoxy (Chris Chulos, Christine Worobec),[107] and religious diversity in Russia (Roy Robson, Heather Coleman, Leonid Heretz).[108] These works serve to elucidate, if gradually, the degree of religious education and knowledge of the layperson, the vital exchange between East and West in Church doctrines and forms over the centuries, and the changing shape of the institution in society. These works also suggest that the relations between the intelligentsia and the Orthodox Church remained much more intricate and perplexing than is often represented.

Most centrally within secondary sources, I draw from and respond to literary studies that discuss the Silver Age or literary engagements with religious tradition, especially Orthodoxy. Olga Matich and Jenifer Presto's seminal works on Russian modernists' rewriting of sexuality and gender illuminate how radically these artists were reenvisioning the body.[109] Matich in particular weaves into her story the decidedly religious ways this topic was discussed, as in the work of Solovyov and in the Religious-Philosophical Meetings. Her study of Gippius's religious poetry along with Bernice Glatzer Rosenthal's monograph on Merezhkovsky are important in understanding these central attempts at bringing together paganism and Christianity, sometimes with special emphasis on Russian Orthodoxy.[110] Several prominent studies offer textured and compelling portraits of non-Orthodox religious traditions in Russian literature (including works by Olga Matich, Maria Carlson, Gregory Freidin, Gabriella Safran, Laura Engelstein, Alexander Etkind, and Nikolay Bogomolov).[111] These works have done much to elucidate how prominent the religious impulse was in this period. A few scholars have begun to explore in productive ways the complex relationship between literature and Eastern Orthodoxy. Steven Cassedy, for one, speaks of "early modern literary aesthetics in Russia" as being "completely dominated by . . . the idealist assumptions underlying Orthodoxy theology and language philosophy."[112] Cassedy and Thomas Seifrid have offered seminal studies of the relations between Orthodox thought and language philosophy.[113] Sarah Pratt and Robert Bird have offered nuanced portraits of individual authors in which they investigate at various junctures the writers' creative engagements with Orthodox culture.[114] Several edited collections make important contributions in this area, too.[115]

Three scholars deserve special notice here—Per Arne Bodin, Olga Meerson, and Ol'ga Sedakova. Bodin addresses multiple aspects of the relations between Orthodoxy and art in Russia across his scholarly oeuvre. But in his far-ranging *Eternity and Time: Studies in Russian Literature and the Orthodox Tradition* he examines this issue across centuries of Russian culture. He not only speaks to liturgical texts as part of the Russian literary tradition but also explores a handful of landmarks of modern Russian literature in light of Orthodox culture.[116] While Meerson does not offer long or systematic studies of Russian literature in the light of Russian Orthodox culture per se, she is unique as a scholar in the conceptually complex ways she treats the literary uses of Orthodox liturgical culture. Both of these scholars, who are immensely informed on the Russian Orthodox tradition, discover and read liturgical references in the light of their context of performance, sequentiality, repetition, and referentiality, revealing the multivalency of both these literary references and the liturgical texts themselves.[117] Ol'ga Sedakova, whose poetic work I consider in the epilogue, has written a scholarly book on the language of the liturgy and also laces her essayistic, critical, and poetic work with references to, considerations, and echoes of the liturgy.[118] Together these three make a convincing case that our readings of key works of Russian literature fall short when we overlook their religious context. Still, much work remains to be done.

Notably, the most sizable body of scholarship directly treating Orthodoxy and literature has emerged in Russian Orthodox intellectual circles in Russia since 1991, represented in particular by the works and edited volumes of V. A. Kotel'nikov, V. N. Zakharov, I. A. Esaulov, and M. M. Dunaev.[119] While the edited volumes draw together a somewhat diverse set of scholars whose work often offers needed insight into authors' echoes of Orthodox culture, the collections consciously hew, on the whole, toward a fundamentally confessional impulse. The more programmatic writings in these collections argue for the vacuity of solely positivistic critical methods and the need to view an essentially religious body of literature (i.e., the Russian tradition) according to religious axioms.[120] In line with this conviction these scholars frequently devote overwhelming amounts of text to citing Orthodox theologians (e.g., Georges Florovsky, Sergei Bulgakov, Pavel Florensky) and Church fathers; consequently their discussion of literary works often feels like a pretext for contemplating what defines Orthodoxy, as reflected in numerous pieces. Frequently the literary texts presumably under examination receive space sufficient only for several direct quotations with little follow-up analysis, so that the overall methodology works only metonymically, by association. In general the most directly accessible articles carry out very focused tasks: investigating authors' religious reading practices, analyzing an explicitly religious *poema* by Aleksei Tolstoy, pointing out citations of liturgical texts within poetic ones.[121] Of particular use is Kotel'nikov's impressive and thorough bibliography of Russian-language critical works on literature and religion from the eighteenth through the twentieth centuries.[122]

Much of the scholarship, meanwhile, can be seen as part of the tradition of "spiritual criticism" ("dukhovnaia kritika") a body of work which several critics in this group take pains to reintroduce—especially Kotel'nikov, who includes a rich sampling of this tradition in his bibliography.[123] In this tradition religious thinkers reflect on secular literature through the lens of spiritual precepts. Indeed, Russian Orthodox theology since the nineteenth century, especially, stands out in its frequent allusions to literary texts—from the poems of Tiutchev and Pushkin to novels of Dostoevsky. As we see in Florovsky's *Ways of Russian Theology* (*Puti russkogo bogosloviia*), literary works can be used to provide illustrations of theological concepts but can also serve as means of defining Orthodox belief and of identifying what, and who, falls within those boundaries.

This body of scholarship surely bears immense value as a community seeks to work out the character and implications of its faith in a still new and shifting context; and it stands as a corrective, of its own kind, to the restrictions of Soviet academic publishing. At the same time, it threatens to create its own restrictive interpretations of "Russian" religion. Still, even if it does not always foster religious openness, it can serve as a reminder of literature's openness to diverse modes of reading, including reading as a religious and even devotional practice. In fact, the poets treated in this volume themselves cast reading as a religious act or ritual. But what constitutes religion for them—indeed, what constitutes Orthodoxy for them—by no means remains within the bounds of any officially recognized Orthodoxy (even when one includes the controversial thought of Sergei Bulgakov and Pavel Florensky). Accordingly, this study treats not so much Orthodoxy comprised by a set of theological propositions or national characteristics, as Orthodox culture and the ways that poets have transposed elements of various Orthodox traditions (especially liturgical culture) into their own literary visions. In doing so, the author seeks to offer a more effective scholarly model of describing the relationship between religion and literature, and especially between Orthodoxy and literary culture.

In an issue of *A New Way*—one that included some of Blok's earliest published verses—editors printed a comment from Father John of Kronstadt in which he criticized the journal's name and what it implied.[124] Father John—an immensely charismatic figure in his day, with huge followings—admonishes "clever idiots [*umniki neumnye*], of the likes of Tolstoy and his followers," by which he means members of the intelligentsia such as those who started *A New Way*.[125] "This journal," he continues, "has set itself the goal of seeking God as though God had not already appeared to people and had not made known to us the true way." The editors responded in the following issue, answering that the "old" way they were abandoning was not that of the Church, but rather "the way of positivism, a lack of spiritual consecration."[126] The new way they propose is, instead, one of "religious depth and inner revelation" and the "consecration of life." The solutions they would invent were, of course, unorthodox by the standards of official Orthodoxy—but it was from other orthodoxies that they initially set sail.

Chapter One

Aleksandr Blok's Other Body

> In Blok's poetry we meet everywhere with the attempt to embody a supertemporal vision in the forms of space and time. She is already among us, with us, embodied, alive, near—the one who is at last recognized as the muse of Russian Poetry—appearing as the Sun, in whom intersect the rays of a newly revealed religion. A battle for this new religion will be the task of our entire life.
> —Andrey Bely, "Apocalypse in Russian Poetry"

> On Mount Sinai, and in the chamber of the most pure maid, and in the studio of the great artist the words resound: "Seek the Promised Land."
> —Aleksandr Blok, "In Memory of Vrubel'"
> (*ABSS*, 5:421–24; here, 423)

RUSSIAN MODERNISTS WANTED nothing more than to take on new flesh. They lived in a world where—thanks to figures like Vladimir Solovyov, Nietzsche, and the French symbolists—poetry offered knowledge that the sciences seemingly could not. It was a world in need of a new body, a new culture, for the old festered in the stagnant forms of the past. Modern (namely, Western) ways of knowing and traditional views seemed inexorably at odds; philosophical trends focusing on individual subjectivity threatened the organic unity of the people. This was the idea, anyway. Dmitry Merezhkovsky wrote as much in his "Reasons for the Decline and New Currents in Contemporary Russian Literature" (1893).[1] Here Merezhkovsky rails against the "rude materialism of dogmatic forms" and the "suffocating, deadly positivism" that imprison and putrefy Russian literary culture in all its "illness, feverish ravings, poverty, bad air, severe spleen."[2] Preferring a new religious vision of literature, he posits, "If we do not want to die in abstraction, emptiness, cold, faithlessness, we must maintain our blood ties with the source of all strength and all faith—the people [*narod*]"; and he finds the greatest source of hope in writers who build on the "divine foundation of the people's worldview, of the people's poetry," returning them to the "living heart of the people."[3] Scary corpses also proliferate in Viacheslav Ivanov's "Crisis of Humanism."[4] Ivanov describes "the old inner form of things becoming decrepit and moribund within us" and argues that the "decaying remains" of this inner form, as a "mummy or a decaying corpse," "infect the personality with miasmas of corruption."[5] Like Merezhkovsky's modern body, Ivanov's is stagnant and cold, a stiffened corpse. For him the person has never before been "so closed and walled-off within his selfhood, so cold of heart."[6] He, too, suggests his own religious resolution—as idiosyncratic as Merezhkovsky's—but aimed at renewing the cultural forms that might reinfuse society and the individual with life.

For many Russian modernists Russian Orthodoxy offered forms that might enable them to forge a unity of the body proper and of the body politic. A tradition theoretically (as in the thought of Merezhkovsky) untouched by modernity and its deadening abstractions, Orthodoxy seemed to offer a bridge to the unWesternized masses and, equally, to a non-dualistic view of the world. As inspired as they were by all kinds of religious forms, ranging from the occult to theosophy to Old Belief, for these modernists Orthodoxy held particular significance as the religious tradition most organically intertwined with Russian history and culture, especially the culture of the *narod*. For modernists, the healthy, living body of the people, untouched by modernity, could be reflected culturally in a poetry that accessed its premodern religious forms. In this chapter I will trace through early poems by Aleksandr Blok the way a key modernist figure used forms from Orthodox culture to flesh out his poetic vision for a changing Russia. In particular, I show how his representation of the body emblematizes attempts by the modernists to utilize Orthodox tradition in envisioning a more integrated, less atomized culture and sense of self. The consummate Russian symbolist poet, Blok fleshes out this vision in his poems by means of sound. Sound moves through his work as a force that penetrates matter, that unites everything in its path with the same rumbles and vibrations. Sound works iconically to transfigure the material world, creating in Blok's poetry the first post-Solovyov embodiments of Sophia.

The call to establish a new, integrated society and selfhood emerges keenly in the notes to the Religious-Philosophical Meetings of 1901–1903. In his opening remarks to the first Religious-Philosophical Meeting, Valentin Ternavtsev speaks of the intelligentsia's responsibility to resolve the "unembodiedness [of Christianity] in life, her unrealized promises" (*nevoplotimost['] ego v zhizni, ego neosushchestvivshi[e]sia obetovani[ia]*).[7] Such language of enfleshment sounds frequently in these discussions as the intelligentsia represent their sense of mission: to give form to a culture whose resources they perceive as too narrowly invested in the life of the spirit and in the world to come. Ternavtsev's comment reflects a pervasive concern with the problem of embodiment that occupied artists of Russia's modernism.

Blok attended these meetings regularly, especially after he had met the Merezhkovskys in spring 1902. When the meetings started up, he was twenty-one years old, and he had just passed through a summer charged with budding romance, mystical intuitions, and electric poetry that would constitute the foundation of his first published volume. But the budding poet was more than a mere audience member: even before he met the meetings' key organizers, Zinaida Gippius and Dmitry Merezhkovsky, he had been reading Merezhkovsky's work, and he caught their attention on their first introduction.[8] The striking, sophisticated, image-aware Gippius and her ambitious, visionary, more pedestrian-looking husband were both poets and prose-writers in their own right; but their chief contribution lay already in their dynamic, innovative, and sometimes peculiar attempts to work out a new aesthetically defined philosophy in life and society. They were ever on the lookout for artists and thinkers to gather into their cause, and Blok was the consummate candidate. Earnest, elegant, unpretentious, he came to them already having absorbed the model of Solovyov's own poetry. One of his closest friends was Sergei Soloyov, a nephew of the philosopher. In Sergei's family home Blok encountered from his teens onward enlivened discussions of Solovyov's thought and poetry, as well as of the "new" art (*APLB*, 1:69–73). But, as Avril Pyman points out, it was the gift of a volume of Solovyov's poetry from his mother at Easter 1901 that most stimulated Blok's first sophianic verses (*APLB*, 1:69). Later Blok began to read Solovyov's philosophy for himself, but poetry was where the influence began. At this early stage Blok was not particularly engaged by Gippius and Merezhkovsky's social aims—that is, their belief that religious exploration by the intelligentsia and the creation of new rituals would help mend fractures in Russian society. That concern would emerge a few years later for Blok—and would define the rest of his poetic career. He had already, however, absorbed Solovyov's and Solovyov-inspired emphases on integrality, on sublimating eros to produce new worlds and on adapting Orthodox traditions to harness mainstream Russian religion to new ends.

All these aspects of Solovyov's thought and of the emerging aesthetic he had inspired make themselves felt in Blok's first book of poetry, *Verses on the Most Beautiful Lady*.[9] Of this collection Blok said in 1916, on his way to war, "*The best* remains the *Verses about the Most Beautiful Lady*. Time should not touch them, however weak I may have been as an artist."[10] These poems, as the volume title indicates, maintain a steady gaze on the often elusive figure of the Eternal Feminine as she appears to the young poet. In an apocalyptic manner the appearance of the Most Beautiful Lady promises to accompany the transformation of the world. We read, "The whole horizon is on fire—and unbearably clear, / And silently I wait—*longing and loving*" ("Predchuvstvuiu Tebia. Goda prokhodiat mimo . . . ," *ABSS*, 1:94). The poems range, though, from expressions of faith and ecstasy to bewilderment and doubt in the Lady and the poet's art. Despite—or maybe precisely because of this wavering vision, the volume became a kind of primer for Russian modernism. Blok's peers and successors learned its lessons well enough to imitate, modulate, and overturn them, but nothing written after this volume appeared could ignore the vision it contained. Because of the cultural and aesthetic significance of this volume, we will concentrate on it in this chapter, with only brief reference to what followed after for Blok. If in the introduction I proposed that Russian modernism sprang from responses to the works of Nietzsche and Solovyov, then this current flowed first through Blok and was forever contaminated by his early art. Indeed, the retrospective works we will discuss later in the present work, by Anna Akhmatova and Boris Pasternak, place Blok at center stage in the masquerade of Russian modernism.

That Blok built his early aesthetic on Solovyov has never been in doubt, as any treatment of his first volumes will show.[11] My purpose here is to show how his early work takes part in the project to create a new "holy flesh," to create visions of bodies and worlds in which the eternal and temporal can interpenetrate. Blok's 1903 poem "I sit behind a screen . . ." pictures an enclosed, solipsistic body that has no hope of the kind of union the poet and his peers seek ("Sizhu za shirmoi . . . ," *ABPSS*, 1:162). Later Blok would add a dedication to Immanuel Kant to this poem, indicating its parallels to the Kantian divide between noumena and phenomena. In a later poem he would also speak of the "boundary of god-knowledge" (*gran' bogopoznan'ia*)—that border that keeps man trapped in his flesh, his earthbound materiality ("Ty ukhodish' ot zemnoi iudoli . . . ," *ABPSS*, 1:77). Already in *Verses*, though, Blok uses images of the body and its relation with other bodies and material objects in space to represent a coming new world that can bear the kind of revelation he seeks to actualize. I will focus on one of the poet's key transpositions of Orthodox liturgical images and types of the deified body, figured most prominently in the liturgical texts and icons for the Feast of the Transfiguration.[12] The poet uses Transfiguration images and types to envision a body in which the poet not only can see his Lady, but can unite with her—and, indeed, with the similarly transformed world around them.[13] Scholars of Blok as prominent as Zara Mints have remarked on this project in Blok's work, but its centrality and outlines have never been treated substantially.[14] Symbolically, though, Blok achieves through his poetic use of the Transfiguration tradition a model for conceiving a new world that has both arrived and has not yet arrived.

In *Verses* Blok crafted an instinctive, unorthodox amalgamation of high Western philosophy, Russian religious philosophy, and Orthodox cultural idiom. His novel cultural form highlights a wider achievement of his period. The concern with reconstructing the body and the bodily accompanies the Russian modernists' sense that Russia had its own word to say to modernity and its philosophies. They would forge this word, as Michael Meerson has shown, from a creative synthesis of contemporary philosophy, Western medieval love mysticism, and the Greek patristic tradition, sustained (and reenacted) in modern Orthodox Christianity.[15] Numerous poems in *Verses* illuminate how such a synthesis seeks (even instinctively) to turn *theosis*, or deification—seen by many as the distinctive doctrine of Eastern Orthodoxy, in all its incarnations—into a concrete answer to the philosophical problems of modernity.[16] As Valerie Kivelson and Robert Greene write of this tradition in *Orthodox Russia*, "The material realm quite literally embodied the incandescent presence of the divine. The sensory and experiential dominated over the textual."[17] Blok was by no means a churchgoing Orthodox believer. He held some kind of faith throughout his life—in true symbolist fashion—in the reality of a sphere beyond the mundane realm: "There are other worlds" (*est' drugie miry*), as he wrote in 1901.[18] Churches, however, made up an important element in his courtship of his future wife Liubov', whose reflections of Sophia he wrote into *Verses*. He and Liubov' would often meet in Petersburg churches, occasionally staying for services, but mostly setting their budding love against a striking, resonant backdrop (*APLB*, 1:91). That he was not "churchy" (*tserkovnyi*) did not keep him from accessing the material he found in the church setting—not only in his romantic rendezvous, but in the piety of people he knew, in the fabric of the culture around him, in Solovyov's work. As I will show, Blok uses and transposes Orthodox liturgical traditions to depict a world in which the material—be it body, poem, or icon—can manifest revelations of truth. Although his hopes in the Beautiful Lady waver and shift throughout *Verses*, we find in all sections adaptations of the Transfiguration scene as well as images of divinized flesh.

Blok's renderings of Orthodox Transfiguration topoi offer a kind of index for the speaker's degree of confidence in his project; one moment we find him standing in a space of radiant revelation and the next in the darkest dungeon. These renderings also provide an index for his own later poetry, as well as for later modernist experiments seeking to depict a flesh shot through with the eternal. Blok's poem "You burn above a high hill . . ." epitomizes Blok's translation of *theosis*—emblematized centrally in Transfiguration tradition—into modernist lyric poetry.[19] And in this poem we discover one of his most hopeful, if not unmixed, expressions of faith in the power of art to transform reality. The Feast of the Transfiguration (August 6), reflected in several poems in *Verses*, seems to filter down into this poem, written two weeks later.[20]

Ты горишь над высокой горою,
Недоступна в Своем терему.
Я примчуся вечерней порою,
В упоеньи мечту обниму.

Ты, заслышав меня издалёка,
Свой костер разведешь ввечеру.
Стану, верный велениям Рока,
Постигать огневую игру.

И когда среди мрака снопами
Искры станут кружиться в дыму,
Я умчусь с огневыми кругами
И настигну Тебя в терему.

18 августа 1901 (*ABPSS*, 1:72)

(You burn above a high hill, / Unapproachable in Your tower. / I will come to you in haste at evening, / In rapture I will embrace a dream. // You, hearing me from afar, / Will stoke your fire at evening. / I will begin, true to Destiny's commands, / To grasp the fiery game. // And when, in shafts, amidst the gloom / Sparks start to swirl in the smoke, / I will hasten away with the fiery circles / And will reach You in the tower.)

The image of the woman with blazing body resembles the radiant body of Solovyov's sophian figure as he presents her in his poems, which Blok knew. Blok quotes one such poem as an epigraph to one of his own poems; in Solovyov's poem "unearthly light" (*nezdeshnii svet*) marks the Lady's appearance.[21] Yet Blok essentially underscores Solovyov's own syncretism, bringing a Gnostic symbol together with references to the Transfiguration, blending tones of tradition into his favored sunset setting, but also transposing that tradition into his own poetic landscape. In the poem the poetic narrator beholds his Lady, above a mountain, shining forth in a body of flames, which she stokes as he approaches. Initially she appears as an unapproachable tower. But the poet predicts that as the sparks fly out and around her more furiously, he will be caught up in this whirlwind and borne to her. Blok's adaptation of the iconic and liturgical tradition of the Transfiguration Feast appear most notably in his use of the elements of the blazing figure, the mountain, the shafts of light sent out from the radiant body, and the disciple's ascent, through transformation into the blazing substance of the central figure.[22] These elements feature prominently in the Russian icon tradition for this feast, such as in Feofan Grek's famous icon, pictured in figure 1.1. Here we see Christ surrounded by a *mandorla*, representing the partial revelation of his radiant divinity.[23] From him shine out rays of his divine energies that pierce the bodies of the disciples who have ascended the mountain with him. The liturgical texts for this feast explicate the theological tradition behind these shafts of light:

> Today Christ on Mount Tabor has changed the darkened nature of Adam, and filling it with brightness He has made it godlike. . . . On Mount Tabor, O Christ, the apostles, bathed in the light of Thine unapproachable glory, cried aloud: "O God of our fathers, blessed art Thou." (*FM*, 469, 489)[24]

These lines describe the light of revelation as accessible only to the chosen, and only to the extent that their spiritual senses are prepared for it.[25] At the same time the tradition holds that the divine energies radiating forth also

Figure 1.1. Feofan Grek, *The Transfiguration*, late 14th century.
Courtesy of the Tretiakov Gallery.

transform those who behold it.[26] In this way those who witness the "unapproachable" light increasingly take on its nature. Blok's references in this poem to the Lady's call to him (blazing as a beacon) and his incorporation into her trailing sparks, uniting him with her, echo these traditional features.

Replacing Christ with his sophianic figure, Blok implies the interpermeation of literary and religious forms. In this sense we find in the poem a prime example of theurgy—and indeed it was first published among the pages of Bely's essay "On Theurgy" in *A New Way* (*Novyi put'*) (*ABPSS*, 1:489n.). Syncretic as it is, Blok's adapted icon with its blazing female body can be seen as an orthodox (in some respects) pastiche of traditional Orthodox elements. Indeed, as he reminds us in his poems "Spring in the river . . ." and "I seek strange and new ones on the pages . . . ," Orthodox tradition grants Mary a flesh of fire in comparing her to Moses's burning bush (*neopalimaia kupina*)—the object that contained God and yet was not consumed ("Vesna v reke lomaet l'diny . . . ," *ABPSS*, 1:100–101; "Strannykh i novykh ischchu na stranitsakh . . . ," *ABPSS*, 1:102).[27] (This is an image found in the icon tradition but also in prominently visible works from Blok's time, such as Vasilii Beliaev's mosaic in the Church of the Savior on Spilled Blood in Petersburg, shown in figure 1.2.)

But beyond creating a symbolic system for a world in transition, how does Blok's poetry seek to effect change? Above all, and as we will see in this poem, he uses poetic form to reconfigure the signifier, gearing it to a projected, signified world where matter is permeable and where all things and beings can know one another fully. Ivanov points to such a need when he describes the "crisis of art" connected with the crisis of humanism and the loss of "inner form." Writing in 1919, he says the artist is "in danger of being cut off from the harmonious system of images that exists in the world of objects."[28] As though reflecting on Blok himself, he speaks of writers in whom "language is becoming vague, incorporeal, and aerial as it moves away from the tradition of the inner form of the word into a dreamy distance that teems with illusions of the possibilities of new inner forms." While applying such a diagnosis to Blok would imply the artist's failure (and Blok would at significant points agree!), nevertheless Ivanov cannily identifies Blok's task—to cast around for ways to represent the forms of a changed world.

Blok presents this new world through sound, above all. For him, as for Ivanov, Bely, and other modernists, the sound of words bears significance far beyond their traditional meanings. Language had failed in its power to convey semantic meaning: words aurally bore magic, but not always a great deal of sense.[29] In "The Magic of Words" (1909) Bely identifies contemporary poetry, with its return to musicality, as a paradigm for "living speech" that opens, through sound, a window onto the essence of things and, simultaneously, creates new worlds.[30] (He opposes this living word to the dead, crystal-

Figure 1.2. Vasilii Beliaev, *Mosaic of the Burning Bush* (*Neopalimaia Kupina*) in the Church of the Savior on Spilled Blood, St. Petersburg.
Courtesy of Father Aleksei Vtulov.

line "word-term," which he connects to abstract, rational thought.) Blok also connects sound with creating new worlds, as in his 1918 "The Intelligentsia and the Revolution": "This is the music which he who has ears should hear," writes Blok, referring to the music of revolution, the sound of the world turning upside down (*ABSS*, 6:9–31; here, 13). This music is that same "*gul*" he describes a decade earlier in "The People and the Intelligentsia," a sound that becomes "more and more distinct by the day" (*ABSS*, 5:318–28; here, 328). This same sound, though, resounds in his earliest poetry and the whirlwinds that blow through them. Blok's allusion to the biblical verse "He who has ears, let him hear" (Matthew 11:15) applies as much to the poem we examine here as for his later work, including the storm of *The Twelve*. Sound is the medium by which the new world will appear, and Blok's use of sound clarifies his vision of material unity.

About a decade after Blok wrote *Verses* the *imiaslavie* controversy would erupt, sparking far-reaching discussions about the power of the word. As Thomas Seifrid recounts, the so-called *imiaslavtsy*, meaning "those who worship the name," were a group of monks on Mt. Athos who believed that the very act of sounding out Christ's name invoked his presence.[31] Church hierarchs strongly objected, and the struggle between the *imiaslavtsy* and their rivals, who came to be known as the *imiabortsy* (literally, "those who fight the Name"), eventually led to a military detachment being sent to Athos with one of the hierarchs to quell the unrest. One of the verbal touchstones for the *imiaslavtsy* was that "the name of God is God himself"—a declaration with far-reaching implications indeed for language and sound. Such a concept and the consequences of embodying this concept in practice inspired numerous literary and philosophical reflections on the power of language and on the identity of the word with the thing it names. Osip Mandelstam wrote defining responses in both prose and poetry.[32] What is interesting for our purposes is how Blok seems to have anticipated many of the issues they would raise.

In this poem Blok begins, from the first line, by confounding our semantic associations and in establishing, in their place, sonic associations.[33] In repeating the syllable "gor-"—"Ty *gor*ish' nad vysokoi *gor*oiu"—he conflates a verb with a noun, action with structural object, and also the translucent nature of fire with the impermeable nature of earth. Moreover, in these elements the earthly and heavenly blend, the former even lifting up the latter.[34] This conflation of fire with putatively impermeable barriers, such as bodies, appears again and again in the poem, and in the volume as a whole. Another key instance occurs in the confusing presentation of the Lady. Any contemporary reader of Blok's would recognize his reference to the Orthodox Transfiguration icon in the first line. In this context, the second line's description of a lady "v teremu"—*in* a tower—cedes much of its locative significance to a metaphoric reading by which the enclosing quality of the tower (and its sense, in Old Russian, of "women's quarters") refers to the "unapproachable" quality of the light emanating from the Lady's transformed body. Here we see the Lady's body and the tower—flesh and encircling structure—merge, into the substance of fire.

This metamorphosis echoes in the poem's stanzaic construction. In each of the first two stanzas, the first two lines (both times beginning with "Ty" [you]) refer to the Lady, and the second two refer to the poetic narrator—effectively separating the poet from his Lady within the stanzas. In the final stanza, the poetic narrator still governs the last two lines, but "sparks" (*iskry*) govern the first two lines. Through stanzaic parallelism we behold the Lady replaced by the sparks that fly out from her flaming body. The poet presents his future self merging with these circling trails of sparks in the next line (the third in the stanza); this move recalls the reader to the shafts of light, the divine energies, which transform Christ's disciples in the Transfiguration scene. As the liturgical text we have seen explains, these beams are what make the followers radiant. Thus the poet's merging with these "shafts" or beams signifies his body's transformation into the same fiery substance of the Lady—enabling him in the final line to reach and merge with her. (This light-penetrated body finds its paradigm in the Transfiguration image.)[35]

Blok also constructs a turning point at the poem's center, the point at which the Lady beckons the poet, and he "will begin" to reach her. In light of Blok's emphasis on the beginning of lines in this poem, the initial letters ("S") of the sixth and seventh lines suggest a connection between the Lady and the poet and, concomitantly, a transition—the end of inaccessibility and the inception of unity. Another interesting sonic feature strengthens this sense of shift: in each of these lines we also find the phoneme 've' repeated twice ("razvedesh' vvecheru," "vernyi veleniiam"). These lines form an axle on which the poem turns, generating its friction and heat, echoed here in "ve" which lies heavier on the lips, slowing articulation and highlighting the change.

Blok forges his convergence of semantic associations most strikingly through his use of sound in the poem. By establishing initial sonic associations and then modulating them, he involves the reader's own body (by way of ear and mouth, enacted or thought) in the unifying transfiguration. Two vowels sound with particular frequency throughout the poem: "u" and "i." The "u" sound seems most connected with the Lady, "Nedostupna v Svoem teremu" ("Unapproachable in Your tower"). (The Lady is further sonically associated with the tower [*terem*] and its final locative "u" through the consonance of "Ty" and "teremu.") This sound appears eight times in both the first and third stanzas. The higher-energy "i" sound burgeons out frequently throughout the poem and explodes in the final stanza.[36] This phoneme associates itself with the poetic persona whose "ia" joins the ranks of "i's" that begin each line of this final stanza. If the "u" sound is initially allied with inaccessibility, the "i" sound associates itself, in the third stanza, with openness. It bears the conjoining powers of a conjunction (as Blok emphasizes by beginning two lines of the final stanza with this connecting word); and it serves further to unite the first and second halves of the stanza by replacing the initial "Ty" (You) with "I" (And). By heavily stoking the final stanza with both of these vowels, the poet creates an undulation between "i" and "u," between poet and Lady, an effect that mirrors the spinning of the sparks around the Lady. Significantly, the heaviest concentration of these two vowels comes in the second half of each stanza—in the half focused on the poet who is striving toward his Lady. Especially in the final stanza sound alternates dizzyingly between "u" and "i" so quickly that these elements seem to blur and converge. Certainly, in the whirling effect of the alternating vowels, we find a rich example of Blok's articulation of the sound of the coming storm that will howl through *The Twelve*. In the poem's final line we find a high concentration of these sounds together (four "i's" and two "u's"). Through this and other features (including identical rhythm) the line establishes an interesting parallel with the final line of the first stanza. The first stanza ends with the line (which bears two "i's" and three "u's"), "In rapture I will embrace a dream." Such a spectral presentation of uniting with the Lady sets in relief the consummation of the poem's ultimate line.[37] That is, we find parallel images that seem to achieve Solovyov's all-unifying *syzygy* relationship—that loving intermixing of opposites figured in the bringing together of the male and female elements.[38]

In its ideal moments, Blok's work in *Verses* presents the world as a body transparent and suffused with light. This representation poetically echoes Solovyov's descriptions of the divine light gradually illuminating the world and bringing all things into unity and their ideal form, just as it adapts elements of the *theosis* tradition.[39] Blok's representation differs from Solovyov's, however, in significant ways. The younger poet essentially removes the historical dialectic so crucial to the philosopher's vision. He seeks to realize transformation in the blink of a poet's eye.[40] In this sense his vision comes much closer to the fearful suddenness of the Transfiguration, which—in Gospel and iconic versions alike—knocks Christ's disciples to the ground. In "You burn above a high hill . . ." we find little of the terror evinced in traditional accounts (or even in others of Blok's poems from this book); nevertheless we do find a subtle tension in the poem that indicates a certain caution. The poet's luminous unification with Sophia—in all its immediacy—strains against the poem's future tense. This tension, too, though, recalls Transfiguration tradition, which views the event as both immediately transformative, but also prefiguring the full glorification at the world's end (at the parousia, Christ's second coming).[41]

Blok follows Soloyvov's call to bring the New Creation to earth by giving form to a restored vision of humanity. He attempts through poetry to realize "total unity" (*vseedinstvo*) by reaching back into traditional religion in a modern world that prefers science and reason. Literalizing images of transparent materiality and "universal mutual permeability" (*vseobshchaia vzaimno-pronitsaemost'*) used by Solovyov, Blok presents his own version of Sophia embodied, with poetry as her flesh ("Obshchii smysl' iskusstva," *SSVSS*, 6:75–92). Beyond Solovyov, though, Blok is drawing on a discourse of iconicity that pervaded linguistic theories of his period—most notably expressed later in Bely's work, as Thomas Siefrid and Steven Cassedy have discussed.[42] The poetic word, or the living word, or the Word, bore the same capacity of the icon to connect the audience with the world beyond and to unite the noumena and phenomena.[43] For Bely, moreover, "The creative word is the incarnate word (word-flesh)."[44] Poetry brings about new worlds through embodying them in its own substance. Blok's conflation, then, of Sophia, Christ, and Mary (the God-bearer) illustrates the modernist appropriation of Orthodox images of divinized or spiritualized flesh.

In his monumental essay from 1905, "The Apocalypse in Russian Poetry," Bely elaborates on the nature and significance of this female figure in Blok's poetry. He writes,

> In Blok's poetry we meet everywhere with the attempt to embody a supertemporal vision in the forms of space and time. She is already among us, with us, embodied, alive, near—the one who is at last recognized as the muse of Russian Poetry—appearing as the Sun, in whom intersect the rays of a newly revealed religion. A battle for this new religion will be the task of our entire life.[45]

In describing the modernists' embattled "new religion" Bely, too, chooses to conflate Sophia with the images of light rays that characterize accounts of *theosis* and the Transfiguration. He thereby demonstrates the relevance of Blok's remaking Transfiguration topoi, even while Bely draws on a later biblical reiteration of the burning body taken from the book of Revelation (12:1).

In *Verses* we find, indeed, other poems that broaden and elucidate Blok's approach to this task. His poem dating soon after the Feast of Epiphany (January 6), 1902, repeats numerous elements we have seen above, elaborating other parts of his poetic landscape. In particular, we find the convergence of body and building through lightened matter, but focused on the image of the church (*khram*), which stands in the cycle as the ultimate sign of the Lady's body.

Мы преклонились у завета,
Молчаньем храма смущены.
В лучах божественного света
Улыбка вспомнилась Жены.

Единодушны и безмолвны,
В одних лучах, в одних стенах,
Постигли солнечные волны
Вверху—на темных куполах.

И с этой ветхой позолоты,
Из этой страшной глубины
На праздник мой спустился Кто-то
С улыбкой ласковой Жены.

18 января 1902. Исаакиевский собор.
(*ABPSS*, 1:91)

> (We bowed before the testament, / Confounded by the silence of the temple. / In the rays of the divine light / The smile of the Lady came to mind. // United and wordless, / In the same rays, in the same walls, / The sun waves reached / Upwards—in the dark cupolae. // And down from this ancient gilding, / Out of this fearsome depth / Onto my feast-day descended Someone / With the smile of the tender Lady. // January 18, 1902. St. Isaac's Cathedral.)

Blok's echo of the service for the Epiphany Feast—marking Christ's baptism and its New Testament theophany—ensconces itself in one of Petersburg's grandest and most prominent cathedrals. (While Blok does not set the poem on the date of the feast, he strongly reflects its central elements, several of which are found in other poems surrounding the date of the actual feast, and leading up to this poem.)[46] The poem narrates a luminous moment when the congregation bows in silence at the reading of the Gospel, and the poet's vision of temple light is transformed into a visitation by his Lady.

Several features of the liturgical text for this service appear in the poem, and most centrally, the images of divine light and the revelation of divine presence. This feast marks the baptism of Christ in the waters of the Jordan by John the Forerunner—an event that, by tradition, both underscores the transfigurative powers of baptism for individuals and communities, and points to the restoration of all creation.[47] In the biblical accounts, when John baptizes Christ, the Holy Spirit descends in the form of a dove, and a voice from heaven declares Christ's divinity (Matthew 3:13–17, Mark 1:9–10). Blok alludes to this narrative in his own manner.[48] His formulation "sun waves" (*solnechnye volny*) picks up on the comparison of the waters of the Jordan (where Christ was baptized) to the symbolism of the Holy Spirit's luminous advent in the waters of baptism. In the canon for the Feast of the Epiphany we hear, "The Lord born from Mary, the Sun of Righteousness, sheds His rays upon the whole inhabited earth" (*FM*, 375).[49] In this phrase Blok transforms water into another light-bearing substance, just as the Blessing of the Waters on the Feast of Epiphany presents Christ's baptism as sanctifying "the nature of the waters" (*FM*, 348).[50] (In other poems, as we will see, water stands as an ambiguating substance, as ready to divide and deceive as to purify and illumine; but here, Blok seems, with the liturgy, to "bless" the waters.) As in his Transfiguration poem, Blok particularly emphasizes this theophanic light, which iconic and liturgical tradition attributes to each instance of theophany (as we have seen in the Transfiguration and Moses's "burning bush"), even when the biblical texts do not offer this detail. (It is absent in the aforementioned accounts of Christ's baptism.) But if the theophanic light accompanies the advent of the Holy Spirit in the liturgical texts, it accompanies the advent of the Lady in Blok's text. Moreover, through such a transposition, Blok replaces Christ with his represented self, the poet; for the Lady descends, dove-like, not into the celebration of Christ's baptism, but "onto my feast-day"!

Once again, though, the liberties Blok takes with this scene may initially obscure some substantial connections with other parts of the Epiphany topos and important aspects of Blok's creative revision. In particular, Blok adapts the ways Mary is presented in the liturgy and especially in festal canons (see appendix), in which Mary pictures the salvation of the whole creation through her bearing Christ. These images—notable in the Epiphany Feast—position Mary as a kind of spacious tabernacle not only for God but also for the restored cosmos. In contiguous canons for the Forefeast of the Epiphany we hear,

> The earth has been sanctified, O Word, by Thy holy birth, and the heavens with the stars declared Thy glory. . . . Let the whole earth rejoice exceedingly, let heaven be glad, let the world leap for joy. . . . The mystery of the Virgin is past speech: for she had been shown forth as Heaven and Throne of the cherubim, and as the light-bearing Bridal Chamber of God the Almighty. . . . Let the wilderness of Jordan blossom with flowers. (*FM*, 302, 309–10)[51]

In some canons Mary is actually pictured as a temple, and so Blok's uniting of cosmic images with this marian-church space seems either an intuitive or a knowledgeable adaptation of common liturgical tropes.[52]

Blok echoes these images of the assemblies unified even across the barriers of space and time in his depiction of the congregation in St. Isaac's. Unusually for Blok in this cycle (and for the lyric in general), he begins the poem with the first-person plural pronoun, offering the bowed congregation as his opening image. Through his use of sonic parallelism and iconic association, he presents a communal image of transfiguration. His use of the ending "-ny," in particular, associates the first adjective describing the congregation, "smushcheny" (confounded), with the Lady (here, "Zhena") and the transforming light (the rays which are "[e]dinodushny i bezmolvny" [one-souled and wordless] and the "solnechnye volny"). He compounds the association through poetic sequence, for the fifth line seems initially to describe the congregation, with its parallel adjectives to that in line two; but in fact, the adjectives describe the rays of light streaming through the cathedral. By association, then, the gathered people bear the same interpenetrable, light-filled nature as we have seen in the previous poem.

In their fiery unity the congregation reminds us of the Lady who burns "above a high hill"—and, in association with Epiphany, recalls the image of the Burning Bush (*Neopalimaia Kupina*, in the Russian liturgy, literally, the "unburnable" or "unconsumable" bush—the bush that burns but is not consumed). While this image is not unique to Orthodoxy, its centrality in Orthodox liturgical culture is unusual. The image of the Burning Bush appears repeatedly as a way to picture the body that contains God, the transformed body, and it served as one of the key images in the Hesychast tradition and its emphasis on the divine energies.[53] Blok uses this tradition to his advantage. He makes a similar connection in his eulogy for Vrubel', writing that

> on Mount Sinai, and in the chamber of the most pure maid [*v svetlitse prechistoi devy*], and in the studio of the great artist the words resound [*razdaiutsia slova*]: "Seek the Promised Land" [*Ishchi Obetovannuiu Zemliu*]. (*ABSS*, 5:421–24; here, 423)

Mount Sinai stands in Christian tradition as the location of several of Moses's encounters with God (see Exodus 3, 19:16–25, 24:9–18), and indeed, the earliest and prototypical iconic image of the Transfiguration is the great mosaic in the apse of St. Catherine's Church, built on Sinai. Here Blok explicitly, and rather orthodoxly, compares Moses's theophanies with Mary at the moment of the Annunciation, the inception of God within her.[54] (The image of Mary alone in a chamber occurs in the iconic tradition specifically in scenes of the Annunciation.) In his poem, then, Blok transforms *theosis* elements into a poetic celebration of the realization of new flesh, linking it with the Annunciation. This, too, follows liturgical tradition, for the Feast of the Epiphany also raises images of the marian body; texts for the feast compare the theophany at Christ's baptism and the streams which will water creation, miraculously restoring creation, with the conception in Elizabeth's barren womb and Mary's virgin womb.[55]

Blok's contemporaries perceived this connection in his early poetry. In his first poems published in *A New Way*, the journal's editors interspersed Blok's verses with reproductions of paintings of the Annunciation from two Renaissance artists (Leonardo da Vinci and Fra Angelico) and contemporary artist Mikhail Nesterov.[56] (See figures 1.3 and 1.4.) The Annunciation (in which God's angel appears to Mary to bring her news of her conception of God's son, the world's savior) blossomed as a favored subject for Renaissance artists, in particular, as they sought to depict the perfect human form and to invest human construction of the world with the divine imprimatur. Blok's appropriation of this motif underscores his intent (a sophianic intent, to use the term as Valliere describes it) to body forth a new civilization and a new humanity by religious means.[57] In a poem from 1901, Blok even realizes this transformation in the Petersburg cityscape, as he pictures the Lady walking along the Neva ("Ne ty l' v moikh mechtakh, pevuchaia, proshla . . . ," *ABPSS*, 1:67–68). The poetic narrator recalls, "You walked as a star to me, but walked in noontime rays, / Sanctifying the paving stones of the squares and streets." The conclusion of this poem underscores the sudden, revela-

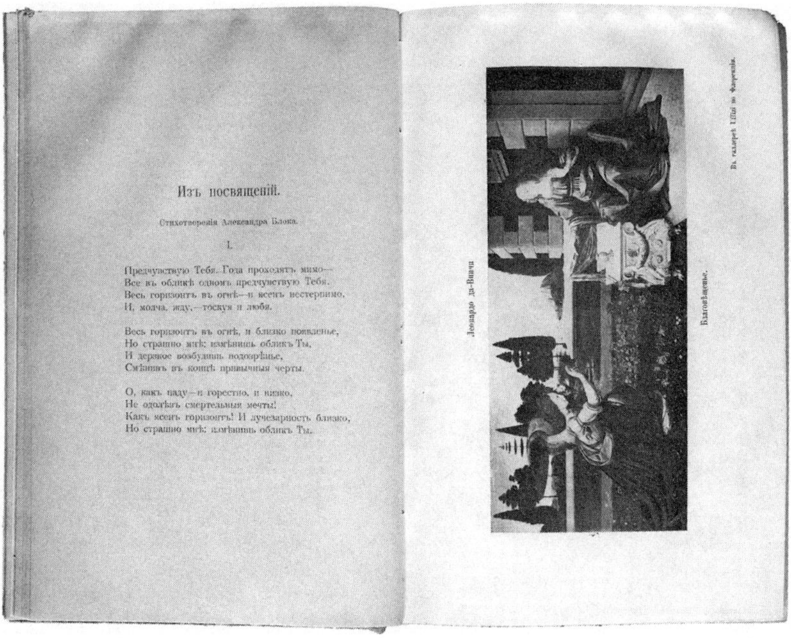
Изъ посвященій.

Стихотворенія Александра Блока.

I.

Предчувствую Тебя. Года проходятъ мимо—
Все въ обликѣ одномъ предчувствую Тебя.
Весь горизонтъ въ огнѣ—и ясенъ нестерпимо,
И, молча, жду,—тоскуя и любя.

Весь горизонтъ въ огнѣ, и близко появленье,
Но страшно мнѣ: измѣнишь обликъ Ты,
И дерзкое возбудишь подозрѣнье,
Смѣнивъ въ концѣ привычныя черты.

О, какъ паду—и горестно, и низко,
Не одолѣвъ смертельныя мечты!
Какъ ясенъ горизонтъ! И лучезарность близко,
Но страшно мнѣ: измѣнишь обликъ Ты.

Figure 1.3. Spread from *A New Way* (*Novyi put'*) journal (no. 3, 1903) with Aleksandr Blok's "*Predchuvstvuiu Tebia* . . ." and a reproduction of Leondardo da Vinci's *Annunciation en face*.
Courtesy of the University of Chicago Library.

tory aspect of Blok's vision, his sense that humanity and culture are so intricately intertwined that they must change all at once. For though the Lady disappears, the poet pronounces, "But I believe that you will arise, and the scarlet twilight will blaze forth."

In this poem, as in others like it from Blok's volume, we witness the poet's collapsing of the Kantian a priori category of space—which move he manages sheerly through a transformation of materiality into bodies that interpenetrate and necessitate no separation. (Sound is the primary index of this transformation in "You burn . . .".) This inextricable metamorphosis of space and material appears especially in images of rivers and wilderness—"bezdorozh'e" (lit., roadlessness)—elements which Blok links functionally. We find a key example in the Paschal-themed poem "Spring in the river breaks the ice floes . . ." ("Vesna v reke lomaet l'diny . . . ," *ABPSS*, 1:100–101).[58] Here the poet proclaims, "Having conquered my summits, / I have forgotten winter's enclosures / And I see the light-blue yonder." Blok combines this image of opening out with the image of melting water and, ulti-

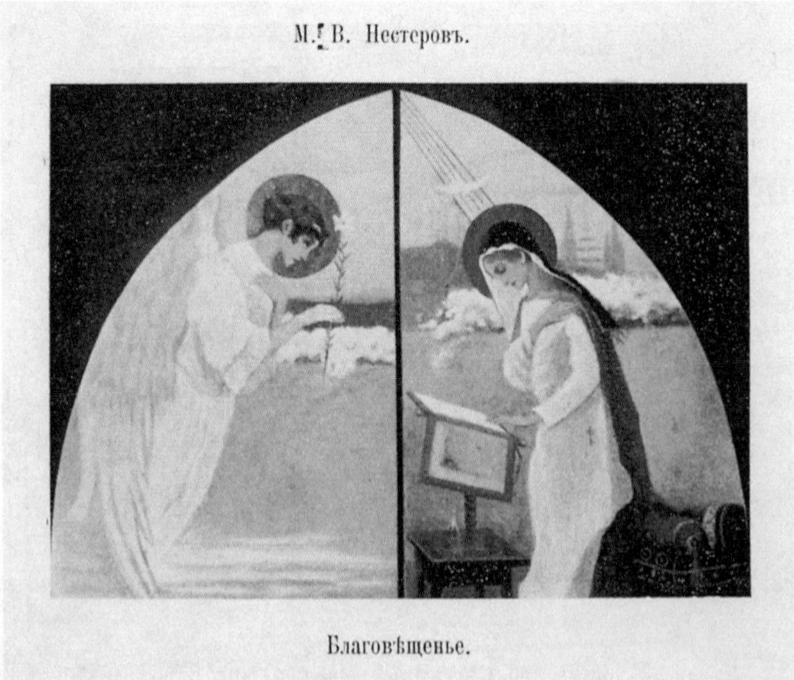

Figure 1.4. Page from *A New Way* (*Novyi put'*) journal (no. 3, 1903) with a reproduction of Mikhail Nesterov's *Annunciation*.
Courtesy of the University of Chicago Library.

mately, the theophanic Burning Bush—or "Moses's bush," as it appears here. This conflation of the opened landscape with images of running water and material (theophanic) light appears also in "We live in an ancient cell . . ." ("My zhivem v starinnoi kel'e . . . ," *ABPSS*, 1:95). In this poem the arrival of spring (everywhere in Blok connected, even when obversely, with hope for revelation of the Lady) brings waters right up to the door of the monk's cell. The poetic voice connects this "light-filled blue" (*svetlaia lazur'*) with the fulfillment of a covenant (*zavet*), declaring, "We will rush toward the wilderness / Into unspoken light." By identifying the wilderness and waters with materialized light, Blok inscribes his ideal landscape, in which no obstacles or boundaries obscure vision or knowledge. In his article on the spatiality of Blok's poetry, John Bowlt calls this space—the "there" of Blok's poetry—a "space beyond space."[59] We find such an image in the brief poem "I'll meet you somewhere in the world . . . ," on meeting at the "final feast," where the poet prefigures the new age in a space "beyond the stretch of stony roads" ("Tebia ia vstrechu gde-to v mire . . . ," *ABPSS*, 1:119.)

This "wilderness" space, unencumbered by limits and boundaries, represents a striking move away from Kantian categories, according to which knowing entails fixed (a priori) spatial and temporal differentiation. Blok, however, is not alone in this position, for scholars have noted a distinct understanding of space in Eastern Christian traditions in general, when compared with Western Christian (and post-Christian) religious and philosophical models. The work of cultural and religious historian Peter Brown echoes, from a more anthropological point of view, Blok's poetic representation of overlapping spaces of divine and human, eternal and mortal being. Brown locates the roots of modern cultural developments of and divisions between Eastern and Western Europe in the soil of medieval Mediterranean religion. He centers his discussion on notions of the "holy" that shaped these cultures, speaking of the rise of the Christian Church as "intimately connected with a drastic redistribution and re-definition of those points at which the holy was thought to impinge on human affairs."[60] According to Brown, East Roman religious accounts characterize the holy as

> a power that "manifested" itself in a manner that was as vivid as it was discontinuous with normal human expectations. If this is so, then we are in a very ancient world indeed. It is the world of the *epiphaneia*, of the sudden appearances of the gods. It is not enough that the divine should exist, it must be seen to exist, in the occasional flash of clear vision.[61]

Brown explains this momentary and "epiphanic" quality of the Eastern experience of holiness as standing in contrast to the more institutionalized and precise definitions of the "holy" in West Roman accounts. According to Brown, this particular notion of holiness plays itself out in regards to the liturgy, for "liturgical expectations were articulated in terms of potential *epiphaneia*—trembling, in many sources, on the edge of breaking forth—with the presence of the angel at the altar and the *epidemia*, the *adventus* of the divine in the Eucharist."[62] He goes on to define the "holy," for the East Roman, as "all that was non-human in any situation and all that could be suddenly 'manifested' from beyond human consciousness."[63]

The work of Thomas Torrance, a contemporary Western theologian versed in the Eastern Christian tradition, brings to bear the spatial implications of the notion of holiness that Brown's work delineates and Blok's work echoes. In his work *Space, Time and Incarnation*, Torrance describes the spatial and temporal conceptions of Eastern Orthodoxy as bearing a particularly "open-ended" character.[64] He argues that the traditions of Western thought, with its Aristotelian bent, led to rigid notions of the structure of the universe, and that the rigid spatial conceptions exemplified by Newtonian physics find reflection in Western theology, with its emphasis on the rather controlled nature of holiness—that is, its treatment of the sacred as something material that must needs be dispensed by the Church in cups, bread, water, or relics. He explains,

> From early times Latin Christianity had assimilated the idea of the receptacle into its theology where it affected deeply the form in which the doctrines of the Church, Sacraments and Orders were developed. Supernatural grace was widely thought of as contained in ecclesiastical vessels and capable of being handed on in space and time by means of them.[65]

According to this tradition, then, holiness works within certain boundaries that the Church (as God's manifest power on earth) regulates. Eastern Orthodox theology, on the other hand, offered a more open notion of the spatial manifestations of holiness, in which man can meet God outside of a strictly regulated dispersal of the divine. Torrance describes, in regard to the thought of Eastern Christianity, a

> concept of space in terms of the ontological and dynamic relations between God and the physical universe established in creation and incarnation. Space is here a *differential* concept that is essentially *open-ended*, for it is defined in accordance with the interaction between God and man, eternal and contingent happening.[66]

The "space beyond space," the "other world" which Blok presents in *Verses* seems to present a poetic conception of this relational (rather than fixed, or a priori) space, where man comes into contact with the divine in an epiphanic, even eschatological moment that can occur before the apocalypse or the end of historical time. Such spatiality resembles that found in "Forms of Art" (1902), and later also in "The Magic of Words," where Bely designates sound (or living speech) as a unifying element that generates space, time, and happening.[67] Blok himself couples the revelatory state with such an "open-ended" space, writing in 1910 of such a world, in which exist "no cause and effect, no time and place, no embodied and disembodied."[68] Such an approach, which defines the open-ended nature of space "in accordance with the interaction between God and man" emphasizes the *relational* nature of holiness, in which God reveals himself to believers who experience intimacy with him. Torrance's work focuses, indeed, on what he terms the "relational conception of space" that Eastern Christianity preserved from the Nicene Council.[69] Brown speaks to this notion of relationality as it developed in the East Roman context, asserting that the place of the "holy man" in this tradition was secured through the notion that he had won "intimacy with God—παρρησία (*parresía*)."[70] Such intimacy recalls that body which both contains but also dwells in union with the rest of the world.

The transcendent materiality which Blok represents dwells in its peculiar space defined by oneness with the Lady; yet in those moments when Blok views only blind matter, untransformed, the space, rid of its boundaries, becomes a place of encounter with terrifying shades and nightmares. A comparison of two poems, "I believe in the Sun of the Covenant . . ." and "Houses grow, like desires . . ." illustrates the way Blok's transformed space can breed angels or demons. "I believe in the Sun of the Covenant . . ." stands as the apotheosis of Blok's Transfiguration poems ("Veriu v Solntse Zaveta . . . ," *ABPSS*, 1:95). With its epigraph from the Revelation According to John, the poem envisions a "golden middle ground" (*zolotaia mezha*) leading into the wilderness (*bezdorozh'e*), a space filled with lilies (a symbol of the Annunciation) and angels' wings; here streams of "light inaccessible" (*nepostizhnogo sveta*) tremble in the gaze of the Lady. In the volume's final poem, "Houses grow, like desires . . . ," however, the poetic narrator surveys his visionary landscape only to find that "there, where once stood a white building / You will see a black stench" ("Doma rastut, kak zhelan'ia . . . ," *ABPSS*, 1:131–32). Proclaiming, "Thus all things change place / Imperceptibly fly upwards," he prepares to throw himself into the river—that constructed space of revelation. Over his body a flower will float up and bob in the current. Here the poet condemns himself to a space where revelation drowns in illusion, in the poet's artificial creations of what he desires to see. And here, finally, he rejects his own body, and, along with it, the possibility of embodiment, turning now not to the liturgy, which hangs on the reenactment of embodiment, but rather to the paragon of classical lyricism, Orpheus: "You, Orpheus, have lost your bride— / Who whispered to you, 'Look back . . . ?'" In this poem Blok rewrites the Orpheus myth in several ways—most prominently in presenting the singer's death as suicide rather than murder by frenzied Maenads. Here the focus we find in, for instance, Ovid's account on re-embodying Eurydice cedes place to Orpheus's willed destruction of his own body.[71] The flower that bobs up to the surface entraps the poet in the elegiac mode, by which he must create substitutes for the absent beloved instead of truly uniting with her. Thus the dead weight of the poet's untransformed body calls forth the insubstantial tokens of traditional lyric poetry and a corresponding chronotope.

In such a space we find what John Bowlt has described as the poet's inability to "apprehend optically the middle ground," explaining that while the middle ground exists for Blok, it consists of haze and objects that neither the poetic narrator nor the reader can discern.[72] Bowlt cites the importance of the middle ground in painting as serving to provide an "interdependence of the primary and secondary episodes and, therefore, to enable the viewer to understand the inner logic of the whole work." He goes on to explain that Blok "sees the penumbra but not the center." This is a wonderful description of Blok's poetry, filled as it is with shades and long light of the liminal hours of the day. In fact, Bowlt notes, this perception of objects as merely "penumbra" is "our normal optical response to sunset and twilight," at which times we can see distinctly what lies near to or far from us, but can see only the vague outlines of what lies in between.[73] On the other hand, Bowlt fails to credit Blok with also creating his "golden middle ground," in which bodies are transformed into light, and all things can dwell within one another. What Bowlt describes as Blok's inability to apprehend the middle ground represents, in fact, Blok's rejection of a Renaissance-type perspective, and his elimination of the middle ground or, in another sense, his transformation of it into a place where bodies and objects permeate one another rather than respecting the divisive properties of dumb material. Pavel Florensky has most famously described this space of encounter in his 1922 work *Iconostasis* (*Ikonostas*).[74] At times this space of meeting in Blok appears golden, at times murky as a nightmare.

Looking back at this early book Blok often comments on the transmogrified shadow space. As he writes in "On the Current Condition of Russian Symbolism" (1910), once the "golden sword," is lost, the symbolist artist dwells in depths in which "the predominant color is one that I would call purple-lilac (although this name is perhaps not quite precise)" (*ABSS*, 5:425–36; here, 427). Such a color—so hazy that even the poet cannot fix its name precisely—appears throughout Blok's work, even in *Verses*, which is considered his most optimistic and hopeful work. These colors, as Blok delineates in this essay, become increasingly associated in his poetry with the demonic. Here he describes the poet's increasing entanglement in his own "web of deceits—the more cunning, the more magical the lilac gloom surrounding him," where demon-doubles carry out his will, where he obtains the end of his darkened desires, the "doll beauty" (*krasavitsa kukla*) (*ABPSS*, 5:429). Such a threshold space calls to mind Kant's lyrical prelude to the third section of his "Analytic of Principles," where he cautions his reader who will explore the boundaries of the domain of "pure understanding":

> This land, however, is an island, and enclosed in unalterable boundaries by nature itself. It is the land of truth (a charming name), surrounded by a broad and stormy ocean, the true seat of illusion, where many a fog bank and rapidly melting iceberg pretend to be new lands and, ceaselessly deceiving with empty hopes the voyager looking around for new discoveries, entwine him in adventures from which he can never escape and yet also never bring to an end.[75]

The year 1905 brought about not only the first of Russia's three revolutions, but also an evolution in symbolist self-understanding. The failure of this revolution to achieve greater changes in Russian society and politics helped spur the symbolists to question the pertinence of their aesthetic theories and activities to society as a whole. At the same time as Russia was experiencing upheaval, Blok's experiences of love and art (inextricable for him) were shifting quickly. He had experienced the loss of his ideal vision of his muse and wife Liubov'; he had begun to suspect that art—and his art in particular—was by nature demonic; and he had begun to embrace this more demonic spirit, not least in the proliferation of doubles in his verse (*APLB*, 1:145–92). The 1905 Revolution inspired in Blok a greater attention to the role of the intelligentsia in Russia. Late that year he published a piece on Ivanov in the journal *Questions of Life* (*Voprosy zhizni*), a kind of sequel journal to *A New Way*, where he castigated modernist writers like Ivanov for ignoring social problems and political events (*ABSS*, 5:7–18; cited in *APLB*, 1:215). Russia as a nation and as a people took a more central place in his poems. But even this increased sense of social mission did not lessen his awareness of the changes taking place within his sense of self and of his art. The radiant visions we find in his first tome become more and more overtaken by visions of terror, vertiginous ecstasy, and confusion—qualities that first strongly characterize his volume *The Snow Mask*. In this collection and in many works that follow it, we perceive the increasingly Dionysian nature of Blok's aesthetic. Blok knew Ivanov's work on Dionysius as a precursor to the suffering Christ, published in *A New Way* in 1904.[76] He then met Ivanov in late 1905 at the first Tower meeting, to which Bely had secured him an invitation (*APLB*, 1:228–29). Moreover, as Edith Clowes has shown, the notion of Christ-Dionysus gained centrality for the symbolists in general, each of whom adapted Nietzsche in their own way—Merezhkovsky and Bely especially.[77] But Clowes speaks in particular to Ivanov's impact on Blok in this regard.[78] The Dionysian surrounded Blok, and it rang increasingly true in his religious-artistic experience.

Blok's thirty-poem cycle *The Snow Mask*, composed between December 1906 and January 1907, exemplifies this new mode in Blok's verse. In these poems, inspired by an intense affair Blok was having, the female beloved becomes yet darker and more changeable with a pronounced streak of sadism. The poet associates her with night, wine, and snakes, but also with snow and ice. The poet's world still filters through the lens of his erotic love, but with the greater darkening of his love, the world appears yet murkier and more terrifying. Despite these notable shifts, Blok's attention to the substance of the represented body and its aesthetic-spiritual implications never wavers. Throughout this cycle we find Blok taking the fiery elements of the Transfiguration body and simply transforming them into their opposites—that is, into snow and ice, into elements that freeze, obscure, and block rather than illuminating and opening. As in "You burn above a high hill . . . ," the Lady's body is made of and sends out swirling sparks, but in this new setting the sparks are made of snowflakes. Instead of light rays piercing the body, the speaker of "Overtaken by a Blizzard" writes of "snow needles" (*snezhnye igly*); and the Lady becomes—not a whirling fire, but the blizzard itself (*ABSS*, 2:217). In another poem, "The Heart Is Handed Over to the Blizzard," the poet repeats and intensifies these images, exclaiming, "Pierce me, / Winged gaze, / With the needle of the snow fire!" (*ABSS*, 232).

But it is in the poem "Second Christening" where we discover Blok's most overt and self-conscious translation of the Transfiguration elements into this new, stormy, and frigid setting.

Второе Крещение

Открыли дверь мою метели,
Застыла горница моя,
И в новой снеговой купели
Крещен вторым крещеньем я.

И в новый мир вступая, знаю,
Что люди есть, и есть дела.
Что путь открыт наверно к раю
Всем, кто идет путями зла.

Я так устал от ласк подруги
На застывающей земле.
И драгоценный камень вьюги
Сверкает льдиной на челе.

И гордость нового крещенья
Мне сердце обратила в лед.
Ты мне сулишь еще мгновенья?
Пророчишь, что весна придет?

Но посмотри, как сердце радо!
Заграждена снегами твердь.
Весны не будет, и не надо:
Крещеньем третьим будет—Смерть.

3 января 1907 (*ABSS*, 2:216)

(Second Christening // The blizzards have opened my door, / My room has grown cold, / And in the new snowy font / I am christened with a second christening. // And stepping into the new world, I know, / That there are people and deeds to do. / That the way is open probably to paradise / For all who walk the ways of evil. // I am so tired of my friend's caresses / On the earth that is freezing over. / And the precious stone of the whirlwind / Flashes like an icicle on the brow. // And the pride of the new christening / Has turned my heart to ice. / Do you promise me a moment more? / Do you prophesy

> that spring will come? // But see how glad the heart is! / The firmament is blocked with snows. / There'll be no spring, we need none: / The third christening will be—Death. // January 3, 1907)

As previously, Blok unabashedly articulates his poetic experience in directly liturgical terms, pointing to ritual realia such as the baptismal font. The poem recalls in its own way the "sun waves" (*solnechnye volny*) of "We bowed before the testament . . . ," with its references to the Feast of the Epiphany and the Blessing of the Waters. But here the all-penetrating rays of light that manifest God's spirit transforming flesh transform into the icy currents of a blizzard. Like the divine rays of light, this blizzard pierces to the poet's heart but turns it to ice instead of fire. A precious stone bedecks his brow, bringing to mind the jewels in Solovyov's poetry that reflect the divine light.[79] And as the poet hoped for his poetry, he enters here into "a new world," but with important differences. Whereas the knowledge of his earlier model is relational and experiential, the knowledge gained in this new world is cerebral; in this new world, the poet states, "I know." The mystery is gone, and the poet's entrance into knowledge brings not transformation and unity but, rather, pride and further isolation. Instead of experiencing the bringing together of here and there, of you and I, he witnesses a firmament "blocked off by snows." In reversing the elements of the Transfiguration body and Transfiguration space, Blok, however, is not undoing his own earlier project. In fact, by reiterating its elements, even through their opposites, he asserts its continuing relevance. The problem of the solipsistic Kantian body compounds itself, along with a desire to break out of it. What has changed is the degree of faith that he and his contemporaries can bring about the age of integrality—the sophianic age—that they so desire.

Blok's work continued to develop, and personal and political situations continued to shift. As time went on Blok thought and wrote with increasingly greater frequency about the responsibility of the intelligentsia in Russia. While some of the most ecstatic elements of his Dionysian shift receded, he came more and more to imagine, believe in, and represent the notion Ivanov had articulated of the artist as suffering Christ-figure, whose sufferings are expiatory for the nation. Blok viewed expiatory suffering not least in the consequences he would experience from his drunken revelries and strayings from the "path" (a word he often used regarding both art and the moral life)—experiences, after all, that fueled his intoxicated nighttime visions. As he wrote in August 1907 to Bely, who was distressed by Blok's apparent metamorphosis, "*All these things I have experienced and they are a part of me*—I bear my own psychological characteristics like a cross" (cited in *APLB*, 1:295; italics in the original). Through all these developments Blok never lost sight of the aesthetic ideal he had sought to realize in his youth, his desire to make art that would unite individual experience and social reality. Glimpses of this ideal surface now and then. In his famous cycle "On the Field of Kulikovo" ("Na pole Kulikovom") Blok retells an event of great patriotic pride, a milestone victory over the Mongols, therefore turning his pen to national themes and concomitantly incorporating national history into his sophianic narrative (*ABSS*, 3:249–53). In the cycle's third poem a warrior (and poetic speaker) encounters the Lady before battle; she appears in his tent with "light in [her] flowing clothes" (*v odezhde svet struiashchei*) (*ABSS*, 3:251), and her image flashes the next day on his shield. In this scene we recognize the familiar outlines of Blok's Eternal Feminine, with the light-filled body she would transmit to all of the earth. But now she is basically removed from an erotic and therefore more lyrical (personal) setting, and Blok has resituated her in an epic action of national consequence.

Blok moved, then, from the heady hopes that he could help realize a new age in clear delineations, that he could help channel that elusive, eternal, other world into earthly forms, transforming earth and earthly experience at the same time. He would not, he concluded, embody Sophia. Instead, he could embody a Christ-figure to be ripped apart—that is, a figure ultimately defined by its destruction of form. He transports us from *Verses on the Most Beautiful Lady* to his last masterpiece *The Twelve* (1918), where Jesus Christ appears in the final line, unveiled as the leader of a murderous, rather incontinent division of Red soldiers (*ABPSS*, 5:7–20). In this controversial long poem about the October Revolution change emerges not via armed divisions and ideologies, but by elemental forces external to the human world—forces pictured by Blok in the ever-present wind that builds into an ever-more-blinding blizzard. The scene, then, recalls *The Snow Mask*. But the scene also recalls *Verses* and even suggests that the cosmically Dionysian situation has realized Transfiguration flesh in an unprecedented and unexpected way. Surrounding the twelve revolutionary soldiers are "fires, fires, fires" (*ABPSS*, 5:11). Voices cry out, "We will blow and spread a worldwide fire, / A worldwide fire in blood— / Bless us, oh Lord." As in "You burn above a high hill . . . ," the sound of transformation penetrates the substance of that world: "The blizzard alone overflows / With laughter in the snows" (*ABPSS*, 5:19). Nowhere do we find the kind of stasis, captivity, inevitability, and enclosure of *The Snow Mask*. Hard ice appears only in the first few lines and then cedes to currents of whirling snow that overtake the whole scene: in the work's penultimate section we watch the Twelve march "down blind alleys, / Where the blizzard alone fills the air" (*odna pylit purga*) (*ABPSS*, 5:18). Seeming embankments of snow are mere fluff (*sugroby pukhovye*) (*ABPSS*, 5:18). The world is radically unified, radically permeable. Gone are the clear Kantian divisions. The world's very substance is changed into something rather like the sophianic body of "You burn above a high hill . . . ," except that blindness, not light results. What is missing is religion. Someone recalls how a priest ". . . used to walk around / With his belly sticking out, / And his belly shone with a cross / On the people" (*ABPSS*, 5:9). Throughout the poem voices intone pious formulations from liturgical culture: "Okh, Little Mother-Intercessor!" "Rest, oh Lord, the soul of Thy servant," "Oy, what a blizzard, Saviour!" (*ABPSS*, 5:7, 17, 18) But these phrases sound out as relics of the past, and the narrator tells us that the Twelve walk not only "without a cross," but also "without a holy name" (*ABPSS*, 5:11, 12, 18). In a radical way Blok both preserves and destroys the sophianic project: Christ and his transfigured world come into being, but it looks nothing like what he had expected two decades before, and no human attempts help actualize this Second Coming. Even and especially the structures of religion, its names and signs and cycles, are powerless and are swept into the ecstatic chaos of the new world.

Marina Tsvetaeva's *Verses to Blok*

TWO YEARS BEFORE BLOK composed *The Twelve*, a young female poet from Moscow had begun to write poems on Blok himself, in part as a way to negotiate her place as a woman in the world of poetry—that is, as a fleshly being in the world of spirit. Marina Tsvetaeva presents Blok in *Verses to Blok*, a series of poems written in 1916 and added to in 1920–21, as pure spirit and presents herself (that is, her poetic persona) as firmly flesh.[1] But even as she positions Blok as the quintessentially male poet—and therefore legitimate—she takes up some of the very questions he poses poetically about whether flesh or any human form at all can manifest spirit. The tension between flesh and spirit features constantly in Tsvetaeva's writing, a basic fact many scholars have discussed.[2] It is instructive to compare her treatment of this problem to the sophianic paradigm that the early Blok first amplifies, for in her approach to the problem she tests out the limits of the paradigm and even seeks to correct aspects of the sophianic program. In accordance with Solovyov's writings, Blok never really lets go of the idea that a mortal needs unearthly, sublimating restraint if he would actualize Sophia on earth. Tsvetaeva experiments in much of her verse to see whether not only the earthly, but even the earthy—the passionate, the unrestrained—can in fact construct at least moments of integration between flesh and spirit.

Like Blok, Tsvetaeva tests out this question not infrequently with reference to Orthodox liturgical culture. Mary as Mother of God is a key figure for her and an image for how flesh can potentially bear spirit—a theme evident in her two poems about the Feast of the Annunciation.[3] In the Matins service for the Feast of the Annunciation we hear the words pronounced by the Theotokos, "The descent of the Holy Spirit . . . has made of me a Temple that contains God, a Tabernacle divinely adorned, a living Sanctuary, and the pure Mother of Life" (*FM*, 455).[4] And in the liturgy for the Feast of the Nativity (Christmas), we hear Mary addressed as "thou Living City of God the King, in which Christ has dwelt" (*FM*, 285).[5] In "Annunciation Eve" Tsvetaeva takes up this liturgical theme of Mary's integrative role, addressing her as "Mother to the Sun" (*K Solntsu—Materi*). Many readers of Tsvetaeva have discussed the status of motherhood in her writings, and the most convincing readings present motherhood in a (complicatedly) complementary position to creativity.[6] One such scholar, Sibelan Forrester, has shown how church architecture in Tsvetaeva's poetry takes on this miraculous marian quality of containing the uncontainable (that is, containing God) and therefore legitimizes the female body as a channel for poetry.[7] As Tsvetaeva proclaims in "Annunciation Eve," "Blessed is the fruit / Of your womb, Virgin / Dear!" Therefore when Tsvetaeva associates herself with Moscow's many churches, as in her *Verses on Moscow* (also from 1916), she gestures at and validates her own constructive power.

But in her Blok poems she accesses further elements of Orthodox culture, including Orthodox hymnography and Orthodox devotional practices; and she employs these elements in her struggle with the male poetic tradition. In the first poem of this series she draws on current debates about the religious power of the word to assert her own verbal powers over Blok and what he represents.

Имя твое—птица в руке,
Имя твое—льдинка на языке,
Одно единственное движенье губ,
Имя твое—пять букв.
Мячик, пойманный на лету,
Серебряный бубенец во рту.

Камень, кинутый в тихий пруд,
Всхлипнет так, как тебя зовут.
В легком щелканье ночных копыт
Громкое имя твое гремит.
И назовет его нам в висок
Звонко щелкающий курок.

Имя твое—ах, нельзя!—
Имя твое—поцелуй в глаза,
В нежную стужу недвижных век,
Имя твое—поцелуй в снег.
Ключевой, ледяной, голубой глоток . . .
С именем твоим—сон глубок.

15 апреля 1916 (*MTSS*, 1:288)

(Your name is a bird in the hand, / Your name is an icicle on the tongue, / One single movement of the lips, / Your name is five letters. / A ball caught in flight, / A silver bell in the mouth. // A stone thrown into a quiet pond / Will sob as you're named. / In the light click of nighttime hooves / Your loud name thunders. / And the noisily clicking cock of a gun / Calls it at our temple. // Your name—oh, I mustn't!— / Your name is a kiss on the eyes, / On the tender hard frost of immobile eyelids, / Your name is a kiss on the snow. / A spring-water, icy, light blue gulp . . . / With your name—sleep is deep. // *April 15, 1918*)

Irina Shevelenko and others discuss the poem's references to Hesychast practices and the debates in the early twentieth century about the practice of *imiaslavie*—literally "praising the name."[8] Indeed, as Shevelenko sees it, Tsvetaeva uses the occasion of her poetic rivalry with Blok primarily to play out the modernist discussions of this phenomenon, discussed in the previous chapter. Osip Mandelstam's 1915 poem inspired by these events—"And until now on Athos . . ." ("I ponyne na Afone")—was especially influential: Shevelenko discusses the Blok cycle in connection with Tsvetaeva's and Mandelstam's relationship around that time. In this poetic dialogue, then, we see Tsvetaeva's engagement with the larger modernist conversation about the relation of spirit to flesh.[9]

In her poem Tsvetaeva explores some of the issues raised by the "name-praising" monks on Athos. Above all she raises the problem of whether the word shares in the essence of what it names—and therefore whether the word, in its connection with flesh and form, can call forth spirit. In this sense *imiaslavie* touches on the heart of sophianic concerns. Tsvetaeva, then, presents herself here as testing out the sophianic premise. On one hand, the poem appears to praise Blok's name—yet his name is not pronounced. The poet's refusal to articulate Blok's actual name seems in this context a refusal to invoke him, preferring instead to emphasize her own potential to do so. She builds her poem on descriptions of sounds that bodies and material objects make and that resemble the sound of his name, as though the most mundane movement can call him forth—a ball caught, a bell, a stone thrown, a kiss. Therefore she could, she shows us, hold Blok in her hand, on her tongue, in her mouth; she could catch him, throw him, stamp him, click him down the barrel of a gun, swallow him.

If Tsvetaeva cannot assert herself as pure spirit, at least she can wield the powers of her flesh, and so she exercises her bodily (earthly, mortal) power over spirit (and therefore over other, airier worlds) throughout the cycle. In subsequent poems the poetic voice invokes Blok in a series of names appropriated from the liturgy—"God's righteous one" (*bozhii pravednik*), "gladsome light" (*svete tikhii*), "of the holy glory" (*sviatyiia slavy*), "almighty" (*vsederzhitel'*), "sun," "bearer of light" (*svetonosnyi*).[10] (Michael Makin, Ol'ga Sedakova, and others discuss the links to liturgical hymnography in this cycle.)[11] But these comparisons of Blok to God do not culminate in her submission. Indeed, it seems that her position as a praying practitioner enables her to command the ethereal Blok: in her second poem she concludes, "Dear phantom! / I know that this is all just a dream. / Do me a favor: / Amen, amen, dissolve! / Amen" (*Milyi prizrak! / Ia znaiu, chto vse mne snitsia. / Sdelai milost': / Amin', amin', rassyp'sia! / Amin'*) ("Nezhnyi prizrak . . . ," *MTSS*, 1:288–89; here, 289).

Although the tension we find in her work between flesh and spirit never fully abates even here, nevertheless as this cycle progresses Tsvetaeva increasingly associates body with power and spirit with irrelevance, thereby elevating the mortal sphere. She draws on Blok's own poetry and also symbolist aesthetics to relegate Blok to the realm of the spirit and therefore to set in question the viability of his poetic legacy. He is a "tender phantom," a figure made of snow, a dream, a "dead angel," a whirlwind, a dead saint-singer, one whose "kingdom is not of this world." (*MTSS*, 1:288, 288, 289, 291, 296, 299, 295). She also compares him to a dead Christ, whose "resurrection lies idle" (*voskresen'e prazdnuet*) (*MTSS*, 1:292). As we proceed through the set of poems, Tsvetaeva's language and images remind us more and more of Blok's 1910 essay on the "crisis of symbolism," where he speaks of symbolism's progeny as Frankensteins—or, in his words, "doll beauties" (*krasavitsy-kukly*) that horrifically feign life (*ABSS*, 5:425–36; here, 429). Rather, that is, than creating new forms of life and culture through *zhiznetvorchestvo* (life-creation) and *mifotvorchestvo* (myth creation), symbolism generates not merely death in the sense of mortality, but death that masquerades as life, masking its own impotence.

The symbolist Sophia, Tsvetaeva seems to suggest, will never transform the world. Kuzmin and Akhmatova will echo this sentiment, but, like Tsvetaeva, they will not abandon the sophianic project itself. Like Tsvetaeva, they—along with Pasternak—will reassert the possibility that human cultural forms can embody spirit. But it is Kuzmin and Pasternak, far more than Akhmatova, who affirm with Tsvetaeva the power of the carnal—the erotic and the passionate—to channel spirit. Where the poems of Kuzmin and Tsvetaeva especially resonate is in the ways they challenge the gender constructs of the Solovyovian and symbolist Sophia.

Chapter Two

Sex, Love, and Liturgy: Mikhail Kuzmin's Revisions of Sophia

> The thought—that here is a person in whose presence the thought arises: if only these eyes, lips, cheeks, body belonged to me, really to me, so that I could without shame caress and stroke him—intoxicates me. It was to my delight and surprise to find that he knows and loves churchgoing and the services, and he even asked me to give him songs for the current feasts so that he could sing them.
>
> —Kuzmin, diary entry, December 18, 1905

WHEN THE TOPIC OF RELIGION in Russian modernism comes up, Sophia can dominate discussions. There are good reasons for this, not least the tremendous and oft-acknowledged influence of Vladimir Solovyov on Silver Age writers and thinkers, especially in the ways he offered and inspired new ways of relating religious (and especially Eastern Christian) traditions to modern life and modern discourses. But scholarship has often tended to confine discussions of this religious sophianic task to terms particular to Solovyov: as each of the poets discussed here—and especially Kuzmin—make manifest, many Sophias inhabit Russian modernist writings.

The work of Mikhail Kuzmin reveals at once the limits of common sophianic discourse in this project and also the broader undercurrents that fostered—among other things—the revival of Sophia. Images of Sophia per se are rare enough in Kuzmin's poetic world, with its overall tendency to highlight male homoerotic desire (albeit not exclusively). Kuzmin challenges the gender-normative sophianic paradigm, and he offers his own, male muses—the angelic-warrior guide (*vozhatyi*), most prominently.

Yet, as this chapter will discuss, his work also demonstrates the principles on which Sophia's rise is premised. Indeed, his work captures the essence of Russia's religious renaissance, with its fervent embrace of materiality, its desire to overcome the perceived divide between knower and known, subject and object. In reality the sophianic impulse simply emblematizes a moment that would transform not only Russian literature, but also Russian religious thought and Eastern Orthodox theology as a whole. Paul Valliere has described the underlying impulse that unites sophiological thought, in all its diversity, as the attempt to adapt Church tradition to a modern context.[1] Kuzmin's work confirms such an approach to Sophia. In this chapter I will consider Kuzmin's oeuvre as an ongoing attempt to embody religious tradition in a modern setting, and in this sense as a sophiological project. While focusing primarily on Kuzmin's poetry, I will draw comparison with the overtly sophiological writings of Solovyov and Pavel Florensky, as one way of demonstrating how Kuzmin's work exemplifies his epoch. Because of his refusal to ally himself firmly with any one group or movement, many readers have seen him, or at least treated him, as a marginal figure. In fact he is a consummate—perhaps *the* consummate Russian modernist; and this status reflects not least in his deeply religious concerns.

While Kuzmin's work offers few obvious references to Sophia, his 1921 volume *Otherworldly Evenings* (*Nezdeshnye vechera*) includes a cycle *Sophia: Gnostic Poems (1917–1918)* (*Sofiia: Gnosticheskie stikhotvoreniia [1917–1918]*). I will read its first and title poem, "Sophia," as an aesthetic manifesto in which Kuzmin distills defining elements of work across his career through his own, distinct sophiology. I will also begin to trace how the poem—like the larger body of work it represents—intervenes in the broader sophiological discourse of the period.

В золоченой утлой лодке
По зеленому пространству,
По лазури изумрудной
Я ждала желанных странствий.
И шафранно-алый парус
Я поставила по ветру,
У кормы я прикрепила
Вешний пух пушистой вербы.
На расплавленном просторе—
Благостно и светозарно,
Но одна я в легкой лодке:
Сестры, братья—все попарно.
На престоле семистолбном
Я, как яхонт, пламенела
И хотеньем бесхотенным
О Тебе, Христос, хотела!
Говорила: "беззаконно
Заковать законом душу,

Самовольно ли, невольно-ль,
А запрет любви нарушу!"
Расковались, оборвались
Златокованны цепочки . . .
Неужель, Отец, не вспомнишь
О своей любимой дочке?
Солнце вверх летит, что мячик . . .
Сердцем быстрым холодею . . .
Ниже, ниже . . . видны горы . . .
Тяжелею, тяжелею . . .
Прорасту теперь травою,
Запою водой нагорной,
И немеркнущее тело
Омрачу землею черной.
Вот, дышу, жених, и помню
Про селения благие,
Я, распятая невеста,
А зовут меня—София!

(*MKSS*, 2:247–8)[2]

(In a gilded, fragile boat / Floating on a green expanse, / Floating on the emerald azure / I awaited longed-for journeys. / And I put to the wind / The saffron-scarlet sail, / I fixed to the stern / The willow's vernal fluff. / In the molten expanse— / All was blissful and radiant, / But I was in the light boat alone: / Sisters, brothers—all in pairs. / On the seven-pillared throne / I flamed like ruby, / And I wanted you, O Christ, / With unwanted wanting! / I said, "It is unlawful / To enchain the soul by law, / Willingly, unwillingly, / But I'll destroy love's prohibition!" / We were unchained, we broke asunder / The gold-forged chains . . . / Surely, Father, you've not forgotten / Your most beloved daughter? / Like a ball the sun flies upwards . . . / My heart races, I grow cold . . . / Lower, lower . . . hills appear . . . / Heavier, heavier I grow . . . / Now I will spring up as grass, / I'll pour forth draughts of mountain water, / And the never-fading body / I'll darken with black earth. / There, I'll breathe, my spouse, and remember / The blessed dwelling places, / I, the bride crucified, / And my name is—Sophia!)

In this poem Kuzmin engages with and makes his own mark on the sophianic discourse of his period. As scholars have noted, Kumin's knowledge of Gnosticism—including the sophian writings that attracted the attention of Solovyov and other contemporaries—was both significant and influential for his writing, although he applied it creatively and with a rather Christian emphasis.[3] His narrative recapitulates, in its broad outlines, a classic sophianic narrative; but specific elements distinguish his poetic approach, which always emphasizes the compatibility of spirit and flesh. In Kuzmin's "Sophia," as in the classic Sophia narrative, the feminine figure, emblematically associated with the earth (e.g., as the "World Soul"), falls into a state of disunity with God; yet her state of union with the world also sustains the possibility of a renewed cosmic union, a version of which Gnosticism terms *Pleroma*. Kuzmin invokes this term in "Basilides," the poem that follows "Sophia" (*MKSS*, 2:79–82). Different writers offer differing versions of this tale, as we can see even from a comparison between Kuzmin's and Blok's sophianic poems. (Indeed, as Judith Kornblatt shows, one can find multiple versions of Sophia even within the work of one writer, Solovyov.)[4] In terms of *fabula*, Kuzmin's version of Sophia begins in a state of solitary splendor—flaming on a "seven-pillared throne"—resembling Blok's Lady who "burn[s] above a high hill"—and also recalling the same throne in one of Solovyov's most important Sophia poems ("U tsaritsy moei est' vysokii dvorets . . . ," *SSVSS*, 12:12).[5] But in terms of plot, Kuzmin, unlike Blok, first places his Sophia on a level with the reader, as she compares her state to the experience of sailing alone. Indeed, Kuzmin's use of the first person introduces the reader directly into Sophia's point of view. Instead of the lyrical hero's sublimated desire leading him to spiritual ascent, *she* is the one who desires, *she* is the one who undergoes transformation. Indeed, she undergoes death—unlike Solovyov's feminine ideal.[6] (Solovyov's model seems to be in mind here in additional details Kuzmin borrows—the colors of gold and azure, as well as mentions of precious stones.)[7] Whereas Blok's vision accompanies the hero into a spiritualized state, Kuzmin's vision accompanies Sophia into a state of enfleshment—her "unfading body" growing heavy and dark with earthly substance. Precisely through her fall and through this act of enfleshment does she ensure earth's redemption, in her emblematic crucifixion. In this distinct narrative we find the marks of Kuzmin's sophiological art: its emphasis on adapting traditional religion to a modern context in practicable forms (both figured in Sophia's incarnation), and its emphasis on the deeply interpersonal nature of being (figured in Sophia and Christ, rather than, say, Tiutchev's impersonal forces of chaos and cosmos).

This poem provides an apt picture of what Valliere describes as sophiology's "conceptual representation of the dialogue between the Orthodox theological tradition and modern liberal civilization"; that is, Kuzmin uses Sophia to emblematize how his art adapts religious tradition to a contemporary context.[8] This adaptive approach manifests in several ways. First, in his *Sophia* cycle, as the title poem demonstrates, Kuzmin offers a spiritual vision that is blatantly syncretic in nature, at once Gnostic and Christian; this syncretism aligns him squarely with his modernist contemporaries—Solovyov, Viacheslav Ivanov, Andrei Bely, to name a few—who wanted to bring the

Orthodox Christian tradition into conversation with other spiritual traditions. Second, Kuzmin, like his contemporaries, advocated a non-dogmatic approach to religion—seen here in Sophia's rejection of any "prohibition" to love. In the light of Kuzmin's larger body of work, this move speaks to the poet's embracing his own homosexuality as compatible with religious, even Christian, belief.

As evinced by the ongoing discussions of sex and dogma in the Religious-Philosophical Meetings, Kuzmin's peers, the representatives of contemporary artistic and literary culture, similarly rejected the Church's claim to regulate sexuality and decried what they saw as its negative attitude toward the body. (Olga Matich offers a focused account of this aspect of the meetings in *Erotic Utopia*.)[9] Notes from the tenth meeting especially reflect the intelligentsia's desire to foster a positive view of the body and bodiliness. In this meeting participants responded to Merezhkovsky's discussion of "holy flesh" (*sviataia plot'*) that he formulated in a talk on Gogol.[10] One enthusiastic respondent, V. V. Uspenskii, affirmed Merezhkovsky's idea by appealing to the language of the Easter season in which the meeting was set: noting that the feast spoke "so eloquently and inexpressibly" of the "resurrection precisely *of the body*," he called for a new "Christian culture of the body."[11]

We can see what scandalous associations such ideas bore not only from the comments at the meetings, but also from a response to it in the Christian press, an excerpt of which made it into *A New Way*. A writer for a "missionary journal" offered a parodic description of a "decadent liturgy" that mixed together snippets of *Ruslan and Liudmila*, *Blue Beard*, and Mozart with readings of the Song of Songs and the Apocalypse, as well as of Blok and Gippius. Outlining how the space might be decorated, he writes, "Above the entrance will hang a notice in verse (how shameful!—in verse!!)":

> "Пред всезрящими очами Господа"
> Одежда—"грех Анании и Сапфиры":
> Скрывать от Бога святое тело "не чистосердечно,"
> В храме тепло,—скидайте все и все одежды.[12]

("Before the Lord's all-seeing eyes" / Clothes are "Ananias and Sapphira's sin": / To hide the holy body from God is "not pure-hearted," / The temple's warm—take all your clothes off, all of them.)

In his own way, this writer understands precisely the project of the intelligentsia—to create sites in which sacred tradition and worldly culture could meet, and where religion and sexuality might share a broader expanse.

We find in Kuzmin's "Sophia"—as in his art more generally—what we might well call a new "Christian culture of the body," affirming the project his peers express in *A New Way* and the Religious-Philosophical Meetings. This emphasis arises first and foremost in the role Kuzmin ascribes to flesh in the spiritual path: for him spiritual transformations take place via physical experiences, wisdom comes through the body. In this sense his art represents a more radical implementation of the attempt we have already seen in Blok's work to unite subject and object, knower and known. Accordingly images of the spiritualized, sophianic body appear alongside images of the earthly body.

The importance to Kuzmin of embodiment also emerges in his embracing of cultural forms, including practiced rituals, as potential instantiations of eternal values. Despite his evident suspicions of dogma Kuzmin does not hesitate to appropriate a Christian narrative of incarnation and salvific self-sacrifice; at the same time he embeds this narrative in the cultural practices that Orthodoxy associates with it. Throughout his work we will find that he adapts Orthodox liturgical traditions to express how the divine becomes increasingly immanent in the mundane. His sophianic art is one worked out through praxis, over time—one that embraces and remakes ritual.

Finally, as in "Sophia," Kuzmin's vision of the spiritual path and of the nature of being is deeply personal—that is, best known and expressed in interpersonal relations. Love is an eternal theme for him, and his love is never abstract, always having a concrete object, even when that object also instantiates a cosmic love in which the poet has faith. In "Sophia" the lover's transformation is motivated by her desire for a specific other. In Kuzmin's opus the desired other always plays a crucial role in the growth of the poetic protagonist. This other appears in his work at times as Christ, but more often as an angel, an angelic guide, a travel companion, a cupid, or simply a lover. Regardless of the particular form, this other always serves to guide the poet figure to greater heights—even if by betrayal. This emphasis on the interpersonal nature of being and (hence) the spiritual path characterizes sophiology as a whole, with its attempts to frame the world's spiritual realities in terms of an interpersonal drama. (Indeed, some of the greatest controversies over sophiology have arisen over concerns that Sophia might represent a fourth person in the Godhead.)[13] As we will discuss further below, the work of Pavel Florensky especially parallels Kuzmin's in its insistence on the personal aspect of knowledge—reflected even in the epistolary form of his 1914 theological work *The Pillar and Ground of Truth* (*Stolp i utverzhdenie istiny*), in which Sophia and sophiology feature centrally.[14]

In this chapter on Kuzmin I will trace these four aspects that I have presented as sophiological: an adaptive approach, an emphasis on embodiment and praxis, and an insistence on the personal. I will draw on works (primarily poetic) from throughout Kuzmin's career with the understanding that certain concerns remain constant for him, even as they evolve—a point made by numerous other scholars.[15] As I hope to demonstrate by my discussion of Kuzmin's revised sophiology, this poet represents the heart of his epoch, though he is often treated as a marginal figure. His position at the margins stems at least in part from the fact that what readers often overlook in Kuzmin, they overlook in the epoch as well—a fervent but complex religiosity that engages critically with Christian, and especially Eastern Christian, tradition. Kuzmin's open and creative approach to his own homosexuality exemplifies this dynamic: his greatest work springs from a quest to express his sexuality in religious and especially Christian terms—as his Sophia puts it—to "destroy love's prohibition." As we will see, he believes in a universe held together and directed by love, and therefore what prohibits love falls outside the bounds of his orthodoxy. Kuzmin's central interpreters have noted how the poet incorporates elements of Christianity into his vision; in this chapter I will offer a more extensive and systematic treatment of this topic in order to demonstrate how Kuzmin represents the creation of a new religious aesthetic that advances the sophianic movement of his time.[16]

SOPHIA AS ADAPTATION

In the fall of 1905 eschatological sentiments waxed large in Russia, stirred up by January's Bloody Sunday and the defeat of the Russian fleet at Port Arthur, as well as widespread unrest and a sense that Russia's social and political structures would not hold. Blok's poetry, as we have seen, anticipates a new world—but it was one that depended on the decline or destruction of the old one—a stance best articulated in his dramatic poem *The Twelve*. In the fall of 1905 Kuzmin wrote in his diary,

> As I was walking home along a narrow, dark street, I was thinking that I find the beauty and delight of life most of all in the Renaissance and in the XVIIIth century; but complex, obscure moods under smoky sunsets in big cities, heart-wrenching attachment to the flesh, the sadness of things that are coming to an end, a readiness to renounce anything, a kind of prophetic joy, a bacchic spirit, mysticism, voluptuousness—all of this presents itself to me either in ancient syncretic cultures [*v drevnikh kul'turakh smeshannykh*]—Rome, Alexandria,—or almost in the yet-to-come contemporaneity.[17]

Kuzmin remained true to this intuition throughout his writing career and life, both of which express a profoundly religious sensibility and a religious sensibility that is profoundly syncretic. For Kuzmin the syncretic impulse characterized all times of cultural upheaval ("things that are coming to an end"), including his own time, with its sense of standing at the threshold of some new moment—a "yet-to-come contemporaneity." As I will argue in this chapter, Kuzmin draws his fundamental religious categories from Christian tradition, but he is always adapting them to the world in which he finds himself. His references to Rome and Alexandria bear out this contention: as we see in his writing more generally, the Rome and Alexandria he reimagines are the Rome and Alexandria of the early centuries of the Common Era, the centuries that gave birth to the Christian Church. Judith Kalb addresses this epochal interest in *Russia's Rome*, though the fullest treatment in regards to Kuzmin can be found in Lada Panova's *Russian Egypt: The Alexandrian Poetics of Mikhail Kuzmin* (*Russkii Egipet: Aleksandriiskaia poetika Mikhaila Kuzmina*).[18] In this work Panova offers the most complete picture yet of Kuzmin's syncretistic borrowings from these centuries, while she underscores the ultimately Christian coloring Kuzmin lends to philosophies that attracted him from this time period, including Neoplatonism and Gnosticism.

His perspective at (what turned out to be) the end of his life is not much changed, as his diary of 1934 indicates. Here he writes, in a section entitled "Everyday Life and Religion" ("Byt i religiia"),

> My constant inner struggle continues with Christianity because of its international character. In my opinion religion is such a national [*narodnaia*], domestic, native, intimate thing that it can't possibly be international. It is tied to the character of locality, with the climate, with customs, hair color, tombs. . . . What is a Christian way of life [*khristianskii byt*]? There's no such thing. There's a country's way of life, consecrated by religion. There are no Christian countries. Especially in the beginning. I feel a cold revulsion to the public from whom were recruited the Christians of the third and fourth centuries. Then everything turned into bureaucracy, and such saints as St. Francis and St. Ignatius, they represent Italy and Spain, not Christianity.[19]

In these lines Kuzmin rejects any identification of a "public" or a culture as Christian. This diary entry, too, links his own epoch ("my constant inner struggle with Christianity") with early Christianity, and it points to his own highly individualized approach to religion, his abhorrence of any religious stance that is not dynamic, syncretic, adaptive.

On the other hand, his religion is embodied, not abstract or empty of content, and as such always launches from concrete traditions. Plentiful evidence of Kuzmin's investment in the Christian tradition clarifies the nature of his syncretic trajectory. Biographers have discussed Kuzmin's early forays into Catholicism and Old Belief, and the poet himself tells of these periods in his brief autobiographical piece, "Histoire édifiante de mes commencements."[20] The poet did not come from an Old Believer background, but he did explore Old Belief and visit Old Believer communities in his early adulthood, and these experiences seem to have attuned him to the potentialities of ritual. Judging by his account of Old Belief in *Wings* (*Kryl'ia*), as well as by letters he wrote, Kuzmin seems to have witnessed a fervent engagement with ritual and a keen sense of a living tradition unlike anything he had known before (*MKP*, 1:179–321).[21] This context seems also to have inspired his interest in icons, offering him one aesthetic way to engage with Eastern Christian tradition.[22] At the same time the young man's remarks on art at this time reveal his struggle with the disapproval that Old Belief traditionally bears toward secular art.[23] If Old Belief inspired Kuzmin's interest in ritual, the explorations of religion that followed in his art and life embraced much wider swaths of tradition.

In a formative trip to Italy in 1897, Kuzmin was introduced firsthand to Roman Catholic culture—to its churches, its history, and its hierarchs (*MBMK*, 71). After an unhappy love affair, he studied and lived for some time with a Catholic monsignor, Canon Mori, who struck the young man by the easy balance he found between religion and a rich cultural life. Kuzmin casts fictional reflections of this time in his most famous work, *Wings*, in which the young hero Smurov stays with a Catholic cleric Mori in Rome in a kind of prelude to his realization and acceptance of his own homosexuality. This period seems, as Malmstad and Bogomolov have remarked, to have reconciled Kuzmin with a life in art, which he began to embrace fully in 1906, when he moved from any allegiance to Old Belief into a sense of identity with the artistic elite of Petersburg. It seems also, though, to have reconciled the poet with his faith in the goodness of the body and of the material world. In subsequent poetic reflections Catholicism—especially as embodied in Rome—appears as a font of civilization and as a bastion of high art.

But from Eastern Orthodoxy sprang the traditions the poet most consistently engages—his most plentiful and accessible raw material. An early devotion to Old Belief evolved over time into a consideration of Eastern Christian tradition more broadly. Kuzmin's experience and study of Orthodox Christian tradition was notable. Readers of Kuzmin's prose and published diaries will already know that he read avidly hymns and the lives of the saints in various collections.[24] Less known is the fact that Kuzmin read or owned an immense number of service books, devotional texts, religious-historical books, and theological works.

Undated notebooks in his archives reflect a voracious appetite for learning across multiple traditions and disciplines, containing numerous long lists of works, often with prices and publication dates. These seem, as Panova has noted, to represent the poet's reading lists, and likely included a number of works he owned and collected.[25] Some lists include works by his Russian contemporaries, for example, Valery Briusov's *Urbi et orbi* (priced at two rubles), Zinaida Gippius's *Verses* (*Stikhi*), Sologub's *Verses* (*Stikhi*) (*RGALI-MK*, 49:103v). Others list music by Mozart, Bach, Handel, and other German, English, Italian, and French composers and paintings by Italian painters (*RGALI-MK*, 49:79v–90v, 91v, 139r–52r, 174r).[26] Elsewhere he lists many foreign (Italian, French, English, German, classical) works of literature—by Gabriele d'Annunzio, Flaubert, Walt Whitman (or "Witman," as he writes), Boccaccio, Hoffmann, Walter Pater, Huysmans (*RGALI-MK*, 49: 91v, 64r–71r, 106r–19r, 156r–61r).[27] Dostoevsky's *Demons* (*Besy*) finds its place in his lists (*RGALI-MK*, 49:162v). This collection of entries fits neatly with any picture of a Russian fin-de-siècle aesthete.

But much of the content of these notebooks is religious and in its variety and detail illustrates how Kuzmin especially, but also many of his contemporaries (if to a lesser extent), brought together Western modernity with a religious quest that looked long and hard at Russian Christian traditions. One notebook seems especially focused on Italian and French mystical writings, such as letters by Catherine of Siena and the writings of Madame Guyon, a French Quietist: he transcribed long passages from each (*RGALI-MK*, 46:48r–78r, 107v–121r). He transcribes Bible verses and lists of saints' days and church feasts (*RGALI-MK*, 44:101r–101v, 101v, 141r–46r). He fills much of another notebook with his transcriptions of sermons in Slavonic, several of them on Lenten themes (*RGALI-MK*, 25:1r–53r). In another notebook he lists hundreds of volumes of various church service and devotional works, with multiple editions of each, from the sixteenth through the nineteenth centuries (*RGALI-MK*, 47:25r–77r). These volumes include the Lenten Triodion and the Pentekostarion (*Triod' postnaia* and *Triod' tsvetnaia*—containing the liturgical texts for services specific to Lent and Pentecost, respectively), the Service, General and Festal Meneia (*Mineia Sluzhebnaia*, *Mineia obshchaia* and *Mineia prazdnichnaia*—containing the offices for daily services throughout the year), but also volumes containing saints' lives and other devotional reading and teachings, including the Spiritual Meadow (*Limonar'*), the Prologue (*Prolog*), and various *paterikon*. It is fitting that the Church book for which the composer and poet lists the most editions is the Psalter, filling a full six pages, rather than, as with many of the other volumes, half a page at most (*RGALI-MK*, 47:50r–52v). Interspersed into this list of liturgical and devotional volumes are numerous volumes of a theological nature, ranging from *The Faith of the Orthodox Eastern Church* (*Vera pravoslavno-vostochnoi tserkvi*) to *The Moral Teachings of Theology* (*Bogoslovnonravouchitel'noe*) to numerous works of early Desert Fathers and Mothers and the Greek Church Fathers—Ephrem of Syria, Basil the Great, Athanasius of Alexandria, Gregory the Theologian, Gregory of Nyssa, and others.[28] In this same notebook we also find pages and pages of Kuzmin's transcriptions of traditional Russian Orthodox musical notations, Znamennyi

Figure 2.1. Page from Mikhail Kuzmin's notebook with transcriptions from a book on *Znamennyi* chant.
Courtesy of the Russian State Archives of Literature and Art (RGALI).

chant, which after Nikon's reforms tended to be preserved mainly by Old Believers (*RGALI-MK*, 47:233v–317r, 318v–358r).[29] (See figures 2.1 and 2.2.)

Kuzmin's literary works reflect elements of these lists; we will begin with an example in one of his best-known works of how the writer adapts his studies of Eastern Church tradition to a modern literary setting. We find this in his most famous work, the *Roman à thèse Wings*, which brings together an apologia for homosexuality with an interest in Eastern Christian tradition through the lens of Old Belief. Evgenii Bershtein has argued that "the aesthetic and erotic philosophy formulated in *Wings* corresponded very closely to Kuzmin's personal quest."[30] The story tells of the coming of age of Vanya Smurov, who with the guidance of his aesthetically inclined English teacher and mentor Shtrup, comes to embrace learning, art, and the beauty of homoerotic love. The novel resonates in many ways with the reading lists in Kuzmin's notebooks, suggesting that these undated notebooks may be contemporaneous with its composition. Like Kuzmin, Shrtup begins "to study Russian antiquity"—that is, Old Belief—with great intensity, explor-

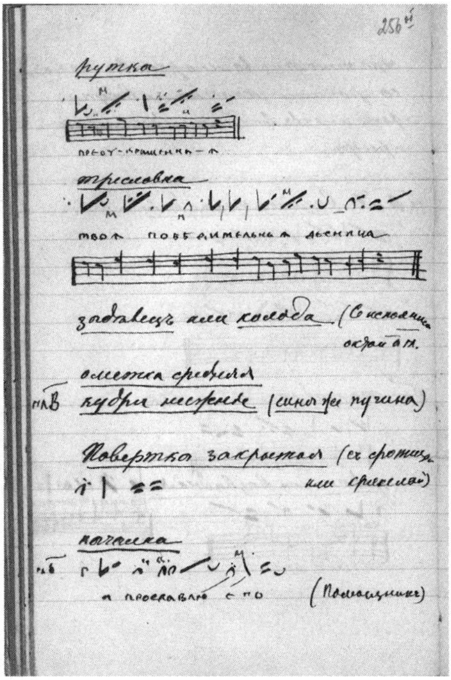

Figure 2.2. Page from Mikhail Kuzmin's notebook with transcriptions from a book on *Znamennyi* chant, including phrases from liturgical hymns.
Courtesy of the Russian State Archives of Literature and Art (RGALI).

ing its icons and its musical traditions. He exclaims to Smurov, "I was completely unfamiliar with this little corner of the world spirit" (*zakoulok mirovogo dukha*).[31] Like his character Shtrup, Kuzmin went through a period of intense study of Znamennyi chant, and he also studied and made lists of icons.[32] (Kuzmin discusses at length his opinions on new and old Russian church music in a letter of 1900 to Grigorii Chicherin.)[33]

But the most potent source by far of Kuzmin's knowledge of Orthodoxy lay in the services themselves. We find references to services and particular holidays throughout his literary and autobiographical writings. In his notebooks daily calendars list church services—presumably that he attended or planned to attend. One Wednesday, for instance, lists *Vsenoshchnaia* alongside the weekly gathering at the Ivanovs' (*RGALI-MK*, 49:41r). Other entries list services (*Vsenoshchnaia, obednia*) alongside eclectic reading lists (the Bible, *The Tempest*, d'Annunzio, Balzac) and places visited (the public baths, the library) (*RGALI-MK*, 49:103v). As suggested by his long lists of Church volumes, his knowledge of the services must have been impressive.

These lists, of course, do not tell the whole story: much of Kuzmin's approach to religion—even down to his fervent study of early Christian tradition—developed in conversation with his peers. One of those was Viacheslav Ivanov, with whom Kuzmin was on very close terms for several years, before a falling out in 1912.[34] Ivanov was one of the most important thinkers of the "Russian religious renaissance," and it was in frequent gatherings at his apartment, the "Tower," that many poets, artists, and religious philosophers encountered one another. His erudition, especially as regards religious cultures, myth, and ritual, was paralleled by few in his time. His poetry, like his publicistic and scholarly works and his efforts at fostering new religious conversations, sought to instill, as Robert Bird has described, "new rituals" into modern life.[35] As a topic of investigation the parallels between Ivanov's and Kuzmin's religious-aesthetic visions deserve ample space; here I will merely outline key points of resonance between Ivanov's thought and Kuzmin's creative work in order to underscore more forcefully the syncretic Christian nature of Kuzmin's approach and also how representative it was of its time. Ivanov's best-known work was and is his 1903 series of lectures, published in *A New Way* (*Novyi put'*), on Dionysus as a lens for the Hellenic-Christian tragedy of the suffering God that catalyzes cathartic experiences by which individuals and societies renew themselves. In these lectures as in much of his work Ivanov reaches into other religious traditions (here pagan antiquity) as a way of reframing the legacy of Christianity in terms that would speak to his peers—a creative syncretism, very much in keeping with the work of modernists across Europe and the United States. Another key aspect of Ivanov's work that resounds in Kuzmin's is his God's fleshiness—shown especially in Christ's capacity, like Dionysus, to embrace the world and die a gruesome death. This myth of Christ-Dionysus was one, as Edith Clowes has shown, adapted from Nietzsche and increasingly current in Kuzmin's surroundings. Ivanov offered some of its most powerful adaptations.[36] The fleshiness of God appears, for Ivanov, not only in his capacity for suffering, but also in concrete religious rites; accordingly he worked constantly to foster new ritual—of a faith embodied in innovative, shared practices.[37] Kuzmin seems to take this injunction and run with it.

We can see in Kuzmin's work his own attempts to body out a new Christianity that would draw on available sources of tradition, and especially the Orthodox liturgy. As we see in our epigraph, his sensuality is ecumenical: his sense of the poetic unites sex and the liturgy in one breath. His poetry itself offers a bold and breathtaking account of the modernist quest to forge a new religious aesthetic, but one grounded in the immediate context—as we read above from his 1934 diary, a "national [*narodnaia*], domestic, native, intimate thing."

SOPHIA AS EMBODIMENT

From his earliest poetic successes Kuzmin gained a reputation as a poet who loved the earthly and fleshly; he attends, too, to the spirit, though, and we will explore his love of the body in this light. Kuzmin's concern with embodiment bespeaks itself in so many features of his work, from depictions of human intimacy, to appropriations of ancient myths about divine-human progeny and Christian narratives of incarnation, to iterations of the ritual calendar. But we find the most apt expression of his passion for the flesh in his declarations of love for the body itself. His cycle *Alexandrian Songs*, which first brought him to the attention of a reading (and writing) public, centers on the delights of the sensual life—the taste of ripe fruit, the fragrance of flowers, the tender shock of a caress, a sweet kiss (*MKSS*, 1:167–231). Lines from the cycle's penultimate poem sum up the attitude conveyed by the poetic personae:

Мы знаем,
что все—превратно,
что уходит от нас безвозвратно.
Мы знаем,
что все—тленно
и лишь изменчивость неизменна.
Мы знаем,
что милое тело
дано для того, чтоб потом истлело.
Вот что мы знаем,
вот что мы любим,
за то, что хрупко
трижды целуем!

(*MKSS*, 1:196)

(We know / that everything's changeful, / that it leaves us and doesn't come back. / We know / that the dear body / is given so it might then decay. / That's what we know, / that's what we love; / because it's fragile / let's kiss it thrice over!)

Because of this cycle Kuzmin gained a reputation as a poet with epicurean sensibilities, and clichés of a carefree, earthy spirit have characterized descriptions of his work from his early reception to the present. The growing body of scholarship on him shows a much more complex picture. Nevertheless, the poet's embrace of the flesh is foundational to all his work; what must be added to this picture is that his approach to the flesh is essentially sophianic—that is, like Blok, Solovyov and his other contemporaries, his art nurtures a vision of spiritualized flesh—flesh that through the practice of faith becomes lit through with eternity's rays. As noted in the introduction, Ivanov's summary in "Two Elements of Contemporary Symbolism" of Solovyov's call to artists pictures "a world-transfiguring revelation of supernatural reality and the emancipation of true beauty out from beneath the coarse coverings of matter."[38] Though Kuzmin rarely depicts flesh and matter as "coarse," he does, as per Ivanov and Solovyov, advocate matter's capacity to show forth a more eternal beauty.

In the following section we will look further into Kuzmin's depictions of bodies to see how he presents art as a kind of *theosis*—the increasing permeation of human flesh with divine presence. Our investigation will move in a sequence that follows the descent of Kuzmin's Sophia, as we have seen her above. We will look first at images in his poetry that portray the sophianic flesh—that light-filled, spiritualized flesh we witnessed in Blok's work. From there we will turn to images of incarnation and crucifixion that portray the sophianic body as it encounters the realities of living in the world—therefore portraying how art incorporates even the darker aspects of existence. From there, we will investigate how his poetry depicts the very process of the earth's transformation into Sophia's own flesh—the process by which art is made. Specifically, we will trace a new ritual order that Kuzmin institutes. Here embodiment works on multiple levels: in his depictions of sex as a repeated sacrament, as well as in his depictions of a new kind of ascetic practice, the body and embodied practices work together to advance the individual on his spiritual, creative path. And finally, we will turn our attention to how Kuzmin speaks into the personalistic nature of the sophianic vision.

We saw in Kuzmin's "Sophia" a depiction of her flaming "like a ruby"; we might also note that the seascape around her shimmers like light streaming through jewels or glows like molten metal. These details may recall the light-permeated bodies and light-filled expanses Blok imagines. Kuzmin offers his own version of the sophianic body and the sophianic earth, and we see its images radiate outward from one central image: the red and flaming body that he compares multiple times to the Burning Bush, the bush that burns but never burns away—*Neopalimaia Kupina*, an emblem of earthly flesh indwelled by the divine—Mary the God-bearer and her progeny Christ. As we find in more overtly sophianic writings, Kuzmin's contemporaries adopted this image as a central emblem for Sophia. In a poem entitled "Burning Bush" ("Neopalimaia Kupina") Solovyov describes Moses's theophanic encounter as the conception of a new Israel, indicating that for the philosopher this image lies behind his notions of Sophia as the emblem of a new world, a counterpart to Mary's divine conception of Christ (*SSVSS*, 12:30–31). In like vein Florensky, in his letter on Sophia in *The Pillar and Ground of Truth*, speaks of Mary as "the Carrier of Sophia" (*Nositel'nitsa Sofii*) and offers a long and variegated list of marian titles that manifest her connection to Sophia as a figure of ideally transformed flesh. In this passage he writes of this Sophia-bearing Mary, "She is the '*Burning Bush*' [*Neopalimaia Kupina*], wrapped in the flame of the Holy Spirit, a living preliminary manifestation of the Spirit on earth."[39] While Kuzmin does not refer directly to the Burning Bush in "Sophia," he does in other places—even including the icon (one exemplar of which is pictured in figure 2.3) by this name in a list of icons in his notebooks (*RGALI-MK*, 47:102r). Indeed, the Burning Bush comes to emblematize the heart inflamed by that very love that directs the soul upwards.

We find the most blatant appropriation of this image in Kuzmin's 1908 long poem *The Rider*, where the poet adjusts a chivalrous tale so that the hero finds his true love not in a damsel but in a young cupid-figure (*Amur*, or *Amour*) whom he liberates to culminate his quest (*MKSS*, 1:183–96). Kuzmin uses Dante's terza rima, cannily linking his work to the *Divine Comedy*, with its classic representations of the love that holds the spheres together and that appears through the beloved.[40] Once freed, *Amour* leads the knight by the hand to a door with a mark above it—a "flower of love" that "gleamed in the

Figure 2.3. Icon of the Mother of God of the Burning Bush (*Neopalimaia Kupina*). Russia, ca. 1750.
Courtesy of the Museum of Russian Icons, Clinton, Massachusetts.

shadow, burning but not burning up" (*goria i ne sgoraia*) (*MKSS*, 1:427). They enter the room. "In the middle was a bush, where each petal / Could be compared to ruby flames." The allegorical nature of this poem enables us to pinpoint the Burning Bush image as a kind of destination for the poet—a depiction of love's apex. He underscores how this state embodies the permeation of the human by the divine, or the temporal by the eternal, by connecting the image back to its traditional source, as in the final poem of his cycle *The Feasts of the Most Holy Godbearer* (*Prazdniki Presviatoi Bogoroditsy*). In this paean to Mary the poet proclaims, "You are a red dawn to the world! / You burn for an age but are not consumed!" (*Ty ne sgoraesh', vek goria!*) (*MKSS*, 1:465).

The image of flesh that burns with eternal light runs like a scarlet thread through all of Kuzmin's work. We find it most prominently in his images of the heart, depicted most vividly in the cycle *Streams*, in his first volume *Nets* (*Seti*, 1908), alongside *Alexandrian Songs*. The first poem of the cycle sets up this image of the heart and connected images that we find throughout Kuzmin's opus.

Сердце, как чаша наполненная, точит кровь;
Алой струею неиссякающая течет любовь;
Прежде исполненное приходит вновь.

Розы любви расцветающие видит глаз.
Пламень сомненья губительного исчез, погас,
Сердца взывающего горит алмаз.

Звуки призыва томительного ловит слух.
Время свиданья назначенного пропел петух.
Лета стремительного исполнен дух.

Слабостью бледной охваченного подниму.
Светом любви враждующую развею тьму.
Силы утраченные верну ему. (*MKSS*, 1:155)

(The heart, like an overflowing cup, sheds blood; / In a scarlet stream flows love that won't dry up; / What was before fulfilled returns anew. // The eye sees the blooming roses of love. / The flame of destructive doubt has vanished, burnt out, / The diamond of the heart that summons burns. // Hearing catches sounds of the stirring call. / The rooster has sung out the time of the appointed meeting. / The spirit is filled with swift flight. // I'll lift the captive in pale weakness. / With love's light I'll dispel the hostile gloom. / I'll return to him his lost forces.)

In this brief poem Kuzmin manages—more deftly than in "Sophia"—to unite physical description with metaphysical imagining. He vividly brings to mind the organ of the heart, with its constant pumping that refreshes the blood; but he also envisions this organ as a vessel of light—a radiant diamond with which he can dispel the powers of darkness and doubt. Kuzmin paints so many of his landscapes, skyscapes, and faces with the color scarlet and its variations (*alyi, rumiannyi, krasnyi, shafrannyi*)—and with each iteration he recalls the force of love and the way it can permeate the world, even if primarily in the lover's imagination. Images of hearts and roses also echo in images of rosy lips and blushing cheeks; these physical tokens serve for the poet to instantiate love's immortalizing force in the world. And like the diamond of the heart in this poem, when his settings are inhabited by love, he often also describes them, as we see in "Sophia," with reference to jewels, molten metal, gold, amber, or honey—substances that carry and seem to solidify light—a detail in which he seems to amplify the light-filled jewels found in Solovyov's poetry. Kuzmin's favorite landscape is lit with the sun, or with flames that recall it, perhaps the guttering light of an icon-lamp. Even battle's spears and the arrows of *Amour* appear as gold and shafts of light![41]

As this poem, though, so strikingly reminds us, the heart appears not merely as a symbol for love, but as the very real organ for the body's blood—and so in his own version of sophianic flesh, Kuzmin incorporates the potential for pain and loss. In this sense his version is much more embodied than Blok's or Solovyov's since even in its spiritualized state his sophianic flesh bears the reminders of the cost of incarnation. Other poems in this same cycle stress this aspect. In one, the poetic persona, the lover, declares to his beloved,

> Ты как воск, окрашенный пурпуром, таешь,
> Изранено стрелами нежное тело.
> Как роза сгораешь, сгорая не знаешь,
> Какое сиянье тебя одело. (*MKSS*, 1:162)

(You melt like wax, colored purple, / A tender body wounded by arrows. / Like a rose you burn up, and burning do not know, / What radiance has clothed you.)

Here cupid's arrows—and those arrows that pierce the soul in Plato's account (a connection scholars have explored in Kuzmin's work)—draw blood as part of the transformative process.[42] We also seem in these lines to glimpse an image of Saint Sebastian, so often depicted as a beautiful youth pierced through with arrows—a saintly image with homoerotic coloring, embraced in many modernist settings. In Kuzmin's work only those who love to the point of suffering gain immortality, and his art, like them, displays the wounds of the past to prove its sacred status. In yet another poem in this cycle the poetic persona also depicts his own suffering on the road to love's transformation:

Но к алой ране я привык.
Как прежде истекаю,
Но нем влюбленный мой язык.
Горю, но не сгораю. (*MKSS*, 1:128)

(But I've grown used to the scarlet wound. / As before, I bleed, / But my loving tongue is mute. / I burn but do not burn up.)

Interested as he is in depicting flesh that bears in itself the eternal, Kuzmin also adapts Christian images of incarnation and crucifixion that emphasize the transformative role of suffering in life and art. (One of the sermons he transcribes in his notebooks offers a meditation on Christ's sufferings on the cross [*RGALI-MK*, 25:1r–27r].) In his 1918 volume *The Guide* (*Vozhatyi*), which contains some of his most religiously tinged verse, he offers a meditation on this aspect of embodiedness, inspired by the sight of a mother and child. He writes,

Ведь всякая мать—Мадонна,
И всякий ребенок свят!
Потом настанут сурово
Труды, волненье и страсть,
И где найти тогда слово,
Что не дало бы упасть? (*MKSS*, 2:19)

(In truth each mother is a Madonna, / And every child is holy! / But then will come in force / Labors, worry and passion, / And where does one then find the word / That helps you not to fall?)

In one breath the poet ties the holiness of each person to the trials, the "passion" they must undergo in their life. Poems on Christmas and the Magi dot Kuzmin's work, each fitting the traditional account of the Incarnation to a modern context and sensibility; and each carries a reminder of the mortality into which the God-child is born—and therefore a reminder of the place of suffering in the spiritual walk.[43]

Incarnation always, for Kuzmin, entails crucifixion, as in another poem from *The Guide*.

Просохшая земля! Прижаться к ней.
Безсолнечную смену мертвых дней
Ясней позабывать и холодней!

О, твердая земля, родная мать!
Научишь мудро, просто понимать,
Отвыкнет бедная душа хромать.

Как сладок дух проснувшейся травы,
Как старые ручьи опять новы,
Какой покой с высокой синевы!

Раскиньтесь, руки, по земле крестом!
Подумать: в этом мире, в мире том
Спасемся мы Воскреснувшим Христом!

Кто грудь земли слезами оросил,
Кто мать свою о помощи просил,
Исполнится неистощимых сил. (*MKSS*, 2:26)

(Desiccated earth! Press yourself to her. / It's clearer to forget for a while / The sunless exchange of dead days and the cold one! // Oh, solid earth, our native mother! / You'll teach us to understand wisely and simply, / The poor soul will learn not to limp. // How sweet the spirit of grass that's just awoken, / How new again are old streams, / What peace from highest azure! // Arms, stretch out on the earth like a cross! / To think: in this world, this very world / We'll be saved by Resurrected Christ! // He who bedews earth's breast with tears, / Who asks his mother for help, / Will be filled with inexhaustible forces.)

This poem recalls "Sophia," with its image of the ethereal body blackened and heavy with earth, even nailed to it. What stands out in greater relief in this poem, though, is the resonance of these pictures with the one Dostoevsky presents in *The Brothers Karamazov*—of Alyosha's conversion moment, where he throws himself down on the ground and waters it with his tears.[44] This passage has been seen as Dostoevsky's depiction of an authentic Russian faith, with its return to the earth and to the faith of the people, its turn away from the abstraction of European philosophy and modern secular life. Kuzmin's echo of such a famous passage speaks volumes about his own attempt to express a native faith.

SOPHIA AS PRAXIS

But Kuzmin is as interested in the process of getting to resurrection, or immortality, as he is in the goal itself. That is *also* to say that he likes to depict the process of making art (the sophianic process), rendering things new in the world. As Vladimir Markov and others have noted, he very often situates his poems as stages in novel-like narratives; in this section we will explore how he embeds his poems in liturgical seasons and ritual practices.[45] We will look especially at how he depicts love's practices—especially sex—as rites, steps in a spiritual journey; and how he adapts Eastern Christian ascetic praxis to a modern, worldly setting.

In his letters and notes, as in his poetry, Kuzmin routinely associates "ritual" and the "everyday" (*byt*).[46] We find a special emphasis on ritualizing life in his first three volumes of verse, *Nets* (*Seti*, 1908), *Autumnal Lakes* (*Osennie ozera*, 1912), and *Clay Doves* (*Glinianye golubki*, 1914), although this aesthetic of praxis extends throughout his work. An early poem in *Nets* exemplifies this approach. In "Oh, lips, kissed by so many . . ." he speaks of kisses as Eucharistic participation, sacred and eschatologically communal, bringing oneness through discrete, physical (and thus temporal) experiences.

Ах, уста, целованные столькими,
Столькими другими устами,
Вы пронзаете стрелами горькими,
Горькими стрелами, стами.

Расцветете улыбками бойкими
Светлыми весенними кустами,
Будто ласка перстами легкими,
Легкими милыми перстами.

Пилигрим, разбойник ли дерзостный—
Каждый поцелуй к вам доходит.
Антиной, Ферсит ли мерзостный—
Каждый свое счастье находит.

Поцелуй, что к вам прикасается,
Крепкою печатью ложиться,
Кто устам любимым причащается,
С прошлыми со всеми роднится.

Взгляд мольбы, на иконе оставленный,
Крепкими цепями там ляжет:
Древний лик, мольбами прославленный,
Цепью той молящихся вяжет.

Так идешь местами ты скользкими,
Скользкими, святыми местами.—
Ах, уста, целованные столькими,
Столькими другими устами. (*MKSS*, 1:49)

(Oh, lips, kissed by so many, / So many other lips, / You pierce with bitter arrows, / Bitter arrows, hundreds. // You'll bloom in animated smiles / Like radiant springtime bushes, / Like a caress by gentle fingers, / Gentle, dear, sweet

> fingers. // A pilgrim or a daring thief— / Each kiss finds its way to you. / Antinous or vile Thersites— / Each finds his own happiness. // As touches you, the kiss / Lies down like a strong seal. / Who communes with a lover's lips / Is linked with all past lovers. // The gaze of prayer left on the icon / Will lie there like strong chains: / The ancient countenance, by prayers made glorious, / With that same chain binds those who pray. // And so you walk in slippery places, / In slippery, sacred places.— / Oh, lips, kissed by so many, / So many other lips.)

This poem presents sex as religious service and physical union as Eucharistic communion in an unorthodox Orthodox key. Images in the first stanzas of "bitter arrows" and lips that blossom (like a rose? like a burning bush?) indicate, as we can see by now, the sophianic implications of the poet's story—that is, he is telling us something about the union of flesh and spirit. He does so provocatively, though—opening his sophianic portrait with a picture of unfaithfulness, and of promiscuity as a means of uniting many people together. This is hardly what Solovyov had in mind by "total unity."[47]

And yet Kuzmin insists that the expression of love in all its aspects does bind not only couples, but also cultures. In his vision, love's binding power works not merely through disembodied imagination, but by shared, repeated acts that shape lives—by common rituals, by praxis. Kissing, caressing, gazing—these physical acts of love take on sacramental qualities, as when one venerates an ancient, well-known icon or partakes of the Eucharistic feast. Kuzmin even draws on religious images of sealing to drive home the binding power of praxis. In the fourth stanza he speaks of the kiss as a seal, bringing to mind the verse from Song of Songs (which Kuzmin knew well), "Set me as a seal upon your heart, / As a seal upon your arm; / For love is strong as death" (Song of Songs 8:6–7). This image of sealing appears again in the following stanza, as the gaze on an icon—a possible reference to Byzantine theories of icons, where, as Bissera Pentcheva discusses, the seal on the icon spoke to "the imparting of spirit to matter."[48] (It is a detail the poet may have known from his intent period of studying icons.) For Kuzmin, as we will see especially in our final section, any act of love—even (perhaps especially?) when shot through with "bitter arrows"—leaves an indelible mark on the lover. If the lover himself is faithful to love's practice, he—like art—will grow in his capacity to experience the immortal in the most mortal of moments.

The representation of sex as sacrament appears frequently in Kuzmin's work and, especially in that first volume *Nets*, seems a way of his purposefully reconciling his homosexuality with his religious faith. In one poem the lyrical speaker lights a candle before an icon in anticipation of a "wise meeting" (*mudraia vstrecha*) that we understand at once as the beloved's arrival and a sacred encounter ("Stekla stynut ot kholoda . . . ," *MKSS*, 1:131). Another poem also represents the lover's tryst as sacrament—"We exchanged rings, we took communion, / We exchanged kisses / At the window"; this sacrament renders passion productive ("I'll cover passion with purity") and removes all threat of shame ("Gde somnen'ia? gde tomlen'ia? . . . ," *MKSS*, 1:115.). The poem concludes, "I'm still the same, but with his tender gaze / My angel / Blocks my path to shame."

In general scholarship has failed to recognize the aesthetic resonances in Russian literature with Orthodoxy, in large part because scholars tend to approach religion via approaches developed according to Protestant tradition. Arnold Eisen makes this point in his study on Judaism in modernity.[49] According to Eisen, Kant's critiques of tradition and authority in "What Is Enlightenment?" (1784) along with his emphasis on religion as morality have been definitive for scholarship, as has as a Weberian-Durkheimian model according to which ritually dense religions are seen as more primitive and therefore not normative for modernity.

Ritual scholar Catherine Bell concurs, and she offers a model focused on performance that helps clarify what role ritual plays for Kuzmin. For Bell ritual enables participants "simultaneously [to] create a ground and foreground"—that is, to invoke tradition even while acting upon it.[50] Much of what gives ritual this capacity is its "physical reality," an aspect that accesses much more—psychically, culturally, and socially—than belief alone.[51] Bell discusses a major shift in the second half of the twentieth century of religious traditions and the study of religion toward an increasingly positive view of ritual, particularly as a way of creating or reinvigorating personal and cultural identities.

Kuzmin and his contemporaries (such as Ivanov) seem to anticipate this trend, as in Florensky's *Pillar and Ground of Truth*, where liturgical texts play a crucial and constant role. In this work Florensky tries to make the experience of faith legible to the modern person. In this attempt he integrates multiple modern secular discourses of math, philosophy, anthropology, psychology, and more with the Jewish and Christian scriptures, Church theology from the times of the Cappadocians and Desert Fathers and Mothers to his time, and also with frequent quotes from the texts of church services. (Just to read through his footnotes is a fascinating glimpse into the amazing breadth of works and disciplines he engages!) As he explains in a telling moment in the text, the liturgy bodies out the Church and its teachings in the world.[52] For Florensky the liturgy awaits interpreters, a task felt and initiated by others in and following that period, such as the more orthodox Alexander Schmemann in his foundational work in liturgical studies.[53]

The lyrical speaker's proclamation we read above, "I'll cover passion with purity," speaks through terms of ascetic discourse, which aims to describe a path by which individuals tame the passions and thereby become more intimate with God ("Gde somnen'ia? gde tomlen'ia? . . . ," *MKSS*, 1:115). This resonance is hardly an anomaly in Kuzmin's work: given his great interest in picturing the sophianic process, we should not be surprised that he labors in his work to adapt ascetic traditions to a modern sensibility.

The poet was not without precedent here: Richard Gustafson has shown how Solovyov's picture of transformation revises ascetic discourse. In his work, Gustafson argues, the philosopher expands the discourse of *theosis*, or deification, to include all people and not only monks.[54] Beyond Solovyov, though, Kuzmin's seemingly idiosyncratic turn to an ascetic way of life resonates with the massive revival in Russian monasticism that began in the nineteenth century, a revival most fully described by Scott Kenworthy.[55] As Kenworthy shows, this revival helped promote greater appeal for Orthodoxy in Russian society as it opened up monasteries to non-elite classes, as postulants or pilgrims. He writes, "The monastery became the locus par excellence of encounter with the divine, above all through its solemn liturgies, the relics of revered saints, and miraculous icons—all of which drew believers by the millions."[56] He goes on to describe how the institution of eldership and also related devotional practices spread rapidly and widely from these monasteries, ensuring "levels of religious practice that were far higher than in Western Europe." These phenomena are reflected in Dostoevsky's *Brothers Karamazov*, with its two elders and their mass appeal; they are also reflected in the pilgrimages made by prominent cultural figures such as Solovyov, Dostoevsky, and Tolstoy to monasteries with famous elders. By accessing ascetic discourse, then, Kuzmin cannily speaks to popular religious interests.

The poet, however, like his contemporaries, is particular about his asceticism, rejecting some forms and adapting others. In his early religious searchings Kuzmin more than once considered taking monastic vows (*MBMK*, 54). But, as with the members of the Religious-Philosophical Meetings (in particular Merezhkovsky and Rozanov), the ascetic tradition taken as a whole seemed for Kuzmin a denial of the world rather than its affirmation.[57] This view is reflected in *Wings*, in Smurov's reaction to an Old Believer elder who rejects the body for its mortality, and in the comments of a musician who speaks of asceticism as "the most unnatural phenomenon of all" (*naibolee protivoestestvennoe iavlenie*) (*MKP*, 1:260, 284). Yet Kuzmin does not reject the ascetic tradition wholesale; instead, he incorporates it into his vision of transformation over time, and of life lived in accordance with ritual. Indeed, a considerable portion of Kuzmin's work features his adaptation of the Orthodox tradition of asceticism and its disciplines in faithfulness, comprised in the liturgical tradition.[58]

He hints at this tradition even in several poems in his first cycle—focusing on the poet's deprivation of the presence of his beloved, and his deprivation of bodily intimacy. Early on he presents modern love as an arena in which faithful expectation takes on an ascetic aspect. Indeed, poems five to twelve of *Love of This Summer* present the poet as residing in the country, away from his beloved, who remains in the city (*MKSS*, 1:52–62). In these eight poems the poetic voice moves from loneliness to disorientation to existential boredom to anticipation of reunion. In each poem of this cycle the poet is faithful to the "flowers" of the "gay earth," in the sense that he faithfully transcribes the poet's state at each season of love. In deprivation of the beloved, time stretches out unbearably. And yet, in its very protraction, time takes on particular meaning as it measures the poet-lover's faithfulness: "The progression of protracted hours, / Of the self-same love—there is no betrayal" ("Ia iznemog, ia tak ustal . . . ," *MKSS*, 1:58). In the eleventh poem the poet figures himself as counting time until he meets his beloved again: "I count the remaining days and hours, / No longer do I write or stroll or read" ("Nichego, chto melkii dozhd' smochil odezhdu . . . ," *MKSS*, 1:59). And he portrays this act of counting time as an act of accruing value to the relationship to which he is faithful: "What tenderness I save up in separation, / That much stronger will be the sweetness of our kiss." This theme of accruing value to love through deprivations of the flesh resonates with the ascetic traditions of Orthodox Christianity. From his works modeled on saints' lives, such as his drama *Aleksei, Man of God* (*O Aleksee, cheloveke Bozh'em*), to frequent references in his diaries to hagiographic literature, to poems about ascetic figures, to endless references in his diaries to the poet's attending liturgy, in which saints' lives are frequently read aloud, Kuzmin's deep familiarity with and intense in interest in the Orthodox traditions of sainthood cannot be doubted.[59] He is a poet of all of love's seasons, and some of his best poetry treats love's dry and wintry seasons, touching these times with the brush of asceticism.

Kuzmin takes the themes of abstinence and fasting and casts his modern concerns and solutions in their mold. In particular, he brings to the fore, in poetry and diary alike, the theme of Lenten deprivation; here he reframes in modern terms that central point of the traditional liturgical calendar, the long period of fasting and practical mourning before Easter's celebration of the Resurrection and new life. He describes in his diary an Easter Eve service of April 1, 1906:

> I attended the liturgy at Nikolaevskii [. . . .] I hurried home to break the fast I had kept for Communion. Despite my bad spirits, I still experienced that moment of light-filled expectation, when those left in the church await with candles the return of the cross procession. Oh, all times of expectation, how splendid you are, how gloomy would life be without expectation, without the expectation of liaisons, of happiness, of changes.[60]

Wittingly Kuzmin transcribes time-honored tradition—and his own religious practice—into the vocabulary not only of modern life but also of modern love, with its "liaisons" and "changes." As in "Oh, lips, kissed by so many . . ." he elides the Eucharist with communion of lover with beloved(s). For Kuzmin the relation of these two moments constitutes not a metaphor or an analogy, but rather an isomorph: in both cases the ritual actor accrues spiritual experience via physical means and repeated (i.e., ritual) practice—the rites of love. Kuzmin here takes up the theme of expectation—*ozhidanie*, or the act of waiting—and he compares to it his own periods of loneliness and longing, casting them as spiritual discipline that bears rewards all the sweeter for their delay.

In other writings the poet not only pictures ascetically styled deprivation, but he revises a monastic setting to fit modern secular experience. (Here I use "secular" in the more traditional sense—as referring to life outside a religious vocation.) Kuzmin writes increasingly explicitly about links between a lover's and a monk's faithful existence. This theme appears notably in the cycle *Autumnal Lakes* (*Osennie ozera*), dating from August 1908 to March 1909 (*MKSS*, 1:243–57). The first poem of this cycle introduces all the major themes the cycle will treat, particularly the theme of separation from the beloved as a stimulus for ascetic practice and kenotic deed.

Хрустально небо, видное сквозь лес;
Усталым взорам
Искать отрадно скрытые скиты!
Так ждало сердце завтрашних чудес,
Отдав озерам
Привольной жизни тщетные мечты!
Убранство церкви—желтые листы
Парчой нависли над ковром парчовым.
Златятся дали!
Давно вы ждали,
Чтоб желтым, красным, розовым, лиловым
Иконостасы леса расцветить,
Давно исчезла паутины нить.
Надежду сменит сладостная грусть,
Тоски лампада,
Смиренней мысли в сердце богомольном,
И кто-то тихий шепчет: "Ну и пусть!
Чего нам надо?
Грехам простится вольным и невольным."
Душа внимает голосам недольним,
Осенней тишью странно пленена,—

Знакомым пленом!
И легким тленом
Земля дохнет, в багрец облечена.
Как четки облака! стоят, не тая:
Спустилась ясность и печаль святая! (*MKSS*, 1:243–4)

(The sky is crystalline, visible through the forest; / May tired gazes / Joyfully seek out hidden sketes! / The heart so awaited tomorrow's wonders, / Having relinquished to the lakes / The vain dreams of careless life! / Yellow leaves, the church's ornamentation, / Hung like brocade over a brocade blanket. / The distance flashes with gold! / Long have you waited / For the iconostasis of the woods to bloom / In yellow, red, pink, lilac, / Long ago the spider's web vanished. / A sweet grief will replace hope, / The icon-lamp of languor, / Meeker than a thought in a devout and prayerful heart, / And someone quiet whispers, "So be it! / After all, what do we really need? / Sins are forgiven, willful and careless alike." / The spirit heeds unearthly voices, / Strangely captivated by autumn's hush,— / By a familiar captivity! / And with light decay / The earth breathes out, swaddled in crimson. / The clouds are like rosary beads! they stand, not melting: / Clarity and a holy sadness have descended!)

This cycle, like *Love of This Summer*, proceeds according to seasonal progression, though it covers the year's dying into winter, the decline of the summer in the country that the earlier cycle describes. Whereas the first cycle opens with an air of nonchalance and languor, *Autumnal Lakes* begins with a sense of barely repressed exaltation that accompanies the relinquishment of summer's hopes and expectations. The opening lines bespeak clarity of vision in its double mention in one line of translucence and visibility (*khrustal'no*, *vidnoe*); and it links this newfound clarity with both the approach of the contemplative life, pictured in the "hidden sketes," and the relinquishment of "tomorrow's wonders" and the "vain dreams of carefree life." The opening few lines include two exclamation marks, the first of many that pepper the poem. The poem's lexicon and syntax, meanwhile, create a mellifluous and understated feel, so that by contrast the use of exclamation marks suggests relieved acceptance, and surprise at the joy found in the meeker season.

This sense of glad relief in the ascetic season is mirrored in the poet's unusual use of meter. Long lines of iambic pentameter alternate with short lines of iambic dimeter—a metrical line that makes only rare appearances in the Russian poetic tradition. While the first two lines present one each of these metrical lines—first the longer, then the shorter line—gradually longer lines outnumber increasingly the shorter lines. We begin with a one-to-one correspondence, then two to one, three to one, four to one, then two to one, three to one, ending with three lines of iambic pentameter. While the first line of the poem offers a very standard metrical pattern that tends to give a casual feel to the verse line (a conventional characteristic of iambic pentameter), the second line, by contrast, cuts short the easy rhythm of the first line, creating a sense of emphasis and urgency. These two first lines, then, set up the reader to perceive the iambic pentameter in a different way—as a marked meter, whose length takes on a protracted and suspenseful feel in contrast to the brevity of the dimeter line. Kuzmin next underscores this sense of protraction by creating longer clusters of the pentameter lines and interpolating in between these clusters single (or, at most, paired) dimeter lines. These continual waves of protraction and abbreviation, accompanied by the periodic exclamation marks, highlight the sense of escape from long expectation, pinpointing the joys of even *this* season.

This rhythmic picture also couples with the poem's setting to emphasize the poetic persona's retreat into a place of greater simplicity and into contemplation. Here the poet pictures himself as entering into the woods, away from urban, if not from all human society. On his approach to the "hidden sketes" the poet depicts a setting more suited to the season's exigencies on poetic practice than the constructions of culture: the woods as a place for worship and ritual. The brocade of the yellow leaves ornaments his retreat sanctuary, and autumn's natural and perishable palette stretching from ground to sky replaces the cathedral's central window onto eternity, the iconostasis.[61] At the same time the liturgy and its trappings play out in the interior space of the poet's contemplation, lighting the "icon-lamp of languor" (*toski lampada*); and the "pious and prayerful heart" forfeits its claim to anything but forgiveness. The poet finally connects autumn's melancholy and the absence of the beloved with a kind of hermit's life, when he clinches the poem's lonely and contemplative mode with the last line's "clarity and a holy sadness."

Kuzmin's interest in monasticism as a model for embodied spirituality reveals itself in numerous works of poetry and prose: this interest, too, demonstrates his closeness to concerns of his time. Indeed, the theme of asceticism emerges in the Religious-Philosophical Meetings, as well as in journalistic essays, where members of the intelligentsia argued with representatives of the Church over monastic traditions and their role in society. Vasily Rozanov, an important voice in these meetings, wrote extensively about asceticism—often of his dislike for it as a way of life that rejects the natural. He compares monasticism negatively to the unnatural act of castration.[62] On the other hand, in his piece "Optina Pustin'," on the famous monastery, he paints a very positive picture of the Elder Amvrosii, renowned in his day and visited by a number of Russia's most important writers of the time—his list includes Aleksei and Lev Tolstoy, Konstantin Leont'iev, Dostoevsky, and

Solovyov.[63] For Rozanov Amvrosii exemplified an embrace of life, a delight in it that was not typical for the monastic setting. Concluding his piece on the Elder, Rozanov comments, "Asceticism is wonderful, if it's not official, not 'out of obligation,' but is a personal, biographical event, chastely modest and unpretentious."[64]

Kuzmin would agree. The asceticism the poet invokes resembles Dostoevsky's Zosima and Rozanov's Amvrosii (on whom, after all, Dostoevsky based Zosima), for it is one fueled by love. In collection of notes made from 1916 to 1921, which Kuzmin entitles "Fish Scales in the Net (For Myself Alone)" ("Cheshuia v nevode"),[65] Kuzmin includes numerous theological ruminations that foreground the place of love in his cosmic outlook. As he writes in one entry, "Love joins. The source of love is God, and creation is the work of His love. The primal law—love. The revelation of this law—truth. Truth and love—Divine Wisdom."[66] Ephrem the Syrian, whose writings were used in the fundamental handbooks of modern Russian monasticism, plays a meaningful role in Kuzmin's articulation of this outlook; and the poet embraces his teachings on love above all.[67] From his early notebooks, we see that Kuzmin read Ephrem, listing more of his works than any other single Church figure (*RGALI-MK*, 47:35v, 36r, 457r). In "Fish Scales" Kuzmin sees in the eminent ascetic's work "a magnificent specimen of Platonic soaring combined with Syrian fieriness" that invigorate his depiction of the Incarnation and its revelation that "love is the source, the salt of all creation."[68] Tellingly, while Kuzmin admires these qualities, he deplores "a certain asceticism" that undergirds Ephrem's works—a seeming reference to the more extreme culture of asceticism that distinguished anchorites, as Kenworthy points out, of the Egyptian and Syrian deserts, from the cenobitic, or community-based ascetic tradition more prominent in Russia.[69] In Kuzmin's poetry and some of his prose works, we see that Kuzmin values the aspects of asceticism that can cultivate love toward fellow humans over asceticism that focuses on fleshly deprivation and mortification.

In "Two Elders" Kuzmin imaginatively revives the debate over two distinct forms of asceticism. A narrative voice sets the scene, telling how

Жили два старца
Во святой пустыне,
Бога молили,
Душу спасали.
Один был постник,
Другой домовитий,
Один все плакал,
Другой веселился. (*MKSS*, 2:97–100)

> (Two elders lived / In the holy wilds, / They prayed to God, / They saved their soul. / One fasted much, / The other kept house, / One wept much, / The other rejoiced.)

Told as though adapted from a tale from the Prologue, the narrative poem recounts how two elders disagree over whether the soul is saved through fasting and solitude or through rejoicing and breaking bread with others. In many ways the poem presents the same paradigm as does Dostoevsky in *The Brothers Karamazov*, where one elder (Ferapont) attracts recognition for his strict fasts and harsh treatment of his own body, and the other (Zosima) attracts recognition (and censor) for his love of hospitality and the delight he takes in earthly things—flowers, jam. The poem continues with a test to reveal which elder most pleases God: two withered birches appear in a meadow, and each elder waters one, waiting to see where God will deign to pour down his restorative grace. Both birches are restored, but the joyful elder's birch "paradisically blossomed" (*raiski raspushilas'*). The poem ends,

> Господь Милосердный
> Всех вас приимет.
> Спасенью с любовью,—
> Спасу милее.
> Слава Тебе, Боже наш,
> Слава Тебе
> И ныне и присно
> И во веки веком
> Аминь.

> (The Merciful Lord / Will receive you all. / Salvation with love— / Is sweeter to the Savior. / Praise to You, our God, / Praise to You / Both now and forever / And to ages of ages / Amen.)

Kuzmin takes this "salvation with love" and adapts it to his own poetic faith.

Elsewhere in "Fish Scales" Kuzmin notes, "Religion—the goal—is the union of our sensual with our intellectual nature, and love of self with love of God."[70] For the poet the physical aspect of sexuality can foster spiritual growth, and accordingly he reimagines ascetic practice, depicting a monasticism that embraces the sexual. Such a depiction is not in every way farfetched, as he seems to indicate in "Fish Scales," where he cites passages from monastic accounts in the Prologue, the Spiritual Meadow, and the Reading Menaia where religious figures encounter and acknowledge the sexual body. He retells, for instance, the following story:

> In a vision Saint Mina commanded a lame man to lie with a woman stricken with dumbness. The man resisted, but at last submitted. The woman cried out with fright and that paralytic ran away. Thus both were healed.[71]

While themes of asceticism appear in many of his poems, Kuzmin offers a host of poems centered on the monastic motif. By means of this motif he both sexualizes the central male figure and inscribes the trope into his treatment of love's experience of time. The first poem from his 1907 cycle *Joyous Traveler* (*Radostnyi putnik*) embodies Kuzmin's peculiar blending of sexuality with asceticism.

> Светлая горница—моя пещера,
> Мысли—птицы ручные: журавли да аисты;
> Песни мои—веселые акафисты;
> Любовь—всегдашняя моя вера.
>
> Приходите ко мне, кто смутен, кто весел,
> Кто обрел, кто потерял кольцо обручальное,
> Чтобы бремя ваше, светлое и печальное,
> Я как одёжу на гвоздик повесил.
>
> Над горем улыбнемся, над счастьем поплачем.
> Не трудно акафистов легких чтение.
> Само приходит отрадное излечение
> В комнате, озаренной солнцем не горячим.
>
> Высоко окошко над любовью и тлением,
> Страсть и печаль, как воск от огня, смягчаются.
> Новые дороги, всегда весенние, чаются,
> Простясь с тяжелым, темным томлением. (*MKSS*, 1:119)

(A light-filled chamber is my cave, / My thoughts are call birds: cranes and storks; / My songs are cheerful akafists; / Love is my lasting faith. // Come to me, you who are bewildered, who are glad, / Who have obtained, who have lost your betrothal ring, / So that I might hang like a cloak on a nail / Your burden, shining and sad. // We will smile over grief, over happiness we will weep. / The reading of light akafists is not difficult. / Joyful healing will come on its own / In the room lit by the sun, yet not stifling. // High is the window above love and decay, / Passion and sadness, like wax from heat, will soften. / New roads, always of springtime, are hoped for, / Bidding farewell to heavy, dark languor.)

Here the poetic voice frames himself as a monk who offers restoration to his visitor. On one hand, the blending of elliptical allusions to undressing and making love with the trope of monastic retreat threatens to immerse the poem in irony. And yet the poem totally lacks such a tone; indeed, it frames domestic love over time as a hopeful path to "joyous healing." The rays of the sun through a high window witness love and decay. Both "passion and grief" lose their acuteness. Here the world itself comes to bear the marks of the Easter-kissed new creation, of an eternal spring.

Kuzmin's lyric protagonist often presents himself as a monk, or as someone shut away in a monk's cell. Sometimes this picture serves to contrast the faithful lover with his unfaithful beloved, as in a poem from his volume *The Guide*, where the lyric hero notes, "I'm a hermit, you're a flighty horse / That neighs and flicks his ears in glee" (*MKSS*, 2:46) At other times he describes his beloved and himself as bound by a vow to love's asceticism. We read in "Trip to Assisi" of a radiant day spent in the home of Saint Francis, which the lovers conclude with their own sacred, uniquely ascetic practice:

> Дома сладко и счастливо
> Ляжем и потушим свет,
> Выполнив благочестивый
> И любовный наш обет. (*MKSS*, 2:356–57; here, 357)

(At home sweetly, happily / We'll lie down and put out the light / When we've fulfilled our vow / Of piety and love.)

Kuzmin articulates this trope of enduring (and bodily) love, bringing healing and transformation, as the "rites of love" in a 1911 cycle *Spring's Return* (*Vesennii vozvrat*), where he writes of "submitting to the rites of love" (*liubvi pokorstvuia obriadam*) ("Kak radostna vesna v aprele . . . ," *MKSS*, 1:281). His poetry offers and frames such rites for recollecting and restoring embodied and mortal creation, as well as for modeling the way art's faithful memory immortalizes the transitory.

If the sexualization of the monk figure seems a merely decadent touch, it is worth considering that much ascetic literature, including Climacus's *Ladder*, represents as its apogee a state of pure love. In *The Ladder to Paradise*, which Kuzmin lists among the other volumes in his notebooks, Climacus describes a spiritual path structured as a ladder "leading upwards from the earthly into the holy of holies, at whose summit appears the God of love" (*vozvodiashchuiu ot zemnogo vo sviataia-sviatykh, na vershine kotoroi utverzhdaetsia Bog liubvi*).[72] Indeed, the scriptural and highly sensual love song the Song of Songs plays a particularly important part in the ultimate "Step Thirty" of Climacus's *Ladder*, where spiritual perfection is rendered as burning, illuminating love. The Song of Songs is traditionally read—both in Jewish tradition and by the Church Fathers—as an allegory for the union of God and man, and more specifically of God and Israel or of Christ and the

Church.[73] And as religious historian Jean Daniélou notes, the early Church Fathers viewed the Song of Songs as "a complete figure of the sacraments as a whole."[74]

It should come as no surprise that the Song of Songs represents one of the books of scripture most appealing to Russian modernists. A poem of love that celebrates the physical, we read in vivid passages of delightful bodies, gardens, kisses, and caresses. The interest of Silver Age artists in the Song of Songs is indicated by Bely's reference to them in his memoirs in the same breath as he invokes the "world soul."[75] Kuzmin's enduring interest in the Song of Songs is reflected in a foreword he wrote in 1916 to a poetic translation of this book into Russian by Lev Iaroshevskii.[76] Here Kuzmin attributes the relative unfamiliarity of the Russian reading public with the Song of Songs to its canonic, scriptural status:

> It is hard for us to view a sacred book from any other standpoint than a theological, dogmatic or ethical one; it is hard for us to perceive all the poetic freshness and delight of this book because we have grown used to viewing it with reverence alone.[77]

In many ways we find in this statement about the Jewish-Christian scriptures' chief love song a fitting summary of Kuzmin's approach to Orthodoxy: revitalizing the perception of religious tradition in a modern setting.

Through his bold rewriting of asceticism Kuzmin manages to have it both ways—affirming at once earthly love, even homosexual love, and traditional spiritual disciplines. While his embrace of homosexuality explicitly controverts Orthodox teachings on sexuality, nevertheless his embrace of physical, even sexual pleasure resonates with a growing emphasis, evident in the monastic revival, on the innate goodness of the sensual world. Florensky makes this point strongly and repeatedly in *The Pillar and Ground of Truth*, with its sophianic thrust. Florensky argues that "only in Christianity did [creation] find its religious meaning" and, furthermore, that the natural sciences were made possible by Christianity's embrace of materiality.[78] Indeed, as we have seen already, this emphasis has become a key way in which modern Orthodoxy—emphasizing its teachings on *theosis* and the transfiguration of the created order—seeks to distinguish itself from other Christian traditions.

SOPHIA AS MODEL OF PERSONHOOD

But for Kuzmin the spiritual path consists in more than the increasing faithfulness of the individual: throughout his work he represents a poetic faith that is intensely interpersonal—that is, ever shaped by encounters with the other—a theme that unites all sophianic thinkers, including Solovyov, Florensky, and Bulgakov. This aspect of his work especially demonstrates its closeness to sophianic thought even and especially in his re-genderings of Sophia. We saw in "Sophia" that Kuzmin uses the feminine point of view to represent desire for a male beloved—here Christ; he uses this approach from time to time. More often he explicitly represents a homoerotic view. Yet the underlying impulse remains the same: the conviction that persons develop in fullness only in intimate relation with other persons. This basic conviction also helps explain the references Kuzmin makes in his poetry here and there to the Trinity, an explicitly Christian doctrine that, as we will see, particularly inspired religious philosophers and theologians of Kuzmin's time but was also creatively rendered by writers.

In this section we will pay closest attention to the male figure of the angelic guide—the *vozhatyi* figure who predominates over other male instantiations of Sophia, including that of the monk, as the figure most connected in Kuzmin's poetry to spiritual growth and ascent. A poem published in Kuzmin's first volume *Nets* delineates the key features of the angelic guide, who appears in consistent profile in numerous volumes.

Где сомненья? где томленья?
День рожденья, обрученья
Час святой!
С новой силой жизни милой
Отдаюсь, неутолимый,
Всей душой.
Вот пороги той дороги,
Где не шли порока ноги,
Где—покой.

Обручались, причащались,
Поцелуем обменялись
У окна.
Нежно строги взоры Ваши,
Полны, полны наши чаши—
Пить до дна.
А в окошко не случайный
Тайны друг необычайной—
Ночь видна.

Чистотою страсть покрою,
Я готов теперь для боя—
Щит со мной.

О, далече—легкость встречи!
Я беру ярмо на плечи—
Груз двойной.
Тот же я, но нежным взором
Преграждает путь к позорам
Ангел мой. (*MKSS*, 1:83–84)

(Where is doubt? Where is turmoil? / Day of birth, of betrothal / Holy hour! / With new force of dear life / I surrender, unquenchable, / With all my soul. / Here are the thresholds of that road / Where the feet of sin have not walked, / Where there is peace. // We exchanged rings, we took communion, / We exchanged kisses / At the window. / Your gazes are tenderly severe, / Full, full are our cups— / Let's drink to the dregs. / And in the window the appointed friend / Of the extraordinary secret— / Night appears. // I will cover passion with purity, / Now I am ready for battle— / I have my shield with me. / Oh, farther on the lightness of meeting! / I will take the yoke on my shoulders— / A double burden. / He is myself, but with tender gaze / He blocks the path to shame, / My angel.)

In this poem Kuzmin adapts the tradition of the guardian angel to his notion of the guide-double. For the poet, divine guidance comes to him in the form of a lover, who at once embodies the transcendence, the physicality, and the immanence that characterize his overarching theology. Kuzmin innovatively combines rituals of the birthday with rituals of betrothal and communion—and consummation of wedding vows. Additionally he layers in references to Christian concepts of the "way," the spiritual path—with its surrendered soul, the road untouched by sinful feet, purity, battle, and the yoke—the latter a reference to Jesus's words, "Take my yoke upon you and learn from me, for I am gentle and lowly in heart, and you will find rest for your souls" (Matthew 11:29). The image of the yoke underscores the concept of the double: the guardian-angel-double embodies Jesus's promise to lighten the burden on the path to holiness.

Kuzmin's "guide" (*vozhatyi*) figure shows several consistent features. He is a warrior with shield and spear who protects the poetic hero from harm. He is bound or betrothed to the poet, and the tokens of this binding appear in such objects as a ring or mirror. He is, or is associated with, the beloved, and though the poetic hero may find a new love, the guide's selfsame gaze looks out from the faces of each subsequent lover portrayed. And finally the guide is a mystical figure whose presence is often associated with holy rituals (here even the Eucharist) and with holy secrets, or mysteries.

The figure of the angel bears a somewhat different profile in Eastern Orthodox tradition than in Western, especially post-medieval tradition. Angels in the Orthodox tradition do not appear as chubby cherubs but rather as figures of might. They are often depicted as warriors, as with the Archangel Michael, the poet's namesake, who appears in icons and liturgical texts alike as a military leader of God's heavenly hosts. (See figure 2.4.) Kuzmin's depiction of angels in his work evidences knowledge of this tradition, on which he was at one time preparing a study, a "Book about Holy Warriors" ("Kniga o sviatykh voinakh"), which he never finished or published (*MBMK*, 186). Kuzmin's notebooks show that he also was interested in the works of Pseudo-Dionysius, who authored the single most important source text (after the Bible) for the understanding of angels in Christian tradition, the *Celestial Hierarchy* (*RGALI-MK*, 47:432r, 492r).[79] In this work, which, along with his other writings, deeply marked Eastern Christianity, angels are described in their progressive hierarchies that reflect progressive degrees of power and of intimacy with God.[80] As such, angels aid in relaying God's word to humans and in raising humans toward God, enacting the possibility of *theosis*. While we cannot be sure whether Kuzmin read this work or exactly what sources he was working from in his depictions of angels, the writings of Pseudo-

Figure 2.4. Icon of the Archangel Michael. Balkan, ca. 1600.
Courtesy of the Temple Gallery, London.

Dionysius do recall elements of the poet's work, with its insistence on the angelic guide who leads the faithful toward God. Pseudo-Dionysius speaks of angels as messengers "who first are granted the divine enlightenment and . . . who pass on to us these revelations which are so far beyond us."[81]

Lines from a poem from his third volume of poetry, *Clay Doves* (*Glinianye golubki*), offer us a picture of the angelic warrior guide.

Не ты ль от Божьего престола,
Плащем прикрывши прелесть плеч,
Держа в руках копье, иль меч,
Пришел для предрешенных встреч
К тому, кто звал тебя из дола?
Нет, не обманчивы мечты:
Пускай пути мои опасны,
Пускай грехи мои ужасны,—
Те ангелы, они напрасны,
Когда вождем мне послан ты.
("V obmanchivom, trevozhnom sne . . . ," *MKSS*, 1:506–7)

(Was it not you, who from God's throne, / Covering the delight of your shoulders with a cloak, / Holding in your hands a spear, or sword, / Came for appointed meetings / To him who from the valley summoned you? / No, dreams are not deceptive: / My paths are dangerous—so be it, / My sins are terrible—so be it— / Those angels are needless, / When my guide has sent you to me.)

This poem shows clearly how Kuzmin takes pains to distinguish his poetic faith from traditional Orthodoxy, with its views on sexuality that preclude central elements of Kuzmin's vision, with its Platonic views of male love. Here and elsewhere we find brief apologias for his beliefs, all traceable to his fundamental belief that love, even in its physical manifestations, is always holy. As the poet writes in one place, "I don't remember what made me fall in love. / Whatever happens is holy. Everything is in bloom" ("Nynche prazdnik, pakhnet miata, vse v tsvetu . . . ," *MKSS*, 1:395) As Lindsay Watton has written, in this attitude Kuzmin, like Rozanov and many of their contemporaries, manifests an "intentionalist" approach to theology—that is, he insists that an action's goodness or sinfulness is determined by the intention behind it rather than how doctrine categorizes that action.[82] Such an approach is echoed in the transcribed conversations from the Religious-Philosophical Meetings, where from the outset representatives of the intelligentsia insist on the imperative for "freedom of religious conscience."[83]

Indispensable to the image of the angel-guide is the traditional notion of the angel as a messenger sent from God to intervene in human affairs; in Kuzmin's work this feature is deeply tied to the idea of providence, a foundational notion for him. When the poet writes, "Love has not made me sinful, people. / It is I who am sinful before love" (*Ia ne liubov'iu greshen, liudi. / Pered liubov'iu greshen ia*), he justifies his choices by insisting that love has been sent by God himself to save him: "From the heavens' boat a gangplank lowered, / And the tender hand of the Lord / Drew me up from the abyss" ("Ia ne liubov'iu greshen, liudi . . . ," *MKSS*, 1:526). The theme of providence can be found in much of his work. Indeed, many of Kuzmin's ascetically themed poems count submission to providence as an important spiritual discipline. A poem from *Autumnal Lakes* offers a refrain that sums up this aspect of Kuzmin's poetic theology: "The Lord of heaven gives it all" (*Vse daet Vladyka neba*) ("Nam rozhden'e i konchinu—vse daet Vladyka neba . . . ," *MKSS*, 1:386).

In Kuzmin's approach to faith the emphasis on divine intervention in human affairs by means of companions is a sophianic theme that strongly echoes in the work of Kuzmin's religious-philosophical contemporaries who emphasize the interpersonal aspect of divine and human being. This theme runs throughout Solovyov's work, stated explicitly and as an underlying concept. In his *Lectures on Godmanhood*, for instance, he writes that "the many beings do not have genuine existence in their separateness or in unconditional particularization, but each of them can exist in itself and for itself only in so far as it is at the same time in a state of interaction and interpenetration with the others, as inseparable elements of a single whole" (*SSVSS*, 3:3–181; here, 61–62).[84] The Sophia myth, with its story of separate beings who must be reunited, reflects this theme, as does Solovyov's "The Meaning of Love," with its insistence that individuals can find their true being only through (erotic) relationship with the other ("Smysl' liubvi," *SSVSS*, 7:3–60; here, 24).

Florensky, too, underscores the centrality of human mutuality in defining the person. This idea is a basic premise of his *Pillar and Ground of Truth*, written as a series of letters addressed to a friend. In some senses his work is even more apt for Kuzmin because he addresses himself to and yearns for a male other who, for him, fulfills a sophianic function. His letter dedicated to "Friendship" ("Druzhba") fleshes out his basic contention that the "manifestation of personality" (*vyiavlenie lichnosti*) happens only in intimate, faithful relationships.[85] The closeness of Kuzmin's conception of the personal aspect of the sophianic path in art and life to Florensky's is reflected especially in the parallel analogies they draw. Both resort to the Platonic image of the other as a mirror in which the person sees his true, ideal self.[86] What is more, both represent those guiding, intimate relationships in terms of a monastic vow. We have seen this theme in Kuzmin's poetry; Florensky states it directly. Still speaking of friendship, he writes,

> Every friendship, like every Christian life is in this sense monastic. Every friend submits to his life's travel companion [*smiriaetsia pred svoim sputnikom zhizni*] without a murmur, like a servant to his master. . . . Faithfulness to a friendship once bound and the indissolubility of friendship are like the indissolubility of a marriage, firmness to the end, to the point of shedding "the blood of martyrs."[87]

Kuzmin, too, as we have seen, calls on the other as guide and travel companion in life, and his concept of faithfulness, like Florensky's, extends to the point of accepting wounds inflicted by or caused in protecting the other. For Kuzmin this "travel companion" (*sputnik*, to use Florensky's term here—but appropriate to Kuzmin with his many images of travel) could change form—be instantiated in different people—more easily than for Florensky; yet both acknowledge in strikingly similar terms the centrality of the other in shaping one's spiritual path.[88]

In his emphasis on human mutuality as the basis of personhood we find yet another aspect in which Kuzmin represents his period and its "sophianic" undercurrents. As we find in the thought of Florensky and Solovyov, but also of Merezhkovsky—with its Hegelian-like progression through history as progressive stages of manifestation of the three aspects of the Godhead—many who were part of the "Russian religious renaissance" took great interest in Christian formulations of the Trinity and creatively applied them to their own art and thought.[89] Michael Meerson's study *The Trinity of Love in Modern Russian Theology* shows how Solovyov and the central Silver Age figures Ivanov, Berdiaev, Florensky, and Merezhkovsky, among others, are united in their project to work out a religious philosophy or theology (depending on their respective discourses) based around the notion of personhood as classically formulated by the early Church Fathers.[90] Meerson gives special credit to Solovyov for this shift, arguing that he "made the doctrines of the Trinity and Incarnation relevant again for the Russian educated public."[91] He speaks of a developing "personalist exemplarism," according to which all these thinkers based their constructs of the human person and human society on the Trinitarian model of three interrelating divine persons.[92] Their approaches and contributions vary, but all prefer to a system of abstract principles one based on personal interrelation and human experience.

Kuzmin was particularly aware of and sought consciously to adapt this legacy. His study and innovative uses of the theological achievements of the Church Fathers were not unusual for his time. The monastic revival we find refracted in his poetry and prose was stimulated by creative readings of the Church Fathers, thanks especially to the efforts of an Optina Pustyn' monk Makarii (Ivanov), who with the help of Slavophile Ivan Kireevsky and others, published in Russian translation for the first time many important patristic works.[93] Not only did these texts become, at places like Optina Pustyn', required reading, but we find them mentioned casually in such a text as Bely's *Petersburg*, as though—as Timothy Langen has pointed out—any self-respecting member of the intelligentsia might read them.[94]

In the lists of Church volumes Kuzmin makes in his notebooks, as described above, we find all three of the fourth-century Cappadocian Fathers, as Basil the Great, Gregory the Theologian (or Gregory of Nazianzus), and Gregory of Nyssa are known, including editions of the latter two that were published by the Moscow Theological Academy at the end of the nineteenth century.[95] Along with Athanasius of Alexandria (also in Kuzmin's lists), this small but immensely important group of theologians is best known for shaping the Christian doctrine of the Trinity, and especially for their formulation of the persons of the Trinity as hypostases (*RGALI-MK*, 47:492r). As Augustine Casiday writes in his brief history of Orthodox theology, the Cappadocians "roughed out terminological distinctions, which when subsequently refined would become landmarks of patristic doctrine."[96] Here again Kuzmin's interests resonate with those of Florensky and Solovyov, who regularly cite these theologians.[97] We have already seen how in "Fish Scales" Kuzmin defines religion above all by love. In this same sequence he goes on to contemplate,

> Is not this the secret of the Trinity? God is fullness, Creation, oneness. As soon as there is a creation, there are two: the Creator and the created. Division. But at once there is love as union and active fullness. That is why there is no Nirvana, no inertia.[98]

We can read even this theological statement sophiologically: if creation brings division, love creates fullness, *pleroma*, union. It is characteristic of Kuzmin, with his constant portrayals of the active spiritual ascent and the ongoing journey that he would pick up especially on the dynamic aspect of the Trinitarian doctrine, the never-ceasing interrelating of the hypostases: a love with no inertia.

At the end of his poetic career Kuzmin's presentations of love and the spiritual path had not greatly changed. His masterful long poem (*poema*) *The Trout Breaks the Ice* (*Forel' razbivaet led*) reiterates those central concerns we have described here as sophianic. Crafted in fifteen sections with twelve sections representing months of the year and stages in love, the *poema* tells the story of lovers who meet, are separated, and then reunited. After a dramatic consummation and move toward a more settled domestic life together, the beloved departs for a woman who then betrays him and reduces him to a depressive, automaton-like state. The lover never forgets his departed, unfaithful beloved and one day finds him in a collection of oddities like a specimen in a freak show. At their reunion and return home to celebrate the New Year together, the eponymous trout breaks the ice.

The work is rich and complex enough to deserve extensive investigation; here I will note simply how Kuzmin uses it to advance his poetic project. An overarching metaphor of a fish beating its way through the winter ice represents the lover seeking union and then reunion with his beloved, "exchange" (*obmen*) with whom gives him life and sustains it. After being abandoned by his female lover, the beloved visits his former male lover (the lyrical narrator) and declares,

> Наш ангел превращений отлетел. . . .
> . . . Тогда я, прах,
> И возвращаюсь в прах! Во мне иссякли
> Кровь, желчь, мозги и лимфа. Боже!
> И подкрепленья нет и нет обмена!
> Несокрушимо окружен стеклом я
> И бюсь как рыба! . . . (*MKSS*, 2:456)

> (Our transforming angel has flown away . . . / . . . And now I'm dust, / And I'm returning to dust! Blood, bile, brains and lymph / Have dried up in me. God! / There's no invigoration, no exchange! / I'm surrounded indestructibly by glass, / And I'm beating like a fish! . . .)

In these lines and in the poem as a whole the individual relies for fullness of life on the other, on the beloved—echoing the personalistic tones of sophianic art and thought as we have seen it. When the lovers are reunited we find, also, images of that sophianic flesh: the lover and beloved call and respond, "—And can your soul blaze again? / —Fire melts steel into gold!" (*MKSS*, 2:461). Praxis, too, gets its due: the reunited lovers return home to celebrate the New Year, and the narrator comments playfully, "Observing age-old rituals, / The cork from the bottle—pop!" (*MKSS*, 2:462). In a familiar blend of phallic images and religious vocabulary Kuzmin reiterates his poetic consecrations of the rituals of love. We find the adaptive impulse, here, too. As researchers have shown, the work brings together Platonic and Christian concepts with opera and folk belief, and through all this Kuzmin still conveys his belief in the power of love to sustain the individual's hope and his sense of connection with eternal forces. Indeed, even while upholding the sophianic project Kuzmin reaffirms in the *poema* his belief that love conquers all dogma. We find this emphasis especially in a "Ballad" at the center of the poem, meant to picture mythically the poem's plot. Here a sailor leaves his betrothed and returns again decades later to marry her, although he has long been assumed dead. The bride notices that he does not observe the wedding rituals, does not kneel or say "Amen." But when she sees him magically transform into a radiant ageless figure, she proclaims, "It may be I'll destroy my soul, / From satan you may be: / But I love you as you are, / I, your wife 'til death!" (*MKSS*, 2:455). *The Trout Breaks the Ice* lacks the more overtly theological elements of some of Kuzmin's other verse; nevertheless here we find the same spirit of a world imbued and guided by love, where love is expressed in the goodness of the material and cultural world, where love inspires faith in life's meaningfulness, and where love transforms all that is transitory into something radiant and immortal.

Chapter Three

"Through Dark Vaults": The Byzantine Imaginary of *Poem without a Hero*

Батюшка-Питер бока нам повытер, братцы-заводы унесли годы, а матушка-канава совсем доконала.

(Ole father Peter roughed us up; our brothers, the factories, took years off our lives; and ole mother ditch did us in.)
—Russian folk saying

But, though my style and manner of writing may be fragmentary and disjointed, my thinking is not so . . .
—Nikolai Berdiaev, *Self-Knowing*

IN 1917 AKHMATOVA wrote,

Я в этой церкви слушала Канон
Андрея Критского в день строгий и печальный,
И с той поры великопостный звон
Все семь недель до полночи пасхальной
Сливался с беспорядочной стрельбой,
Прощались все друг с другом на минуту,
Чтоб никогда не встретиться . . .[1]

(In this church I heard the Canon / Of Andrew of Crete on a day solemn and sad, / And since that time Great Lent's tolling, / All seven weeks right up to the Paschal midnight, / Has merged with disordered shooting, / Everyone bid each other farewell for a moment, / Never to meet again . . .)

The February Revolution took place in the first week of Lent, a week liturgically permeated by the solemn and poetic Great Canon of Andrew of Crete (c. 660–740), a penitential poem.[2] In Akhmatova's imagination the ritual sounds of Lent—its services and bells—blend together with the revolution's "disordered shooting," creating a new fabric of life. Things have changed irrevocably, and yet she insists on and fosters a certain kind of continuity; in her brief poem Akhmatova demonstrates both rupture and continuity via the liturgical calendar. The poetic narrator positions herself on the threshold of Easter, in the same church where she celebrated Lent's beginning; but many who celebrated with her there those seven weeks ago have not returned, having "bid each other farewell for a moment," not foreseeing the events that would soon disrupt so much. The poem seems to balance precariously on this midnight threshold: it is as though the congregation's incompletion threatens the Paschal culmination. Accordingly the poem seems to break off a line and a half early, disrupting the metrical expectations it builds in its first four lines, of iambic pentameter with alternating masculine and feminine rhyme. Its single, nearly unpaused sentence ends abruptly in the middle of a line like the jarring end of a long sequence that once seemed as though it would go on forever. In a fascinating move Akhmatova depicts revolution's disrupting force through a disruption of liturgical and poetic expectations; but she also depicts the possibility for resolution via the implied Paschal trajectory and the sense of standing on the brink of a new day, a new world.

Eighteen years later she is still doing the same thing. That is, in her monumental poem *Requiem* (1935–40) she tries to make poetry stand in the gap—the gap that revolution, civil war, world wars, and social and political restructurings evinced in Russian society (*AASS*, 3:21–30).[3] Akhmatova wrote this much-discussed cycle as a kind of religious-poetic ritual for the dead, filling a major gap in a political setting where people and the past were quickly disappearing and new rituals were being created all the time to reform Russian society.[4] (As a whole the work existed for many years in furtive samizdat and in the memories of readers who would recite it, a virtual requiem for the victims of terror.)[5] We have seen how Kuzmin adapted liturgical culture to foster a relatively individualized religious-poetic practice in a Soviet context. Akhmatova—as she herself liked to point out—never emigrated, and, unlike Kuzmin, she consciously presented herself in her later work as a figure around whom the Russian people might congregate and cohere. This much is clear from the image she raises of her suffering mother self at the end of *Requiem*: "And if some day in this country / They think to raise a monument to me, / I give my permission for that festival" (*AASS* 3:29). Her placing herself at this national center also appears in *Requiem* as a placing of herself at a liturgical center. Her lyrical persona speaks of herself in relation to the unnamed suffering Russian people thus:

О них вспоминаю всегда и везде,
О них не забуду и в новой беде,
И если зажмут мой измученный рот,
Которым кричит стомильонный народ,
Пусть так же они поминают меня
В канун моего погребального дня. (*AASS* 3:29)

(I commemorate them everywhere and always, / Nor will I forget them when new trials appear, / And if they will shut my tortured mouth / By which the people—a hundred-million—cry out, / Then let them instead commemorate me / On the eve of the day of my burial.)

Despite the tremendous differences between *Requiem* and *Poem without a Hero*, in the latter, even more complex work Akhmatova is still positioning herself as a central agent for cohering the Russian nation. Clare Cavanagh has written eloquently of the ways Akhmatova poetically complicates this relationship between artist and people in *Poem without a Hero*, "deferring indefinitely the questions of personal and poetic responsibility that [the work] both raises and deflects."[6] I concur with Cavanagh that Akhmatova knowingly complicates her role, but I also believe that the poet finds a strategy via Orthodox liturgical culture to reinstitute herself as a kind of ultimate representative for her people.

If we recall the aims of symbolists such as Merezhkovsky, Gippius, even Blok, poets were to draw on Russia's religious tradition to help create a common culture, to unify intelligentsia with *narod*. While Kuzmin is working somewhat within this paradigm in that he is elaborating his own version of a specifically religious aesthetic, nevertheless with him this more political aspect recedes somewhat behind other interests. We can say this in another way by returning to our language of Sophia. For Blok, the difficulty of conjuring Sophia and her new world all at once leads to a major realignment of vision, by which only a Dionysian shattering of form can introduce a new world. For Kuzmin, Sophia (or her male equivalent) appears, but only in an aggregate image cobbled together from glimpses and experiences across time. In her late work Akhmatova essentially returns to Blok's foundational vision—that Sophia and the new world must appear together all at once—that is, a new age can appear, but the poet cannot bring it about by her lone efforts. She has learned from her predecessors, and she has learned from all that has passed in Europe and in Russia over the first decades of the twentieth century. And so she reignites the sophianic vision only to suggest its impracticability: she recalls the religious strivings of the modernists as doomed to fail, and she replaces Sophia with Mary, Mother of God. For Akhmatova, the artist cannot bring about a new age (the sophianic idea), she can only cultivate an expectation of it—and so the pregnant Mary takes center stage. We will examine Akhmatova's late work as a way, therefore, both of evaluating the Russian modernist religious project and of discerning how Akhmatova adapts it to craft her own religious-poetic solution to problems of a national character.

In its clear engagement with ritual tradition, *Requiem* makes an excellent case for the claims of the present study. But even more relevant for our purposes—and, I would argue, amplifying a similar concern with ritual—is a work Akhmatova began around the same time and never exactly finished, a work in which she attempts to evaluate and correct the modernist religious project: *Poem without a Hero*. Akmatova began this work in 1940 and kept working on it—finishing and then restarting—until 1963. It is notoriously hard to pin down both identities and final meanings in this long poem (*poema* is the word used in the title, generally applied to long narrative poems), but its central, most obvious story tells a kind of morality tale about the dangers of erotic passion and also of art that sacralizes erotic passion. The larger scene the work paints is filled with fin-de-siècle decadent types who live for revelry and turn themselves into works of art. Akhmatova clearly renders the Silver Age world of life-creation (*zhiznetvorchestvo*), with its Pierrots and Columbinas and Harlequins, and all its masked revelers dressed for Epiphany celebrations (*sviatki*), who make a religion of artifice.[7] (For a description of the Orthodox Feast of Epiphany, see appendix.) A markedly Blokian subtext in the poem makes his key lyrical drama *The Puppet Theater* (*Balaganchik*, 1906) resonate, with its filtering of commedia dell'arte and its perennial love triangles through mystical questionings. In this famous and influential play (for which Kuzmin composed the music) Blok projected on stage artistic doubles of himself, Liubov', and Bely as commedia dell'arte figures, turning their complicated love triangle—as well as their complicated ideas about art—into art, albeit of a parodic variety. At the same time Blok emblematizes the ways that he and his contemporaries turned art into reckless play. Akhmatova reuses these figures to her own purposes, referring to multiple people, but clearly echoing Blok's theme of making heedless play out of heady aesthetic theories.

Akhmatova characterizes this fearsome harlequinade setting most starkly in an embedded narrative of a young hussar (Pierrot) who kills himself when his lover, a decadent femme fatale dancer-artiste (Columbine), betrays him with someone else (Harlequin). In this story Akhmatova fictionalizes an actual event that took place in 1913, the suicide of poet and officer Vsevolod Kniazev in response to dancer and artist Olga Glebova-Sudeikina's betrayal of him. Kniazev had also been a lover of Mikhail Kuzmin, whose fictional counterpart lingers menacingly in the shadows of Akhmatova's poem, evidencing no grief for Kniazev's death. The affair came to emblematize the fin-de-siècle elite's careless revelry and myopia in the face of historic developments that were threatening the very fabric of European society and Russia especially, and Akhmatova accentuates this aspect of the myth. The playful masks of her bedecked modernist revelers come in the poem to cover up a terrifying emptiness that betokens evil in its most essential form—echoing, as Colleen McQuillen has shown—folk and Orthodox Christian associations of masks with the demonic.[8] The scene opens somewhat innocently in chapter 1:

"Вас я вздумала нынче прославить,
Новогодные сорванцы!"
Этот Фаустом, тот Дон Жуаном,
Дапертутто, Иоканааном;
Самый скромный—северным Гланом
Иль убийцею Дорианом,
И все шепчут своим дианам
Твердо выученный урок. (*PBG*, 875)

("I've decided to laud you now, / New Year's madcaps!" / This one as Faust, that one as Don Juan, / As Dapertutto, as Baptizer John; / Most modest of all, as the Northern Glan / Or as the murderer Dorian, / And all whisper to their Dianas / The well-learned lesson.)

But the threat lurking beneath these masks reveals itself soon in the poet's vision, just a few lines later:

Я надеюсь, Владыку Мрака
Вы не смели сюда ввести?
Маска это, череп, лицо ли—
Выражение злобной боли,
Что лишь Гойя смел передать. (*PBG*, 876)

(I hope you did not dare / To bring in here the Prince of Darkness? / Whether it's a mask, a skull or a face— / An expression of malicious pain / That only Goya would dare convey.)

Presenting her memories of the modernist period as a nightmare, Akhmatova makes use of the ways *sviatki* rituals mark the New Year as a moment when the border between this world and others, between the living and the dead, is permeable.[9] She suggests, then, that the modernist impulse not only to create new worlds but to incarnate otherworldly realities reaped dire consequences, inviting in sinister forces.

The work itself is daunting in form—fragmented, elliptical, quickly shifting from one scene or thought to the next—and we can see in this method a firm rejection of the deceptively smooth surfaces she depicts as characteristic of the modernist world she once inhabited. While Akhmatova indeed inherits a certain fragmentation of form from modernism, she uses and amplifies stylistic fragmentation in order to critique Russian modernism's promise that art will ultimately bring about a sense of unity lacking in modern experience. Art's sophianic mission to create a synthetic and even integral vision becomes not only quixotic but even Luciferian in *Poem without a Hero*. Akhmatova seeks to rectify the artist's understanding of her task. In one of the work's three (!) dedications we find her employing her fragmentary method even as she gives us one of her first keys to its aim: an image of pregnancy that will come to represent how art should always defer its unifying resolution.

Второе Посвящение

О.С.

Ты ли, Путаница-Психея,
Черно-белым веером вея,
Наклоняешься надо мной,
Хочешь мне сказать по секрету,
Что уже миновала Лету
И иною дышишь весной.
Не диктуй мне, сама я слышу:
Теплый ливень уперся в крышу,
Шепоточек слышу в плюще.
Кто-то маленький жить собрался,
Зеленел, пушился, старался,
Завтра в новом блеснуть плаще.
Сплю—
она одна надо мною,—
Ту, что люди зовут весною,
Одиночеством я зову.
Сплю—
мне снится молодость наша,
Та, ЕГО миновавшая чаша;
Я тебе наяву,
Если хочешь, отдам на память,
Словно в глине чистое пламя
Иль подснежник в могильном рву.

25 мая 1945.
Фонтанный Дом.
(*PBG*, 872–73)

(Second Dedication / O.S. / Is it you, Confusion-Psyche, / Waving your black-and-white-fan, / Leaning over me, / Wanting to tell me in secret / That you've already crossed the Lethe, / And breathing of a different spring. / Don't dictate to me, I hear it myself: / A warm rain has leaned into the roof, / A little whisper I hear in the ivy. / Someone small has gotten ready to live, / Has turned green, has fluffed up, has tried / To shine tomorrow in a new cloak. / I'm asleep— / she alone is over me— / She whom people call spring / I call loneliness. / I'm asleep— / I dream of our youth, / Of that, the cup that passed HIM by; / I will give it to you for real / If you wish, for memory's sake, / Like a pure flame in a clay jar / Or a snowdrop in the mouth of the grave.)

May 25, 1945
House on the Fontanka[10]

This "Second Dedication" resembles a traditional invocation to the muses, combined with the romantic trope that associates poetic creation with dreaming. Apart from these generic aspects, however, the casual reader of this work (if such a reader exists) may find this section little help as an introduction, with its vague references to specific figures from the Russian Silver Age (Sudeikina and Kniazev) and its hazy setting. Past and present and even future blur as the poet addresses a dead person and offers a poem as a souvenir to help the dead remember their shared past. Throughout the poem this superimposition of time layers echoes in the poem's disorienting sequence, its constant elliptical shifts from one thought or image to the next, its refusal to explain who's who and to clarify what is literally happening. The work retains throughout its sense of pregnant meaning (ever averring final explanations), and so an image of pregnancy in the middle of this section takes on particular portentousness. As the muse ("Confusion-Psyche"/Sudeikina) appears, we also witness the implantation of "someone small" into the walls of the room where the poet sleeps. This space comes to harbor ghosts for the poet, but also the promise of salvation, of renewal and release. But the work will proceed true to its title, *Poem without a Hero*: the awaited savior will never emerge. This passage, then, serves to illustrate a basic principle of the work as a whole: a resistance to closure, encapsulated in the difficult form but also in images of pregnancy that will never result in birth. What takes center stage, then, is not the satisfyingly shaped work of art but an endless procession toward it, Sophia's endless deferral. That is to say, in the work's marian subtext we discover the promise of a new, transfigured flesh, a new age; but the artist appears powerless to actualize this transfiguration and works only, instead, to generate forms appropriate to a period of expectation.

In *Poem without a Hero* we find Akhmatova reorienting modernist aims to fit a Stalinist context, in which a determined endurance appears more effective than bold intervention. By the time she began writing this poem, her husband the poet Nikolai Gumilev had been executed in 1921 as an anti-revolutionary, White officer; her son Lev had been arrested and imprisoned in the Great Purges of the late 1930s; she had witnessed the silencing of most prominent modernist voices (through exile, execution, or more subtle methods); the doctrine of Socialist Realism had been established in 1934, with suppression of all works falling outside its parameters ensuing; she had moved from a position of privilege and recognition to one of great instability, where she could be upheld as exemplary one moment only to be castigated the next. In 1946 she would fall victim, with writer Mikhail Zoshchenko, to the repressive campaigns of Andrei Zhdanov, secretary of the Central Committee of the Communist Party, lambasting her and writers like her as anti-Soviet, immoral throwbacks.

Akhmatova displays, then, a keen awareness that her bid to extend the religious-aesthetic task of the intelligentsia into the Soviet setting remains problematic. But the problematic nature of this move stems not only from her political situation: in certain ways like her Soviet detractors, Akhmatova uses her poem to condemn decadent revelers, among them herself. How can she, then, speak as one implicated in the sins of the past that she evaluates? What is more, how can she speak for the Russian people when she enjoys a status that is privileged, in its own unpredictable way? In 1941, for instance, the poet was flown out of Leningrad to spare her the immense deprivations and dangers of the great siege. Akhmatova inscribes this problem and its artistic solution, too, into her work, in images of willed descent, even burial. Indeed, she sends the poet figure down into the very wombs she uses to reorient the figure of artistic transformation. She therefore also leverages these womb images to picture her immersion in the sufferings of the Russian people. If *Requiem* ends with a monument to the representatively suffering poet, *Poem without a Hero* takes the poet into the depths and implants her in the very walls of her city. *Requiem* may seem to present a rather sophianic ending—with a vision of art's unifying power, the all-embracing feminine figure embodied most concretely. *Poem without a Hero*, however, demonstratively shifts the focus from the Sophia figure and the restored wholeness she emblematizes to the Mary figure who suffers and labors as she, too, awaits a redeeming hero . . . whom we will never encounter in the space of this artwork.

In this sense, Akhmatova's long poem explores an aspect of Orthodox liturgical culture that the modernists largely overlook: the ritual procession. Whereas we tend to see in earlier modernism momentary and often triumphant adaptations of liturgical services, Akhmatova takes the long view, comparing life to a seemingly unending ritual procession of the kind that takes place in seasons such as Lent, imitating Jesus's road to the cross.[11] We have seen how Kuzmin, too, steps back to survey whole liturgical cycles and appreciates the value of longing, but his vision of faithfulness over time contains heady doses of delight and pleasure and unmistakable moments of consummation—features to which Akhmatova may well have objected by this time. In *Poem without a Hero* Akhmatova presents an unflinching advance into the very heart of suffering along a road that she travels with her people. Here, too, Mary's pregnancy replaces Sophia's embodiment. The new age is deferred indefinitely but its hope rehearsed. This ritual and poetic procession constitutes the mode of the poem—and this will be the focus of this chapter—how we should read *Poem without a Hero*, and how reading *Poem without a Hero* can make us reread Russian modernism. In this work Akhmatova critiques the particular religious aesthetic of her modernist peers but also asserts her own, corrected religious aesthetic. In fact, she offers what may be the most identifiably Russian Orthodox aesthetic of the poets gathered here, and indeed she seems to assert her greater understanding of the thrust of Orthodoxy over the modernist artists who preceded her. Akhmatova is not alone in her task of revaluating modernism via reappropriations of Orthodox liturgical culture: Boris Pasternak, too, joins in this task—and we can see their projects as rival projects in certain ways.[12] But Akhmatova finds in *Poem without a Hero* an immensely innovative solution to the problems she perceives in modernism's sophianic vision.

The great temptation of *Poem without a Hero* is to read it as a rebus, a text in need of deciphering—as many of the most influential readers of this text have done.[13] Such a hermeneutic extends the obsession with wholeness that Sophia personifies. The form of the poem seems to invite such decoding. Akhmatova offers in it one of the most complex texts in the Russian literary canon, with its three main parts and many more subdivisions, and numerous versions combining variously a pastiche of stanzas composed at different times and in different places. (Recently Natalia Kraineva, who curates Akhmatova's archives in St. Petersburg, has published an authoritative edition of the work, based on its ninth and final version. So complex was the task of reconstructing the twenty-six-page authoritative version that it required nearly fifteen hundred pages, including an intricate scholarly apparatus [*PBG*].) The text shifts between scenes of the Soviet present, irruptions of the Silver Age (embodied in the 1913 narrative) into the author's world, and self-conscious (often ironic) commentary on the writing process. The poet figure, cloistered in her room, experiences dizzying visitations by ghosts of her past, who come to her as masked, Epiphany mummers; her writing robs them neither of their power nor presence, as stanzas of commentary attest. If the poet-narrator finds it difficult to distinguish dream from reality and self from dream double, so much more the reader! Glimpses of war and prison camps linger disturbingly at vision's edge.

Readers of this poem have tended to see in it a kind of encoded cultural repository, a network of veiled references to key cultural events and figures of Russia's twentieth century.[14] The text stands, for them, as an account in need of deciphering by those privy to cultic knowledge, as Galina Rylkova indicates in her recent study of the legacy of the Silver Age.[15] If we could piece together all the references, we would reconstruct Akhmatova's representation of what the twentieth century was *really* like . . . for people like her, for the intelligentsia. This understanding hews to what Rylkova has called an "archaeology of anxiety"—a compulsion in Soviet and post-Soviet periods to reconstruct the recent yet distant modernist past. By this account *Poem without a Hero* constitutes an encoded memoir, unlocking which will restore history and culture to greater fullness. The specter of wholeness may have compelled modernist artists and later interpreters alike; but for the Soviet-period Akhmatova such wholeness is precisely and never more than a specter. Such a reading (a kind Rylkova observes with critical eye) has held its ground because it comes close, I would argue, to being right—but misses the mark: in her *poema* Akhmatova makes of her quasi-memoir an enigma, not an encoding. The difference lies in mode: an encoding obscures a static and finite image that one must reveal, while an enigma orients along a dynamic, infinite trajectory that one must pursue. Akhmatova's poem is byzantine, labyrinthine, and in this way she defies the modernist project to unite and consummate. Her poet-narrator comments wryly on her work, "This box has a triple bottom. // But I'll admit that I've used / Invisible ink, / I write in mirror writing" (*PBG*, 891–92).

We have said that the poem's womb images never culminate in birth. Likewise, true to her word, the author fills her poem not only with wombs but also with many varied images of enclosed spaces that seem to contain sought-after secrets but at the bottom of which we find "a triple bottom." We never get to the real bottom of it. To amplify the pursuit, Akhmatova introduces many images of mirrors that project a mis-en-abîme—both within the poem's fractured narratives and in the reader's experience. Some of Akhmatova's most successful readers have perceived the poem's resistance to closure and have abandoned the task of "decoding."[16] The text, like its bottomless boxes and mirrored halls, extends itself endlessly. It is in this mode in particular that Akhmatova rejects the modernist pretension to realize a new kind of person and a new kind of world; whatever hero may eventually arrive, she relinquishes the right to project him, or her, in any kind of clearly perceptible form.

It is precisely in her enigmatic mode—a mode that instigates endless procession—that Akhmatova uses Orthodox liturgical culture to assert her superior religious aesthetic. In this chapter I will argue that the mode of *Poem without a Hero* is an iconic one, one that deploys a Byzantine imaginary, and therefore one that joins in the sophiological task of refitting Orthodox tradition to a modern context but that also tries to avoid the mistakes of the past, the too literalistic attempts at incarnating a new world. When I speak of the "iconic" mode of the work, though, I have in mind not merely the visuality of an icon in isolation, but the icon as embedded in a liturgical context—the icon as a liturgical emblem. Byzantinist Bissera Pentcheva has most vividly evoked this aspect of the icon in her work *The Sensual Icon: Space Ritual, and the Senses in Byzantium*.[17] Here she shows how icons were traditionally made to come to life in a liturgical context, with its candles, movement, scents, sounds, and cavernous cathedral space. The icon, therefore, implies and entails procession, and it is in this sense that I refer to it here. In *Poem without a Hero* Akhmatova engages with a distinctively Eastern Christian visual economy, an Eastern Christian aesthetic mode that suggests an extension of the modernist project even as it critiques it. Indeed, Akhmatova uses this mode to extend her own influence in the precarious landscape of Russian letters.

I will draw especially on the work of French philosopher Marie-José Mondzain, *Image, Icon, Economy: The Byzantine Origins of the Contemporary Imaginary*. Mondzain speaks of the icon as art that models and calls forth a kenotic procession—a movement out of oneself in order to open oneself to what lies beyond. Other scholars of the icon, including Orthodox thinkers such as Pavel Florensky, have discussed the significance of kenosis in an iconic and liturgical context. What makes Mondzain's thought especially relevant for our purposes, however, is her characterization of this kenotic-oriented medium as in fact a medium of imperial projection. She takes the iconic mode right back to its Byzantine origins and shows how the kenotic economy works to extend imperial power (and therefore entails not only liturgical but also political procession). As such, Mondzain argues that the notion of "representation" insufficiently describes what the image does, and that instead we should understand it as a "reiteration"—that, in other words, the work of art does not so much point beyond itself as guide the audience through a "kenotic" (self-emptying) process to inscribe the viewer into its own economy, an imperial economy (*MIIE*, 95). That is, in order to realize a new reality, art instills the constant emptying out of form rather than the sophianic construction of new forms. (In liturgical terms, art emphasizes the procession above all—and the icon's economy is a specifically liturgical one.) For Mondzain it is precisely the marian body that models this kenotic aesthetic, that models art's successful colonization of cultures.

Akhmatova, too, prefers the motherly female body to the seductive one, and she embeds within her poem images of wombs that stand in contrast to the un-progenied play of the modernist-revelers. By setting up this contrast and identifying her poetic self with the pregnant body, Akhmatova therefore downplays the sophianic idealization of the sexualized female body even as she keeps the female body at the center of her project. (Tsvetaeva's representations of feminity never fall down quite so firmly on either side.) In Akhmatova's poem sophianic desire seems a pretext for bad behavior, a way the intelligentsia could avoid the truly hard work of world-transformation; yet she in no way rejects the theurgic (and liturgical) calling, as Solovyov, Ivanov, and others describe it. Poets should still be priests of culture. She therefore replaces the sophian body with the marian one. A critique of Russian modernism and its sophianic project, this vision bears its own problems.

A brief biographical (and literary-biographical) note. There are many indications that Eastern Orthodox tradition, particularly its marian and icon traditions, constituted part of the fabric of Akhmatova's life and work and her attunement to liturgical culture via the liturgical calendar. One might start at the poet's name, Anna—the name of Mary's mother, whose *zhitie* (saint's life) the poet knew. Poems also indicate her particular interest in Mary: *Requiem*, but also a host of poems from throughout Akhmatova's career. This is not the place to trace that arc, but Wendy Rosslyn, for one, has described it at length.[18] And one of the poet's biographers, Roberta Reeder, notes frequently how Akhmatova drew on realia from the Orthodox context.[19] Certain details from her life indicate it, including a moment witnessed by Lydia Chukovskaia, who recounts seeing Akhmatova venerate an icon of Mary with marked devotion—perhaps a Kazan' Mother of God (pictured in figure 3.1), to which icon a central cathedral of Petersburg is dedicated.[20] Of icons we know that Akhmatova's third husband, Nikolai Punin, was a highly regarded art historian who in fact wrote a review, for the modernist journal *Apollo*, of the seminal Exhibition of Old Russian Art that took place in March 1913.[21] His concern with icons reflected a major resurgence of interest in the icon around the turn of the twentieth century, critical and artistic responses to which Akhmatova could not have missed.[22] In fact, as she only began publishing verse in 1912, much of what she wrote would have been informed by the growing awareness of icon tradition around her, especially in response to the March 1913 exhibition.

Akhmatova's attention to Anna and veneration of the marian icon confirms a particular interest in Mary; this interest is also clearly reflected in her poetic oeuvre, not least in works like *Requiem*, where the poetic speaker patently identifies herself with Mary, even quoting words about her from the Lenten liturgy.[23] Other poets, such as Pasternak, responded to such poems by also figuratively associating Akhmatova with Mary, Mother of God.[24] Given, moreover, that Akhmatova sets her *Poem* in the season of Epiphany—when Russians also traditionally celebrate Christmas, the role of Mary takes on particular significance. Through Mary God made himself incarnate in human flesh. Mary, therefore, supersedes Sophia by far, since Sophia must be embodied by humans, who are, by her accounts here, feckless, misguided

Figure 3.1. Icon of the Kazan' Mother of God. Russia, ca. 1650.
Courtesy of the Museum of Russian Icons, Clinton, Massachusetts.

and even narcissistic. We can say, therefore, that Akhmatova sets up a marian model in order to set in relief the failings of the sophianic one.

This marian model encompasses not only the birth of transfigured flesh, but also the pain of death and loss; for this reason Mary better answers a time of suffering and oppression. Mary's life, as Church tradition has it, constitutes a kenotic model second only to Christ's. Mary empties herself to take in God, and she gains incomparable status, but she also undergoes suffering as she awaits and then witnesses her son's death. In the liturgy for the Nativity of Christ, we hear, "Thou hast shone forth from a Virgin, O Christ, Thou spiritual Sun of Righteousness. And a star showed Thee, whom nothing can contain, contained within a cave." Further on in the service we hear, "The Virgin is now more spacious than the heavens" (*FM*, 259, 263).[25] Mary—here as throughout liturgical culture—is made a God-container. She is his cave, his room; but she is also figuratively his tomb. The liturgical culture—service texts and icons alike—frequently connect Mary's life-giving power with the mortality she bestows on God-made-flesh. In the service for the Epiphany, or Baptism, of Christ, we hear, "The Lord, incarnate of the Virgin, having clothed material flesh with the immaterial fire of His divinity, wraps Himself in the waters of Jordan, for He has been glorified" (*FM*, 367).[26] But only moments later we hear, "O Word without beginning, Thou hast buried man with Thee in the stream" (*FM*, 368).[27] Jesus's baptism, like his birth, prefigures his death and time in the grave. It is this time in the tomb that Akhmatova pictures in *Poem without a Hero*, where she embeds images of wombs that she superimposes on images of graves. While the poet sets her late work during Epiphany, Lenten themes shine through, the "snatches of Requiem" (*obryvki Rekviema*) that she invokes in the *Poem*'s second section (*PBG*, 605).

The figure of Mary is so central to *Poem without a Hero* that it comes to obscure and replace modernism's Sophia: for Mary, indeed, stands as the model of humanity awaiting and passively receiving God's new life and not artists' self-directed, hell-bent production of a new world, their so-called life-creation (*zhiznetvorchestvo*) that seemed to produce death. And yet we might also see here a differently pitched rendition of the sophianic task. As I will show in this chapter, elements of descent and assimilation appear throughout *Poem without a Hero*, and these elements, according to Paul Valliere, epitomize a sophiological approach. As Valliere writes in *Modern Russian Theology*, in the Russian school (including Solovyov and Bulgakov) "the humanity of God is connected first of all with kenosis, the self-emptying of God in the incarnation."[28] What is missing in Akhmatova's *poema*, in contrast to other sophianic writings we have seen, is the birth of the Word: here transfiguration exists only in potential, awaited in the absent hero.

Although there is much theological work on both the icon and Mary, Mondzain's work is particularly appropriate here because it helps obviate the imperial impulse that Akhmatova adapts from the icon. Although all artists may be said to work to leave their mark through the art they produce, Mondzain's work on the icon speaks precisely to the power Akhmatova finds in *not* bringing resolution but rather in stimulating further pursuit. Therefore it helps explain how the poet seeks to transform her own apparent lack of power (in the Soviet context especially) into immense influence. For now, I will summarize the key concepts and terms from Mondzain that will direct our reading of *Poem without a Hero*. For Mondzain the icon serves as a means of propagating power, imprinting the ruler's image onto ever-expanding territories, assimilating those territories. What propels this act of assimilation is the legitimating narrative of divine incarnation: God assimilates himself to finite human form in order to restore the divine image in humankind. But this assimilation constitutes an ongoing act of emptying himself of the divine—an act of kenosis. The mark he makes in the form of Jesus betokens God's constant withdrawal, his absenting, his abstraction; but it is this very abstraction that perpetrates the expansion of his realm via the image. One must infinitely pursue God in hopes of catching sight of him. Therefore the icon acts as a vector: it models an emptying out of self that paradoxically enables the self to adapt endlessly to new terrain, to colonize it. The notion of kenosis has a significant presence in Russian studies, but it often figures as passivity and as a dispersal of selfhood—whereas for Mondzain it is precisely kenosis that establishes the influence of the self. (Mondzain's view is consistent with that of Florensky, who sees in this act the potential for a fullness of self enabled by union with another.)[29]

And here is where Mondzain becomes especially apt for Akhmatova: the marian womb offers the form par excellence that best describes the iconic economy (*MIIE*, 100–101). In *Requiem* Mary appears in the pose of the grieving mother at the cross, but in *Poem without a Hero* the work operates by analogy with the marian womb. Mary's womb is a surface—in Mondzain's words, "panel, canvas, blank page, veil, vaults, unknown lands," inscribed with the seed of the Father's voice via the annunciation; here the Word implants itself, circled about but never circumscribed, always just beyond comprehension (*MIIE*, 101). Just as God empties himself into human form in order to propagate his image, Mary opens herself to God's inscription, so that her own act of kenosis also constitutes the universalization of her image. Likewise, Akhmatova pictures the prophetic word implanting itself in the vaults of her memory, the depths of her psyche, as though pressed into a page; what emerges is an image of the poet who, like the word, pours herself into an alien shape in order to secure an audience. The constant act, therefore, of assimilating to new forms overtakes the more properly sophianic act, as we have previously seen, of crystallizing new forms.

It is this at once kenotic and imperial mode that defines *Poem without a Hero*, and this mode enables Akhmatova both to critique the sophianic project and to refit it to her Soviet context. We find already in *Requiem* that Akhmatova places herself in a privileged position vis-à-vis her nation: we read in the epigraph, "No, not beneath a foreign firmament, / Not under the shelter of foreign wings: / I was with my people then, / There, with my people in their misfortune" (*AASS*, 3:21). In *Poem without a Hero*, too, the poet depicts her special solidarity with the people (*narod*, as used in these lines from *Requiem*), but her pose no longer appears stable. Akhmatova must redouble her efforts to prove her relevance to the Russian people—not only because of Soviet claims of her irrelevance, and even accusations of irrelevance by certain contemporaries, but also because of special protections she nonetheless received from the government. So over and over in her poem she reiterates a downward vector, a motion into the depths, where the Russian people seemingly founder. By such an act of condescension—understood here as the intelligentsia's assimilation to the non-Westernized *narod* and therefore as "kenotic"—she can inscribe her own image as that of a co-sufferer. But her assimilation also constitutes an act of identification:

she inscribes an image of the collective with the poet's self-abnegation, and so to regain a vision of the collective one must pursue the poet's trail. Her enigma initiates a pursuit.

Akhmatova subtitles her work "A Triptych," gesturing at its capacity for endlessly unfolding, opening up one thing inside another. Just as she continually shifts scenes, references, and images and interposes different moments in time, she also unapologetically mixes and moves between genres, underscoring her refusal to settle on one form or approach. This formal hybridity compounds the work's difficulty. In order to honor Akhmatova's mode of constant assimilation but also to help clarify and relate layers in the work, I will offer three interwoven readings of *Poem without a Hero*, as container, memoir, and icon—all demonstrating how Akhmatova subverts the sophianic image to replace it with a more directly marian one. In the first reading, I will pursue a set of images of enclosed spaces—wombs, rooms, and houses—whose enclosing power the poet seeks to overcome in her downward procession. In the second reading, I will show how Akhmatova participates in the memory projects of her period but resists their tendency to objectify past events, to settle on a fixed interpretation, and chooses instead an existential immersion in the past that ascetically denies a satisfying and unifying explanation. In the third reading, I will show how Akhmatova replaces the sophianic image with the iconic line, a mode of representation that draws the artists and audience into a sacred, liturgical procession rather than the self-satisfied production of artistic doubles. In each reading I will demonstrate how Akhmatova adapts certain sophiological-modernist impulses to her Soviet context, how she creates a kenotic vector that draws the reader into the fabric of national history in hopes of constructing the shared identity the modernist artists desired but never achieved. In each reading I will highlight Akhmatova's motif of the work as a womb, an organ describing a space where the imperializing poetic image can embed itself and grow. I will also, finally, show how this downward vector constitutes in the poem a liturgical procession of its own kind, and therefore a new ritual suited to a very particular modern context.

CONTAINER

It is difficult to say where *Poem without a Hero* begins, both because its main narrative is so fragmented and because Akhmatova changed the text so much over many sittings, shuffling pieces so dates appear in no clear chronological order; yet in a very real sense one can say that the work begins with a house, and most certainly a haunted one.[30] After the title and subtitle (*A Triptych* [1940–1963]), the first words we read—"Deus conservat omnia"

(God preserves all)—quote the crest on the gates of the House on the Fontanka, where Akhmatova lived from 1926 to 1952 (*PBG*, 898). This place provides the primary setting for Akhmatova's "hellish harlequinade," as she calls her work (*PBG*, 889). It was also the closest thing she had to a home in her adult life—but as we will see, she presents "home" in her *poema* as a deeply troubled notion—"Home—a jolly word— / Now known to none" (*PBG*, 896). Akhmatova's years in a wing of this grand house saw an incomprehensible string of traumatic events—her fall into public disfavor, her son's arrests and sentencing to labor in Siberia, the Stalinist purges, the beginning of the gruesome Siege of Leningrad, and the horrors of World War II. Most of all it is the place she associates with memories of her friends who were repressed, imprisoned, executed, and forced into exile. For her, the house—true to its coat of arms—guards its ghosts. And the entrapping house comes to constitute a central womb image in the work.

This hungry quality of inner spaces suits Akhmatova's purposes well—indeed, she dots the terrain of her poem with sites into which the poet-figure can fruitfully descend. Hellish, enclosing spaces pictured in the work include the tomb (*PBG*, 872, 873), a lonely room (*PBG*, 873), a mirrored hall (first on *PBG*, 875). Many more such containing spaces appear in the poem, but the mirrored hall especially comes to represent a hellish space the poet enters and inhabits. (The mirror is also associated with *sviatki* divination rituals, and therefore with otherworldly—and potentially sinister—realms, a theme Pushkin plays upon famously in *Eugene Onegin*.) Ol'ga Sedakova has written about the motif of what she varyingly calls "emplacement" (*vnutripolozhnost'*) or "one in another" (*odno v drugom*) across Akhmatova's poetry, with special reference to *Poem without a Hero*.[31] Sedakova locates this motif in the unusual proliferation of prepositional phrases governed by "in/into" (*v*), of container objects, of narrative trajectories directed *inwards* and of concepts of inwardness. But as Sedakova shows, these instances are often characterized by a dynamic tension: the "one in the other" strains to break out (or in), manages to break free, or dwells in antithetical tension with that which seems to contain it.[32] Indeed, in Akhmatova's *poema* the speaker constantly wavers between a desire to escape these spaces and the sense that her work will emerge specifically from them. Container-figures in Akhmatova's *poema*, then, picture the kenotic vector of the poetic word, conceived by a voice cast into the depths (the speaker in her confined space), ever yearning to break out as a new word, a new hero—who never arrives.

Rooms, Apartments, Houses

A good acmeist, Akhmatova bends architectural images to her purpose, making of them sites where the poetic word can implant itself. Like the House on the Fontanka, interior spaces in her poem are hellish ones so that entering them becomes a kenotic act. To enter these spaces is to reenter the womb, relinquishing distinct form and therefore burying oneself alive, entering the realm of death unprotected. The hell the poetic speaker experiences in the womb-like rooms she inhabits is a hell she chooses, a path of suffering she elects. In her first "Dedication" Akhmatova compares her poem to a composed funeral march—"*Marche funèbre* . . . / Chopin . . ."—and throughout the work she refers to funerals and describes impending death (*PBG*, 872). She describes the poet herself as on the verge of death: "I myself, like a shade on the threshold, / Preserve the last comforts" (*PBG*, 875). But Akhmatova does not stop there: she pictures her poetic self, in fright, entering into the realm of death, into the hellish space:

Но мне страшно: войду сама я,
Кружевную шаль не снимая,
Улыбнусь всем и замолчу.
С той, какою была когда-то,
В ожерелье черных агатов,
До долины Иосафата
Снова встретиться не хочу . . .
Не последние ль близки сроки? . .
Я забыла ваши уроки,
Краснобаи и лжепророки!—
Но меня не забыли вы.
Как в прошедшем грядущее зреет,
Так в грядущем прошлое тлеет—
Страшный праздник мертвой листвы. (*PBG*, 877)

(But I'm afraid: I will go in myself, / Not removing my lace shawl, / I'll smile to all and fall silent. / I do not wish to meet again . . . / Before Jehoshaphat's valley / With the one I was at one time, / Bejeweled with black agates. / Are not the end times close? . . . / I've forgotten your lessons, / rhetoricians and false prophets!— / But you haven't forgotten me. / As in the past the future ripens / So in the future the past decays— / A frightful festival of the dead leaf.)

The poem for the poet becomes a portal into hell—even letting her recapitulate the apocryphal marian descent into hell (*khozhdenie po mukam*), that immensely popular story for Russians about the merciful intercession of Mary even to damned souls. In Akhmatova's "Third and Last" dedication the poet speaks of "the Poema's mortal flight" (*Poemy smertnyi polet*) (*PBG*, 874). She seems to mean this entering into the realm of death that includes judgment for past sins—suggested here in the image of the Valley of Jehoshaphat, which the poet describes in her notes as "the presumed location of the Last Judgment" (*PBG*, 897). (The reference is to Joel 3:2.) Akhmatova's poetic self enters this hellish space, however, not as a sinless saint, and therefore not entirely as Mary. For the poet this realm is terrifying because there she will meet with her former self and her doubles, whose way of being she desperately wishes to disavow. She will have to undergo the judgment she is about to carry out on the modernist religious project. Interestingly, Akhmatova pictures her willed immersion in this haunted space as a way of expiating the sins of the past. Many have noted the role of conscience and guilt in the poem. The poet shares her room with shades who play out a tragedy that Akhmatova sees as emblematic of the sins of Russian modernism—the hussar, the seductress, a shadowy male tempter figure who lingers in the background, and whom readers have linked both to Blok and Kuzmin.[33] In *Poem without a Hero* all these personae step forth as types, representatives of their age—to whom the poet-narrator says, "You are one of my doubles" (*PBG*, 883).

I would argue, though, that this image of entering into an overpopulated hell *also* points in more literal ways to Akhmatova's living situation in the House on the Fontanka. In the Soviet period she lived there as one resident of a communal apartment. Two recent investigations of Akhmatova in the Soviet period—by Rylkova and Irina Paperno, respectively—remind us how prominent the experience and notion of the communal apartment was for the poet.[34] From 1926 on, Akhmatova lived in others' rooms in the House on the Fontanka and had no home of her own. Akhmatova, then, refers to her own life in a communal apartment to stress her solidarity with ordinary Soviet citizens and the discomforts they endured. Akhmatova seems to be placing herself in a position of strain and difficulty; indeed, the poet herself (as reported by Lydia Chukovskaia) referred to her living quarters in her communal apartment with the word *zastenok*—literally "behind-the-wall-space"—but used figuratively to mean "torture chamber."[35]

There is evidence not only that Akhmatova emphasized her living situation in solidarity with the Russian people via literary means, but also that she chose to align her life with her desired literary image as the people's representative by rejecting better living situations. From what we are told, Akhmatova refused more than one offer of a living space of her own.[36] One might propose that this refusal stemmed from a desire to remain in her "torture chamber" as a gesture of solidarity with Stalin's victims in gulag and grave, as well as with the living conditions of average Soviet citizens. Such a literary and literal move would enable her, therefore, to reiterate her imperial kenotic trajectory—to maintain her position of influence in the Russian national imaginary. Robert Bird argues that the genre of the long poem in Russia—the *poema*—posits itself above all as a vehicle for the *collective* voice.[37] In her recent reading of *Poem without a Hero* (technically, *Poema without a Hero*) Clare Cavanagh interrogates the problem of how Akhmatova navigates the task of nurturing a collective voice for the Russian nation when she is considered of public irrelevance.[38] For Cavanagh, Akhmatova attacks the problem by dissolving the individuality of the poet in the poetic text—hence the lack of a "hero." I would suggest, rather, that the poet transforms her figure into a self that self-empties—that is, a marian or Christ figure. The poet digs in. Surely this act of intent identification hovers behind the emphatic prefatory lines:

ИЗ ГОДА СОРОКОВОГО,
КАК С БАШНИ, НА ВСЕ ГЛЯЖУ.
КАК БУДТО ПРОЩАЮСЬ СНОВА
С ТЕМ, С ЧЕМ ДАВНО ПРОСТИЛАСЬ,
КАК БУДТО ПЕРЕКРЕСТИЛАСЬ
И ПОД ТЕМНЫЕ СВОДЫ СХОЖУ.

25 августа 1941
Осажденный Ленинград
(*PBG*, 874)

(FROM THE YEAR 1940, / AS FROM A TOWER, I LOOK DOWN AT EVERYTHING. / AS THOUGH I'M BIDDING FAREWELL ONCE MORE / TO THAT TO WHICH I LONG AGO BID FAREWELL, / AS THOUGH I HAVE JUST CROSSED MYSELF / AND DESCEND NOW THROUGH DARK VAULTS. // *August 25, 1941 / Besieged Leningrad*

In these lines we find one of the only moments where the speaker describes herself as *seeing*—that is, where she rules a verb of sight. Here she pictures herself looking down from above, with a bird's-eye view—commanding a vista where distance makes things look clear. Then she bids farewell to this distanced, objectified perspective and even disavows it as something to which she "long ago bid farewell"; and she announces her ultimate intent for her work—to "descend through dark vaults." This descent into the vaults seems a descent into the grave. Through this move Akhmatova symbolically ascends into the vaults of memory to join the deceased friends she recalls in her *Poem*. But she also thus symbolically participates in Orpheus's descent into Hades and Christ's descent into the grave and hell—and even Mary's apocryphal ascent into hell to visit and bring relief to sinners (*khozdenie Bogoroditsy po mukam*). Joining the womb with the tomb, Akhmatova becomes Mother, Savior, and Poet all at the same time.

Visions in a Hall of Mirrors

The poet's kenosis, her insistent identification with her suffering nation, marks her attempt at reestablishing the poet's relevance in the social sphere;

she figuratively identifies with the Russian people by descending into "dark vaults." But she also plays out this notion of identification on a more abstract level—at the level of vision and representation. Akhmatova essentially eschews a mode of vision (and therefore representation) premised upon a distance between subject and object. And she figures this undistanced, identificatory mode of vision especially in images, appearing throughout the poem, of a room walled entirely by mirrors. In these rooms one cannot visually distinguish a real self from an image, so the distinction between subject and object effectively disappears. The facing mirrors that Akhmatova sets up create a space for reflection, but one where she cannot distinguish her own image from those that memory calls up, a space of vertiginous identification. The motif of the "double" repeats throughout the work, and the poet-narrator brings herself, in fright and disgust, to embrace them. She speaks of a person who "as though in a mirror one frightening night / Raves like one possessed and will not / Recognize himself": the very refusal constitutes an admission of identity with the mirror-double (*PBG*, 885).

In this kind of specularity the poem recalls the icon, which Mondzain describes as "a gaze and not an object"; that is, the icon institutes a relationship between the source of the image and the one who seeks to imitate the image, or conversely between the image-maker and the imagination he seizes (*MIIE*, 70). Many scholars of the icon have described the icon's "inverse" or "reverse" perspective, which works to incorporate the viewer into the perspective of the image itself, and not the other way around (i.e., not the Renaissance way of linear perspective).[39] Reading Akhmatova's poem via this concept, but also taking into account her power play, we can say that the poet-narrator casts her living image in among shades, and her assimilation to (identification with) them restores them—but only by her incorporating their legacy into her own project. The imperial nature of her appropriation—and Alexander Zholkovsky and Rylkova have spoken to this element of her biography—is evident not only in her identification with figures such as Olga-Glebova Sudeikina—a "Petersburg doll, an actress," "so ostentatiously exposed"—but also in the way she pieces together her text out of quotes from and references to others' poems (*PBG*, 883, 880).[40] Indeed, Akhmatova's speaker begins by proclaiming to her dead contemporaries: "I am writing on your manuscript" (*Ia na tvoem pishu chernovike*) (*PBG*, 872).[41]

At the same time, however, there is one image that takes priority even over the poet's—the image of one long awaited. Akhmatova sets up this mirror scene with reference to the work's Epiphany subtext—not only to the mummers who appear in that space, but also to the tradition of young women divining who their future spouse will be, by means of a mirror and candle used at midnight—a folk tradition associated with *sviatki*. She uses this figure of fortune-telling and expectation to brings us back to the sophianic task—that is, the artist's aim of producing a new word that will embody a new world. In among all these specters we glimpse a different kind of figure. In a section visually marked off from the stair-step placement of the lines surrounding it in "Nineteen Thirteen: A Petersburg Tale," we read:

Б *Звук шагов, тех, которых нету,*
По сияющему паркету,
Е *И сигары синий дымок.*
Л *И во всех зеркалах отразился*
Ы *Человек, что не появился*
Й *И проникнуть в тот зал не мог.*
Он не лучше других и не хуже,
Но не веет летейской стужей,
З *И в руке его теплота.*
А *Гость из Будущего!—Неужели*
Он придет ко мне в самом деле,
Л *Повернув налево с моста?* (*PBG*, 877)

W The sound of steps of those who aren't,
Along the shining parquet floor,
H And the blue cigar smoke.
I And in all the mirrors reflected
T A person who did not appear
E And who could not penetrate that hall.
He's no better or worse than the others,
But the Lethe's chill does not waft from him,
H And there is warmth in his hand.
A The Guest from the Future!—Will he really
L Come to me, in actual fact,
L When he turns left at the bridge?

In the midst of the spectral ruckus appears an infinitely refracted image ("in all the mirrors") of someone who promises to bring life and resolution. Unlike the masked phantoms from the past, he remains in the mirror, and his image seems prior to hers, waiting in the vaults of her creative and commemorative space. Though his image and hers presumably elide, his seems to determine hers since, as we read further on, he is the one who will speak the "*Word that will defeat death / And solve the riddle of my life*" (*PBG*, 886; italics in the original). In this sense the title of Akhmatova's *poema* might best be translated as *Poem without* the *Hero*, since the work projects not merely a missing protagonist, but an awaited messiah.[42]

The hierarchical iconic relationship of supplicant to savior appears in the strange format of these stanzas. The vertically placed words "White Hall" seem to represent a solid barrier, a threshold one can cross from neither direction—a screen. The block letters take on an iconic quality, suggesting that they point to larger meanings; but their relation to the words opposite them is unclear, opaque. The poem's walls, then, seem the very mark of the hero's absence. This, too, recalls the icon's mode, its trace of the absenting God whose image draws the viewer in pursuit of him. Mondzain writes that this absence, "by the trace that it leaves and the lack that it incarnates, produces the very essence of the visible" (*MIIE*, 94). Akhmatova's *Poem without a Hero* describes a lack, invokes the hero's image as his withdrawal, reiterates this withdrawal in scenes of the poet's own emptying herself out into shades and masks. Make no mistake: the absent hero's priority does not mitigate but rather strengthens the poet's imperial impulse since she identifies with his image. In a way she is the absent hero of her own poem. "*To incarnate oneself*," Mondzain proposes, "*is to empty oneself, or what amounts to the same thing, to become similar to one's own image*" (italics in the original). Akhmatova has made herself into the long-awaited Sophia, even as she makes Sophia appear rather more like Mary.

Poetic Progeny and the Ruptured Womb

My contention that Akhmatova's work traces the marian womb as icon does not rest on these architectural images alone, and the pictured descent into them: indeed, concealed in the poem we find images of wombs. Some are barren and some fertile; some emblematize the fruitlessness of modernist "life-creation," some promise to give birth to the Guest from the Future, to produce a restored, unified Creation—someday. None of them release their progeny in the poem's purview.

The narrator comments on the work in part 2, "The box has a triple bottom" (*U shkatulki troinoe dno*) (*PBG*, 891). This image of the poem suggests that several poems exist in one poem, several spaces recess in one space. It also suggests that the poet makes some aspects of the poem less accessible, perhaps its most troubling aspects. One such aspect, I would venture, is a set of images of murdered infants and/or terminated pregnancies. Several scholars have described a deep ambivalence Russian modernists held toward physical progeny—in part inspired by Solovyov's utopian vision that depends on individuals' sublimation of their desire.[43] This ambivalence seems to carry over into Akhmatova's project, and the poem wrestles with its legacy.

One prominent association with a narrative of a murdered infant emerges in the poem's references to Goethe's *Faust*, in one of the stage directions we have already seen (*PBG*, 290). Akhmatova refers twice to the Brocken scene in *Faust*, where Mephistopheles leads Faust to witness a witches' sabbath. It is at this scene where Faust has a vision of Margarete, the woman he has seduced, with her throat slit.[44] He returns to find her incarcerated for murdering the infant he had fathered. She has the opportunity to escape but resolves to remain imprisoned and pay for her terrible sin. This resolve reminds us both of the poet-figure's determination to remain in her "torture chamber," as well as of the narrator's description elsewhere of the "epoch that has taken a vow of silence" (*bezmolvie velikoi molchal'nitsy-epokhi*) (*PBG*, 888). The similar choice of fate suggests similar causes, similar sins to expiate. In her other *Faust* reference in part 3, the narrator depicts herself in Akhmatova's evacuation flight out of Leningrad:

> Все вы мной любоваться могли бы,
> Когда в брюхе летучей рыбы
> Я от злой погони спаслась
> И над полным врагами лесом,
> Словно та, одрежимая бесом,
> Как на Брокен ночной неслась . . . (*PBG*, 896)

(All of you could have admired me, / When in the belly of a flying fish / I was saved from evil pursuit / And over woods full of foes, / Like that other, possessed by a devil, / I was borne over Brocken by night . . .)

Here we find the Akhmatova-figure firmly ensconced in her customary space, manifestly a type of womb—in a "belly." She places herself inside a womb, but she also bears a womb, here (the box with the "triple bottom"), as a witch flying over Brocken as though for the occult rites. Interestingly, Goethe echoes the image of the murdered child in this very scene, in the Witches' chorus, when they sing of their journey:

> The road is wide, the road is long,
> Ah, what an antic, frantic throng!
> The pitchfork pokes, the broomstick thrusts,
> The infant chokes, the mother busts.[45]

(Der We gist breit, der We gist lang, / Was ist das für ein toller Drang? / Die Gabel sticht, der Besen kratzt, / Das Kind erstickt, die Muter platzt.)[46]

In the scene they describe, frenzied as the fearful carnival of Akhmatova's *poema*, the wild ride results in the death of the child in the womb.

Early on in the poem, in the "Second Dedication" we read above, Akhmatova identifies her work with a child in the womb, and this image raises a host of comparisons between physical and artistic progeny—a fitting motif for a work that revisits the modernist project to produce transfigured materiality. The narrator declares to her muse,

> Не диктуй мне, сама я слышу,
> Теплый ливень уперся в крышу,
> Шепоточек слышу в плюще.
> Кто-то маленький жить собрался,
> Зеленел, пушился, старался,
> Завтра в новом блеснуть плаще. (*PBG*, 873)

(Don't dictate to me, I hear it myself, / A warm rain has pressed against the roof, / I hear a whisper in the ivy. / Someone small has gotten ready to live, / Has turned green, burgeoned, tried / To shine tomorrow in a new cloak.)

In this scene the poet lies in her bed in the enclosed space of her room, and the rain hitting the roof portends the conception of "someone small," implanted into the walls of the poet's room, as though it were itself a womb. The image recalls the myth of the conception of Perseus, when Zeus comes to Danae in the form of a golden rain and impregnates her. But who fathers the work is in question: to the poet's double Sudeikina the poem asks, "Beautiful lady, is your paladin / Gabriel or Mephistopheles?" (*PBG*, 882). One announces God's impregnation of the chaste womb, another heralds the sacrifice of physical progeny for intellectual progeny. One foretells transformed flesh, another ghoulish visions—Sophia or her horrifically failed embodiments.

The Marian Womb

This womb image introduced so early on is one that Akhmatova associates specifically with the womb of Mary, Mother of God, or God-bearer (*Theotokos* in the Greek). A few lines down from the initial conception image of "someone small," we find a set of images that echo liturgical enumerations of womb and container images associated with Mary:

> Сплю—
> мне снится молодость наша,
> Та, ЕГО миновавшая чаша;
> Я ее тебе наяву,
> Если хочешь, отдам на память,
> Словно в глине чистое пламя
> Иль подснежник в могильном рву. (*PBG*, 873)

(I'm asleep— / I dream of our youth, / Of that, the cup that passed HIM by, / I will give it to you when awake, / If you wish, for memory's sake, / Like a pure flame in a clay jar / Or a snowdrop in the mouth of the grave.)

Each of these images—the cup, the flame in the jar, and the flower in the grave's mouth—is comprised of a vessel whose contents we can see. Akhmatova, then, depicts her *poema* itself as a vessel—which contains, the second two images suggest, fragile, flickering life. In taking this gift, however, one drinks a bitter draught. Those of Akhmatova's contemporaries that perished (like Kniazev) avoided the suffering that would later arise—less from political repression than from the knowledge of their complicity in Russia's fate. Akhmatova's work is a vessel for bitter memories—*gorech'* (a bitter drink) or "poisoned wine" (*otravlennoe vino*), as she mentions elsewhere in the poem (*PBG*, 894, 896). The drink is redemptive, however. Those who drink it imitate Christ, who asked the Father to let the cup of suffering pass him by and yet drank it to its dregs.[47]

The image of the work as a pregnant, virginal womb, and therefore a vessel of life and light, resonates deeply with the way the liturgy imagines Mary, as we see especially in the final odes of the festal canons and also throughout the marian feasts. In the canons Mary appears as God's throne (*FM*, 284), is addressed as his "Living City" (*FM*, 285), the Ark of the Covenant (*FM*, 457) and in endless other variations as a container in which God dwells and through which his grace flows.[48] (See also appendix.) We find a virtual catalogue of such pictures in the foremost liturgical text in the Eastern tradition connected with Mary—the sixth-century Akathist hymn, celebrated in the fifth week of Lent, just a few days after the service for the Great Canon, about which Akhmatova composed the poem opening this chapter. The Akathist, along with its accompanying canon, uses Mary's bearing God to picture the theology of the Incarnation, and it endlessly innovates images of the womb—addressing Mary as "orchard of pure fruit," sheepfold, "book," "fount," shell, "bridal chamber," "enclosure of God whom nothing can enclose," but also "ladder," "bridge," "vine," and "gate"—figuring not spaces so much as sites and passages.[49] An important marian icon—the Mother of God of the Sign (figure 3.2)—visually represents Mary as a kind of container of God. As one who used marian images and venerated marian icons, Akhmatova seems likely to be drawing from this most important marian liturgical motif.

The notion of the marian womb—and by analogy Akhmatova's work—as a passage rather than a self-sufficient image or work is an important one. In *Poem without a Hero* reified, "total" images inevitably implode. Throughout the poem wherever we encounter totalizing, impenetrable forms, we also witness the destruction of those forms. Akhmatova therefore not only

Figure 3.2. Icon of the Mother of God of the Sign (*Znamenie*). Russia, ca. 1600.
Courtesy of the Museum of Russian Icons, Clinton, Massachusetts.

uses images of the pregnant womb to debunk the modernist creation of full-blown new worlds, but she pointedly raises and then explodes such forms. In one of the scenes, for instance, where she describes the hellish modernist masqued ball, the narrator invokes a precariously swelling figure: "But for them the walls have stepped back, / The light has flared up, the sirens have sung, / And the ceiling has swollen out like a cupola" (*PBG*, 876). As we know according to the poem's central narrative, the masquerade culminates in disaster. Akhmatova makes this point vividly in the scene when the hapless Kniazev figure witnesses his idealized female-figure Sudeikina betray him: "He has seen.—The buildings collapse . . ." (*PBG*, 886). The poet who has survived, then, into the Stalinist period and even into the Thaw, takes more caution than the artists she depicts. Instead of erecting grand constructions, she makes of her poem a shape-shifter, an enigma that always evades comprehension.

Instead of glorious figuration, spectacular resolution, Akhmatova offers abnegation, an entering into the depths. That is, she offers the way of the Russian people, with whom she wishes to identify as a poet. This identification emerges in numerous ways, but especially in some telling lines of a folkloric nature that she inserts into her sophisticated poem. In chapter 2 of part 1 Akhmatova partially quotes a folk saying that brings this contrast between deserved and salvific suffering to light, in the lines "And around me the old city Peter, / That roughed the people up, / (As the people used to say)" (*PBG*, 881). The full saying (which the context suggests Akhmatova knew) vividly figures Petersburg's and Russia's construction on the backs of the peasant populace: "Ole father Peter roughed us up; our brothers, the factories, took years off our lives; and ole mother ditch did us in" (*Batiushka-Piter boka nam povyter, brattsy-zavody unesli gody, a matiushka-kanava sovsem dokonala*).[50] In this saying as in Akhmatova's *poema* the Russian people pour their lives into the ground and fabric of their nation's construction, into "our old mother ditch." Their downward procession provides the motion and substance on which Russia is built. The repentant poet follows them and crafts her own aesthetic descent, perhaps even drawing in her reader, on the path to restoration.

MEMOIR

Akhmatova uses spatial and container images to figure her work as a descent into the depths, thereby establishing herself more firmly as an artist for the people. In this way she works to recoup the status that the intelligentsia and artistic elite held in imperial Russia, as well as to perpetuate a religious aesthetic. But we can see Akhmatova working at the level of genre, too, to create a poem that will move beyond modernism's failed attempts to realize a new world. While her title itself highlights the main genre she chooses—the *poema* or long poem—Akhmatova also incorporates elements of memoir. This move is strategic in a number of ways. First, it allows her better to position herself as someone who has shared in the hardships of the Russian people over the past few decades. Second, this move enables her to participate in a genre that takes on special prominence in the Thaw; in this period after Khrushchev's "secret speech" debunking Stalin, a new, if limited, openness allowed writers publicly to take stock of the recent past and to assert their own authority in its interpretation and legacy. Third, her move toward memoir allows Akhmatova to disavow the ivory tower of the prophetic, elite poet—to reject a poetics of distance and clarity on the human condition in favor of a poetics of participation, where the poet has no special view into the future but takes on a new, more viable role.

In this section I will argue that Akhmatova, in her attempt to highlight her own legacy, takes over and outdoes the genre of memoir with her poem. I will discuss her poem in relation to contemporaneous memory projects, with special reference to Nikolai Berdiaev's autobiography, a work she knew. And I will show, through references to sight and sound, how she privileges a perspective that only brooks the chaos of what it describes, rather than a perspective that objectifies from a distance. That is, Akhmatova contends poetically that the poet's immersion in the suffering she depicts lends her authority. Framed in terms of the sophianic task, Sophia's necessary incompletion speaks to the power of Akhmatova's more marian model and its emphasis on pregnant potential.

To reiterate, Akhmatova's late work comprises a commemoration, a *procession into and through* memory—but always with an eye to the shape of the poet's life. And so we can read *Poem without a Hero* as a poetic memoir, albeit an enigmatic one, one that defers final interpretation of a life and the history it processes. In *Stories of the Soviet Experience: Memoirs, Diaries, Dreams*, Irina Paperno explores autobiographical texts in the late Soviet period as loci where individuals seek to make sense of a period whose end they sense by embedding a "story of intimate life" in a whole society's "catastrophic history."[51] These texts, moreover, bear special import for the intelligentsia, as their authors, readers, collectors, and editors seek to reestablish a sense of community through them, a "community where those who lived through the Soviet era can gain access to the intimate, inner recesses of one another's lives."[52] While Akhmatova seems to be responding to Berdiaev's autobiography, its own kind of memory document, we can also see her poem as propagating the mythology that these late-Soviet memoirs will incorporate—that is, the notion that the intelligentsia in some way speaks for and embodies the fate of the nation. We can in this sense see *Poem without a Hero* as a kind of poetic memoir or proto-memoir—a genre that helps make sense of Akhmatova's disorienting mix of the personal and national, lyric and epic in her *poema*, as well as her concern in the work with what role the privileged poet-*intelligent* can realistically play on the national scene.

In her study Paperno especially examines Lydia Chukovskaia's diary of Akhmatova's life, *Notes about Anna Akhmatova*, in which, unbeknownst to the poet, Chukovskaia records minute details from their many exchanges over seventeen years, including frequent conversations about the troubled composition of *Poem without a Hero*. Chukovskaia's text for Paperno exemplifies the way that authors and readers alike can use autobiographical forms to create a sense of identity. Readers attested in their own accounts that they "felt admitted to Akhmatova's apartment" via Chukovskaia's diary.[53] Akhmatova's poem-memoir, meanwhile, practically forces the reader into her apartment (her "torture chamber") and into even more intimate experiences of its unsettled isolation. It draws the reader into Akhmatova's struggle to reconcile her privileged status with her sense of the poet's obligation to her people.

Akhmatova's adaptation of the memoir genre suggests itself in powerful resonances between her work and Nikolai Berdiaev's "philosophical autobiography," which she was reading as she composed the *Poem*, as we know from her notebooks of the period. Berdiaev was not only an important Silver Age religious philosopher, but he was a prominent figure in modernist circles—closely acquainted with Gippius and Merezhkovsky and engaged in their journalistic activities, a leading member of Viacheslav Ivanov's inner circle for a time, involved in the Religious-Philosophical Meetings, and friends and collaborator with Bely. He not only took part in the Russian "religious renaissance," but he was one of its earliest commentators, publishing in 1907 *The New Religious Consciousness and Society*. Berdiaev was forced by the Bolsheviks to leave Russia in 1922, along with 160 other purportedly anti-Bolshevik thinkers and writers, and soon he and his wife settled in Paris. In Paris he played a central role in the intellectual and cultural life of elite Russian émigrés. He kept writing philosophy, but he also sought to interpret the events that had led up to the Bolshevik Revolution and the authoritarian turn it had taken. As Stuart Finkel notes, Berdiaev and other émigré thinkers with him offered "a devastating criticism of the intellectual milieu and mentality that they believed had led directly to the October Revolution"; yet they believed the intelligentsia should play a continuing role in the life of the Russian people, in Russia and abroad.[54] From Paris Berdiaev not only set up his own school to advance Russian philosophy, but he also published many works that became seminal in Russia and the West alike for interpreting Russia's recent history and role in world culture.

The work that Akhmatova seems to have been reading, however, is his 1949 *Self-Knowing: An Experiment in Philosophical Autobiography*, or *Dream and Reality*, as the English translation is known (*NBSP*).[55] In this work Berdiaev seeks to deal with both historical and philosophical questions via autobiography, evaluating a Russian half-century and its larger meanings through the lens of his own life. Two of the topics he treats most centrally in the project are the role of the intelligentsia in Russia (historically and currently) and, in connection, the place of creativity. Both topics boast prominent places in much of his writing, including his essayistic journalism from earlier in the century, as found in *Landmarks* (*Vekhi*), a defining 1909 collection of essays on the intelligentsia in Russia.[56] In numerous places throughout *Self-Knowing* Berdiaev takes aim at "Classicism," meaning art that produces placid and ordered forms, because for him such art monstrously misrepresents the nature of life, creating "the illusion of perfection in the finite" (*NBDR*, 30; *NBSP*, 42).[57] In these terms Berdiaev speaks out against utopian projections of modernist sophianism, with its attempts to envision a perfected world. As an alternative, he proposes moving away from art, as he understands it, toward non-artistic genres, as he imagines them. For Berdiaev works of art evoke above all "the disparity between the creative impulse and creative product" (*NBDR*, 214; *NBSP*, 233). Likewise, the forms of philosophy Russia has appropriated from the West inadequately express reality, due to the tradition's tendency to "exalt the subject-personality but then suffocate it with its objectivizing approach" (*NBDR*, 304; *NBSP*, 336). He seeks to temper both problems by proposing (and practicing) writing that is not quite art and not quite philosophy: "Only confessions," he writes, "diaries, autobiographies and memoirs break through this objectivizing approach toward existential subjectivity." The Russian novel, he concedes, in the fully developed form it attained in the nineteenth century, also became a means of "self-knowing" (*samopoznaniia*—employing the same word as his own work's title) and philosophical insight. Berdiaev cites the "metaphysical" novels of Dostoevsky, in particular. Such genres as the memoir, that is, avoid the pitfalls of Classicism because they are better able to reflect life's messiness, its refusal to take on a final form. Poetry is notably lacking in his list.

Akhmatova seems, then, to take Berdiaev's discussion of art, philosophy, and knowledge as a kind of challenge, shaping her own poetry into a memoir-poem, or her poem that leans into memoir. That is, she seems to shape *Poem without a Hero* as a poem that bends form to life's unfinalizable quality. She wants to create a new kind of art that reflects human life more accurately and that therefore avoids the pitfalls of a more utopian sophianic approach. That Akhmatova read *Self-Knowing* is not in doubt. The poet comments on *Self-Knowing* in two places in her *Notebooks*. In one entry she comments,

> Now that I've finished reading B[erdiaev], I feel we had every reason to see the tower the way we did.
>
> A lot of what B[erdiaev] writes "doubles" and "triples" in my *poema*; something is guessed there, maybe even the main thing.
>
> I know the siren verse of Akhmatova
> Sounds of me, so far away.[58]

In these short lines Akhmatova sheds light on her project as a whole and the larger tasks she sets herself in it. She characterizes the poem as, like Berdiaev's work, a personal and retrospective glance at modernism: she speaks of how "we" "saw" the period, as embodied in Viacheslav Ivanov's "Tower" apartment. Following Berdiaev's suit, she, too, takes aim at these Wednesday gatherings that, as we have already seen, so shaped the age and that she first attended in 1910.[59] Berdiaev comments numerous times in his philosophical autobiography on Ivanov and the "Tower," which for him exemplified the initially well-intentioned but ultimately unwholesome and isolating quality of artistic life in the early decades of Russia's twentieth century. In terms that recall Akhmatova's poem he observes, "When I remember those 'Wednesdays,' I am struck by contrast. In the 'Tower' the most gifted cultural elite carried on refined conversations, while beneath them the revolution was raging" (*NBDR*, 161; *NBSP*, 167). Akhmatova goes on, in her comment on Berdiaev's book, to connect the evaluative look backwards with her *poema*, remarking on the closeness of their projects.

But Akhmatova does more than just agree with Berdiaev here. In her three-tiered comment and the poem it reflects, Akhmatova at once acknowledges Berdiaev's implicit challenge to modernist poetry and also sets herself in competition with him as though she might more legitimately speak to the legacy of the Silver Age. Fascinatingly, she directly employs Silver Age poetry in her diary entry to mark out her territory, when she quotes, "I know the siren verse of Akhmatova / Sounds of me, so far away."[60] On their face these lines, quoted from her first husband Nikolai Gumilev (who was executed in 1921), seem a paean to Berdiaev and others "far away," in exile, imprisonment, and death, and a way of giving them voice. But they also place Akhmatova in a superior position to Berdiaev and others: they speak from "far away," but she speaks out of the tomb itself, she speaks from the crucible of Soviet Russia. Although she is quoting someone else's lines, the effect is to emphasize her importance as a poet and as a mouthpiece for Russian letters. After all, these lines speak of her own sounding out, legitimized by the male voice of the martyred Gumilev.

What is more, in her mention of the "siren voice" Akhmatova also draws on a motif that appears in *Poem without a Hero*, a motif by which she associates the female poet with powerful female voices from classical mythology. Sirens appear in *Poem without a Hero* when the "hellish harlequinade" begins: here we read, "The light has flared up, the sirens have sung" (*PBG*, 876). In this moment Akhmatova is aligning her past self with the decadent seductress, the erotically charged female artist. But the reference to the Siren also brings to mind other female voices Akhmatova invokes from classical mythology—specifically those of women prophets, as in a stanza from "The Flip Side" ("Reshka"):

> Посинелые стиснув губы,
> Обезумевшие Гекубы
> И Кассандры из Чухломы,
> Загремим мы безмолвным хором . . . (*PBG*, 890)

(We've pursed our blue lips, / Hecubas who've lost our minds, / And Cassandras from Chukhloma, / We'll start rumbling, a silent chorus . . .)

Akhmatova's comment on Berdiaev's work, then, places her front and center in the scene she evokes, painting herself, effectively, as a "Cassandra from

Chukhloma," a provincial Russian town near the historic Golden Ring cities. By associating herself with these particular female figures, she lends herself the allure and legitimacy of prophets who, unheeded and unglorified, suffer no less than their nation. In her indirect polemic with Berdiaev, then, she crafts herself as the more authoritative voice to speak for contemporary Russia. She rejects the distanced stance of Berdiaev, suggesting that she is better equipped to speak to the realities of the Russian present and recent past than he. She pictures herself wading into the struggle and chaos, into the prophetic sound that rumbles up from the smallest Russian towns.

The Embedded Gaze

There is another way to describe how Berdiaev's project is relevant and may have informed Akhmatova's. That is, in *Self-Knowing* he addresses both directly and indirectly the problem of how one accounts for past events, both personal and historical. He interrogates philosophy itself and contends that memoir-related genres, where the subject narrates his experience of events, come closer to presenting accurate knowledge of the world. That is, Berdiaev eschews what he sees as a false distance between the subject and the object of investigation. Akhmatova, too, strongly indicates in *Poem* that the poet is most clairvoyant when she is immersed in the turbulent events she narrates. This theme of sight and insight suggests itself in the way Akhmatova uses images of seeing. In fact, I will argue that Akhmatova brings together her motif of the womb with images of sight in order to upset the primacy of the distanced perspective; furthermore, I will argue that this subversive literary act works to overturn fundamental notions about seeing and representation in the tradition of European art and philosophy.

Akhmatova uses her inter-resonant images of the hall of mirrors, the room or house, the tomb, the womb, the vessel to picture the poem as a medium through which she comes to terms with the legacy of the Silver Age; but these images also reveal a vision of broader import—a vision, that is, of how one sees. *Poem without a Hero* indicates its investment in defining vision through its sparse and strategic use of eyes and verbs of sight. The poem also explores the problem of the role of the poetic elite—and, by extension, the intelligentsia—in Russian society. Akhmatova's imperial wish to identify herself with the suffering Russian people is complicated by her privileged status as a well-known poet. Her special position resulted, for one, in her evacuation from Leningrad during the great German siege of that city, lifting her up and out of the most horrific suffering her city saw. Not one to shy away from challenges, Akhmatova recalls this moment and reshapes it so as to incorporate her self-mythology in this text. "All of you could have admired me / When in the belly of a flying fish / I was saved from evil pursuit" (*PBG*, 896). Even her VIP flight, then, morphs into a recessed womb image. Akhmatova's "descent" constantly betokens her identification with the suffering nation and, more notably, with their way of seeing. Her *poema* concludes, "With dry and downcast eyes / And wringing of hands, Russia / Walked east before me" (*Opustivshi glaza sukhie / I lomaia ruki, Rossiia / Predo mnoiu shla na vostok*) (*PBG*, 896). In these lines the poet takes the Russian people as model; her descent, then, comprises as much a realignment of vision as participation in the nation's suffering.

This vision Akhmatova proposes casts the gaze downwards, strips it of its distance and clarity; it embeds the gaze in the flesh of things. In *Downcast Eyes: The Denigration of Sight in Twentieth-Century French Thought*, Martin Jay describes an increasing revolt against the regime of "Cartesian perspectivalism," and the trajectory he presents finds deep resonances in *Poem without a Hero*—even beyond the coincidence of his title with the poem's final lines.[61] The "perspectivalist regime" Jay describes posits a single disembodied eye, separate from its object and unimplicated in its materiality. It views the world as its domain, able to be known through distanced observation—an assumption "shared by modern science and Albertian art."[62] As the twentieth century wears on, figures such as Georges Bataille, Jacques Lacan, Michel Foucault, and others increasingly challenge the status of sight as a premier vehicle of knowledge. Jay's study furnishes helpful tools for investigating sight in the later Akhmatova, though ultimately her conception and solution diverge from those of her French contemporaries as she engages her uniquely Russian context, with its tradition of icon veneration in a liturgical setting.

In keeping with the memoir genre as Paperno has described it, Akhmatova interrogates a whole society through the lens of her own life. Her work constitutes self-reflection, an inwardly directed gaze that must also identify common impulses in her society as a whole. As with Descartes, the look within, into the depths, promises knowledge; but as with her French contemporaries, she revises his terms. To Descartes's famous dictum she might respond: "I reflect, therefore we are." We have seen how the poet-figure refuses to disengage her own reflection from the dream doubles who visit from her past. She implants herself firmly in the mirror walls of her vision-space. As we have seen, this act of re-implanting constitutes a willed self-emptying, which allows her to make her mark on a greater territory. In the poem the poet embeds herself in the very walls of the city, addressing besieged Leningrad, insisting as she escapes: "You and I are inseparable, / My shade is on your walls, / My reflection in your canals, / The sound of my steps in the Hermitage halls" (*PBG*, 895).

Akhmatova, who was familiar with Freud's work, uses her conceit of the poem as dream to investigate the idea of gaining knowledge (insight) through delving into personal experience.[63] In particular she uses the topos of the dream to project a world that *is* the poet herself—the imperial imprint, indeed! Akhmatova sets the scene for her poem as a look inward in "Second Dedication," where the narrator proclaims, "I'm sleeping. . . . I'm sleeping— / I dream of our youth." References to dreams and dream states abound in the work. Paperno discusses the use of dream accounts in memoirs as stories used "to communicate 'truths'" about the self and its circumstances, but with an air of inaccessibility.[64] This notion fits with the poet-narrator's treatment of the specters who visit as her own doubles. This morphing of reflection into dream, then, serves further to entangle the poet into her look at things, as these things constitute projections of her own psyche. Freud's work, of course, deals not simply with dreams, but with their interpretation; his seminal 1899 work on this topic treats the dream as an instrument that channels insights previously not available to rational thought.[65] He uses many case studies to demonstrate how with the right tools one can quarry and tame dreams by analyzing them, transforming them into rational discourse. Akhmatova, however, refuses to usher her dream-visions into the bounds of logos thus conceived, and instead maintains her identity with them. She eschews a vision based on analytical distance.

This rejection of interpretation declares itself most boldly in part 2 of her "Triptych." This section seems at first glance to shift radically from the apparent chaos of part 1 and to offer a more objective and reasoned look at the work's task. It offers twenty-five stanzas of equal length, in contrast to the four chapters and numerous stanzas of very diverse length, as well as multiple and irregular sections that often begin with several lines of prose. Part 2 promises that "the hellish harlequinade of nineteen-thirteen has just passed through," and its first stanza offers hope that we have escaped the dream realm and may soon behold the work's hidden meaning from a safe distance:

Мой редактор был недоволен,
Клялся мне, что занят и болен,
Засекретил свой телефон
И ворчал: "Там три темы сразу!
Дочитав последнюю фразу,
Не поймешь, кто в кого влюблен,

Кто, когда и зачем встречался,
Кто погиб, и кто жив остался,
И кто автор, и кто герой,—
И к чему нам сегодня эти

> Рассуждения о поэте
> И каких-то призраков рой?" (*PBG*, 888)

(My editor was not happy, / He swore he was busy and ill, / Got an unlisted number / And grumbled: "There are three themes at once! / Even when you've read the last phrase, / You can't tell who's in love with whom, // Who met, when and why, / Who died and who's still alive, / Who's the author, who's the hero— / And why in times like these we need such / Arguments about the poet / And such a swarm of specters?")

After the editor's rant the reader awaits the author's reasoned answer, and indeed, the narrator begins to explain . . . and then stops short. Her explanations prove as enigmatic as the poem she is asked to clarify, and she proclaims, "There's no escape from the music." "A dream," she proposes, "is also a thing, after all" (*A ved' son—eto tozhe veshchitsa*) (*PBG*, 889). Such a posture confounds clear vision if vision is understood as making sense of things from a distance, but not if vision is understood, per Berdiaev and Akhmatova and their hybrid memoirs, as marking the territory of the past with one's own image.

Retraining the Gaze

But Akhmatova's presentation of sight and insight extends beyond the dream topos; she presents a series of images of *looking* that picture how perception works in her poem. She illustrates biographically her close involvement in the events she represents, but she also illustrates through certain images the principle of non-distanced perspective. Throughout the poem she pictures gazes and eyes actually embedded in the scene they are witnessing. We have previously seen how in the 1913 narrative Sudeikina's betrayal of Kniazev causes his world to fall down around him: "He has seen.—The buildings collapse . . ." But just before he experiences the existential collapse of his world, the poem pictures Kniazev paralyzed in the act of witnessing his beloved's betrayal. In the section's first lines of verse we read, "Who has frozen at the darkened windows, / On whose heart is the 'pale golden lock,' / Before whose eyes is mist?" In these lines we seem to glimpse the outlines of the Medusa myth with Freudian outlines: the male frozen—or petrified—in beholding the Gorgon, which is for Freud, a figure of female sexuality.[66] As previously shown, the poem's clearest womb image ("Someone small has gotten ready to live . . .") itself gestures at the Medusa myth, with its rain-shower conception as Zeus fathers Perseus, the great Gorgon hunter. Perhaps Akhmatova remembered Ivanov's essay "The Precepts of Symbolism" (1910), where he wrote of the crisis of Russian symbolism, when the world suddenly seemed reduced to a

> mound of "ashes," watched by the Gorgon's petrifying gaze. . . . The Beautiful Lady seemed like a "cardboard bride" to her paladin. The image of the expected Woman began to double and be confused with the apparent image of a whore.[67]

The collapse of buildings that follows, then, reads as an image of castration (as well as of the ruptured womb discussed above). The modernist seductress's (and, in a sense, the decadent Sophia's) rampant sexuality destroys the possibility of fruitful generation. Kniazev, a poet himself, will not produce a new world through sublimating erotic desire; he will bear neither artistic nor physical progeny.

Akhmatova works to develop a mode of vision that can see all the horror and chaos of the hellish harlequinade and what follows, yet not be blinded or petrified by it. In another passage where the poet revisits this very scene of betrayal, she presents a different mode of vision, one that can save her from the shortcomings of modernist selves. Concluding an ambivalent paean to the Sudeikina figure, the narrator speaks to her of the betrayed Kniazev:

> Всех влюбленных в тебя суеверней
> Тот, с улыбкой жертвы вечерней,
> Ты ему как стали—магнит,
> Побледнев, он глядит сквозь слезы,
> Как тебе протянули розы
> И как враг его знаменит.
> Твоего я не видела мужа,
> Я, к стеклу приникавшая стужа . . . (*PBG*, 884)
>
> (The most superstitious of all those in love with you, / The one with the smile of the evening sacrifice, / You were to him like a magnet to steel. / Gone pale, he gazes through tears, / At how someone hands you a rose, / At how famous his enemy is. / I did not see your husband, / I, the hard frost clinging to the window . . .)

In this passage, too, we see the witnessing Kniazev's frozen gaze, and here it turns him not merely to stone but to steel. In fact, we find *another* picture of the frozen gaze a few lines down—the "hard frost clinging to the window"; but Akhmatova uses this image to set up her own, superior mode of seeing. This second gaze belongs to a distinctly female subject. This gaze, moreover, buries itself in the structure it views—here lines of frost on the window of a house. In this detail as in so many other elements of the poem the speaker descends into the thick of things. This figuratively embedded gaze outdoes the frozen male gaze, seeming even to commandeer it. If according to Freud the male subject's petrifaction signifies an erection steeled to defy castration fear, then the womb here offers an alternative to the phallic gaze which can be castrated: her model reorients the gaze, directing it into the position of the "downcast eyes" she idealizes in the poem's final lines. Olga Matich has written about the stakes for Russian modernists of symbolic castration in the Salome story—an adaptation of the biblical account of Herod's stepdaughter who dances for her stepfather and demands in return the head of John the Baptist.[68] The *Poem*'s repeated evocation of the seductress-dancer Sudeikina in concert with the poem's reference to John the Forerunner ("Iokanann," *PBG*, 875) suggests Akhmatova's own adaptation of the story; but here the poet redeems the gaze by assimilating it to her womb-form. Rejecting the perspectivalist gaze and its stultifying objectifications, she offers instead a gaze that looks out from the depths. Mondzain writes that the gaze (and not the form) serves as the index for the icon, and this distinction applies well to *Poem*, where the gaze relentlessly pursues the absent hero, who is not the earnest Kniazev, not the daemonic Blok, not the mummers whose masks cover nothing.[69] The poet's roaming gaze passes over and leaves its impress on the terrain of the past, projecting its line into an undetermined future.

In *Downcast Eyes* Jay describes a number of disturbing images Georges Bataille deploys to combat the West's tradition of ocular-centrism. In one image Bataille pictures an enucleated eye shoved into a vagina.[70] This moment seems to echo elements of Akhmatova's "embedded" gaze, the eye repositioned in the lining of the womb—however, their massive difference in presentation tips us off to the distinctness of their solutions to the problem of "Cartesian perspectivalism." Bataille aggressively employs horrific visual and visceral violence to pursue his cause, while Akhmatova takes a more measured line of attack, one that preserves the basic human form but subtly curbs it to her own purposes.

The Sound of Nascence

Akhmatova insists throughout *Poem without a Hero* on an artistic mode that identifies with its subject and refuses to offer the easily graspable representations that one might find in a more sanguine mode. Yet another way she illustrates this more difficult artistic mode is in multiple references to a particular kind of sound in the poem. We have seen Akhmatova use sight to figure her preferred mode of knowing and showing; likewise she uses sound to figure how the poet's voice emerges precisely from *within* the chaos it seeks to present. She uses sound to indicate how the Word implants itself in the depths to emerge as a directive.

It is not my intent here to explore the full texture of sound in *Poem without a Hero*; instead I want to show how Akhmatova figures sound itself, drawing it into the kenotic vector the work persistently reiterates. In particular she accesses sounds from the modernist past and makes them echo through her work. We find this not least in her constant quotes of and reference to others' poems, as mentioned above. She also strikes that portentous note of which Blok in particular spoke, as we saw in an earlier chapter on him.[71] Given Blok's massive presence in the *Poem* one might surmise a reference to his essay "The People and the Intelligentsia" in Akhmatova's use of his repeated key word "*gul*" (rumble) when her narrator intones, "And ever in the stifling chill, / Pre-war, lecherous and ominous, / Dwelt some kind of future rumble" (*Zhil kakoi-to budushchii gul*) (*PBG*, 885) ("Narod i intelligentsiia," *ABSS*, 5:318–28). This sound for Akhmatova, as for her contemporaries looking back on the century's early decades, represents, on one hand, the gross inability of Russia's intelligentsia to understand their situation and thereby foresee and respond to crisis. On the other hand, it also represents the potential for the intelligentsia to assume a "visionary" role, newly understood. The one who can perceive and partake in that sound can marshal a whole society through times of massive uncertainty, landscapes of ruin. She can claim legitimacy as a poet who has moved beyond modernism's sophianism into her own Sophia-inspired marianism.

"The Flip Side" ("Reshka"), with its ironically playful thematics of interpretation, helps elucidate the way Akhmatova figures sound to represent her overall vision; like sight, sound finds it most resonant position in the depths. We saw above how in this section the poet begins to explain her work to her editor. Indeed, she tries to stand with the editor, at a distance from the work, and she concedes, "And I myself was not glad / Of this hellish harlequinade, / Hearing its sound from afar" (*PBG*, 889). She gives up her attempt at an objective distance as the poem itself begins to burgeon out and overshadow the interpretive task. "There's no escape from the music," she cries. She reverts to her position in the depths of the work, and in the process, she presents us with what we might consider the poem's key stanzas:

Карнавальной полночью римской
И не пахнет. Напев Херувимской
У закрытрых церквей дрожит.
В дверь мою никто не стучится,
Только зеркало зеркалу снится,
Тишина тишину сторожит.

И со мною моя "Седьмая",
Полумертвая и немая,
Рот ее сведен и открыт,
Словно рот трагической маски,
Но он черной замазан краской
И сухою землей набит. (*PBG*, 890)

(But it does not smell like a midnight / Roman carnival. The Cherubic hymn / Trembles by closed churches. / No one knocks at my door, / Mirrors only dream of mirrors, / Silence guards silence. // And with me is my "Seventh," / Half-dead and mute, / Her mouth is open and turned down / Like the mouth of a tragic mask, / But it's smeared with black paint / And filled with dry earth.)

In these consecutive stanzas we encounter further iterations of the womb/ container image—the closed church, the hall of mirrors, the work in a tomb (like the light in the clay jar promised in the "Second Dedication"). But this time these images are rendered in terms of sound, and with added emphasis on the status of the work of art (notably feminized, as though in a nod to Sophia). The "hellish harlequinade" that visits the poet—hall of mirrors, ephemeral dream—turns out, under further scrutiny, to resemble a closed church. The poet's creation (her Sophia) lies half-dead in . . . a grave?—her mask-mouth stopped with earth. While there is some question about what Akhmatova refers to precisely by her "Seventh," it is clear that she intends a work of art—her own poetry or Shostakovich's famous *Leningrad Symphony*.[72] Neither music nor poetry sounds out here, however. In fact, silence seems to reign—but in the larger context of the poem, we will find that silence coexists with what we might call incipient sound, or nascent sound—pictured in the oxymoronic description of Akhmatova's prophetess-doubles who "rumble in a silent chorus." Indeed, in part 1 we read that "Silence herself speaks" (*PBG*, 886). Likewise in the "Afterword" to part 1, the "*poema* lies there / Silent, as is her wont," but "suddenly like a theme that breaks forth, / There is a knock by a fist at the window" (*PBG*, 887). The vibrating rap of an unpersoned hand circles the "silent" *poema* back into the phantom ruckus of the hall of mirrors.

Just as the poem's new being stops short of birth, and sight stops short of perspective, vibration—the rumble—stops short of full sound. The poet retains her position in the resonant but non-articulate depths. Indeed, the sounds that emerge in *Poem without a Hero* tend toward the rumble, toward vibration, when they are not simply ghost echoes of long-ago carnivals. Knocks and footsteps sound out (*PBG*, 887, 877), sleigh runners, clocks, and church bells ring (*PBG*, 882, 875, 884, 886), a drum beats (*PBG*, 885). The one distinct voice recalled—that of opera titan Fyodor Chaliapin—emerges as "the echo of mountain thunder" (*PBG*, 881). A music box "rumbles" (*gremit*) (*PBG*, 889), and a church "rumbles: 'Dove, come forth!'"—turning even the words of the wedding hymn into vibration (*PBG*, 883). The landscape itself vibrates: as we behold the poet's flight at the work's end, we read that the Urals "started rumbling" (*zagremel*) (*PBG*, 896) and the earth itself "hummed underfoot" (*pod nogoi gudela*) (*PBG*, 894). These vibrations can be heard, apparently, by one who is attentive: the verb "to hear" and its derivatives appear frequently—and especially by the poet, whose narrator figure governs the verb six times. But the hearer, the mother, responds by storing her knowledge deep inside:

Враг пытал, "А ну, расскажи-ка!"
Но ни слова, ни стона, ни крика
Не услышать ее врагу.
И проходят десятилетья,
Пытки, ссылки и смерти. Петь я
В этом ужасе не могу. (*PBG*, 890)

(The enemy tempted, "Tell me, come on!" / But no word, no groan, no cry / Would her enemy hear. / Decades pass by, / Torture, exiles and punishments. I cannot / Sing in this horror.)

She cannot and will not sing, but she will break forth in her "silent chorus" that mimics the silence of frozen waterfalls (*PBG*, 885), the eloquent "silence of our brothers' tombs" (*PBG*, 895). She will, that is, avoid the errors of male Logos that would embody Sophia too quickly. Akhmatova's chorus, after all, merely evokes, without resolving, voices and fragments from the past. As the narrator writes in her opening section about those "who perished in Leningrad during the siege," "I hear their voices and remember them when I read the *poema* aloud, and that secret chorus has come for me to justify this thing" (*PBG*, 871).

ICON

But Akhmatova's poem may also be seen as a kind of holy icon, in the Byzantine tradition. We have proceeded from image to genre, and now we will observe how Akhmatova propels her poem over the bounds of medium. On all these planes of her triply recessed box we find the same, kenotic, imperial vector along which the poet pours herself into what she recounts in order to master the legacy of the past and assert how Russia should move forward. To the image of the artist as the promiscuous body that produces specters,

Akhmatova opposes the virginal body that immaculately conceives (but does not yet relinquish) the Word. As with Tsvetaeva, Akhmatova uses the pregnant, marian body to recalibrate the Sophia figure to one of potential. But Akhmatova is much more insistent than Tsvetaeva on the primacy of potential within a sophianic vision, and she does much more to align her vision with religious norms. The pregnant virginal body plays, of course, a central role in the icon. As Mondzain describes it, this virginal body is a surface with a self implanted in it, a self whose identity consists in masterful assimilation (*MIIE*, 100).

Akhmatova's attachment to the image of the virginal body that nonetheless promises to produce progeny asserts itself not just in her poems but also in other kinds of texts pertaining more directly to her biography. We find evidence of it, for instance, in her personal copies of the Reading Menaia (*Chet'i minei*), containing saints' lives for each day, now held in the archives of her house-museum in the House on the Fontanka. She marks very little in these volumes that help guide the reader through the liturgical calendar, but she does leave neat red underlinings in a text that mentions the prophetess Anna, who, according to Gospel accounts, spoke to Mary and Joseph of the significance of their son when they presented him at the temple.[73] More significantly for our purposes, there is strong evidence that Akhmatova not only read but perhaps displayed the pages corresponding to the saints' day for Saints Joachim and Anna, parents of Mary: the binding shows a notable gap here, unique to all these twelve volumes, indicating that she left the volume open to this *zhitie* for an extended length of time. It is tempting to see in this attention not just interest in a namesake, but, more grandly, a claim to a legacy.

This feeling is somewhat fortified by Akhmatova's unfortunate attacks on Kuzmin, whose own *poema* she knew so well. There is more here than a rivalry of two retrospective long poems: Kuzmin was an early mentor of Akhmatova's, writing the preface to her first volume, *Evening* (*Vecher*, 1911)—a preface, incidentally, that she repeatedly includes in lists made in her diary/notebooks.[74] But in 1923 he wrote publicly of her irrelevance to Soviet society, as a poet who had outlived her time.[75] During the time she was composing *Poem* she made some comments about Kuzmin that have gone down in history, castigating his homosexuality and calling him "malevolent, spiteful."[76] I believe these comments go beyond sex, and even beyond an anxiety of influence, touching on an aesthetic vision that Kuzmin threatens. As we saw in an earlier chapter on this more senior poet, Kuzmin adapted Orthodox tradition to embrace a homosexual aesthetic, whereby same-sex love produces ritual-poetic progeny. Akhmatova's nasty comments seem territorial markings: Kuzmin's differently-sexed religious aesthetic threatens Akhmatova's own sexless one. Her imperious thrusts reiterate the imperial dissemination of orthodoxy.

Flights into the Infinite

As she works to establish the preeminence of her art in the Soviet space, Akhmatova is countering not only Kuzmin's aesthetic and its account of liturgy, but also Berdiaev's, who in his account of the Silver Age rejects any art that purports to represent truth in its finite forms. Although he affirms creative activity, he sees creativity's projects as disfigurations. He writes in *Self-Knowing*:

> Creativity, in my view, is not a form-making in the finite, or the creative product itself: rather it is an opening up of the infinite, a flight into the infinite; not an objectification, but a transcendence. Creative ecstasy (the creative act is always an *ex-stasis*) is a breakthrough into the infinite. (*NBDR*, 209; *NBSP*, 227)

Akhmatova, too, views the creative act as a flight into the infinite, as a pursuit—but instead of rejecting "the creative product itself," she innovates a kind of "finite" form that manages to underscore its own incompletion and point beyond itself. This view of artistic form accords with the icon aesthetic, as Mondzain and others describe it. Mondzain writes of the icon as "a vector, always active" and of icons as "mobile dwellings of a power that their matter does not limit" (*MIIE*, 98, 144). These holy art objects trace the infinite along the forms of the finite, assimilating and laying claim to profane space (*MIIE*, 144). David Bentley Hart, a contemporary theologian who discusses the aesthetic of the icon, also affirms the capacity of artistic form to reflect the infinite, seeing in the icon a relentless pursuit of God, whom, in his infinitude, finite form can never comprehend.[77] The line of the icon, for Hart, pictures an ever-unfolding aesthetic surface of response to the excess of divine glory that spills into the bounds of human vision.[78]

In keeping both with the autobiographical genre as he understands it and with descriptions of him as an existentialist thinker, Berdiaev focuses on his inner experience of the failure of human projects to gesture at the infinite. In *Poem without a Hero* Akhmatova addresses concerns Berdiaev raises but to a rather different end. We can see in Berdiaev's autobiography a rejection of the sophianic project of creating new ideal forms. If every artistic embodiment is ultimately a monster, a nasty deformation of the artist's vision, then by all means let us stall its birth: Akhmatova's womb-tomb poem, accordingly, looks hell-bent on thwarting a neat, closed form. Yet Akhmatova manages to reinstate the sophianic project in a much-revised form: instead of rejecting art's progeny she uses the kenotic line to project an openness, to transform finitude into radical unfinishedness. She keeps starting over, diving in, pushing the appearance of the "hero" further into the future. If for Berdiaev the artistic text always culminates in a miscarriage, for Akhmatova in *Poem without a Hero* it remains pregnant, pushing out toward the possible but never erecting itself into a monument, a tower with a vista, a phallic word. This solution frees her from Berdiaev's dilemma—the untenable rejection of form for line. It also frees her to intervene in the project this study has been describing—the Russian modernist project to figure a sophianic or "holy flesh," an inner unity of form and essence, phenomena and noumena.

The Flesh and Fabric of Ritual

Ironically, Berdiaev seems to anticipate Akhmatova's solution in his statement of disgust, that "any attempt to ascribe a sacred character to finite things was repulsive to me" (*NBDR*, 45; *NBSP*, 58). Akhmatova embraces the finite, and she transforms it by depicting it as pushing out toward a new (marian-sophianic) reality. Akhmatova animates her surface-depths, impels the finite into a process, into a procession that is ritual in character.[79] She even gives us literal images of processions and specifically of liturgical ones. We begin the work with mention of a funeral procession (*marche funèbre*) and find references to processions and ritual series throughout. In these images, in concert with the rest of the work, we see her depicting the delay of the "hero" (or really of Sophia) as a sacred collective act, a kind of liturgical procession of its own. In this way her work resists narrative culmination but not a narrative trajectory. Accordingly, Akhmatova repositions her narrator-poet not as ultimate arbiter—an *intelligent* with enough distance from the Russian people to analyze and diagnose—but as ritual expert, one who participates and only thereby models.

Playing with genre, Akhmatova not only creates memoir out of poetry, but she also creates a novel liturgical procession out of memoir. We see her make this move most notably in the work's "explanatory" section, "The Flip Side." The speaker sets the scene:

> The hellish harlequinade of nineteen thirteen has just passed by, rousing the wordlessness of the great century that has taken a vow of silence [*bezmolvie velikoi molchal'nitsy-epokhi*] and leaving behind the disorder characteristic of every festal or funereal procession—the smoke of torches, flowers on the floor, sacred souvenirs forever lost. The wind howls in the stovepipe, and in this howl one can divine fragments of Requiem, cunningly hidden way down deep. What seems to appear in mirrors, well, best not to think about it. (*PBG*, 888)

Here the carelessness of an earlier epoch yields to a willed enduring, a religious vow, a religious procession whose force wells up in waves of commemoration, an elemental Requiem. And again, less obliquely, in the fifteenth stanza:

> И была для меня та тема
> Как раздавленная хризантема
> На полу, когда гроб несут.
> Между "помнить" и "вспомнить", други,
> Расстояние, как от Луги
> До страны атласных баут. (*PBG*, 891)

(And that theme was for me / Like a crushed chrysanthemum / On the floor, when they carry a coffin. / Between "remember" and "recall," friends, / Lies a distance like from Luga / To the country of satin gowns.)

In these lines Akhmatova deploys scent and sound—the recurrent musical theme—to picture her work's memory as a ritual procession, here a funeral. She also privileges procession in her verbs, contrasting the imperfective *pomnit'* with the perfective *vspomnit'*. The first she associates with a provincial Russian town outside Petersburg, and the second with Venice and the carnival setting that raises such problems in the author's retrospective gaze. In the context of the funeral procession the verb *pomnit'* also brings to mind its cognate, *pominanie*—the ritual remembrance of the dead, to which *Requiem* directly refers (*AASS* 3:29). Throughout the long poem Akhmatova's speaker continually casts herself as a chorus, and this move comes to make sense as a strategic gesture of solidarity with the processing, suffering *narod*. Indeed, at the work's end we find the narrator-poet following *behind* Russia ("Russia / Went east before me") in a long funeral procession spreading out into Siberia—"And that funeral path was long / Amidst the solemn and crystalline / Silence of Siberian earth" (*PBG*, 896).

This image of the procession seemingly embedded in the frozen, encrusted earth brings us back again to the image of the womb whose walls push outwards but do not yet give way. This ritualization of the womb image points us directly to the role Akhmatova constructs for the poet in Soviet Russia—one modeled after the God-bearer, whose very flesh partakes in the suffering that will bring forth salvation. By casting herself as a pregnant Mary, one bringing forth poetic progeny, she accesses the imaginary that holds together the Orthodox liturgy and thereby the ritual life of the Russian people. She also reconfigures the poet's sophianic task as carrying a torch rather than setting the world alight. Two moments in the poem in particular indicate how conscious was this decision. We saw above the image of the poet ensconced in the "belly of the flying fish": the liturgy adapts this image from the Jewish scripture account of the prophet Jonah in the belly of the whale, setting it in parallel—in each festal canon—with pictures of Christ in Mary's womb (and also Christ in the tomb).[80] (See appendix.) While Akhmatova sets her *poema* in the liturgical period of Epiphany with its sinister folkic traditions of mumming, she also mixes in themes of Lent—with its willed suffering and endurance in pursuit of holiness—the "snatches of *Requiem*" (*obryvki Rekviema*) she mentions in the *Poem*'s second section (*PBG*, 605). This image of the person in the belly of the fish is a Lenten image if there ever was one, recalling as it does, per Christian tradition, Jesus's time in the grave. The chronotope of Lent also announces itself in the image, cited above, of the Cherubic hymn that "trembles by closed churches" (*u zakritykh tserkvei drozhit*). This hymn signals in the Eucharist service the joining of the congregation to the chorus of angels worshipping God and thus signals a collective preparation for the advent of the Son.[81] The image is ambiguous: it could signify the sound of the hymn rumbling through closed doors. The line that follows points to Akhmatova's room, declaring, "No one knocks at my door." By placing these two images side by side Akhmatova thus draws a parallel between her "torture chamber" and the "closed churches" where the Eucharist is about to take place—underscoring the promise of secret, nascent life from these centers of power.[82] In another reading, the hymn stands, personified, trembling outside in the cold—a vivid way of picturing both the hymn's ritual exclusion from key services during Lent and thereby a delay of Christ's appearance. In both readings Akhmatova uses the image insistently to forestall a culmination. But the pulse of the work proceeds ever ahead.

Osip Mandelstam's Eucharist

EARLY ON IN *Poem without a Hero* Akhmatova tantalizes us with the hero's near arrival. We read, "A cry: 'Our hero is coming out to the proscenium!'" (*PBG*, 879). But no one arrives—in fact, everyone else runs off, leaving the narrator face to face with her onslaught of memories that portend, instead, her long poem's burgeoning. The narrator hears a whisper, a message that she will be sole survivor, and then a "clear voice" declaring, "I am ready for death." Instead of her awaited hero the narrator hears, plain as day, words that Osip Mandelstam once spoke to Akhmatova, in 1934, as he prepared for his fate at the hands of Soviet power.[1] Early versions of *Poem without a Hero* follow this line with an epigraph for the next section—lines from the Russian romantic poet Evgeny Baratynsky that read, "Resplendent shade, you are more passionate, / More bodily than the living" (*PBG*, 168, 201).

In these early concatenations, at least, this epigraph seems addressed as much to the shade of Osip Mandelstam as to any other shades that come to haunt the poet who survived. It was Mandelstam who wrote, "I've been given a body—what should I do with it?"[2] Mandelstam was as concerned with the problem of body and spirit as any of his peers, and he, too, turned at times to Orthodox liturgical tradition to picture an integration of the two. He appears in Akhmatova's retrospective meditation in the paradoxical position that he expressed in his own poetry: a position where flesh and spirit, mortal embodiment and ethereal eternity, coexist uneasily. Still, they coexist in a mode more manifest than we find in *Poem without a Hero*: even if in their measured way, Mandelstam's poems display a sense of immediate possibility that Akhmatova abandons.

He wrote some of the most pointedly liturgical stanzas of the modernist era in Russia, as we see from an early poem, from 1915.

Вот дароносица, как солнце золотое,
Повисла в воздухе—великолепный миг.
Здесь должен прозвучать лишь греческий язык:
Взят в руки целый мир, как яблоко простое.

Богослужения торжественный зенит,
Свет в круглой храмине под куполом в июле,
Чтоб полной грудью мы вне времени вздохнули
О луговине той, где время не бежит.

И Евхаристия, как вечный полдень, длится—
Все причащаются, играют и поют,
И на виду у всех божественный сосуд
Неисчерпаемым веселием струится.[3]

(There, the pyx, like a golden sun, / Has hung poised in the air—magnificent moment. / Here only the Greek language should sound out: / A whole world taken into the hands like a simple apple. // The solemn zenith of the liturgy, / The light in the round edifice below the cupola in July, / That with our whole breast we might sigh outside of time / For that meadow where time does not fly. // And the Eucharist, like the eternal noonday, lasts— / All commune, play and sing, / And in full view for everyone the divine vessel / Streams with inexhaustible delight.)

In these verses Mandelstam depicts the height of the liturgy—the sharing of the Eucharistic meal—held in its special vessel, here a "pyx" or *daronositsa*.[4] The time Mandelstam portrays here differs keenly from the extended, earthbound, expectant procession we find in *Poem without a Hero*. Here, instead, in this "magnificent moment" time becomes timeless, bringing a foretaste of the "eternal noonday"—that state of fullness promised at the end of time, on the so-called eighth day. Comparing this poem from 1915 with Akhmatova's work that she shaped over a quarter-century, we encounter the differing modes of *chronos* and *kairos* that characterize different layers of liturgical experience. (Gregory Freidin has spoken of these two modes in "There, the pyx . . ." as "mutable time" and "permanent time.")[5] Theologian Oscar Cullmann distinguishes between *kairos* as the "point of time" or "convenient season" and *chronos* as the "duration of time" or "extent of time" (*aion* or *chronos*).[6] He envisions the primitive Christian conception of time as a continuous chronological line punctuated by *kairoi*, points of time that have "a special place in the execution of God's plan of salvation."[7] According to this model, both the terms *chronos* and *kairos* can convey eschatological significance—that is, both types of time offer the realization of Christianity's telos of redemption or full spiritual enlightenment.[8] *Chronos*, on one hand, figures the *eschaton* as the final point on a continuous—chronological—line, while *kairos*, on the other hand, offers a periodic opening out of time, in which humankind experiences the fullness of the *eschaton* before its chronological occurrence. Moments of the Eucharist or miraculous events celebrated by the liturgical feasts are understood as *kairoi*.

Mandelstam embraces the shape of *kairos* in his descriptions of time as paused, even as he suggests its impossibility. We witness the golden sun hanging in the air, its precarious pause extended by a dash in the middle of the second line; the July light caught perfectly beneath the cupola; the meadow where time does not pass; the further extension of the Eucharistic moment in the third stanza where everything moves into a radiant present. We witness nothing less than a transfiguration of the "divine vessel," from which light pours in Theophanic streams. We might well read the penultimate line as suggesting the transfiguration of all gathered, since the line can read both, "Before everyone's eyes the divine vessel . . ." *and*, "In full view everyone's divine vessel . . ." Nothing in Akhmatova's later long poem manifests *kairos* so hopefully. Yet even the young Mandelstam is not a starry-eyed Blok—or even, for that matter—a jaded Blok. He quietly tempers this vision of glory with shades of uncertainty. The poem's third line suggests that the situation "should" be different from what it is—the Byzantine service has been embodied in a Russian form. On one hand, we could read this line as a hearty affirmation of the transfigurative moment if we read it through the lens of Mandelstam's essay "On the Nature of the Word": here he writes of Russian as "a Hellenic language" because it carries forth the "mystery of free incarnation" and thus has become "*resounding and speaking flesh*" (italics in the original).[9] Indeed, as scholars have shown, the idea of a certain continuity with and even revision of Hellenism is central to Mandelstam's poetics.[10] But the fact remains that in this poem, "should" grammatically injects a note of conditionality. Mandelstam subtly reminds us that all liturgical forms, and all artistic realizations and cultural forms in general, are improvisations, adaptations—a prominent theme in his well-known poem "Silentium," where he urges Aphrodite to "remain as foam" and the word to "return to music" that they might retain their links with "primordial life."[11] We find a similar tension in the second stanza, where "we" sigh for that place where time no longer passes even as we ourselves experience what it is to be "outside of time."

Still, Mandelstam's poem does not shy away from presenting earthly containers that can contain the divine, and from presenting them in all their glory. The prime container he depicts—the "pyx" (*daronositsa*)—finds parallels throughout the poem: the sun, the hands containing the whole world, the building containing all the worshippers in July light. If the containers Akhmatova traces in her poem hold their secret for now, these vessels reveal theirs—at least in this brief and endless moment that Mandelstam depicts. Mandelstam scholars have addressed Mandelstam's attempts to revise and move beyond the symbolist aesthetic, with its sophianic, Solovyovian underpinnings, while retaining some of its concerns—extending the problem of form and spirit, but cautiously.[12] In his late novel *Doctor*

Zhivago Boris Pasternak returns to Blok under very different circumstances: the symbolist thread has already snapped, and nostalgia replaces anxiety of influence. Pasternak will follow both Blok and Mandelstam in representing flesh shot through with spirit, but he will explicitly and unapologetically adapt Blok's sophianism. What is surprising is that he does this at nearly the same extended moment that Akhmatova was composing *Poem without a Hero*.

Chapter Four

Cultural Transformation as Transdisfiguration in Pasternak's *Doctor Zhivago*

BORIS PASTERNAK WAS one of Akhmatova's few peers who survived in Russia well into the period during which she composed *Poem without a Hero*. Pasternak certainly knew of Akhmatova's *Poema* project—even though its outlines were constantly changing—and Akhmatova knew of his novel-with-poetic-cycle, *Doctor Zhivago*, in which he sought to depict Russia's previous half-century in order to make sense of recent upheavals and indicate a path toward national and cultural integration.[1] In a very real way these writers were, de facto, competing to define a legacy and therefore potentially to shape Russia's future—a point Edith Clowes has made eloquently.[2] Clowes even shows that these two writers—modernist relics in the Soviet period—compete primarily over who will best sustain and define what she describes as Russia's "Orthodox legacy" in the Stalinist period. Like Akhmatova, Pasternak essentially placed himself prominently at the center of his own work, modeling his protagonist's life in many ways on his own experiences. He also gives the final word to this semi-autobiographical protagonist by ending the novel with Zhivago's cycle of poems that therefore purport to speak not only for the whole novel but for the whole half-century it depicts. If it is the poet's word that defines an era and shapes the next, then Pasternak claims significant power for his creative output.

Like Akhmatova—and like Blok and Kuzmin—Pasternak in his own way extends that dual sophianic task, as we have described it, of creatively adapting Russia's religious tradition to contemporary circumstances while working to produce a transfigured reality through art. Unlike Akhmatova, Pasternak affirms a more canonical sophianism, with its emphasis on sublimating eros. And while extending this project, he also depicts it in positive terms: in *Doctor Zhivago* Pasternak traces the emergence of sophianic thought at the turn of the twentieth century and its life through five tumultuous decades in Russia. His novel focuses on a poet and doctor, Yurii Zhivago, whose personal life disintegrates in parallel with Russian society as a whole;

but Zhivago leaves behind a cycle of poems that outline a vision of personal and social reconstruction and transformation along which Russia might fruitfully proceed. As the narrator takes pains to indicate, much of that vision constitutes a creative and original rendering of the religious-philosophical thought of Zhivago's uncle, Nikolai Vedeniapin, elements of whose ideas resemble Solovyov's (as others have discussed and as I discuss elsewhere).[3] As such, Pasternak's novel provides its own artistic commentary on the Russian modernist project. Whereas, however, Akhmatova and even Blok represent the impossibility of the artist's satisfactorily embodying Sophia, Pasternak takes pains to craft a Sophia—and therefore an art—that lets eternity shine through the most mundane of details. He thereby recoups the sophianic project as one that can be realized in the here and now, but, aware of previous critiques, he also qualifies the project.[4]

In this chapter I will argue that Pasternak depicts art as a force that realizes new worlds, but that it does so by willfully (and playfully) deforming old ones. That is, Sophia comes into being precisely through acts of disfiguration—that disfiguration so feared by Akhmatova, Berdiaev, and others is what makes Sophia viable in the human world. Moreover, Sophia remains in existence by the artist's constant adaptation to new circumstances, by his playful willingness to see her and realize her in all kinds of incongruous places. Sensitive to critiques of the modernist project, Pasternak acknowledges that art can never rest in the forms it has established. He does not, however, present his reuse and adaptation of old forms as particularly transgressive, but, rather, playfully productive. While *Doctor Zhivago* ends more with a fizzle than a bang, there is something decidedly triumphant about its reinvocation of the modernist project in a Soviet setting—especially in comparison to the muted and enigmatic *Poem without a Hero*. Pasternak's interest in extending the sophianic task into the Soviet period can be especially discerned in his persistent references to Blok in and around the writing of his novel. Writing in 1945, for instance, to a fellow poet who was in a labor camp, Pasternak charged him to "write prose that is genuine and seizes one with its content. Forget all this Leftist-Acmeist, un-Blok-like, anti-Christian garbage, and may God help you."[5]

Using Mondzain's terminology, we spoke of a vector in *Poem without a Hero*, making of the work an endless procession, an arrow toward an ever-distant future; in *Doctor Zhivago* we find emblematic lines, too, but with important differences. Pasternak offers multiple and distinct images of an arcing line, consciously presenting it as an index for the artist's labor and effect. This line expresses a force—inspiration, grace, love—that surges up and then curves gracefully downward to meet and follow the landscape, the artist's response. His line overtly celebrates and amplifies the sources of his inspiration; his line makes manifest. Unlike Akhmatova's line that obscures itself, ever tracing the inner depths, the womb-walls, Pasternak's line follows and amplifies the outward and visible curves of the erotic female body. Zhivago improvises regularly, for instance, on the forms of Lara's curvaceous arms, seeing everywhere around him the same curves—in brook and film reel alike. And Pasternak uses Zhivago's reveries about Lara's body to picture how the art process works. If we speak in terms of how these lines characterize distinct aesthetic modes, we might say that the line in *Poem without a Hero* represents form forestalled, whereas the line in *Doctor Zhivago* represents form amplified: the artist distorts what he observes in order to exaggerate what he finds beautiful about it. If Akhmatova uses images of the chaste and pregnant female body to privilege the potentiality of artistic form, then Pasternak uses images of the curvaceous and sexualized female body to emphasize the imaginative, erotic element in art. Like Tsvetaeva and Akhmatova in particular, Pasternak compares his Sophia to Mary the Mother of God at certain moments. Yurii's mother, for instance, is buried on the day of the Feast of Mary's Protection (*Pokrov*). And his first wife, Tonia, in fact, resembles Mondzain's description of Mary Mother of God in the scene where she has just given birth. Here Yurii sees her as a ship that has transported precious cargo between the land of the dead and the land of the living and now lies at anchor, "with all the emptiness of her lightened sides" (*DZh*, 116). We are reminded of the liturgy's representations of Mary as a vessel of God and a passageway. This is the "Mary" whom Yurii abandons. Clowes shows that Pasternak associated Akhmatova, via her poetry, with the Mother of God.[6] But, in keeping with their artistic rivalry, Pasternak effectively rejects Akhmatova's de-eroticized mother type. In the figure of Lara he combines images of Mary the Mother of God with Mary Magdalene, the redeemed temptress. Several scholars have described Tsvetaeva's particular identification with Mary Magdalene, and Catherine Ciepiela has shown at length how Pasternak drew on this Tsvetaevan heritage in his novel.[7] It is as though he and Akhmatova offer competing revisions of sophianism—one where Sophia is promised but can never be realized in the world as it is and is therefore effectively replaced by the pregnant Mary God-bearer, versus one where Sophia emerges now, always as a beautiful figment of the artist's imagination, but also as an echo of the deep, eternal truths that lie just beneath the surface of life and nature. Akhmatova's revision is more subversive in many senses, but especially as regards the distinctly gendered nature of the sophianic vision—and, as we have seen, of conventional artistic vision in general. Pasternak's revision is both more traditionally gendered and more aesthetically traditional. He reinstates the romantic notion of the (male) genius, and this move allows him to revisit the original sophianic project in a doggedly anachronistic mode.

Several scholars, Susanna Witt most comprehensively, have discussed

Pasternak's representations of "distortion" in his novel; here I will read Pasternak's "distortions" as part of a larger process in the novel that envisions imaginative disfiguration (recall, for instance, Blok's "doll-beauties" and Akhmatova's miscarriages) as a method of transforming life and society.[8] Pasternak is not embarrassed to affirm art generated from male erotic reverie—not even in light of his move toward Orthodox praxis and apparent belief after World War II. We know from numerous sources that Pasternak began regularly attending Orthodox services in the postwar period (*FBP*, 259). Christopher Barnes notes that the writer even knew and could sing the liturgical texts (*BBP*, 245). Pasternak was at the same time highly aware of the powerful ascetic traditions within Russian Orthodoxy, traditions advocating great restraint over the bodily appetites and passions. In *Doctor Zhivago* he not only references these traditions but turns them to his own purposes: he recasts asceticism as channeling rather than rejecting eros. In his novel Pasternak brings together the discourse of asceticism with images of the Transfiguration body so prominently used by Blok. I will speak of the art process that Pasternak depicts as "trans*dis*figuration"; for not only does he exaggerate forms to make his art, but he also overtly adapts Orthodox traditions, especially liturgical ones, in ways that, as even his characters acknowledge, run somewhat counter to received traditions. Pasternak not only practices such productive disfigurations (adaptations of existing forms and modes), but he actually figures this revised sophianic process itself in his images of arcing lines. In his emblematic arcing line as in the adjustments he makes to liturgical and ascetic traditions, Pasternak represents a religious aesthetic according to which individuals transform society through creative misappropriations of its spiritual and cultural traditions. In keeping with his emphasis on adaptive continuity, he therefore either misses or dismisses some of the opportunities Akhmatova takes to critique and transform the art process more radically.

Pasternak's "Gospel according to Zhivago," as his late novel has been called (ironically and otherwise), was conceived in the wake of loosened restrictions on literature and religion in World War II—a time when the author held renewed hope for Russia's future (*FBP*, 224, 260). Pasternak starting writing *Doctor Zhivago* in the summer of 1945, just as this period of relative freedom was coming to an end—that is, just before Zhdanov's August attacks on Akhmatova and Zoshchenko. These raised and dashed hopes confirmed in Pasternak a firmly but quietly dissident spirit that would characterize his novel and cause him trouble in the Nobel affair that ensued in 1958 (*BBP*, 234). Through the novel Pasternak hoped to take stock of how Russia had changed over the tumultuous past few decades, but he also hoped to model a way of building a Soviet future through creative continuity with the Russian past. Russia had experienced immense changes that entailed massive rupture with its past; the time, Pasternak felt, for radical change had now passed, and the job of building culture would be made easier and surer by assimilating preexisting cultural tradition. He looked especially to the period of modernism, seeing in it useful tools for constructing a new world—an aim the so-called decadents shared with their revolutionary peers. Pasternak turned, that is, to sophianism. But in order to make it relevant for the new Soviet setting, he had to bring it back to life in print for those who had rejected it or suppressed it inwardly and also for those who had never known it—younger generations and Soviet citizens who were never part of the intelligentsia or even the educated middle class. To this end Pasternak follows the fictional life of a poet-doctor from his coming of age around the 1905 Revolution, through the 1917 Revolution, into the Russian Civil War, in which he participates, and, finally, to Moscow, where he returns to practice medicine, dying in 1929. His beloved Lara ends up being arrested in Stalin's purges in the late 1930s. Zhivago is no hero, but he leaves behind a cycle of poems in which he depicts his life experience through all these decades in decidedly sophianic terms—meaning both that he figures a world transfigured by his love for an erotically cast feminine figure (Lara), and that he adapts many elements of Orthodox liturgical tradition in his art, gearing them to a contemporary setting, as scholars have noted variously.[9]

Numerous scholars have discussed the image of the line in this novel, most of all in reference to its treatment of post-revolutionary theories of transforming society and culture. As David Bethea and Boris Gasparov have described, Pasternak emblematizes the Soviet approach in the character Strel'nikov (Lara's husband, formerly Pasha Antipov). Associated, for Pasternak's protagonist Yurii, with "straightforwardness" (*priamolineinost'*) (*DZh*, 450) and, throughout the novel, with the image of the train, Strel'nikov epitomizes "linear logic" (Gasparov) and "a straight line into a better future" (Bethea), as well as a complete break with the past, a "radical turning point."[10] Yurii is associated with, and idealizes, another kind of line—the curve or arc. Gasparov describes Yurii's "contrapuntal" line as an overcoming of the mortality associated with linear logic and linear time; and Bethea identifies Yurii's relation to space as the seasonal cycle (an "open circle"), thus rendering a history open to extra-temporal revelation. Relatedly, Olga Raevsky-Hughes links Pasternak's novel with the eschatological time of the Eucharist, which connects eternity and chronological time. Per Arne Bodin describes Yurii's "line" as a "chain" (*stseplenie*), creating a connection between past and present, I and Other, and, ultimately, a kind of "cosmic interconnection."[11] And Mary Catherine Gannon finds a transgressive line, a movement to cross boundaries and to create a "cross-identification" between diverse elements.[12] But the arc (the non-straight line) also bears other associations within the novel, crucial to understanding Pasternak's aesthetic vision. The arc stands, in particular, for the disfigured and amplified line, the line that explodes with the inspirational force of eros but that also accommodates itself to the landscape, the context, to alien elements it encounters, to restraining forces. It is the line that connects the eternal life force with the immediate forms of earthly life, transforming them in the process.

In view of the ascetic-liturgical discourse Pasternak introduces into his novel, we can also speak of this disfigured line as an "ascetic" one. The saint, like Yurii's namesake Andrei Iurodivyi (Andrew the Holy Fool), disfigures his natural bodily form to curb and restrain his passions. If Yurii is ascetic, it is certainly not because he curbs his passions: a significant portion of the novel's central narrative follows his ardent and adulterous relationship with Lara. Pasternak does, however, represent Yurii as ascetic in the way that he channels his passion and his experiences into poetry (which is also to say that Pasternak represents art-making as ascetical). In this sense Pasternak reshapes the straight line into an arc, picturing how Yurii's art and art in general respond to the down and dirty conditions of human life.[13] *Doctor Zhivago* suggests that this adaptation to and therefore transformation of actual human life characterizes the Orthodox liturgy as a whole. Pasternak's use of the liturgy in this work has been noted by numerous scholars, but not in terms of its relevance to Pasternak's overall figurative method.[14] Pasternak shapes his transdisfigurative line according to the Orthodox Paschal narrative, known most centrally through its Lenten and Paschal services.

As the liturgy presents it, the fall of humanity from a state of perfection comprises an erosion of man's original beauty, a marring of his original form. The "Great Canon" of Andrew of Crete, which sets the tone for Lent (in its recitation across the first four evenings of Lent and then as a whole on the fifth Thursday of Lent), touches frequently on this idea, as in the following lines:

> Woe to thee, miserable soul! How like thou art to the first Eve! For thou hast looked in wickedness and wast grievously wounded. . . . I have lost the beauty and glory with which I was first created. (*LT*, 378, 382)[15]

In the Easter sequence, Christ experiences death—recapitulating humanity's fall in the defacement of his own perfect form; but then in his resurrection and defeat of death, he restores humanity to its original beauty.[16] Within this tradition, impurity—the lack of holiness, separation from the radiant divine communion—appears as the corrosion of man's ideal form. In the Great Canon—which evokes Andrew of Crete's indexical linking of *theosis* to the Transfiguration—we find, "I have discoloured Thine image and broken Thy commandment. All my beauty is destroyed and my lamp is quenched by the passions, O Saviour" (*LT*, 404).[17] The progression of the Lenten and Paschal cycle, then, demonstrates the link between asceticism and Christ's experience of death: both involve a willed surrender to the corruption of the flesh, the given form, in order to defeat those deadly forces which, unchecked, would not only disfigure but destroy both body and soul. Appropriately to tradition, Pasternak also associates the key image of the Transfiguration with this picture of life proceeding through death and corruption—the eternal encountering the earthly. For in the Orthodox Christian tradition as expressed by the liturgy, transformation proceeds not only by willed curbing of the passions, but, inseparably, by Christ's imparting his resurrection glory to earthly things, to mortal humanity. The Transfiguration's images of the divine energies—shafts of light—provide Pasternak with an alternate type of transformative force: not the aggressive line of post-revolutionary programs, but the line cast to the drowning, connecting the living and the dead. In Transfiguration tradition, these divine energies (as we will see below) reach out to transform the human body—not only soul—into divine substance; similarly, for Pasternak the art impulse touches and transforms all of life. It connects what was before not connected, accommodating the shapes it encounters. Per-Arne Bodin's discussion of the "chain" or "linkage" (*stseplenie*) in Pasternak's aesthetics demonstrates how fundamental this connective impulse is in Pasternak's presentation of the world.[18]

Such linkage, though, entails not only a reconciliation of form, but also a divestment and reshaping of form. The notion of a constructive *dis*figuration, or transdisfiguration, permeates Pasternak's novel on many levels. Most obviously, we find images of productive, imaginative distortion in Yurii's creation of a poetic cycle about Holy Week out of his story with the paradigmatic fallen woman, Lara. In his cycle, he creates of Lara a saint—Mary Magdalene; and of himself, Christ. On the level of language in the poems, he blends liturgical reference with the most ordinary diction. His novel, though, also purports to present transformation on an epic scale, and so in it we find a portrait of how change begins and spreads, contaminates and transfigures a whole culture, through unlikely figures and ways.

In the thirteenth chapter of *Doctor Zhivago*, "The House with Figures" ("Protiv doma s figurami"), Pasternak crystallizes his vision of his epic-and-poetic work's projected effects. Here a Siberian townswoman named Sima (whose views Lara declares "strikingly similar" to Yurii's) parses passages from the Holy Week liturgy to illustrate the relation between cultural production and historical evolution (*DZh*, 405–8). Her reading spells out, as it were, the notion of transformation that Pasternak has shown vividly in the two preceding chapters, where Yurii undergoes a series of three visions modeled on the liturgy. In her reading, as in the visions, we discover a process of creative change by which the individual imaginatively adapts and blends forms from innumerable and diverse sources to transfigure himself and the world around him. This creative process at once disfigures the forms it borrows, but also uses them to produce new forms to feed the cultural imagination. In a passage key to the novel's aesthetic mode, Sima describes the liturgy itself as a text that blends elements from diverse epochs, creating marvelous juxtapositions that evince both the nature of historical development and of daily, individual life. Her discussion culminates in a reading of a *troparion* from the Holy Wednesday service, which centers on the harlot Mary Magdalene's washing of Christ's feet.[19] For Sima, this service illustrates arrestingly the liturgy's boldfaced blending of diverse elements. She notes the text's blending of profound religious concepts with references to the everyday. Here, she points to Magdalene's expression of her repentance in the language of ordinary things (*veshchestvenno*—literally, "thingly"), comparing God's act of forgiveness (releasing her from sin) to her act of letting down her hair. Most likely, Sima uses the word "veshchestvenno" polemically, for we find this very word in the Great Canon, but in the liturgical text it is linked with the passions (*strast'*), and thus loaded with negative connotation.[20] Sima also marvels not only at the juxtaposition within the story itself—incarnate God's contact with a harlot—but also at the location of this story within the liturgical calendar: the service recalling the harlot stands at the very threshold of Easter.

In Sima's discussion "about what life is" (*o tom, chto takoe est' zhizn'*), we find not only a comment on the liturgy's mimesis of life's often unexpected sequence, but also an indication of Pasternak's picture of art as he presents it within the work as a whole. In this context Sima comments simultaneously on the harlot's speech and on the shape of the liturgical text, exclaiming, "What brevity! What parity of God and life, God and person, God and woman!" She finds remarkable, that is, the improbable parallel status granted to such obviously unequal figures and elements, by rights separated into the realms of the holy and the unholy. And she presents this conjoining as a kind of sacred, redemptive contamination, a fruitfully distortive blending of apparently incongruous narratives.

In a passage that reminds us of Kuzmin's critique and revision of asceticism, Sima fulminates against the traditional discourse of purity and reclaims a place for sensual passion on the redemptive path. Earlier in her discussion of the liturgy, she embarks on a brief and vigorous discursus on traditional ascetic interpretations of the notion of "passion." Here she protests against a group of Lenten readings that elevate the "reining in of the senses and the mortification of the flesh" (*obuzdaniia chuvstvennosti i umershchvleniia ploti*); she describes these texts as devoid of poetry, written by "fat-bellied" monks. For these hypocritically fat monks, passions denote something to put to death on the road to holiness. While noting the more central definition of "passion" as referring to Christ's suffering, she also implicitly privileges the connotations of sensuousness and desire. Conversely, she rejects the idea of seeking purity and restoration of ideal form through denying the actual human body, even to the point of its physical disfiguring. Sima's disgust for radical forms of asceticism resonates more broadly in Pasternak's insistence that spiritual transformations embrace the most mundane reality and materiality—including earthly passion. These very qualities surround the fleshy Mary Magdalene figure, who apparently achieves an equal status to God. Yurii's visions, too, engage and flesh out this notion of productive passion, as well as of the fruitful incongruity—between texts and figures—that Sima extols in her discussion of the liturgy. It is important to note also that in Sima's discussion of beauty, passion, and the liturgy she is drawing on the ideas of Nikolai Vedeniapin, Yurii's uncle and a philosopher whose thought Pasternak has modeled directly on Solovyov. Vedeniapin propounds a religious-aesthetical philosophy overtly based on Christianity, and he asserts that love—and especially erotic love—forms the basis for all of humanity's creative endeavors (*DZh*, 67). Yurii more than once acknowledges his debt as an artist to his uncle, as well as to Solovyov, whose work he had read as a young person.

In the novel's central, eleventh and twelfth chapters ("The Forest Army" ["Lesnoe voinstvo"] and "The Rowan Tree" ["Riabina v sakhare"]), we find the tale of three visions Yurii experiences—visions that either stem from or resemble erotic reverie; and in these three passages we find the key to Pasternak's picture of transformation. While the first of these comprises our only glimpse of Yurii in meditative solitude since his childhood prayer in a forest ravine, the final vision immediately precedes his escape from the partisans and into Lara's curvaceous arms. The sequence, then, marks a narrative turn toward Yurii's new life (with Lara) and new art—the defining poems of the "Zhivago cycle."

Pasternak sets his initiatory picture of transformation in the middle of a forest that is slowly being turned into a dwelling place for humans—thereby even in the setting gesturing toward the act of human creation and social construction. Yurii has come to this place with a group of partisans called the "Greens," who have pressed him into service. In the midst of the forest encampment Yurii comes upon a lush clearing where meetings are sometimes held. The place is empty of people, except for an officer burning some documents. As Yurii walks into the space, the narrator describes in intense sensory details a moment that takes on epiphanic proportions, transposing the visual and verbal language of the Transfiguration.

> Much of the greenery in the forest had not yet turned yellow; its depths they were still fresh and green. The afternoon sun was setting behind the forest,

> piercing it with its rays, and the leaves let the sunlight through and burned from their undersides with the green light of transparent bottle glass. . . .
>
> Ever since his childhood Yurii Andreievich had been fond of evening woods letting the fire of sunset show through. At such moments he felt as if he too were letting these shafts of light pass through him. It was as though the gift of the living spirit were streaming into his breast, piercing his being and coming out at his shoulders like a pair of wings. The archetype that is formed in every child for life and ever after serves as and seems to him his inward face, his personality, awoke in him in its full primordial strength, and compelled nature, the forest, the afterglow, and everything else visible to be transfigured into a similarly primordial and all-embracing likeness of a girl. Closing his eyes, "Lara," he whispered and thought, addressing the whole of his life, all God's earth, all the expanse turned red with sun before him. (*DZh*, 339)

Here the narrator describes elements of the forest space, reimagining them as features in the scene of the biblical and liturgical transfiguration. Through vivid images of the leaves and trees (which he notes prior to this passage are elsewhere in the forest turning yellow), Pasternak sets the scene approximately around the summer Feast of the Transfiguration (August 6)—suggested not only by the images in this passage, but also by the Zhivago poem "August," which names this date and retells the Taboric event (*DZh*, 525–26). In "August" the poetic narrator sets the scene at a dream of his own funeral, ostensibly addressing his friends, and by extension all his readers:

> Вы шли толпою, врозь и парами,
> Вдруг кто-то вспомнил, что сегодня
> Шестое августа по старому,
> Преображение Господне.
>
> Обыкновенно свет без пламени
> Исходит в этот день с Фавора,
> И осень, ясная, как знаменье,
> К себе приковывает взоры.
>
> И вы прошли сквозь мелкий, нищенский,
> Нагой, трепещущий ольшаник
> В имбирно-красный лес кладбищенский,
> Горевший, как печатный пряник. (*DZh*, 525)

> (You walked in a crowd, separately and in pairs. / Suddenly someone recalled that today / Is the sixth of August, Old Style, / The Transfiguration of the Lord. // Ordinarily light without flame / Descends on that day from Mount

Tabor, / And the autumn, clear as a sign, / Forges gazes to itself. // And you passed through sparse, beggarly, / Naked, trembling alder thickets / Into the ginger-red cemetery woods, / Burning like stamped gingerbread.)

In both prose passage and poem, Pasternak offers literal images of the divine energies, flowing into and transforming the individual and his surroundings. As in the icon tradition, these energies figure here as shafts of light piercing the body and the surrounding nature. (See figure 1.1.) As Karen Evans-Romaine has pointed out, the image of light beams in Pasternak's work resonates strongly with Novalis's vision of the transformative power of art.[21] Gustafson, moreover, has pointed out Solovyov's adaptation of German idealist thought, especially that of Schelling, in his representation of spiritual transformation.[22] Pasternak also, though, weds this image to an Orthodox context—not a strange move, given, as Gustafson has pointed out, Schelling's interest in the Neoplatonist elements he found in patristic writings.[23] Revealing his hand, Pasternak pictures Yurii receiving the "gift of the living spirit" (*dar zhivogo dukha*). The language of this description closely resembles traditional ways of describing *theosis*, by which the flesh of the individual transforms into a body of light, becoming godlike—a tradition we have already seen adapted in Blok's poetry.[24]

This passage also echoes another aspect of *theosis*: that is, the transfiguration of all of nature through the transfiguration of its head, mankind, represented paradigmatically in the second Adam, Christ. Indeed, Pasternak uses a term—"archetype" (*pervoobraz*) that is crucial to the theology of the New Creation. This term appears in the canon for the Feast of the Transfiguration, in which Jesus's disciples witness the glory of the transfigured Christ and proclaim, "This is the imprint of the archetype, even our Savior" (*FM*, 493).[25] Here and elsewhere the "archetype" connotes the original perfect form of mankind, and of nature by extension, which is fatally marred by the Fall but gloriously restored in Christ.[26] According to the theology of the Transfiguration (in liturgy and icon alike), the divine body central to the image represents this restored primordial image—anticipated in its fullness in the *eschaton*, but glimpsed in this earthly scene.

The subsequent two visions emphasize the sophianic aspect of restored creation more clearly—that is, the transformed world pictured as the eroticized female; yet we find hints of it here. The awakening of Yurii's archetype "compels" nature's transfiguration, into "the original and all-embracing likeness of a girl" (*pervonachal'noe i vseokhvatyvaiushchee podobie devochki*). We find in this detail a prime example of the kind of constructive "contamination" that Pasternak stages. Not only do the trees seem themselves transfigured into light-bearing organisms, "transparent" as green bottle-glass; but they also join nature in taking on the aspect of what Yurii imagines essentially as a restored sophianic image—a point Bodin has discussed in reference to *Doctor Zhivago*.[27] In this passage as in the whole of Pasternak's novel, the transfigured body is decidedly male, and its transfiguration accompanies union with the more amorphous female force of life. Christ meets Mary Magdalene, cast as Lara, the fallen woman restored, who appears in and through the natural elements around the fixated Yurii. Pasternak's very act, meanwhile, of connecting the theology of Sophia with his depiction of a human character (the "likeness of a girl"—"Lara")—and with his modeling, moreover, this character on an extramarital lover—exemplifies his synthetic creative philosophy. (Pasternak had fallen in love with the younger Olga Ivinskaia in 1946, and their love helped inspire a new wave of intense lyric production and renewed vision of life [*FBP*, 251].)

Pasternak also pictures his "transdisfigurative" approach in the rather Platonic image of the soul growing wings, an image that visually resonates with the wing-like form of a six-pointed star, in the Feofan Grek icon; in this detail, too, then, the author weds the erotic-aesthetic impulse to Christian tradition—a move that is in fact in concert with Christian tradition, as we have seen already in relation to Kuzmin's poetry. He continues to capitalize on this approach in Yurii's second and third visions. Yurii's second vision, which we will see below, takes place as the poet contemplates the creative practices of the folk healer Kubarikha. The partisans with whom Yurii is forced to wander have moved to a new location. At the edge of this new forest encampment stands a small clearing with a rowan tree in the middle. Yurii also notices here a circle of stones that, he reflects, seem to date from ancient pagan magic rituals—which possibility imbues the rowan tree with magical associations (*DZh*, 349). In the novel's twelfth chapter Yurii witnesses, by this rowan tree, not only his second and third visions, but, first of all, poetic and magical performances of the folk healer; and this folk-magical element increasingly imbues his transformational visions.

Through Yurii's eyes, we view Kubarikha's performance of healing a sick cow, and in Yurii's meditations on this performance Pasternak provides another key to his transdisfigurative aesthetics. The narrator recounts the words of the spell that Kubarikha weaves over the cow, and Yurii distinguishes in her words phrases from "the opening sections of a chronicle, Novgorodian, perhaps, or Ipatievan, made apocryphal through accumulated layers of distortions" (*naslaivaiushchimisia iskazheniiami*), passed down orally (*DZh*, 362). Here Yurii sees in Kubarikha's chant a constructive textual corruption both accumulated and acted out. The theme of textual corruption shows up elsewhere—earlier in this same chapter—when Yurii finds two soldiers bearing minuscule transcriptions of Psalm 90 (Psalm 91, in Western Christian texts), a psalm traditionally associated with divine protection (*DZh*, 331). Reading the copy he finds on the body of a young soldier, he rehearses the rather homonymical transcription into contemporary spoken Russian from Church Slavonic—a transcription which is almost comedic in its distortions. A few lines later, Yurii also finds a soldier, of more educated background, whose uncorrupted Slavonic copy of the psalm has—thanks to its casing—saved him from a bullet. Lazar Fleishman ends his article on Pasternak and Christianity with the image of this contaminated text as a symbol of Pasternak's non-dogmatic relation to Orthodoxy (*FBP*, 298–99). His analysis rings true; what is more, this passage emblematizes Pasternak's resolutely revisionist method of appropriating and adapting cultural signs, of "corrupting" the text to his particular aesthetic ends. The subsequent passages suggest Yurii's incorporation of Kubarikha's and the soldier's examples into his own practice.

Yurii's second vision follows right on the tail of Kubarikha's healing ceremony and seamlessly incorporates elements both of her enchantment and of the Orthodox Feast of the Virgin's Protection—the *Pokrov*, in a method not unlike that of the witch's (the narrator calls her a "vorozheia"). Yurii's meditation or erotic reverie begins with his taking one of Kubarikha's vivid images—the opening up of a woman's shoulder to find some secret treasure inside ("from one, a measure of wheat, from another, a squirrel, and from another, honeycomb")—and applying this strange image to Lara (*DZh*, 362). Imaginatively opening her up thus, he finds a long ribbon—much like a film reel—which reveals "the secrets hidden by her soul. Unfamiliar towns she visited, unfamiliar streets, others' homes, unfamiliar expanses." As Yurii contemplates this fantastical quasi-dissection, he marvels at how he can discern no single feature which so draws him to her, but rather that the whole of her, as in an "inimitably simple and swift [*stremitel'noi*] line" enwraps his soul as swaddling does an infant. The next moment picks up this image, again, of the arching line, the living fabric, in an unmistakable incorporation of the *Pokrov* image (and, by extension, the light shaft) into his dream:

> Stretching from one side of the glade to the other, like a huge fabric banner hung over a city street from building to building, Yurii beheld a blurred spectral image, much larger than life, of that astonishing, divinely wrought [*bogotvorimoi*] head. The head wept, and the rain kissed it and poured down upon it with increasing strength. (*DZh*, 363)

On one hand, the image resembles the archetypal "icon not made by hands" (*nerukotvornyi*). This type of icon depicts Christ's face imprinted on a cloth. (See figure 4.1.) But Pasternak conflates this icon type, in Yurii's imagination, with the image of Mary spreading her veil of protection over

Figure 4.1. Icon of the Image Not Made by Hands (*Nerukotvornyi*). Russia, ca. 1700. Courtesy of the Museum of Russian Icons, Clinton, Massachusetts.

the congregated crowd. Whereas his earlier vision refers to the Transfiguration tradition, his second vision refers to the tradition by which Mary appears to Andrew the Holy Fool (Andrei Iurodivyi), during a service in the church at Blachernai. The feast of this icon, pictured in figure 4.2, has become a central one in the Russian Orthodox calendar and is seen to express the special protection of Mary for the Russian nation. In connection with the feast's importance for Russian self-imagination, Andrew was viewed as one of the first Russian saints.[28] Yurii's position as witness here, then, recapitulates the holy fool's function in the culturally generative moment. The link to Mary becomes clearer as we witness Kubarikha's concluding exhortation to the cow's owner, "Pray to the Mother of God. For lo, behold the abode [*chertog*] of light and the book of the living word" (*DZh*, 363). These latter images Kubarikha takes directly from the liturgy, as images of Mary, found, in particular, in the Akathist of the Theotokos, which is read on the fifth Saturday in Lent (Akathist Saturday), and in the canon performed in the Akathist service.[29] If Yurii's first vision embraces himself and nature, this next vision embraces the community around him, and, by extension, the

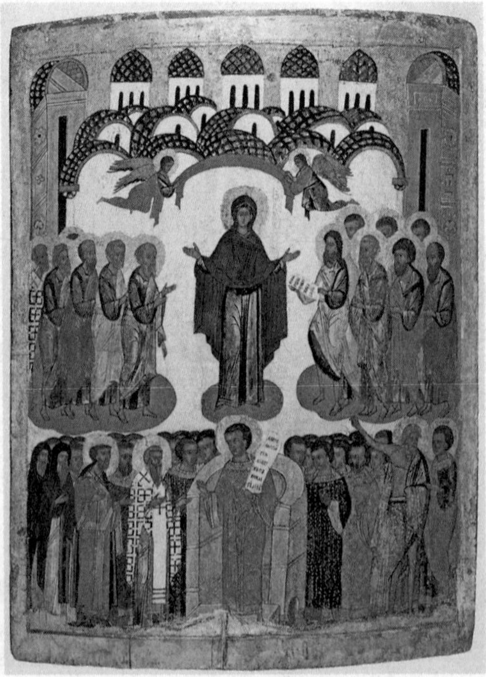

Figure 4.2. Icon of the Protection of the Holy Virgin (*Pokrov*), Novgorod School, 14th–15th centuries.
Courtesy of the Temple Gallery, London.

Russian nation, through the living fabric it imaginatively weaves from the threads of the past. At the same time his eroticization of the marian image works to amplify the ways Mary traditionally links heaven and earth, spirit and flesh.

Yurii's final vision offers the most universal image of the three, the image of the primordial man and woman. In the final paragraphs of this same chapter, we see Yurii return to the rowan tree in the deep of winter, as he makes his escape from the partisans:

> The tree was covered partly by snow, partly by frozen leaves and berries. It stretched out two snow-covered branches toward him. He recalled Lara's big, white, round, generous arms and, reaching out, pulled the branches toward himself. As though in response, the rowan tree sprinkled him with snow from head to toe. He muttered, not even aware of what he was saying:
>
> "I'll see you yet, my fabled beauty, my princess, my rowan tree, my flesh and blood." (*DZh*, 370)

At this moment Yurii embraces an emblem that transformatively intertwines in itself key artistic sources and forces of Pasternak's novel. Not only is the rowan tree associated with pagan magic rituals, and thus with folk tradition generally, but it directly echoes a song which Kubarikha performs in an earlier passage (*DZh*, 358). Yurii takes this improvised folk song of the wandering soldier and his distant love and adapts it to his own narrative. But the tree also seems at once a liturgical, marian image and a sophianic image. In an earlier passage the narrator describes the tree in late autumn blazing with heavy red branches of berries, which it feeds benevolently to gathering birds—an image described as a mother nursing an infant. The image of the strikingly red tree against the steel sky recalls the Mosaic theophany of the Burning Bush (*Neopalimaia Kupina*) (Exodus 3)—that liturgically stands as a prefiguration of Mary. (Sima cites the association of the Burning Bush with the Bogoroditsa in her discussion of the liturgy.) The tree represents, yet again, though, an eroticized Mary, for not only does Yurii embrace it, but he has also stated earlier his plans to gather and eat its berries—and so he positions himself as feeding at his beloved's breast. Pasternak, too, then, as we have seen with other modernists in previous chapters, turns this canonical image of Mary into his own rendition of the sophianic body. Most similarly to Kuzmin, Pasternak has his protagonist associate the Burning Bush image with the sexualized flesh of his earthly beloved. Neither fear presenting aesthetic and spiritual transformation in explicitly sexual terms, though Kuzmin is more liberal than Pasternak in his presentations of gender.

The scene of Yurii's embracing the tree foreshadows the way that Pasternak morphs the Magdalene narrative to his aesthetic purposes—gesturing at how he believes art can restore humanity and its cultural forms through acts of creative (if not radically creative) continuity. This act of embracing the tree directly links to the Zhivago poem “Magdalene I,” in which we see the double image of Magdalene the harlot embracing Christ, into whom she grows “as a graft onto a tree” (*kak s derevom pobeg*), and then embracing the beam of the cross (*DZh*, 536–37). These scenes, with those that follow in “Magdalene II,” depict a redemptive moment, the restoration of fallen humanity, and Pasternak's linking these three scenes establishes Lara as the Mary Magdalene figure. Indeed, Sima's discourse to Lara on the liturgy in the following chapter, as we have seen, presents Magdalene's placement in the liturgy as a key to understanding its arc.

Another conversation in the thirteenth chapter—this time between Lara and Yurii—extends and elucidates the image of the mythic embrace. In this conversation Lara compares herself and Yurii to Adam and Eve, the first man and woman. Speaking of the breakdown of families, of society, and of cultural mores, Lara portrays herself and Yurii both as the original humans, but also as “the last vestige of all that incalculable greatness created on earth in the many thousands of years between them and us" (*DZh*, 397). Her comparison works in two fundamental ways to establish Pasternak's notion of transformation. First, it underscores the casting of Lara and Yurii in Pasternak's tale as primordial man and woman, and thus as the ultimate objects of transfiguration. (Sima refers to this concept when she cites the liturgy for the Feast of the Annunciation.)[30] Second, it emphasizes the necessary correlation between restoration of humanity and restoration of culture, as we will see below.

Pasternak depicts the magnetic attraction between Yurii and Lara as a line connecting diverse figures and elements. While Yurii envisions Lara's diverse experiences merged as though into a film roll, his poetic voice narrates Magdalene's reaching toward Christ as a graft into a tree, or the branches of the rowan tree stretching out to invite Yurii's embrace. The connecting line makes its components into an entirely new, and whole, figure—pictured in Yurii's evocation of the line that describes Lara, and that, by extension, binds his soul. This passionate connective line, though, is ever, for Pasternak, a peculiarly ascetic line. Uniting ascetic traditions on the most fundamental level is the notion of holding back, or restraining, in order to achieve greater fullness and to forestall destruction by disordered passions. Images along these lines appear among Yurii's meditations on Kubarikha's practices, which meditations serve to articulate, as discussed above, his own aesthetic. Hearing Kubarikha's song, Yurii reflects, "A Russian song is like water in a pond" (*DZh*, 358). On one hand, the pond contains the water, and yet the pond is ever fed by underground springs, so that the still surface of the pond belies the current beneath. Likewise, a song, he reflects, uses every means, "repetitions, parallelisms," to "hold back its content, which gradually emerges." This same system of oppositional forces, for Yurii, emerges in the attempt of a "strong yearning" (*tockuiushchaia sila*) to master itself. He concludes, "It is an insane attempt to halt time with words."

As in Kuzmin's work, Sima's discussion of the liturgy, as seen above, highlights a major distinction between one traditional view of ascesis within Orthodoxy and that which Pasternak ultimately prefers, viewing it as more culturally generative. This passage in isolation seems to suggest Pasternak's abjuring, through Sima, the ascetic mode; yet if we return to his discussions of form and force, we find, instead, that he is presenting his own kind of asceticism—the asceticism of artistic (poetic) form. He upholds the artistic form which holds back and channels the poet's overwhelming passion for Lara, which orders and synthesizes the flood of past experiences, which slows the dizzying stream of time that threatens to submerge the individual and destroy whole cultures. His poems, above all, live on and have a force in the world. This idea emerges strongly in the poem "August," cited above (*DZh*, 525–26). Here the poet dreams grandly of his own funeral, seeing it as a moment when his sophianic art will make good. In the scene the poem sets, the "uncorrupted" (*netronutyi raspadom*), "prophetic" (*providcheskii*) voice of Zhivago's poems speaks out to his funeral guests, even as he fades in the grave. Despite his failures and weaknesses, Zhivago will leave behind a legacy that will, the poem implies, transfigure those left behind.

Such a concept gives impetus to the poet, driving him forward as he shapes his sometimes inglorious life events into formal works of art. In this holding back and ordering, passion—in the sense of a driving force, impelling forward time, culture, and the individual—continues to play a crucial role, for the form without the force rings hollow. To understand the relationship between this "passionate" life force and poetic form, one can recall Yurii's impression, upon his return from the front, of Vedeniapin in public settings. The narrator, through Yurii's eyes, describes this Vedeniapin as maintaining his old forms in a changed context, ultimately framing him as a parody of his former self (*DZh*, 176–77). We find other examples in the figures of Gordon and Dudorov, especially as Yurii sees them in the concluding scenes of the novel, spouting platitudes, their speech characterized by a stifling "appropriateness" (*zakonomernost'*). These figures seem all form with no life force. Yurii, on the other hand, seems, ultimately, a wandering force without form. Indeed, his death by heart attack suggests a being for whom the force of passion is too strong, too long unrestrained—as though his heart finally explodes its bounds, figuratively and literally. Differently from Akhmatova's late and radical abjuration of comprehensible form, Pasternak calls for a passionate asceticism, turning erotic experience into something more or less ordered, presentable, and accessible.

Pasternak frequently associates Yurii with Christ—especially with the narrative of his death and resurrection—notably during Yurii's bout with typhus, and at his funeral (*DZh*, 206, 486). Bodin shows the importance of the liturgical tradition of Christ's descent into death (Hell) for Pasternak—especially in the Zhivago poem "Evil Days"—and he links it to Yurii's creative act.[31] Yurii, too, has to enter the forest—a classic locus for transformation, a kind of underworld realm. He emerges disfigured as a holy fool, but also transfigured, his passion for Lara directed and crystallized. Only after Yurii's dark interval in the forest does Pasternak connect him and Lara with the primordial pair at the conception of a new world.

Yet the relation of *Doctor Zhivago* to the Passion Week narrative represents something more complex than a direct allegory: it demonstrates Pasternak's concept of the way that art engages a nation's history. Akhmatova responds to modernism's failure and Soviet repressions by deferring visions of a better future. Pasternak, however, optimistically offers a novel that would bridge the vertiginous gap between pre- and post-revolutionary Russia and that would restore a national culture in a country disjointed by revolution, civil war, and staggering political and social change. Certainly Pasternak is producing, in part, an alternative model to a Marxism imposed from above through scientific principles of a kind; to this he opposes change generated by the individual imagination, drawing in significant part on previously accessible cultural forms. His transfigurations wittingly disfigure, his texts wittingly contaminate, in order to create continuity, restore and make new. As a whole, his novel proposes a continuity with the nation's unusually distant recent past in its reconstruction of the century's first decades, from the vantage point of mid-century Stalinism. It also proposes a continuity between the experience of the individual and the nation—but one not premised on a heroic narrative that would project the triumph of the new Soviet nation through the development of the new Soviet man. In her liturgy discourse, Sima marvels at the functional replacement, within the Christian redemption narrative, of the Jewish nation as vehicle of redemption with the lowly figure of Mary as Messiah-bearer. For Sima, it is precisely this kind of unorthodox, refigurative elision—similar to the liturgical conjoining of Mary the harlot with Christ in Holy Week—that expresses the life of culture.

Yurii's journal reflections on Pushkin reiterate this "ascetic" process of nurturing culture. Here Yurii imagines "light and air, the noise of life, things, essences" pouring in through Pushkin's window and crowding out the "less defined" (*menee opredelennye*) (i.e., more formless) parts of speech (*DZh*, 280). Through this rigorous marriage of form and force, Pushkin established, Yurii suggests, his tetrameter as a "measuring stick of Russian life." Likewise, Pasternak seeks to endow the revisedly sophianic poetry of his unlikely savior, Yurii, with the linking and ordering power that might sustain a cohesive national imaginary.

In this task Pasternak has not come so far from Blok's *Verses on the Most Beautiful Lady*, or, at least, his Soviet-period novel-with-verse develops the task Blok set himself. Pasternak thought so, anyway. Blok cameos in *Doctor Zhivago* as an emblem of the novel's aims; and Galina Rylkova has offered a fascinating and compelling reading of the work as an attempt to "translate" Blok (and by extension the Silver Age) by reconstructing the circumstances under which Blok wrote his early poems.[32] Early on in the work Yurii, still a university student, plans to submit an article on Blok for a student journal. At this same time his well-loved guardian, Anna Ivanovna, is lying ill. Facing the possibility of death and wishing for some kind of continuity of the life she has lived, she proposes to Yurii and her daughter Tonia that they marry. At this portentous moment Yurii looks out the window onto the city street and sees a world filtered entirely through his thoughts about Blok.

> Yurii looked around him and saw what Lara had seen shortly before. The moving sleigh was making an unusually loud noise, which was answered by

> an unusually long echo coming from the ice-bound trees in the gardens and streets. The windows, frosted and lighted from inside, looked like precious caskets made of smoky layered topaz. Behind them glowed the Christmas life of Moscow, firs were lit [*goreli elki*], and guests milled about and mummers fooled about, playing hide-and-seek and hunt-the-ring.
>
> It suddenly occurred to Yurii that Blok was the manifestation of Christmas in all domains of Russian life—in the everyday life [*byt*] of the northern city and in the newest Russian literature, under the starry sky of the modern street and around the lighted tree in a twentieth-century drawing room. There was no need to write an article on Blok, he thought, all you had to do was to paint a Russian version of the Adoration of the Magi, like the Dutch had, with a frozen winter landscape, wolves, and a dark fir forest. (*DZh*, 82)

In this passage I believe we find Pasternak's most vivid and compressed picture of the sophianic project as he understood it at its beginning and as he sought to develop it. We know from the novel that by this point Yurii has read and earnestly considered Solovyov's "The Meaning of Love" (*DZh*, 42). He seems, then, to combine his reading of Solovyov and Blok. Yurii for the first time sees Tonia as his potential bride and therefore as his own manifestation of the Eternal Feminine. This glimpse generates a vision in which the entire contemporary Russian cityscape, with all its mundane and festive details together, is transfigured. Specifically, Yurii sees Moscow as shot through with the light of the Incarnation—God's enfleshment that Christmas celebrates. The jewel images used by Solovyov, and after him by Blok and Kuzmin, to picture transfigured matter reappear here in the windowed, lit homes drawn as caskets of topaz. The Burning Bush reappears in the blazing Christmas trees that do not burn up.

And yet Pasternak inscribes into this luminous scene the kind of fragility that characterizes all the artist's instantiations of the transfigured world and that requires him constantly to generate new visions by willful, idealizing distortions. For the picture to work the narrator quickly has to replace Tonia with Lara, of whose proximity the young Yurii is unaware. More than that, though, lurking at the edges of the picture—Yurii's painting in words—are wolves, dark forests, and *sviatki* mummers with their sinister associations, highlighted centrally in *Poem without a Hero* and Blok's masked doubles. In these details the author inscribes into the scene the terrifying events that will overtake not only Yurii, but also his city and nation—the very destruction of civilization, as Yurii comes to believe. What contemporary readers Pasternak had (mostly his friends, to whom he read portions of his work from time to time) would surely have attended carefully to these darker touches and perceived their significance.

With the retrospective power of a narrator telling a whole life, the young Yurii presents Pasternak's mission for his novel and for reviving the religious aesthetic Yurii finds in "the newest Russian literature"—that is, in the literature of Russia's modernism. By the mode of his novel and the model of his protagonist Pasternak urges his readers to rebuild a safe, well-lit world via acts of imagination. He urges us—as Clowes has affirmed—to find the miracle in the everyday (*byt*), to see and realize God (life, love) in the world around us.[33] Pasternak does not back away from sentimentality. If it gives his novel a touch or two of kitsch, he does not seem to mind. He grew used to his friends' doubts about this work (*BBP*, 275–76). Pasternak's Christmas is as sentimental as they come, as seen also in the Christmas poem Yurii writes years later in place of his Blok article (*DZh*, 530–32).[34] In both prose passage and poem Pasternak sets up this holiday as the paragon of human culture-making, with the Magi—or wise men—who gather to worship God incarnate, rather like poets and religious-philosophers; with its carefully cultivated domestic settings made radiant for guests. In the poem the scene of worshippers gathered around the newborn Christ generates "all thoughts of the ages, all dreams, all worlds, / The whole future of galleries and museums, / All pranks of fairies, all deeds of magicians, / All firs lit up, all children's dreams."

T. S. Eliot's speaker in *The Wasteland*, that monumental modernist work, proclaims, "These fragments have I shored against my ruin." Through this whole long poem Eliot draws together relics of great civilizations in a form as fragmented and elliptical as Akhmatova's. In a way Eliot's project resembles Pasternak's in the impulse to assemble elements of the past; but ultimately their projects are as different as *Doctor Zhivago* and *Poem without a Hero*. Pasternak knew Eliot's work, but, as Timothy Sergay has shown, he sought to disassociate his later work from that of the British-American modernist.[35] He wrote, in fact, to Eliot in 1960 of "the groundless parallels that sometimes have been drawn between your art and my poor first steps."[36] I believe, however, that this seeming modesty in fact speaks to Pasternak's determination to make his work increasingly accessible, to shed the complex lyricism of his earlier, more identifiably modernist ("formalist," in Soviet terms) work—a shift many commentators have described. For him such simplicity relates not merely, though, to gaining readers but to a unity of vision he is determined to establish. Pasternak is not content to shore up fragments: he boldly projects a kind of Solovyovian "total unity" that both Eliot and Akhmatova aver. (Akhmatova, as it happens, includes an epigraph from Eliot's *Four Quartets* within her long poem.)[37]

Pasternak and Akhmatova were writing their retrospective works at about the same time, though Akhmatova began hers a few years earlier. We could, then, finish our story with Akhmatova as easily as with Pasternak—and in fact Akhmatova kept working on her *Poem* well after Pasternak's novel appeared in full (in the West). But I end with Pasternak to show how Russian literature came—if not full circle, then back to itself in a kind of spiral, in the inhospitable (and therefore perhaps apt) context of Stalinism. Pasternak's novel is artistically less sophisticated and groundbreaking than Akhmatova's *poema*—and also, for that matter, than Eliot's. But its attempt at a greater simplicity even where flawed is far from naive. The author knows the terrifying darkness of the world, knows how people can make monstrosities out of ideals; and yet he pointedly, perseveringly prefers to imagine a beautiful, transfigured world.

Epilogue

Ol'ga Sedakova's Religious Humanism

IN THEIR OWN WAYS each of the poets we have examined here worked to build or at least nurture hope in a new world. The early Blok shared the hopes of his symbolist contemporaries that a new world would materialize suddenly and through mystical means. Kuzmin took a more measured approach, working out a new way of life through a new religious-artistic practice. This approach endured and carried him through betrayals, loss, revolutions, massive unrest, official condemnations of his native milieu, penury, and persecution. Tsvetaeva adapted Orthodox traditions in order to pave a way for herself as a woman in the poetic conversation taking place—and through these adaptations she proved that she could speak more authoritatively *precisely as* a woman to flesh's capacity to channel spirit. Through tumult of war, cultural revolution, and repression, the Silver Age religious project persevered. Akhmatova, one of the few Silver Age poets who survived in Soviet Russia, sought in her late poetry to project hope for a restoration of Russian (and European) society—as well as to revise and secure her own place in that legacy. She poetically recalled and rejected the chiliastic visions of the young Blok, who had believed, like many of his peers, that a new radiant age was just around the corner. And she called, instead, for long-suffering endurance. Pasternak, too, sought to restore an imagined unity to mid-century Russian society, but with a more sanguine nod to the young Blok and his Beautiful Lady. In a kind of elation at the brief emergence of greater freedom during World War II Pasternak believed he could write a novel-with-poetry that would help restore a tumultuous Russian society by linking it to pre-revolutionary culture and working out that legacy in terms of a new reality. Even after he realized that his hopes for swift change were ill-founded, he determined to leave a work that would outlast him and provide a kind of blueprint for cultural restoration. Instead of suffering and endurance, he would call upon the forces of eros and imagination to work this transformation, thereby recalling the Silver Age Sophia in her more orthodox aspect.

We began by asking two questions: How do we understand the abundant uses of Orthodox tradition (viewed especially through liturgical culture) in Russian modernism? And what might the Silver Age tell us about religion in the context of modernity? As we have seen, the poets gathered here used Orthodoxy to advance visions of a world that could be changed by beauty. Indeed, for all of these poets no new world could materialize without a grounding in religious tradition. In this attention to the religious in human life and culture, they were true representatives of the Russian modernist impulse, which—in this at least—followed in the footsteps of the Slavophiles and of Solovyov, who insisted that no individual or society could survive in any healthy form while denying the religious aspect of being. We might also see these poets and the epoch they represent as exemplifying that late modern impulse described by Hervieu-Léger and others to find innovative ways of extending religious tradition into modern life.

We might view the interventions of Blok, Kuzmin, Akhmatova, and Pasternak in the sophianic task as a series of religiously oriented responses to the nineteenth-century legacy of the Russian intelligentsia, with its keen sense of responsibility for the Russian nation and its people (*narod*)—an argument already treated to some extent in a volume edited by Irina Paperno and Joan Delaney Grossman.[1] When Viacheslav Ivanov called for symbolists to move *a realibus ad realiora* (from the real to the more real), he had in mind the artist's need to reach toward a spiritual reality that theories of art (if not all writers themselves) had neglected.[2] Accordingly, his contemporaries imbued their works with images of spiritualized flesh—from the blazing Sophia to Mary the God-bearer and their many specters. These images signified not only an embrace of the material and bodily, but also a conviction that new life could express itself through cultural—and especially artistic—forms: not only through official church services, not only through ideas, not only through ideologically motivated action.

As regards the second question more specifically—that is, what might the Silver Age tell us about religion in modernity?—these poets' persistent religious-aesthetic interventions may remind us of conversations taking place currently. That is to say, over the last two decades (approximately), many scholars and thinkers across many disciplines have revisited the "secularization thesis" and sought to reconfirm, revise, or reject it.[3] The writers whose work we have been exploring and many of their contemporaries were responding to a previous generation (the so-called men of the sixties) who proclaimed the end of religion in the civilized world and the beginning of the reign of science. But as Mark Steinberg and Heather Coleman point out in their nuanced discussion of secularization in Russia, we find in many documents from the late imperial period "complex interrelations between religious vocabularies and 'secular rationalism.'"[4] The literary texts we have explored here reveal, accordingly, not so much a return to but rather a deployment of traditional religion—in the service of creating religion that looks rather untraditional, aligning with the varieties of religious "dispersal" Hervieu-Léger and others describe.

In the post-Soviet space, too, religion finds a new place for itself, in ways that look similar and in ways that look very different. In contemporary Russia, too, we find attempts to revitalize a sense of continuity with Russia's Orthodox past—but only after massive (if not total) rupture in that tradition on all levels of society. In this sense Pasternak's model remains the most current in its attempt to reconstruct a culture via shreds of the past imaginatively deployed after a period of radical change and loss. Pasternak has successors in this task, and one of these successors is the contemporary poet, essayist, and scholar Ol'ga Sedakova. Sedakova's adaptations of Russian Orthodox tradition via the medium of poetry is a substantial and largely unexplored topic, and its significance becomes clear only in light of Sedakova's profound knowledge of and engagement with Western European literary and religious traditions.

Sedakova has herself written on the ways the Russian literary tradition draws on the Orthodox Christian context. Introducing her translations of liturgical texts in her new *Collected Works*, she writes,

> The language of Church Slavonic belongs not only to church history but to the entire history of Russian culture. Much in this culture speaks to the powerful, thousand-year presence of this second, "nearly native," "almost understandable," "consecrated" language. The use of this language was limited to church services, prayer, devotional reading: areas where the Russian language was considered inadmissible. Any quote—even the briefest—in Church Slavonic immediately introduces the whole atmosphere of the temple, its color, smells, rhythms, its distinct atmosphere of light.[5]

And to make her point she quotes one of the poems from Tsvetaeva's Blok cycle, where the Silver Age poet cites several phrases from the liturgical hymn "Gladsome Light" ("Svete tikhii").[6]

Like the modernists Sedakova works to sustain a conversation between traditional Russian culture and modern, Western forms and values. While these heuristic categories do not represent elements that can actually be separated in a Russian context, the distinction bears relevance as contemporary official Russian culture (including both state and Church) seeks to delineate a post-Soviet Russian identity often by means of opposition to a non-Russian West—a tactic not entirely different from that of Soviet Russia's official culture. By contrast, in her work Sedakova moves fluidly between Russian and Western European, religious and secular discourses. Here I wish merely to indicate one prominent way she embodies Orthodox traditions in a poetry that sustains the Russian modernist ambition to use beauty to nurture society. That is, Sedakova, not unlike Kuzmin, adapts the discourse of asceticism to speak into a contemporary setting. As one might expect, her emphases are somewhat distinct from those of the modernists. Nevertheless, in both a Soviet and post-Soviet context her work seems to foster a contemporary Russian religious humanism.

I will begin with Kuzmin simply to underscore some parallels between one modernist's and Sedakova's projects. In the chapter on his work we explored how he adapts the theme within ascetic discourse of the soul's working toward a greater capacity of love, which constitutes—for both Kuzmin and the asceticism he adapts—the telos of life's journey. In a poem from *Autumnal Lakes* we find a representation of this path that resonates strongly with traditional ascetic texts.

> Посредине зверинца—ограда,
> А за нею розовый сад.
> Там тишина и прохлада,
> И нет ни силков ни засад.
> Там дышится сладко и вольно,
> И читают любовный псалтырь,
> А кругом широко и бездольно
> Распростерся дикий пустырь.
> Когда ж приоткроют двери,
> Слышут лай и яростный вой,
> Но за стены не ступят звери:
> Их крылатый хранит часовой.
> И все так же тихо и мирно
> Голубой лепечет ручей,
> И медленно каплет смирна
> Из цветочных очей.
> И издали вой, как "осанна,"
> Говорит: "Люби, живи!"
> Но звериная жизнь—обманна
> Запечатанной там любви. (*MKSS*, 1:325)

(In the middle of the menagerie is a fence, / And beyond it a rose garden. / There one finds quiet and coolness, / And there is neither snare nor ambush. / There one breathes sweetly and freely, / And love's psalter is read, / And all around broadly and unhappily / The savage wilderness has spread. / And when they will open the doors, / One will hear the howl and fierce roar, / But the beasts will not step beyond the wall: / A winged watchman keeps guard. / And still just as quietly and peacefully / Murmurs a light-blue spring, / And

> slowly drips the myrrh / From the flower eyes. / And from afar the roar, like "Hosanna," / Says, "Love, live!" / But the beast's life is a counterfeit / Of the love that abides there, set as a seal.)

In these verses Kuzmin seems to present a traditional rendering of a trope commonly used to illustrate the soul's ascent through ascetic endeavor—that is, he presents the soul as a garden whose fruits (virtues) require cultivation and protection from the savage beasts of the passions. This image of the soul as a cultivated garden appears in much patristic literature—from John Climacus to John Chrysostom—and reappears in contemporary Orthodox theology. Gregory of Nyssa writes in the fourth century that to be united with God one

> must become a flourishing garden, having within himself the beauty of all kinds of trees. There must be the sweet fig, the fruitful olive, the lofty palm, the blossoming vine. . . . It is with such trees and plants that the flourishing and well-kept garden is filled. In addition, our garden is closed in on all sides by the fence of the Commandments, so that no thief or wild beast can gain entrance.[7]

Against the background of his poetic oeuvre, meanwhile, we can see how this poem offers one of the most radiant depictions of Kuzmin's religious aesthetic. In this "rose garden" "love's psalter is read"—clear references for us by now to physical acts of love—those "rites of love" he institutes. The "winged watchman" refers in part to the angel guarding Eden so that Adam and Eve cannot return; but it also recalls Kuzmin's angelic warrior guide. And since the lovers are back inside the garden enclosure, the poem suggests that the modern path of love's poetic praxis can culminate in a return to paradise.

Sedakova, too, wittingly interacts with this trope, presenting the garden as a symbol for the cultivation of the soul and of an integral culture. We find a key example of this connection in her well-known poem from 1970 "Surely, Maria . . ." ("Neuzheli, Maria . . .").

> Неужели, Мария, только рамы скрипят,
> только стекла болят и трепещут?
> Если это не сад—
> разреши мне назад,
> в тишину, где задуманы вещи.
>
> Если это не сад, если рамы скрипят
> оттого, что темней не бывает,
> если это не тот заповеданный сад,

где голодные дети у яблонь сидят
и надкушенный плод забывают,

где не видно ветвей,
но дыханье темней
и надежней лекарство ночное . . .
Я не знаю, Мария, болезни моей.
Это сад мой стоит надо мною.[8]

(Surely, Maria, it's not just that the window frames creak / and the windowpanes hurt and are trembling? / If it isn't the garden— / then let me back in / to the silence where things are imagined. // If it isn't the garden, if the window frames creak / because it doesn't get darker than this, / if it isn't the garden we've been covenanted, / where hungry children sit under apple trees / and forget the fruit they once tasted, // where no branches can be seen, / but breathing is darker / and the medicine of night is trustier . . . / I don't know, Maria, what is making me ill. / It's my garden that stands over me.)

This poem—terrifying in its own way—reads as the poet's muse coming in to bend over her, to call her to her labors. The poetic voice speaks as though in a kind of delirium, a state between dreaming and waking—an atmosphere conveyed especially in the halting but unbroken sentence that dominates the second two stanzas and breaks off in an ellipsis. In an unusual move Sedakova identifies this looming, muse-like figure with her garden. As in Kuzmin's poem we find here an image of a return to paradise—pictured in the "hungry children" sitting "under apple trees" and forgetting the original sin of tasting Eden's forbidden fruit. Sedakova represents her poetic work, then, as a cooperative (even theurgic) labor to bring about the New Creation.

Unlike in the earlier poem, however, Sedakova presents this image in a much more recessed way—as a desire, a possibility—and one that can materialize only after facing tremendous fear. Even when dealing with the theme of the lover's betrayal or loss, Kuzmin's poetry tends to balance grief with the comforts of faithfulness. Even the wounded flesh shows forth Sophia's blazing body. In this sense "Surely, Maria . . ." presents an outlook closer to Akhmatova's than to Kuzmin's: both Sedakova and Akhmatova present a much more measured approach to those hopes than Solovyov and the symbolists first articulated.

Sedakova seems in her garden poems to picture the cultivation of ethical qualities, as though acknowledging that the radiant dreams of the modernists will be reached only by long labor—a viewpoint perhaps inculcated in her and Akhmatova by more experience of the late Soviet period. Sedakova has, in fact, described such a process in the work of her contemporary and friend the Byzantinist and cultural critic Sergei Averintsev. She writes of the "spiritual tasks" of the Silver Age and their disruption and the ways that the few remaining artists in Russia—Akhmatova, Pasternak, Mandelstam—introduced a new ethical note. For her, Averintsev reengaged similar problems and fulfills the task begun by others, rounding out the achievements of the Silver Age by incorporating new virtues into this religious-cultural movement: "conscience, sobriety (*trezvost'*—meaning the spiritual virtue of vigilance), endurance, a definitive move away from Russian isolationism, and attention to the other."[9] We find a similar emphasis on cultivating virtues in another well-known poem of Sedakova's, "The Wild Dogrose" (1976).

> Дикий шиповник
>
> Ты развернешься в расширенном сердце страданья,
> дикий шиповник,
> о,
> ранящий сад мирозданья.
>
> Дикий шиповник и белый, белее любого.
> Тот, кто тебя назовет, переспорит Иова.
>
> Я же молчу, исчезая в уме из любимого взгляда,
> глаз не спуская и рук не снимая с ограды.
>
> Дикий шиповник
> идет, как садовник суровый,
> не знающий страха,
> с розой пунцовой,
> со спрятанной раной участья под дикой рубахой.[10]

(You unfold in the expanded heart of suffering, / wild dogrose, / oh, / wounding the garden of creation. // And the wild dogrose is white, whiter than any other. / Who names you will out-argue Job. // As for me, I am silent, disappearing in mind from a lover's glance, / not lowering my eyes and not taking my hand from the fence. // The wild dogrose / goes forth, like a gardener stern, / knowing no fear, // with its crimson rose, / with a hidden wound of partaking beneath a wild shirt.)

Here the garden is a locus for suffering, a microcosm for the "creation" (*mirozdan'ie*) that moves painfully toward some cosmic purpose it cannot grasp—as suggested in the reference to Job. "Wild," that is, introduced from beyond the garden itself, the dogrose acts like a Christ figure as the "stern gardener" (*sadovnik surovyi*) who wounds the "garden of Creation" (*raniashchii sad mirozdan'ia*) in order to cultivate it. In these lines, too, we find echoes of Kuzmin, who associates roses, hearts, and bleeding wounds all with the flesh that has been transfigured through suffering. But again the focus in Sedakova's poem lies more on the suffering incurred in the shaping process than in the luminous results.

Sedakova takes the discourse of ascetic cultivation, then, and shifts its emphasis, connecting it to the poet's task, which she often characterizes as suffering, or an illness—but one that she willingly accepts. She has noted in an award speech, "Poetry, as people have known since the times of Orpheus, softens custom [*umiagchaiet nravy*]. That is, poetry returns to custom its native depth, it tears up the earth so the earth can receive the seed."[11] The here somewhat violent image of disturbing the soil heightens the violent aspect of cultivation, in which poetry—as its own kind of asceticism—takes part. Poetry, then, restores not just the individual but human culture and society.

This aspect of the garden topos emerges particularly in Sedakova's *Chinese Journey* (*Kitaiskoe puteshestvie*), from 1986.[12] This cycle offers one of the poet's extended meditations on nature. In it, the poetic voice endows elements of nature—trees, rivers, the sky—with qualities that enable and foster interpersonal harmony. Nature, that is, becomes a model for society and the individual in society.

The second poem of the cycle exemplifies Sedakova's approach to depicting what fosters the life of the garden.

Пруд говорит:
были бы у меня руки и голос,
как бы я любил тебя, как лелеял!
Люди, знаешь, жадны и всегда болеют
и рвут чужую одежду
себе на повязки.
Мне же ничего не нужно:
ведь нежность—это выздоровленье.
Положил бы я тебе руки на колени,
как комнатная зверушка,
и спускался сверху
голосом, как небо.[13]

(The pond says: / if I had hands and a voice, / how I would love you, / sing you to sleep. / People, you know, are greedy and always hurting / and rip others' clothes / into bandages for themselves. / I don't need anything: / after all, tenderness is healing. / I would put my hands on your knees, / like a house pet, / and would descend from above / in a voice like the sky.)

In this poem and others in the cycle, the natural inhabitants of the garden are characterized, above all, by their active acceptance of what they do not have and by their continued generosity in the face of loss. That is, they exemplify relinquishment—of themselves or of desires to be other than they are. In this act they open themselves up to the hurt and greed of others, but their attitude makes social harmony more possible.

In this and other poems the poetic voice proclaims its own poverty and validates a poetic humility. It recognizes its inability to convey what it desires to convey, and its greatest achievement lies in its renunciation of self. One of the most famous, and perhaps the central poem of the cycle echoes this sentiment and contrasts human society with the organic order of the garden. The poem begins, "Unhappy / is he who speaks with a guest / while thinking of tomorrow's / doings; / unhappy / is he who does what he does and thinks he does it / and not that air and light guide him, / like a paint-brush or butterfly or bee."[14]

This poem bears more of an aphoristic quality than other poems in the cycle, but it spells out in simple terms an important aspect of Sedakova's vision here. Over and over in her poetry Sedakova emphasizes the qualities of renunciation, humility, patience, endurance, willingness to suffer—as well as childlike simplicity. As Benjamin Paloff has pointed out, certain of these qualities are manifest in the form of her poems, too, with their unadorned language and open-ended quality.[15] In her work self-renunciation prepares the way for poetic inspiration, but also for healing of human relations and, more generally, for grace in all its many forms. Here we find powerful echoes of Orthodox ascetic tradition, although she is always also engaging with a broad range of poetic and philosophical traditions—seen not least in the epigraph to *Chinese Journey* from Lao-Tse. Sedakova's poems humbly invite readers to contemplate world and spirit with her, to enter as equal partners into her metaphysical task.

In her emphasis on relinquishment we find the chief distinctive marker of Sedakova's humanism. She introduces into the high Russian tradition of poetry a central ascetic value, the value of humility. More than the modernists we have discussed here—who were most concerned with revitalizing a religious ritual culture in order to consecrate all of life as quickly as possible—she looks to the ethical teachings of the Orthodox tradition as a necessary grounding for social change.

Some of her critical writing clarifies this issue, especially her discussion of the mind, in ways that differ from Western European philosophical notions. In an essay on the work of Pushkin, Sedakova shows how Russia's great poet presents the mind as not primarily cognitive but as a part of a human being that bears moral and aesthetic sensibilities. "Sense (*chuvstvo*)," she writes, "is the more general capacity to perceive (*chuiat'*); it is at once intellectual and emotional: it is openness."[16] Sedakova's description of the mind resonates with that of contemporary theologian Andrew Louth, who writes of mind in terms of the term *nous*, a seminal concept in the Eastern Christian tradition, as distinct from that of the West. According to Louth,

> *nous* is the means by which the soul "aspires to a knowledge that is a direct contact, a 'feeling' (*sentiment*), a touching." . . . This kind of knowledge is contemplation: simple regarding, beholding, without the necessity of seeking to control or manipulate.[17]

We find an emphasis on knowledge as personal contact, as Louth describes it, in the modernists, too. But the difficult work of attuning the mind to the contemplative task, with its radical openness, seems rather different from the way the modernists we have seen almost demand or force a realization of the new world they hope to discover.

In this and other senses Sedakova's work seems rather more traditional than the work of the modernists, from whom she has drawn much. In her wide-ranging creative and scholarly activity, Sedakova has worked on a number of projects meant to reintroduce Orthodox and more broadly Christian tradition into contemporary Russia. She has translated numerous liturgical texts;[18] she has translated classic didactic and devotional readings from ancient Christian tradition;[19] she has written on the poetics of Eastern Slavic burial rites, including those within Russian Orthodoxy;[20] she has, perhaps most impressively and significantly in this vein, composed a dictionary of Church Slavonic words that cause difficulty for translators.[21] This dictionary and her own poetic models help lay a foundation for the much-needed translation of Slavonic texts into contemporary Russian.

And yet despite the continuities she seems to establish, we must remember that they are innovations in their own way—attempts at throwing a connecting cord over a wide chasm, if we speak in terms, at least, of the larger public sphere. Nor does her poetry lack innovation—in form, and also in its breathtakingly deft way of bringing together literary, artistic, and religious traditions from across the world. In this sense we can say that she is a true inheritor of the Russian modernist religious project, in all its daring, its brilliance, and its vertiginous ambition.

Appendix

The Shape of the Liturgy

WHEN I SPEAK of the "liturgy" in this study, I speak of a whole cycle and set of practices and not only that particular service when the Eucharistic feast is shared. Indeed, neither this particular service nor any other service in the liturgical cycle can be properly understood in isolation from the whole ongoing, ever-changing configuration of all the services. As Alexander Schmemann writes in his *Introduction to Liturgical Theology*, the liturgy is

> the life of the Church, the public act [*litourgos* comes from the Greek for "common" or "public action"] which eternally actualizes the nature of the Church as the Body of Christ, an act, moreover, that is not partial, having reference only to one function of the Church (her "corporate prayer") or expressing only one of her aspects, but which embraces, expresses, inspires and defines the whole Church, her whole essential nature, her whole life.[1]

In terms of its foundational elements the Orthodox Christian liturgy consists of several cycles: a daily cycle of services, adapted from the monastic hours (see below for more detail); a weekly cycle of services, which commemorates particular biblical events on specific days of the week—echoing the order of Holy Week; a yearly cycle of "movable" feasts; and a yearly cycle of "fixed" feasts.[2] Because of their prominence and symbolic importance I draw primarily from these latter two, overlapping cycles of "movable" and "fixed" feasts. The "movable" feasts center on Easter, the Church's central holiday, the timing of which is determined by the lunar calendar. The "fixed" feasts occur yearly on the same calendrical date—still designated by the Julian calendar. With Easter standing in a class of its own, the remaining major feasts total twelve, often referred to as the "Great Feasts." I add to this number another of special significance to Russia and therefore to Russia's Silver Age writers: the Feast of the Virgin's Protection (*Pokrov*).

In this brief appendix I will not attempt anything close to a comprehensive summary of the liturgical cycle in all its aspects (though I do include a bibliography for further information); instead, I present some of the cycle's more prominent elements, its main feast days, which services even irregular churchgoers might attend, and which present vividly important aspects of the liturgical imagination. I include a list of these thirteen feasts, along with a brief description and the major motifs their texts contain. The liturgy as we know it was essentially cobbled and woven together over centuries and includes prayers, hymns, and texts of all kinds, from diverse periods and styles. Yet in all their diversity, these texts together reflect both a stability of doctrine and of imagination in the Church. As Hugh Wybrew tells us in his history of the development of the Eucharistic liturgy specifically, by 988, when Vladimir I officially designated Christianity as the primary Russian religion, the central service was "well on its way to attaining its final form," and by the fourteenth century it "had reached the full term of its development."[3] We see stability, though, not only in the historical embodiment of the Eucharistic service but also in images and motifs binding together the diverse texts of the liturgical cycle as a whole. Each feast has its own symbolic cluster and emphases, and yet all of the feasts incorporate and rework some key motifs that picture central points of theology, such as Old Testament prefigurations of New Testament events, Trinitarian doctrine, and the role of Mary in bearing God and interceding for God's people.

The repetition of these motifs has much to do with the structure of the central hymn, or canon, for each feast.[4] Canons are built from nine odes (though in some circumstances particular odes are omitted), each ode of which ostensibly draws on a song from the Judeo-Christian scriptures.[5] The first eight point to moments celebrated by song in the Hebrew scriptures (e.g., the Israelites' crossing of the Red Sea, a prophecy by Isaiah, Jonah's release from the belly of the fish); and the final, ninth ode recalls Mary's *Magnificat*, her song in response to Gabriel's news that she would bear the long-awaited Messiah (Luke 1:46–55). Also recalled in the ninth ode is the *Benedictus*, sung by Zacharias when his son John the Forerunner was circumcised and named (Luke 1:68–79). Each of these scriptural songs speaks to the salvation of God's people; and ancient Christian tradition, as reflected by the canons, explicitly presents the Old Testament events as prefigurations of Christ and the salvation he brings. (See below for a full list of the odes.) Within the canon each ode begins with a section designated as a *heirmos*, or "link," in which the hymn-writer links the feast and its remembered events to the conventional subject for each ode. In this way the events and symbols for each feast become imaginatively intertwined with the most ancient events of sacred history. Moreover, it takes the entire liturgical cycle to perceive just how intertwined all these events become in a larger network of associations: each service comes to reflect a facet of the sweeping liturgical imagination. In referring to one image in the sequence—for instance, Jonah's voyage in the fish—one refers to the entire body of motifs that picture the Christian theology of salvation.

CANONS: ODES IN ORDER

In the list that follows I have drawn the scriptural references (book, chapter, and verse) from a list given in von Gardner, *Russian Church Singing*, 40.

1. The song of Moses after the Israelites have crossed the Red Sea as its waters moved back to form a dry path for them and then flooded back over the soldiers of the Pharoah who were in pursuit of them (Exodus 15:1–19 and 21)
2. A second song of Moses, composed in his last days as he hands over the leadership of the Israelite people to Joshua; the song is full both of reminders of God's provision in the wilderness and also of God's judgment on those who forsake him (Deuteronomy 32:1–43)
3. The prayer of Hannah, who prayed to God for a child when she was seemingly barren and had a son (1 Samuel 2:1–10 [titled as 1 Kings in the Slavonic bible])
4. The prayer of the prophet Habakkuk, who is concerned for the sinful state of his people; in his song he praises God for his glory and faithfulness (Habakkuk 3:1–19)
5. A prayer by the prophet Isaiah, about the awaited salvation of Israel; the book is seen in Judeo-Christian tradition as having special importance in the messianic tradition (Isaiah 26:9–19)
6. A prayer by the prophet Jonah from the belly of the fish who has swallowed him, that he may be released (Jonah 2:1–9)
7. A prayer of Shadrach, Meshach, and Abednego in the fiery furnace for protection from harm; with praise to God for his righteous judgment and faithfulness to the Hebrew people (Daniel 3:26–51a [reference to the Slavonic Bible, not to the Russian Synodal translation])
8. The song of Shadrach, Meshach and Abednego, who are praising God from the fiery furnace, and calling on all elements of creation to praise him (Daniel 3:51b–88)
9. Mary's *Magnificat*—her song of praise to God for the salvation that he will accomplish through her bearing the Christ (Luke 1:46–55); this ode also

refers to the *Benedictus*, a song of prophecy by Zacharias, foretelling God's salvation and the future role of his son (John the Forerunner) in it (Luke 1:63–79)

THE DAILY CYCLE

In a monastic setting—the setting for which this regimen of services developed—all of these services are observed in a given day. Outside such communities however, in regular parish churches and even at cathedrals, only some of these daily services are observed—most commonly Vespers and Matins—and in smaller churches some services may be observed only once or twice a week. For one reader-friendly account of the daily cycle, see Thomas Hopko, "The Daily Cycles of Prayer," in *The Orthodox Faith*, Vol. 2, *Worship* (Syosset, N.Y.: Orthodox Church in America, 1997), 59–68.

1. *Vespers* (*vechernia*): The liturgical day begins, in fact, in the evening, and therefore the first service of the day is Vespers. Typically this service takes place relatively early in the evening.
2. *Compline* (*povecherie*): In a monastery or convent one also celebrates a service later in the evening, after the meal.
3. *Nocturne* (*polunoshchnitsa*): Another service generally restricted to monastic settings is Nocturne, which begins at midnight.
4. *Matins* (*utrenia*): Typically, outside a monastic setting, the second service of the day is Matins, which takes place in the morning.
5. *The Hours*: In a monastic setting other services punctuate the day. These services are the First, Third, Sixth and Ninth hours (*pervyi chas, tretii chas, shestoi chas, deviatyi chas*), which generally take place at 6 A.M., 9 A.M., 12 P.M., and 3 P.M.
6. *The Divine Liturgy* (*bozhestvennaia liturgiia/obednia*): Also known as the Eucharist—and in Western practice as Communion—worshippers partake of the elements of wine and bread, disbursed by a priest. In monastic communities the liturgy is often served daily. Outside that setting, it is most often celebrated only on Sundays, after Matins, and on important feast days.
7. *Vigil* (*vsenoshchnoe bdenie*): Sometimes for feasts of particular importance, including in parish churches and cathedrals, Vespers, Matins, and the First Hour are combined into a Vigil service, which extends from the early to the late evening. For Easter, the service begins early Saturday evening and continues into the early hours of the morning.

LENT, HOLY WEEK, AND EASTER

Easter, or *Paskha*, the central feast for the Christian liturgical year, celebrates the resurrection of Jesus from the dead after he was crucified and lay in the tomb from Friday until Sunday morning. His resurrection marks, in the Christian tradition, not simply the end of the power of sin and death but—more fully—the restoration of humanity and all of creation to its originally intended state. The celebration of Easter is made particularly solemn by the complex array of services and ritual traditions surrounding it. Easter is preceded by a strict forty-day fast, known as Lent. Throughout Lent numerous services mark special moments of the fast and moments in the final weeks of Jesus's life. But by far the most important services of the Lenten period are the services that take place during Holy Week (or Great Week)—the week immediately leading up to Easter. Each day of this week celebrates a significant moment in Jesus's final days and, what is more, sets up the model for the celebration of that day during the weekly cycle as it occurs throughout the year. Most notably, Holy Friday (or Great Friday) recalls Jesus's Passion and Crucifixion, and Holy Saturday (starting on Friday evening) celebrates his burial, as well as the vigil believers keep as they await God's renewal of life and salvation. (Accordingly, on Saturdays in the Church the dead are particularly remembered.) The most solemn service of the year begins on Saturday early evening and extends into the early hours of Sunday morning as worshippers mark the shift from death to life, darkness to light, sin to salvation.

The key liturgical text that sets the tone for Lent is the Great Canon, said to have been composed by Andrew of Crete, who lived in the seventh and eighth centuries. This long hymn is sung in full on the fifth Thursday of Lent, but its themes are found throughout the Lenten services (*LT*, 378–415). The central theme for this text is grief over sin and longing for salvation. The work speaks in the first person, and the hymn's persona throughout laments his sin and asks for God's mercy, also seeking Mary's intercession. An awareness of God's wrath and judgment is strongly felt, and in each section of the hymn the speaker compares himself to biblical figures who sinned against God but also holds out other biblical figures as models and beacons of hope. Christ's salvation is gladly remembered and also fervently requested. The speaker emphasizes across the hymn the notion of flesh corrupted, beauty disfigured, and the need for healing and restoration.

Easter itself celebrates the rising of Jesus, the Christ, from the dead, thereby defeating death. Its services are full of images of light and refer to the purification of sin from the world, the restoration of humanity to its perfect and intended state and also the coming of God's Kingdom, or the New Jerusalem. It stands as the culmination of the liturgical year.

THE GREAT FEASTS (DATES ARE LISTED IN THE JULIAN CALENDAR)

A Note on Marian Imagery in the Feasts

In all of the feasts Mary features prominently as a key intercessory figure. She is invoked throughout with a rather consistent set of titles and images, most of which picture her as a container or a passageway—that is, as a way to and vehicle of salvation—to take just a few from the service for her Nativity, "the Bridal Chamber of the Light, the Book of the Word of Life, . . . the East Gate," "a golden censer," "the Mountain, the Gate of heaven, and the spiritual Ladder" (*FM*, 101, 118, 120).[6] Mary is also frequently addressed as the "Temple of God." Such images are especially prevalent in the services dedicated to her, but they appear in all of the services in some form or another. She is invoked with particular frequency and in various formulations as one who contains that which cannot be contained—that is, the finite human who holds the infinite God in her womb. Another important title and way of picturing her in both liturgical texts and icons is as the Burning Bush (*Neopalima kupina*) that Moses encountered in the wilderness (Exodus 3)—that bush that was burning but not consumed. These images taken together present her first as an emblem of the wondrous because seemingly impossible reconciliation of God and man, heavenly and earthly, spirit and flesh. They also designate her, second, as the most fitting intercessor between God and humankind. Since all of these marian images are so common in all of the services of the Church, I will not make note of them in the individual sections for each major feast, except where marian titles have special emphasis.

These motifs are often complex and interconnected, as with the traditional comparison of the voyage of Noah's ark to the Israelites' crossing of the Red Sea to Jonah's three days in the belly of the fish, Christ's incarnation via Mary's womb, his baptism in the Jordan, and his three days in the tomb—all moments that lead to salvation and point to resurrection, and all moments that image containment and submersion preceding release. It is instructive that in individual services—with the exception of the Easter vigil—we generally find only elements of these symbolic complexes so that we need the entire set of services to demonstrate the whole network of associations and its full effect.

The Nativity of the Mother of God (*Rozhdestvo Presviatoi Bogoroditsy*) (September 8)

This feast begins the liturgical year. It marks Mary's birth to Anna and Joachim, a miraculous event since both parents are of advanced age and apparently barren.

Throughout the hymns and prayers for this feast Anna is compared to apparently dead wood that suddenly blossoms—as in the prophecy of Isaiah, or the miraculously flowering rod of Aaron—symbols that represent hopes for divine intervention and redemption (Isaiah 11:10; Numbers 17 and Hebrews 9:1–5). Mary, then, is compared to the miraculous bloom. Many of the texts meditate on this notion of life divinely conceived out of barrenness—whether from dead wood, infertile soil, or desert ground. In keeping with this notion, we also find numerous images of life-giving water flowing from unexpected places—such as fountains gushing from rock or springs flowing in the desert. Through such images the feast highlights the wondrous nature of God's reconciliation with humanity and with mortal, corruptible flesh and positions Mary and her birth from Anna as emblems of that feat.

The Raising of the Honorable and Life-Giving Cross (*Vozdvizhenie Kresta Gospodnia*) (September 14)

This feast actually commemorates two events—primarily the rediscovery and exhumation by Emperor Constantine's mother Helen of the cross on which Jesus was crucified, but also the dedication of the Basilica of the Resurrection by Constantine in 335 AD.

The services for the feast contain several notable motifs, including the cross as an emblem of the victory of God's people, with the cross viewed as a kind of banner or standard in battle. Some of the hymns and prayers draw a parallel between Emperor Constantine and the Old Testament Patriarchs (Jacob, Joshua, Moses) who lead God's people to victory. Another prominent motif lies in the use of the wooden cross as the picture of a living tree that overtakes and renews the dead wood of corrupted, sinful creation. Along these lines Christ is pointedly remembered as the new Adam, who brings life to a world that was damaged when Adam and Eve ate of the "tree of the knowledge of good and evil" (Genesis 2–3). Mary appears in the ninth ode as the "untilled" yet fertile ground from which will spring a new paradise.

The Protection (Veil) of the Mother of God (*Pokrov Presviatoi Bogoroditsy*) (October 1)

This feast is not generally included in typical lists of the so-called Great Feasts, but in a Russian context it is a holiday of special and national significance. Although the services mark an event from Byzantine sacred history, this event has come to represent God's special favor for and protection of Russia. The feast commemorates a vision by Andrew the Holy Fool (Andrei Iurodivyi) in the church of Blachernai in tenth-century Constantinople, where he saw Mary stretching out her veil over the congregation as a sign of her special protection of and intercession for that city. In the saint's life (*zhitie*) for Andrew, he is referred to as a Scythian, and for this reason as well as Russia's assumed role as successor to Byzantium, the feast came to be connected in Russian tradition with Mary's protection of Russia, and indeed the Slavonic texts include a special prayer for the Russian land.

In the services for this day we are especially reminded of Mary's intercessory role for Christians. Much of the language is influenced by an imperial context, with prayers asking that Mary—here addressed frequently as "Tsaritsa"—intercede for the city, for the tsar, for the emperor, and the people and that she protect them from the attacks of the pagans and drive out and confound the enemies of the Christian people. Mary herself is presented at various moments—in line with other services in the liturgy—as a strong fortress, a refuge, and a wall. Another set of images presents Mary as an adornment of the Church and as the Bride of God—the Church arrayed in beauty. (See "The Entrance of the Mother of God into the Temple," below.)

The Entrance of the Mother of God into the Temple (*Vvedenie vo khram Presviatoi Bogoroditsy*) (November 21)

According to apocrypha, Anna and Joachim take their daughter, the three-year-old Mary, to the temple so that she may serve there until it is time for her betrothal. The priest who receives her and under whom she serves is Zacharias, father of John the Forerunner.

On this day prayers and hymns draw on the symbolism of the temple itself, comparing Mary to a temple that contains the uncontainable God, as well as to the Holy of Holies, the innermost chamber of the temple, which few could enter—and to the Ark of the Covenant that resided in the Old Testament tabernacle. Her innocence from birth is emphasized, along with her purity. Another prominent theme in this feast (as in the Feast of the Protection, which was established several centuries later) is the representation of Mary as the fulfillment of Psalm 45 (Psalm 44 in the Russian Orthodox Bible), in which the psalmist depicts a king's daughter being arrayed for her wedding to another king.[7] Christian tradition has interpreted this psalm as an image of the Christian Church. Mary appears both as this daughter of the king and as the Church's greatest adornment, arrayed in all her virtues. The feast recalls how Joachim and Anna brought young girls from their village to accompany them to the temple, and these girls appear as the maidens accompanying the virtuous bride to her wedding, another reference to Psalm 45.

The Nativity of Christ (Christmas) (*Rozhdestvo Khristovo*) (December 25)

The Nativity of Christ, or Christmas, as it is best known in the West, celebrates the incarnation of God as Jesus, born of Mary but conceived uniquely and miraculously by the Holy Spirit. According to the Christian scriptures Jesus was born in a stable or in a cave where animals were kept while his parents were traveling, having returned to Bethlehem for a census. Shepherds nearby witnessed a choir of angels singing about the event, and they went to find this extraordinary infant. (See Luke 2:1–20.)

The texts for the Nativity emphasize wonder at the possibility that the Creator of the world could come into the world as a helpless infant. Jesus appears as a kind of star, partly in reference to the star that accompanied his birth, which the Magi followed to find him (though they are not pictured here). But in fact many cosmic images appear in the Nativity services, not only representing Jesus as a source of light and of enlightenment, a shining star, but also picturing the miracle of the King of the heavens fitting into the womb of a woman, or in a cave. (Mary's womb is drawn very much in parallel with the cave, container of the uncontainable.) Another prominent set of motifs has to do with the restoration of the world through the birth of Jesus and the events of his life that followed. The feast emphasizes the reopening of the gates of Paradise (in reference to the fall of Eden) and the restoration of Adam through Jesus, the second Adam, and Eve through Mary. The wilderness of the world becomes a flowering garden.

Epiphany (Theophany/The Baptism of Christ) (*Kreshchenie Gospodne*) (January 6)

In Russian Orthodox tradition this feast is much more prominent and elaborate than the feast of the Nativity. It marks the baptism of Jesus in the waters of the Jordan by John the Forerunner (known in other Christian traditions as John the Baptist). In scriptural accounts of this moment the Holy Spirit descends in the shape of a dove, and God's voice is heard revealing Jesus as God's son; thus the name of the feast comes from the revelation of God's presence with humanity, now in the form of a human (Matthew 3:13–17; Mark 1:9–11; Luke 3:21–22). Christian tradition treats this moment as a culmination of previous theophanies retold by the Jewish scriptures, visions of God's glory such as Moses's encounter with the Burning Bush or his encounter with God on Sinai (Exodus 3, Exodus 34).

A major theme across the services for this feast is that of cleansing—not only by water, but also by fire. In addition to many images of water, along with references to moments where the Jordan appears in Jewish scriptures, light and fire feature significantly, especially in connection with the enlightening Christ, who purifies the world both by washing away its sins through his life, death, and resurrection and by the fire of his judgment. In keeping with this motif we find numerous images of dragons and serpents that represent the power of evil in the world and of unbound passions. The texts present Jesus's defeat of the dragon as he is immersed in the water. His immersion also figures his burial (a New Testament account of which is read on the Eve of the Epiphany), and therefore the mortification of flesh in order that it might be renewed and given life immortal. Many of the prayers and hymns marvel that the Master of all takes on the form of a servant and is baptized by a servant (that is, a mere human). Here in particular we find reference to the very important notion of kenosis, God's willed self-emptying in taking on the form of a human in order to save humanity.

The pure and purifying grace-filled light of Jesus's divinity cleanses and renews not only humanity but also all of creation. References to the four elements and their sanctification and renewal abound, along with images of the wilderness blossoming. An especially notable part of this feast is the Blessing of the Waters, which takes place on the feast day itself. In this portion of the service—which can constitute a discrete service itself, in the context of the larger celebration—the priest blesses containers and often even whole bodies of water, sanctifying that element so that it may serve as a protection and means of blessing, healing, and grace throughout the year.

Another important theme in the feast is the revelation of the fullness of the Trinity: the incarnate Son, seen in Jesus; the Holy Spirit, seen in the dove; and the Father, known through his affirming voice. In this sense, too, Christian tradition represents Jesus's baptism as the culmination of previous theophanies.

The Presentation of Our Lord in the Temple (*Sretenie Gospodne*) (February 2)

Mary and Joseph take Jesus to the temple on his fortieth day to sanctify him, as their first-born son, to God, as well as for the purification of Mary after the birth, in accordance with Jewish (Old Testament) regulations. There they encounter Simeon and Anna, two elderly, pious Jews who have been awaiting the appearance of the Messiah and who prophesy about Jesus's role as the appointed Savior. (See Luke 2:22–38.)

The central theme for this feast is the shift Jesus brings about from an economy of law to an economy of grace—a foundational concept in Christian theology. Jesus is seen as fulfilling and satisfying the Jewish law, not only in his parents' faithfulness to these rituals, but also in his manner of living and in his substitution for sinners in his life, death, and resurrection. Through him the requirements of the law are not only fulfilled but are also superseded by God's grace, made manifest in Jesus. Another motif is that of the infinite, eternal, uncircumscribable God being made present in the tiny, seemingly mortal form of an infant.

The Annunciation of the Mother of God (*Blagoveshchenie Presviatoi Bogoroditsy*) (March 25)

Gabriel comes to Mary to tell her that even though she is a virgin, she will conceive and bear the Christ, the one foretold to the Jewish people who will establish a never-ending kingdom of justice and righteousness. Mary responds in surprise, but offers herself as the servant of God. (See Luke 1:26–38.)

As in the feast of the Entrance of the Mother of God into the Temple, we find here many images of containers that present Mary's womb as the ultimate vessel of divine grace that also recalls other vessels of grace from Jewish tradition: the Ark of the Covenant, the fish/whale that swallowed Jonah, the ark of Noah, the throne of God, the bridal chamber, the Tabernacle, Abraham's tent. In these images Mary is shown paradoxically to contain the uncontainable. The image of the Burning Bush appears with prominence, including in the reading of the Genesis passage where the account of this theophany is found (Exodus 3:1–8). In accordance with other marian feasts Mary also appears as a way to God—a ladder, a gateway, a bridge. A particular theme of the Annunciation feast is wonder that the order of nature has been upset in a virgin's conceiving and remaining a virgin. Also significantly, the prayers and hymns frequently recall Eve and the serpent who tempted her, figuring Mary as overcoming Eve's sin through the conception and birth of Christ, and through her own sinlessness.

Entrance of Our Lord into Jerusalem (Palm Sunday) (*Vkhod Gospoden' v Ierusalim*) (one week before Easter)

Jesus rides into Jerusalem on a colt in the midst of the Passover festival. His disciples and crowds gathered to proclaim the coming of Israel's long-awaited king, and crowds spread their cloaks and leafy branches (traditionally palm branches) in his path as he rides into the city. (See Matthew 21:1–10; Mark 11:1–11; Luke 19:28–40; John 12:12–19.)

The services for Palm Sunday focus on the idea of Jesus as King and on his appearance in Jerusalem for his Passion as the incipient realization of his Kingdom on earth. We find comparisons between Jesus's throne among the cherubim and his humble seat on a colt. Images of palm branches appear throughout (and are used in the services themselves), referring to the biblical accounts but also symbolizing the new life that Jesus brings through his life, death, and resurrection. A subtext in the feast is Jesus's raising of Lazarus, who had been dead for four days; this event appears as a prefiguration of Jesus's own resurrection. Another prominent theme in the services is the extension of salvation to the Gentiles, symbolized, according to liturgical tradition (as in the Palm Sunday Vespers) by the colt—untrained and undisciplined but yet visited by God.

The Ascension of Our Lord Jesus Christ (*Voznesenie Gospodne*) (forty days after Easter)

Forty days after his resurrection, Jesus departs from earth and ascends to heaven. (See Mark 16:19–20; Luke 24:50–52.)

The feast marking this event emphasizes Christ's elevating humanity and human flesh from death and hell as he ascends from earth in a deified human body into heaven. A theme running throughout the services is the amazement of the angels and heavenly powers at this change wrought by Christ, the reconciling of man and God, flesh and spirit. Texts for the feast also refer to Jesus's ascension to sit at the throne at God's right hand, from where he will come to judge the earth in the last day.

Pentecost (Trinity Day) (*Den' Sviatoi Troitsy. Piatidesiatnitsa*) (fifty days after Easter)

After Jesus's resurrection and ascension into heaven, his disciples who are gathered together experience the advent of the Holy Spirit as a great wind and tongues of fire that float above their heads. In the number are devout Jews from many nations and tongues. At the coming of the Holy Spirit the apostles spontaneously begin to preach to the gathered peoples in their own languages. (See Acts 2:1–42.) Pentecost celebrates the coming of the Holy Spirit onto God's people and thus is traditionally seen as the beginning of the Christian Church.

Pentecost services speak of the arrival of God's Spirit as the "Comforter." They set side by side images of fire and water to emphasize that the purifying fire of God descends as sweet streams of grace, as rain and dew.

The Spirit also brings the gifts of prophecy and wisdom, and so the services marvel at the Spirit's filling illiterate fishermen (Jesus's disciples) with wisdom, turning them into theologians. Pentecost texts especially present the events as ones shedding a fuller light on the nature of God as Trinity, Father, Son, and Holy Spirit. For this reason the Feast of Pentecost is also often referred to as Trinity Day.

The Transfiguration of Our Lord Jesus Christ (*Preobrazhenie Gospodne*) (August 6)

Before his death and resurrection Jesus takes three of his disciples—Peter, James, and John—up onto Mount Tabor and reveals to them the radiant glory of his divine nature. Moses and Elijah appear beside him, attesting to his divinity and his status as the awaited Savior of the world. Jesus's disciples are terrified and fall to the ground. (See Matthew 17:1–8; Mark 9:2–8; Luke 9:28–36.)

Even though it is not as prominent as Easter and Epiphany, this feast holds tremendous significance for Orthodox Christian theology and praxis alike. The major images of the services feature the penetration of human flesh—the darkened and corrupted flesh of Adam—by divine light as Jesus recuperates humanity as God incarnate. Thus the Transfiguration offers the most concentrated liturgical representation of the notion of *theosis*, or the divinization of the human, humanity's becoming like God through receiving the grace of God's energies, which he imparts to the world. Hesychasm (in Russian, *isikhazm*), a major spiritual tradition within Eastern Christianity, cultivates the stilling of the senses and thoughts through a mystical form of prayer. (*Hesychia* is the Greek word for stillness or quietness). This discipline is meant to make one more receptive to God's divine energies and therefore more able to participate in the divine life. Gregory Palamas, who was most formative in developing *hesychast* theology, pointed especially to the Transfiguration to argue for the possibility of God's divine energies penetrating even human materiality, an idea very much in question at the time.[8] The services for the Transfiguration reflect this heritage.

Services also present the Transfiguration as a moment when something of the fullness of God's glory was revealed in Christ. As such the event came to be seen as prefiguring Jesus's resurrection glory, but also as a fuller revelation than previous theophanies—in some ways like Epiphany. Thus we find in the biblical texts for the feast, as well in liturgical references, accounts of encounters with God by Old Testament figures such as Moses and Elijah (who of course also appear in the biblical and liturgical account of the Transfiguration itself).

The Dormition (Assumption) of the Mother of God (*Uspenie Presviatoi Bogoroditsy*) (August 15)

At the time of Mary's death Jesus's disciples, except for Thomas, return to Jerusalem, and Jesus descends from heaven to take her soul up with him. Mary is laid in a tomb, and three days later Thomas arrives to discover that her body is no longer there, that it, too, has been taken up to heaven. The feast is based on apocryphal writings.

The Feast of the Dormition celebrates the assumption of Mary's deified body into heaven, picking up themes from the Feast of the Ascension—purified and restored human flesh entering the heavenly kingdom, the awe of the angels at this event. But in addition to these themes we find much emphasis in the services on the joy and peace that Mary's assumption into heaven brings to the earth, for now she can act as a special intercessor. Mary appears as a support for kings and a protector for the nations, and as one who brings healing and mercy to all people who ask of her. Images of choirs, singing, and dancing abound in this feast.

SELECTED BIBLIOGRAPHY ON THE STRUCTURE AND DEVELOPMENT OF THE RUSSIAN ORTHODOX LITURGY

The Festal Menaion. Trans. Mother Mary and Archimandrite Kallistos Ware. London: Faber and Faber, 1977.

The Lenten Triodion. Trans. Mother Mary and Archimandrite Kallistos Ware. Boston: Faber and Faber, 1978.

Men', Aleksandr. *Tainstvo, slovo i obraz*. Leningrad: Ferro-Logas, 1991.

Ouspensky, Leonid, and Vladimir Lossky. *The Meaning of Icons*. Trans. G. E. H. Palmer and E. Kadloubovsky. Crestwood, N.Y.: St. Vladimir's Seminary, 1999.

Schmemann, Alexander. *Introduction to Liturgical Theology*. Trans. Asheleigh E. Moorhouse. Crestwood, N.Y.: St. Vladimir's Seminary, 1986.

Sedakova, Ol'ga. *Slovar' trudnykh slov iz bogosluzheniia: Tserkovnoslaviano-russkie paronimy*. Moscow: Greko-latinskii kabinet IU. A. Shichalina, 2008.

von Gardner, Johann. *Russian Church Singing*, Vol. 1, *Orthodox Worship and Hymnography*, Vol. 2, *History from the Origins to the Mid-Seventeenth Century*. Trans. Vladimir Morosan. Crestwood, N.Y.: St. Vladimir's Seminary, 1980.

Ware, Timothy. *The Orthodox Church*. New York: Penguin Books, 1991.

Wybrew, Hugh. *Orthodox Feasts of Jesus Christ and the Virgin Mary: Liturgical Texts with Commentary*. Crestwood, N.Y.: St. Vladimir's Seminary, 2000.

———. *Orthodox Lent, Holy Week and Easter: Liturgical Texts with Commentary*. Crestwood, N.Y.: St. Vladimir's Seminary, 1997.

———. *The Orthodox Liturgy: The Development of the Eucharistic Liturgy in the Byzantine Rite*. Crestwood, N.Y.: St. Vladimir's Seminary, 1990.

———. *Risen with Christ: Eastertide in the Orthodox Church (Commentaries and Translation of Liturgical Texts)*. London: SPCK, 2001.

Notes

INTRODUCTION

1. Several book-length works treat Rilke's relation to Russia. See Patricia Brodsky, *Russia in the Works of Rainer Maria Rilke* (Detroit: Wayne State University Press, 1994); and Anna Tavis, *Rilke's Russia: A Cultural Encounter* (Evanston, Ill.: Northwestern University Press, 1994).

2. All translations are my own, unless otherwise noted.

3. Rainer Maria Rilke, "Du, Nachbar Gott, wenn ich dich manchesmal . . . ," in *Gedichte* (Frankfurt: Erster Teil Insel Verlag, 1987), 256.

4. Pavel Florensky, *Iconostasis* (Crestwood, N.Y.: St. Vladimir's Seminary, 1996), 67; Pavel Florenskii, *Ikonostas* (Moscow: Iskusstvo, 1994), 66.

5. See Dmitrii Merezhkovskii, *Polnoe sobranie sochinenii Dmitriia Sergeevicha Merezhkovskogo* (Moscow: Tipographiia I. D. Sytina, 1914), 17:175–276.

6. Dmitrii Merezhkovskii, "O prichinakh upadka i o novykh techeniiakh sovremennoi russkoi literatury," in *Polnoe sobranie sochinenii Dmitriia Sergeevicha Merezhkovskogo* (Moscow: 1914), 17:173–275.

7. Astradur Eysteinsson, *The Concept of Modernism* (Ithaca, N.Y.: Cornell University Press, 1990), 7.

8. Edith W. Clowes, *The Revolution of Moral Consciousness: Nietzsche in Russian Literature, 1890–1914* (De Kalb: Northern Illinois University Press, 1988).

9. Irina Paperno and Joan Delaney Grossman, eds., *Creating Life: The Aesthetic Utopia of Russian Modernism* (Stanford, Calif.: Stanford University Press, 1994).

10. An in-depth study of this phenomenon in Russia can be found in Olga Matich, *Erotic Utopia: The Decadent Imagination in Russia's Fin de Siècle* (Madison: University of Wisconsin Press, 2005). A less far-ranging but also helpful study along these lines is Jenifer Presto's *Beyond the Flesh: Alexander Blok, Zinaida Gippius, and the Symbolist Sublimation of Sex* (Madison: University of Wisconsin Press, 2008).

11. For a rich and varied account of the theatrical and masquerading impulses of the Silver Age, see Colleen McQuillen, *The Modernist Masquerade:*

Stylizing Life, Literature, and Costumes in Russia (Madison: University of Wisconsin Press, 2013). McQuillen argues that the possibility of wearing masks and playing roles allowed participants to navigate the fluidity of social and personal identity in turn-of-the-century Russia.

12. Irina Paperno, "Introduction," in Paperno and Grossman, eds., *Creating Life*, 1–11; here, 11.

13. On the revival of the tradition of eldership in Russia, in connection with Russia's monastic revival of the nineteenth century, see Scott Kenworthy, *The Heart of Russia: Trinity-Sergius, Monasticism, and Society after 1825* (New York: Oxford University Press, 2010). On the impact of these connected revivals on Russian letters, see Margaret Ziolkowski, *Hagiography and Modern Russian Literature* (Princeton, N.J.: Princeton University Press, 1988).

14. I draw here on Camilla Gray's account of the Abramtsevo circle in "1860's-90's," in *The Russian Experiment in Art, 1863–1922* (London: Thames and Hudson, 1971), 9–36.

15. Aleksandr Benua, ed., "Patriarshaia riznitsa v Moskve: 53 snimka s predmetov (tserkovnye oblacheniia i utvar'), khraniashchikhsia v riznitse," *Mir iskusstva* 12 (1904): 203–36.

16. An excellent recent edited volume, *Alter Icons*, not only addresses the rediscovery of the icon in Russia but also its significance for modernist and modern Russia. See Jefferson J. A. Gatrall and Douglas Greenfield, *Alter Icons: The Russian Icon and Modernity* (University Park: Pennsylvania State University Press, 2010). Gatrall, for one, describes the 1913 icon exhibition and its impact ("Introduction," 1–25; here, 4–5).

17. N. Punin, "Vystavka drevne-russkogo iskusstva (ustroennaia Moskovskim Arkheologicheskim Institutom imeni Imp. Nikolaia II)," *Apollon* 5 (1913): 38. Cited in Gatrall, "Introduction," *Alter Icons*, 5.

18. See Judith Kalb's study, *Russia's Rome: Imperial Visions, Messianic Dreams, 1890–1940* (Madison: University of Wisconsin Press, 2008).

19. The Meetings restarted a few years later, but this time without the participation of the clergy.

20. See Dmitrii Merezhkovskii, *Polnoe sobranie sochinenii Dmitriia Sergeevicha Merezhkovskogo* (Moscow: Tipographiia I. D. Sytina, 1914), 27:175–276.

21. Merezhkovskii, *PSS*, 27:182.

22. Kristiane Burchardi has done the most significant work so far on the Religious-Philosophical Meetings, in *Die Moskauer "Religiös-philosophische Vladimir-Solov'ev Gesellschaft" (1905–1918)* (Wiesbaden: Harrassowitz, 1998). Jutta Scherrer's older work on this group is also a key study (*Die Petersburger religiös-philosophischen Vereinigungen: die Entwicklung d. religiösen Selbstverständnisses ihrer Intelligencija-Mitglieder (1901–1917)* [Wiesbaden: Harrassowitz, 1973]). Avril Pyman has also published a good, if brief, introduction to the meetings. See Avril Pyman, "The Church and the Intelligentsia with Spe-

cial Reference to the Religious-Philosophical Meetings in St. Petersburg, 1901–1903," in Roger Bartlett, ed., *Russian Thought and Society, 1800–1917: Essays in Honor of Eugene Lampert* (Keele: University of Keele, 1984). Olga Matich devotes a chapter in *Erotic Utopia* to the meetings, although in contrast to the present study, she focuses on discussion in later meetings on sex, marriage, Orthodoxy, and decadence ("Religious-Philosophical Meetings: Celibacy contra Marriage," *Erotic Utopia*, 212–35). Contemporaries to the meetings subsequently wrote about them in memoirs and retrospective works; the most famous of these accounts are Nikolai Berdiaev's *The Russian Idea* (Boston: Beacon, 1962) and Nikolai Zernov's *The Russian Religious Renaissance of the Twentieth Century* (New York: Harper and Row, 1963). Georges Florovsky has also written on this movement from a more theological perspective (*Ways of Russian Theology: Part Two* [Vaduz: Büchervertriebsanstalt, 1987]). Often, though, these gatherings receive only brief mentions as an important, if passing, factor in Silver Age culture.

23. See in particular Andrei Bely, *Nachalo veka* (Moscow: Khudozhestvennaia literatura, 1990).

24. These first expressions are taken from V. A. Ternavtsev's initial usage in his opening talk, "Russkaia tserkov' pred velikoiu zadachei" ("The Great Task Facing the Russian Church"), published, along with the transcriptions of the first few meetings of the Society, in the first issue of *Novyi put'* (January 1903): 8. Ternavtsev was a member of the intelligentsia and a teacher at the theological academy who served as a key link between intelligentsia and clergy. The latter reference comes from remarks on the same meeting, written by N. O. Romanov, published in this issue of *Novyi put'* (p. 49).

This thought was echoed by numerous of Ternavtsev's contemporaries, such as Viacheslav Ivanov in his 1909 essay "On the Russian Idea" ("O russkoi idee"), in which Ivanov writes that "the only force ordering the chaos of [Russia's] spiritual body is the free and wholesale acceptance of Christ, as the single all-defining source of our spiritual and outer life" (in M. A. Maslin, ed., *Russkaia ideia* [Moscow: Respublika, 1992], 229.) Ivanov goes on to specify that Russia's religious tradition in particular—that is, Orthodox Christianity, with its emphasis on the mystery of Easter and the resurrection—distinguishes her as the place where modernity can most surely experience spiritual rebirth.

25. Avril Pyman writes in particular on this lack of common terminology. See Pyman, "The Church and the Intelligentsia."

26. Robert Slesinski reflects on the legacy of modern Eastern Orthodox theology in the Christian Church more broadly, suggesting that its emphasis on beauty relates to one of the most pressing current religious questions raised by modernity. For Slesinski the Orthodox embrace of beauty relates to its affirmation of "the possibility of communion between the divine and the human in this world," an issue particularly vexed in a late modern setting. His discussion of beauty and the interrelationship of the divine and human parallels in basic

ways Russian modernism's sophiological impulse (Robert Slesinski, "Postmodernity and the Resources of the Christian East," in *Essays in Diakonia: Eastern Catholic Theological Reflections* (New York: Peter Lang, 1998), 37–51; here, 50.

27. Ternavtsev, "Russkaia tserkov' pred velikoiu zadachei," 10.

28. Ibid., 14.

29. Cited in Pyman, "The Church and the Intelligentsia," 202.

30. Solovyov takes the phrase from Dostoevsky's *The Idiot* (F. M. Dostoevskii, *Polnoe sobranie sochenenii v tridsati tomakh* [Leningrad: Nauka, 1973], 8:317).

31. "Vse khromaem, vsiakii bolee ili menee." This phrase is taken from the central "chapter 10" in the second half of Dostoevsky's *Notes from Underground* (Dostoevskii, *PSS*, 6:135).

32. For a key study on the concern Solovyov and Dostoevsky shared with establishing an "integral vision" of the world, see Marina Kostalevsky, *Dostoevsky and Soloviev: The Art of Integral Vision* (New Haven, Conn.: Yale University Press, 1997).

33. Here I use Boris Jakim's translation, from Vladimir Solovyov, *The Crisis of Western Philosophy (Against the Positivists)*, trans. and ed. Boris Jakim (Hudson, N.Y.: Lindisfarne, 1996), 148.

34. For the translation I have used, see Solovyov, *The Crisis of Western Philosophy*, 93, 13, 112.

35. See Richard Gustafson, "Soloviev's Doctrine of Salvation," in *Russian Religious Thought*, ed. Judith Kornblatt and Richard Gustafson (Madison: University of Wisconsin Press, 1996), 31–48. For a particularly focused discussion by Solovyov of this dialectic and the projected eventual synthesis between Western achievements and Eastern tradition, see the eleventh and twelfth lectures in *Chteniia o bogochelovechestve* (*SSVSS* 3:3–185), and also *Krizis zapadnoi filosofii (protiv pozitivistov)* (*SSVSS* 1:27–170).

36. Gustafson, "Soloviev's Doctrine of Salvation."

37. Judith Deutsch Kornblatt, *Divine Sophia: The Wisdom Writings of Vladimir Solovyov* (Ithaca, N.Y.: Cornell University Press, 2009), 101–8, especially 104.

38. Gustafson, "Soloviev's Doctrine of Salvation," 33.

39. Solovyov refers directly to *theosis* in Lecture 10 (*SSVSS* 3:145), but aspects of this tradition appear throughout the lectures. For example, in the seventh lecture from *Chteniia o bogochelovechestve* Solovyov draws directly on the language of both *theosis* and the Transfiguration (we consider this language in greater detail in the readings of Blok's poetry) when he writes, "distinct rays and glimmers of the divine world must penetrate [*otdel'nye luchi i otbleski bozhestvennogo mira dolzhny pronikat'*] our reality [*deistvitel'nost'*] and bring to bear all the ideal content, all the beauty and truth that we find in it" (*SSVSS* 3:118). Solovyov then goes on to quote about thirty lines from a poem of A. K. Tolstoy's de-

scribing a spiritual transformation with a brief but patent reference to Transfiguration tradition. Consider the lines, "And I came down from the hill's height, / Penetrated by its rays" (*I s gornei vysi ia soshel, / Proniknut ves' ee luchami*).

40. Merezhkovskii, "O prichinakh upadka," 273.

41. Kornblatt has discussed Solovyov's very conscious project of tempering philosophical discourse with more literary and specifically poetic modes. See Judith Deutsch Kornblatt, "The Truth of the Word: Solovyov's 'Three Conversations' Speaks on Tolstoy's *Resurrection*," *Slavic and East European Journal* 45, no. 2 (2001): 301–21.

42. Pavel Florensky, *Stolp i utverzhdenie istiny: Opyt pravoslavnoi teoditsei v dvenadtsati pis'makh* (1914; Moscow: Lepta, 2002).

43. Viacheslav Ivanov, "Two Elements in Contemporary Symbolism," in *Selected Essays*, trans. Robert Bird, ed. Michael Wachtel (Evanston, Ill.: Northwestern University Press, 2003), 13–35; here, 33. In the original, Viacheslav Ivanov, "Dve stikhii v sovremennom simbolizme," in *Rodnoe i vselenskoe* (Moscow: Izdatel'stvo 'Respublika,' 1994), 143–69; here, 160.

44. Judith Kornblatt discusses Solovyov's own embrace of matter as a nuanced response to positivism. She writes, "We might see Solovyov's articulation of Divine Wisdom as a reaction against the prevailing positivist attitudes of the day. Most crucially, however, we need to understand it not as a mere negation but rather as an *incorporation* of materialism, as the union of Solovyov's intangible intuition of ideal reality and the 'facts' of the modern world. It is this role of mediation that most marks Sophia" (Kornblatt, *Divine Sophia*, 27).

45. Paul Valliere, "Sophiology as the Dialogue of Orthodoxy with Modern Civilization," in Kornblatt and Gustafson, eds., *Russian Religious Thought*, 176–92; here, 176.

46. Oliver Smith, *Vladimir Soloviev and the Spiritualization of Matter* (Boston: Academic Studies, 2011), 9.

47. This point is a guiding argument in Kornblatt's book on Solovyov's Sophia writings. See Judith Deutsch Kornblatt, *Divine Sophia: The Wisdom Writings of Vladimir Solovyov*.

48. This is not to say that Solovyov by any means fully rejected the rational and even the positivistic, as Kornblatt points out (Kornblatt, *Divine Sophia*, 27); I describe here, rather, a tendency or corrective.

49. Valery Briusov, "F. I. Tiutchev: Smysl ego tvorchestva," in *Sobranie sochinenii* (Moscow: 1973), 6:203. Cited in Joan Delaney Grossman, "Alternate Beliefs: Spiritualism and Pantheism among the Early Modernists," in Boris Gasparov et al., eds., *Christianity and the Eastern Slavs*, vol. 3, *Russian Literature in Modern Times* (Berkeley: University of California Press, 1995), 113–33.

50. Charles Baudelaire, *Selected Poems from Les Fleurs du mal: A Bilingual Edition* (Chicago: University of Chicago Press, 1998), 90.

51. Stéphane Mallarmé, "Les Fleurs," in *Collected Poems and Other Verse*,

trans. E. H. Blackmore and A. M. Blackmore (New York: Oxford University Press, 2006). Translation here is my own.

52. For an extended discussion of the influence of English letters on Russian modernism, see Rachel Polonsky's *English Literature and the Russian Aesthetic Renaissance* (Cambridge, Eng.: Cambridge University Press, 2006).

53. Carsten Strathausen, *The Look of Things: Poetry and Vision around 1900* (Chapel Hill: University of North Carolina Press, 2003), 30.

54. Ibid., 241.

55. Mallarmé, *Collected Poems and Other Verse*, 12.

56. Numerous scholars discuss concepts and models of "alternative modernities" in the eponymous volume (Dilip Parameshwar Gaonkar, ed., *Alternative Modernities* [Durham, N.C.: Duke University Press, 2001]). In his introduction to *Alter Icons*, Jefferson Gatrall also discusses the usefulness of postcolonial concepts of "counter," "alternative," or "multiple" modernities for the Russian modernist context (3).

57. Fyodor Tiutchev, "Eti bednye selen'ia . . . ," in *Polnoe sobranie sochinenii* (Moscow: Tovarishchestvo A. F. Marks, 1913), 126.

58. See especially Khomiakov's "Some Remarks by an Orthodox Christian Concerning the Western Communions, on the Occasion of a Letter Published by the Archbishop of Paris," in *On Spiritual Unity: A Slavophile Reader*, ed. Boris Jakim and Robert Bird (Hudson, N.Y.: Lindisfarne Books, 1998), 63–116.

59. Merezhkovsky coined this term in his paper "Gogol and Fr. Matvei" ("Gogol' i o. Matveii"), given at the tenth meeting of the Society, and first published serially as "The Fate of Gogol" ("Sud'ba Gogol'ia") in the first three issues of *A New Way*: Dmitrii Merezhkovskii, "Sud'ba Gogol'ia: Chast' I: Tvorchestvo," *Novyi put'* 1 (1903): 37–81; "Sud'ba Gogol'ia: Chast' II: Zhizn' i religiia," *Novyi put'* 2 (1903): 1–41; and "Sud'ba Gogol'ia: Chast' II: Zhizn' i religiia," *Novyi put'* 3 (1903): 123–61. Prefacing his paper, Merezhkovsky delineates the divide he perceives between the Church's ideal and the intelligentsia's ideal. In the transcription of the general discussion in the first meeting, Merezhkovsky remarks,

> The earth has its own ideal, just as "Flesh" has an independent significance, not subordinated to its relationship to Spirit. It is absolutely essential to define the relation of these two ideals; will the content of the heavenly ideal be identical with the content of the earthly ideal? I think there might be a great differentiation here. To clarify that is the task for our subsequent meetings. ("Zapiski religiozno-filosofksikh sobranii," *Novyi put'* 1 [1903]: 32)

60. For two rather different accounts—in form and method, above all—compare Nikolai Zernov's *The Russian Religious Renaissance of the Twentieth Century* (London: Darton, Longman and Todd, 1963) with Bernice Glatzer Rosenthal's entry, "Russian Religious-Philosophical Renaissance," in the *Routledge Encyclopedia of Philosophy*, ed. Edward Craig (New York: 1998), 422–28.

61. Merezhkovsky was particularly important, as David Bethea shows, in rearticulating Joachim of Fiore's notion of the three stages of history, in which the final stage would be the stage of the "Holy Spirit," who would bring the Church universal together and bring the world into a final state of "union," pictured in the apocalyptic marriage of the Bride and the Lamb. Bethea describes Merezhkovsky's post-Nietzschean critique of historic Christianity. His efforts were directed toward the inauguration of a neo-Joachimist "Third Testament," a future time when all the dualities (pagan-Christian, Dionysus-Apollo, East-West, male-female, etc.) that had produced tension and conflict in the past would be unified. See David Bethea, *The Shape of Apocalypse in Modern Russian Fiction* (Princeton, N.J.: 1989), 109n.

In her article on the "Russian Religious-Philosophical Renaissance," Bernice Rosenthal describes this aspect of Merezhkovsky's thought and the vision he had for Russian society in particular, writing,

> Merezhkovskii taught that "historical Christianity" (Christianity as taught by the churches) was becoming obsolete; he expected a New Revelation, a Third Testament, to be granted by Christ himself, whose Second Coming was imminent. At that point, the joyousness of Jesus' Resurrection will prevail over the suffering of Golgotha and the hitherto proscribed pagan values of sensuality, worldly beauty, and self-affirmation will be sanctified. Russians were to prepare for His Advent by studying all religions and by joining Merezhkovskii in his religious quest. At first Merezhkovskii envisaged a new church developing out of the Orthodox Church. Later on, he advocated a complete break with it. (Rosenthal, "Russian Religious-Philosophical Renaissance," 424)

See Solovyov's "Lecture Ten" and "Lectures Eleven and Twelve" for a related formulation of the three-stage historical process (*SSVSS* 3:143–62). Here he describes the divine beginnings of the world, the fall of the world soul from unity into freedom and chaos, and the return of the world soul, through free activity, into unity with the divine, universal idea.

62. Danièle Hervieu-Léger, *Religion as a Chain of Memory* (New Brunswick, N.J.: Rutgers University Press, 2000), 3.

63. Ibid., 168.

64. Valliere makes some account of the divide between the "Neopatristic" and "Russian" schools of Orthodox theology in *Modern Russian Theology, Bukharev, Soloviev, Bulgakov: Orthodox Theology in a New Key* (Grand Rapids, Mich.: Wm. B. Eerdmans, 2000), 14.

65. Hervieu-Léger's study corresponds, for instance, to Thomas Greene's studies of poetry and magic—studies based most firmly on Western European literary tradition (*Poetry, Signs, and Magic* [Newark, N.J.: University of Delaware Press, 2005]). In this work Greene compares conjunctive and disjunctive concepts of language and presents poetry as nostalgia for magic's conjunctive as-

sumptions. For Greene poetry "does indeed involve the merging of word and thing, signifier and signified"; but this merging takes place on the plane of individual projection (19, 28). Accurate or not, such a view lies far afield from the primarily epiphanic conception of poetry being developed by the Russian modernists such as Bely, Ivanov, and others.

66. In *The Word Made Self: Russian Writings on Language, 1860–1930* (Ithaca, N.Y.: Cornell University Press, 2005), Thomas Seifrid sheds light on, among other things, the "conjunctive" tendency within Russian language philosophy of the late nineteenth and early twentieth centuries. For the thinkers, theologians, linguists, and poets he traces—from Hesychasm to symbolism to *imiaslavie*—"language . . . is continuous with essence." Literary studies have also addressed this phenomenon, most notably Stephen Hutchings's *Russian Modernism: The Transfiguration of the Everyday* (New York: Cambridge University Press, 1997). In this work Hutchings shows convincingly that prose narrative of this period manifests a dialogue between Western representational aesthetics and an "Orthodox emphasis on iconic embodiment" (i). Ironically, Hutchings swiftly abandons poetry to the clutches of Western critical approaches, relying on a single collection of essays on the Russian debt to European modernism (Peter Barta and Ulrich Goebel, *The European Foundations of Russian Modernism* [Lewiston, N.Y.: Edwin Mellen, 1991]). As the present study shows, however, Western literary tradition does not have the final word because, inevitably, Russian poets took that word and made it their own, changing it fundamentally. Sarah Pratt's work on Zabolotsky and Oberiu, meanwhile, offers an astute example of criticism demonstrating how one strand of the Russian poetic tradition envisions art as revealing a given essence. See Sarah Pratt, *Nikolai Zabolotsky: Enigma and Cultural Paradigm* (Evanston, Ill.: Northwestern University Press, 2000). In particular, she connects the emphasis in Zabolotsky and within Oberiu on the "thingness of things," the "objectivity of the object," with the icon's "interrelation of material and spiritual" (161, 139, 133).

67. Richard Gustafson describes this emphasis on *theosis* across differing strains of Orthodoxy, and how Solovyov innovated his own version of it, in "Soloviev's Doctrine of Salvation," 31–48. Speaking more generally to the Eastern Orthodox tradition, Sergey Horujy describes *theosis* as "the goal (*telos*) of [the] spiritual process, understood in Orthodoxy as the complete unity of the practitioner's energies with the Divine energies" (in "Slavophiles, Westernizers, and the Birth of Russian Philosophical Humanism," trans. Patrick Lally Michelson, in *A History of Russian Philosophy, 1830–1930: Faith, Reason, and the Defense of Human Dignity*, ed. G. M. Hamburg and Randall A. Poole [New York: Cambridge University Press, 2010], 27–51; here, 28).

68. Irene Masing-Delic, *Abolishing Death: A Salvation Myth of Russian Twentieth-Century Literature* (Stanford, Calif.: Stanford University Press, 1992).

69. Nicolas Zernov, *The Russian Religious Renaissance of the Twentieth Century* (London: Darton, Longman and Todd, 1963), 285.

70. This is the sense in which Alexander Schmemann—father of modern liturgical theology—speaks of the liturgy: as the whole body of the Church's worship as its ongoing "public act," a phrase referring to the Greek *litourgos*, meaning "common action" or "public action." See Alexander Schmemann, *Introduction to Liturgical Theology*, trans. Asheleigh E. Moorhouse (Crestwood, N.Y.: St. Vladimir's Seminary, 1986). This understanding of the term "liturgy" is fundamental to his whole work, but for a specific discussion along these lines, see p. 14. Use of the term "liturgy," meaning the whole cycle of services, is common in Western Christian tradition, too. See, for instance, Gregory Dix's seminal work, *The Shape of the Liturgy* (London: Dacre, 1945).

71. This distinction is fundamental to Matich's monograph, *Erotic Utopia: The Decadent Imagination in Russia's Fin de Siècle.*

72. Richard Taruskin, *Stravinsky and the Russian Traditions: A Biography of the Works*, vol. 2, *A Biography of the Works through Mavra* (New York: Oxford University Press, 1996), 1379.

73. See Simon Morrison, *Russian Opera and the Symbolist Movement* (Berkeley: University of California Press, 2002), 195. Morrison's study of Russian composers (Chaikovsky, Rimsky-Korsakov, Scriabin, and Prokofiev) addresses at numerous points the religious ferment of the age.

74. For one account of this unrealized project, see Andrew Spira, *The Avant-Garde Icon: Russian Avant-Garde Art and the Icon Painting Tradition* (Burlington, Vt.: Lund Humphries, 2008), 133–38.

75. I am drawing my discussion of this phenomenon from two works: Spira, *The Avant-Garde Icon: Russian Avant-Garde and the Icon Painting Tradition*; and Camilla Gray, *The Russian Experiment in Art, 1863–1922* (London: Thames and Hudson, 1971).

76. Spira, *The Avant-Garde Icon*; quote from p. 9. Alexei Kurbanovsky, "Malevich's Mystic Signs: From Iconoclasm to New Theology," in *Sacred Stories: Religion and Spirituality in Modern Russia*, ed. Mark D. Steinberg and Heather J. Coleman (Bloomington: Indiana University Press, 2007), 358–76.

77. Spira, *The Avant-Garde Icon*, 78.

78. Gray, *The Russian Experiment in Art*, 166, 168; Spira, *The Avant-Garde Icon*, especially 71–74.

79. See, for instance, Robert Bird, *The Russian Prospero: The Creative Universe of Viacheslav Ivanov* (Madison: University of Wisconsin Press, 2006).

80. See Olga Matich, *Paradox in the Religious Poetry of Zinaida Gippius* (Munich: Wilhelm Fink Verlag, 1972); and Bernice Glatzer Rosenthal, *Dmitri Sergeevich Merezhkovsky and the Silver Age: The Development of a Revolutionary Mentality* (The Hague: Martinus Nijhoff, 1975).

81. See Michael Makin, *Nikolai Klyuev: Time and Text, Place and Poet* (Evanston, Ill.: Northwestern University Press, 2009).

82. Gregory Freidin, *A Coat of Many Colors: Osip Mandelstam and His Mythologies of Self-Presentation* (Berkeley: University of California Press, 1987).

83. See Catherine Ciepiela's book-length study *The Same Solitude: Boris Pasternak and Marina Tsvetaeva* (Ithaca, N.Y.: Cornell University Press, 2006).

84. Blok's engagement with Solovyov's aesthetics is well known. Avril Pyman points out Blok's interest in Plato and that, indeed, in 1900 Blok read Plato's Socratic dialogues in Solovyov's translation (*APLB*, 1:68).

85. The remark lies at the center of Kuzmin's biography by John Malmstad and Nikolay Bogomolov (*MBMK*, 10).

86. Ol'ga Sedakova, *Slovar' trudnykh slov iz bogosluzheniia: Tserkovnoslaviano-russkie paronimy* (Moscow: Greko-latinskii kabinet IU. A. Shichalina, 2008).

87. Schmemann, *Introduction to Liturgical Theology*.

88. Aleksei Khomiakov, "Some Remarks by an Orthodox Christian Concerning the Western Communions," 110.

89. Aleksei Khomiakov, *Stikhotvoreniia i dramy* (Leningrad: Sovetskii pisatel', 1969), 136.

90. See, for example, I. Iur'eva, *Pushkin i khristianstvo* (Moscow: Muravei, 1998); V. A. Kotel'nikov, ed., *Dukhovnyi truzhenik: A. S. Pushkin v kontekste russkoi kul'tury* (St. Petersburg: Nauka, 1999); and T. G. Mal'chukova, *Antichnye i khristianskie traditsii v poezii A. S. Pushkina* (Petrozavodsk: Izd-vo Petrozavodskogo universiteta, 1997). Numerous articles explore this topic. See, for instance, Pamela Davidson, "The Moral Dimension of the Prophetic Ideal: Pushkin and His Readers," *Slavic Review* 61, no. 3 (2002): 490–518.

91. In her work on Russian poetry and Orthodoxy, for instance, Tatiana Koshchemchuk cites the work of Aleksei K. Tolstoy numerous times, so that he becomes for her in certain respects a paradigmatic example of the Orthodox poet (Koshchemchuk, *Russkaia poeziia v kontekste pravoslavnoi kul'tury* [St. Petersburg: Nauka, 2006]). See Sarah Pratt's *Russian Metaphysical Romanticism: The Poetry of Tiutchev and Boratynskii* (Stanford, Calif.: Stanford University Press, 1984) for links in Tiutchev's poetry to Orthodoxy.

92. Examples of this scholarship include Richard Gustafson, *Leo Tolstoy, Resident and Stranger: A Study in Fiction and Theology* (Princeton, N.J.: Princeton University Press, 1986); Inessa Medzhibovskaya, *Tolstoy and the Religious Culture of His Time: A Biography of a Long Conversion, 1845–1887* (Lanham, Md.: Lexington Books, 2008); Konstantin Mochulsky, *Dostoevsky: His Life and Work* (Princeton, N.J.: Princeton University Press, 1973); Maria Nemcova Banerjee, *Dostoevsky: The Scandal of Reason* (Great Barrington: Lindis-

farne Books, 2006); George Pattison and Diane Thompson, eds., *Dostoevsky and the Christian Tradition* (Cambridge, Eng.: Cambridge University Press, 2001); Steven Cassedy, *Dostoevsky's Religion* (Stanford, Calif.: Stanford University Press, 2005); Leonard Stanton, *Interpreting Nikolai Gogol within Russian Orthodoxy: A Neglected Influence on the First Great Russian Novelist* (Lewiston, N.Y.: Edwin Mellen, 2006); James Muckle, *Nikolai Leskov and the "Spirit of Protestantism"* (Birmingham, Eng., 1978); and Irmhild Christina Sperrie, *The Organic Worldview of Nikolai Leskov* (Evanston, Ill.: Northwestern University Press, 2002).

93. See, for instance, Frank's chapter "A Reading of *Crime and Punishment*," in *Dostoevsky: The Miraculous Years, 1865–1871* (Princeton, N.J.: Princeton University Press, 1997), 96–147.

94. Koshchemchuk, *Russkaia poeziia v kontekste pravoslavnoi kul'tury.*

95. Marcus Levitt, "The Rapprochement between 'Secular' and 'Religious' in Mid to Late Eighteenth-Century Russian Culture," in *Early Modern Russian Letters: Texts and Contexts* (Boston: Academic Studies, 2009), 269–93, here 270; and Levitt, "The Ode as Revelation: On the Orthodox Theological Context of Lomonosov's Odes," in *Early Modern Russian Letters*, 320–38, here 322.

96. For one discussion of the ways eighteenth-century Russian poets adapted Psalms, as well as the ways they innovated in distinct ways from Western European traditions, see Viktor Zhivov, "Tserkovnoslavianskaia literaturnaia traditsiia v russkoi literature XVIII v. i retseptsiia spora 'drevnykh' i 'novyikh,'" in *Istoriia kul'tury i poetika*, ed. L. A. Safronova et al. (Moscow: Nauka, 1994), 62–82. In this article, Zhivov shows, in part, how the Russian odic tradition maintained more continuity with a traditional, medieval vision of religious art than did its European counterparts.

97. Harsha Ram, *The Imperial Sublime: A Russian Poetics of Empire* (Madison: University of Wisconsin Press, 2003).

98. G. R. Derzhavin, *Stikhotvoreniia* (Leningrad: Sovetskii Pisatel', 1957), 92.

99. For the Masonic aspects of this poem, see O. M. Goncharova, "*Vozvrashchenie k sebe* kak natsional'no-religioznoe vozrozhdenie v russkoi masonskoi mistike XVIII veka," in *Vlast' traditsii i "Novaia Rossiia" v literaturnom soznanii vtoroi poloviny XVIII veka* (St. Petersburg: Izdatel'stvo Khristianskogo Gumanitarnogo Instituta, 2004), 52–95.

100. Ruth Coates, "Religious Writing in Post-Petrine Russia," in Neil Cornwell, ed., *The Routledge Companion to Russian Literature* (London: Routledge, 2001), 49–63.

101. Valliere, *Modern Russian Theology*, 2, 7.

102. This phrase comes from Akhmatova's poem about the Stray Dog cabaret, "Vse my brazhniki zdes', bludnitsy . . ." (Anna Akhmatova, *Sochinenii v dvukh tomakh* [Moscow: Pravda, 1990]).

103. Alexander Schmemann, *Introduction to Liturgical Theology* (Portland,

Ore.: American Orthodox, 1966), 12. Schmemann here also quotes briefly from L. Bouyer, *Le Mystère Pascal* (Paris: Les Editions de Cerf, 1947), 9.

104. Patrick Lally Michelson and Judith Deutsch Kornblatt, *Thinking Orthodox in Modern Russia: Culture, History, Context* (Madison: University of Wisconsin Press, 2014), 4.

105. Mark D. Steinberg and Heather J. Coleman, eds., *Sacred Stories: Religion and Spirituality in Modern Russia* (Bloomington: Indiana University Press, 2007); quote from "Introduction," 10.

106. Vera Shevzov, *Russian Orthodoxy on the Eve of Revolution* (New York: Oxford University Press, 2003); Nadieszda Kizenko, *A Prodigal Saint: Father John of Kronstadt and the Russian People* (University Park: Penn State University Press, 2000); Scott Kenworthy, *The Heart of Russia: Trinity-Sergius Monasticism and Society after 1825* (New York: Oxford University Press, 2010).

107. Chris Chulos, *Converging Worlds: Religion and Community in Peasant Russia, 1861–1917* (De Kalb: Northern Illinois University Press, 2003). Christine Worobec, *Possessed: Women, Witches and Demons in Imperial Russia* (De Kalb: Northern Illinois University Press, 2001).

108. Roy Robson, *Old Believers in Modern Russia* (De Kalb: Northern Illinois University Press, 1995); Heather Coleman, *Russian Baptists and Spiritual Revolution, 1905–1929* (Bloomington: Indiana University Press, 2005); Leonid Heretz, *Russia on the Eve of Modernity: Popular Religion and Traditional Culture under the Last Tsars* (Cambridge, Eng.: Cambridge University Press, 2008).

109. Matich, *Erotic Utopia*; Presto, *Beyond the Flesh*.

110. Matich, *Paradox in the Religious Poetry of Zinaida Gippius*; and Rosenthal, *Dmitri Sergeevich Merezhkovsky and the Silver Age*.

111. Olga Matich reads the poetry of Zinaida Gippius through the lens of Gippius's exploratory and unorthodox religious faith (Gippius, *Paradox in the Religious Poetry of Zinaida Gippius* [Munich: Wilhelm Fink Verlag, 1972]). Maria Carlson's study of theosophy in the Silver Age illuminates influential currents of this particular religious movement especially in Russia's elite cultural spheres (*"No Religion Higher than Truth": A History of the Theosophical Movement in Russia, 1875–1922* [Princeton, N.J.: Princeton University Press, 1993]). Gregory Freidin's monograph on Osip Mandelstam successfully illuminates the poet's relation of religion (if not Orthodoxy itself) to culture (*A Coat of Many Colors: Osip Mandelstam and His Mythologies of Self-Presentation*). Gabriella Safran's *Rewriting the Jew: Assimilation Narratives in the Russian Empire* (Stanford, Calif.: Stanford University Press, 2002) explores the complex relations of narrative and religious assimilation in Russia. Russian religious sects are the subject of Laura Engelstein's *Castration and the Heavenly Kingdom: A Russian Folktale* (Ithaca, N.Y.: Cornell University Press, 1999); and Aleksandr Etkind's *Khlyst: Sekty, literatura i revoliutsiia* (Moscow: Novoe Literaturnoe Obozrenie, 1998). Nikolai Bogomolov explores occultism in *Russkaia literatura nachala XX veka*

i okkul'tizm: Issledovaniia i materialy (Moscow: Novoe literaturnoe obozrenie, 1999); and this is also the subject of Bernice Glatzer Rosenthal's edited volume, *The Occult in Russian and Soviet Culture* (Ithaca, N.Y.: Cornell University Press, 1997).

112. Steven Cassedy, *Flight from Eden: The Origins of Modern Literary Criticism and Theory* (Berkeley: University of California Press, 1990), 105.

113. Steven Cassedy, "Pavel Florenskij's Philosophy of Language: Its Contextuality and Its Context," *Slavic and East European Journal* 35, no. 4 (1991): 537–52; Thomas Seifrid, *The Word Made Self: Russian Writings on Language, 1860–1930*; Irina Paperno, "On the Nature of the Word: Theological Sources of Mandel'stam's Dialogue with the Symbolists," in Boris Gasparov et al., eds., *Christianity and the Eastern Slavs*, vol. 2, *Russian Culture in Modern Times* (Berkeley: University of California Press, 1994), 287–310.

114. Sarah Pratt, *Nikolai Zabolotsky: Enigma and Cultural Paradigm*; Robert Bird, *The Russian Prospero: The Creative Universe of Viacheslav Ivanov* (Madison: University of Wisconsin Press, 2006).

115. Two excellent volumes explore the place of Christianity and other religious movements in modern Russian culture: Robert P. Hughes and Irina Paperno, eds., *Christianity and the Eastern Slavs*, vol. 2, *Russian Culture in Modern Times* (Berkeley: University of California Press, 1994); and Boris Gasparov, Robert P. Hughes, Irina Paperno, and Olga Raevsky-Hughes, eds., *Christianity and the Eastern Slavs*, vol. 3, *Russian Culture in Modern Times* (Berkeley: University of California Press, 1995).

116. Per Arne Bodin, *Eternity and Time: Studies in Russian Literature and the Orthodox Tradition* (Stockholm: Almqvist & Wiksell International, 2007).

117. Several essays addressing these issues can be found in Meerson's 2009 *Personalizm kak poetika: Literaturnyi mir glazami ego obitatelei* (St. Petersburg: Izdatel'stvo 'Pushkinskii Dom'). Notably, Meerson's first chapter in this book demonstrates a nuanced methodology for reading liturgy as (a very special kind of) literature (Meerson, "Liturgicheskoe tsitirovanie v kontekste sub"ektnoi organizatsii poetiki i liricheskoi poezii v chastnosti," *Personalizm kak poetika*, 42–77.)

118. Sedakova, *Slovar' trudnykh slov iz bogosluzheniia: Tserkovnoslaviano-russkie paronim.*

119. V. A. Kotel'nikov, ed., *Khristianstvo i russkaia literatura*, vols. 1–4 (St. Petersburg: Nauka, 1994–2002); V. A. Kotel'nikov, ed., *Dukhovnyi truzhenik: A. S. Pushkin v kontekste russkoi kul'tury* (St. Petersburg: Nauka, 1999); V. N. Zakharov, *Evangel'skii tekst v russkoi literature XVIII–XX vekov: Tsitata, reministsentsiia, motiv, siuzhet, zhanr*, vols. 1–5 (Petrozavodsk: Izdatel'stvo Petrozavodskogo universiteta, 1994–2008); I. A. Esaulov, *Kategoriia sobornosti v russkoi literature* (Petrozavodsk: Izdatel'stvo Petrozavodskogo universiteta, 1995); M. M. Dunaev, *Vera v gornile somnenii: Pravoslavie i russkaia literatura v XVII–XX vv.* (Moscow: Izdatel'skii sovet russkoi pravoslavnoi tserkvi, 2002); M. M. Dunaev,

Pravoslavie i russkaia literatura, 6 vols. (Moscow: 2001–2004). These latter volumes by Dunaev are comprised of lectures the author gave at the Moscow Religious Academy (Dukhovnaia akademiia).

120. M. M. Dunaev's writing proceeds centrally from this premise, viewing post-Renaissance literature (thus by extension literary criticism) as fundamentally degenerate. Kotel'nikov, Zakharov, and Esaulov are somewhat more sanguine in their evaluations of modern literature and literary scholarship; nevertheless, they are also engaged in the project to offer a more overtly religious (namely, Orthodox Christian) model of scholarship. See, for example, V. A. Kotel'nikov, "Ot redaktora," in Kotel'nikov, ed., *Khristianstvo i russkaia literatura*, 2:3–8; N. P. Sablina, "'Ne slyshateli zabytlivy slova, no tvortsy'" Ogranichnoe pravoslavie russkoi poezii," in Kotel'nikov, ed., *Khristianstvo i russkaia literatura*, 3:3–25; and V. N. Sakharov, "Russkaia literatura i khristianstvo," in Zakharov, ed., *Evangel'skii tekst v russkoi literature XVIII–XX vekov*, 1:5–10.

121. See, for example, L. A. Il'iuinina, "Krug chteniia A. Bloka 1910-x gg. (Blok i *Dobrotoliubie*)," in Kotel'nikov, *Khristianstvo i russkaia literatura*, 2:334–42; I. K. Gerasimov, "Poema A. K. Tolstogo *Ioann Damaskin*. (K istorii vospriiatiia)," in Kotel'nikov, *Khristianstvo i russkaia literatura*, 2:146–59; N. S. Seregina, "Stikhotvoreniia A. S. Pushkina 1836 goda v svete khristianskoi poezii iz bogosluzhebnoi knigi *Triod'*," in Kotel'nikov, *Khristianstvo i russkaia literatura*, 3:113–27; and also I. I. Iur'eva, *Pushkin i khristianstvo: Sbornik proizvedenii A. S. Pushkina s parallel'nymi tekstami iz Sviashchennogo Pisaniia i kommentariem* (Moscow: Izdatel'skii dom 'Muravei,' 1998). While this latter book-length study still retains a confessional bent (with its focus on establishing Pushkin's status as truly Orthodox), it usefully uncovers networks of references in Pushkin's verse to texts from the Christian and, more specifically, Orthodox tradition.

122. V. A. Kotel'nikov, *Khristianstvo i novaia russkaia literatura XVIII-XX vekov: Bibliograficheskii ukazatel' 1800–2000* (St. Petersburg: Nauka, 2002).

123. See also P. E. Bukharkin, *Pravoslavnaia tserkov' i svetskaia literatura v novoe vremia: Osnovnye aspekty problemy*, in Kotel'nikov, *Khristianstvo i russkaia literatura*, 2:32–60; and for a helpful and focused survey of this tradition, see Diakon V. Pantin, "Svetskaia literatura s pozitsii dukhovnoi kritiki (sovremennye problemy)," in Kotel'nikov, *Khristianstvo i russkaia literatura*, 3:34–58. Pantin defines the notion of the "*dukhovnyi kritik*," writing: "The spiritual critic studies literature with an eye to the question most crucial for the Christian—the question of the soul's salvation; it is in this sense that he analyzes the positive and negative aspects of a given work, a literary tendency, the life and creative path of a writer, his social reputation and the influence he has on the spiritual state of a society" (34).

124. "Religiozno-filosofskaia khronika," *Novyi put'* (March 1903): 253.

125. For a biographical account of this popular and controversial figure, see Nadieszda Kizenko, *A Prodigal Saint: Father John of Kronstadt and the Russian People* (University Park: Penn State University Press, 2000).

126. "Religiozno-filosofskaia khronika: *Novyi put'* i 'put' sataninskii,'" *Novyi put'* (April 1903): 197.

CHAPTER ONE

1. Merezhkovskii, "O prichinakh upadka."

2. Merezhkovskii, "O prichinakh upadka," 211, 215, 263.

3. Ibid., 233, 236, 237.

4. Viacheslav Ivanov, "O krizise gumanizma: K morfologii sovremennoi kul'tury i psikhologii sovremennosti," in *Rodnoe i vselenskoe* (Moscow: Respublika, 1994), 102–12.

5. All translations of this essay are taken from Viacheslav Ivanov, "On the Crisis of Humanism: Toward a Morphology of Modern Culture and the Psychology of Modernity," in *Selected Essays*, trans. Robert Bird (Evanston, Ill.: Northwestern University Press, 2001), 163–75. For the quotes in this sentence, see 165, 170. For the essay in the original, see "O krizise gumanizma: K morfologii sovremennoi kul'tury i psikhologii sovremennosti," in *Rodnoe i vselenskoe*, 102–12; here, 104, 109.

6. Ivanov, "On the Crisis of Humanism," 164; "O krizise gumanizma," 103.

7. V. A. Ternavtsev, "Russkaia tserkov' pred velikoiu zadachei" ["The Great Task Facing the Russian Church"], *Novyi put'* (January 1903): 20.

8. Avril Pyman notes that Blok was reading *Eternal Companions* during his "mystical summer" of 1901 (*APLB*, 1:82).

9. By *Verses on the Beautiful Lady*, I refer to Blok's fifth edition of his early poetry, following *ABPSS*, 1:47–132. One major difference Blok made between his first and later editions was including many more poems from the period.

10. Aleksandr Blok, *Zapisnye knizhki Al. Bloka*, ed. P. N. Medvedev (Leningrad, 1930), 309–10. Quoted in *APLB*, 2:235.

11. Pamela Davidson describes Blok's reading of Solovyov's verse and prose from 1901 and over the next several years (Pamela Davidson, "The Symbolist View of Dante as a Poet of Sophia," in Davidson, *The Poetic Imagination of Vyacheslav Ivanov: A Russian Symbolist's Perception of Dante* [New York: Cambridge University Press, 1989], 74). Zara Mints also notes that Blok "became familiar with the lyric verse, and then with the philosophy of Vl. Solovyov at the turn of the new, twentieth century." She sees echoes of Solovyov in Blok especially in his eschatological vision, his sense of the "high calling of poetry" and "in the image of the beloved," elements expressed in the most essential form in *Verses* (Z. G. Mints, "Lirika 'pervogo toma' (1898–1904)," in *Poetika Aleksandra*

Bloka [St. Petersburg: Iskusstvo-SPB, 1999], 16). For more discussion of Solovyov's influence on Blok and other symbolists, see Samuel Cioran, "The Woman Clothed in the Sun," in Cioran, *The Apocalyptic Symbolism of Andrej Belyj* (The Hague: Mouton, 1973), 92–110.

12. To clarify usage, I capitalize 'Transfiguration' when referring specifically to Church tradition.

13. This union, as I will demonstrate, is in no way fully delineated in its sexual revisions—which tell only a part of the story. For this part of the story, see, in particular, Olga Matich's *Erotic Utopia*. Here Matich describes a model in which the erotic impulse is channeled into the artistic shaping of a new world, a new creation. This new reality is to explode in one cosmic eschatological orgasm, bringing total unity to the world.

14. Zara Mints points to this aspect of Blok's project, not least in his attempt to reveal the noumenal world through the phenomenal world. (Z. G. Mints, "'Poetika daty' i ranniaia lirika Al. Bloka," in *Poetika Aleksandra Bloka*, 390). More recently and at greater length, Tatiana Igosheva has written about this project of Blok's (T. V. Igosheva, "Materialy i soobshcheniia: Religioznoe preobrazhenie v kontekste *Stikhov o prekrasnoi dame* A Bloka," *Izvestiia RAN. Seriia literatury i iazyka*, 63, no. 4 [2004]: 54–62). Quoting figures ranging from Blok himself to Bely, Florensky, Rozanov, and Berdiaev, she persuasively delineates the idea of the "spiritualization of natural flesh" (*odukhotvorenie prirodnoi ploti*), the search for an "eternal substance" (*vechnaia sushchnost'*)—à la Solovyov (54, 55). Yet her readings of *Verses* miss the point, for she nowhere shows such represented transformation, so much as she abstractly connects words and phrases in the poems with concepts from the theoretical discussions she cites.

15. Michael Aksionov Meerson, *The Trinity of Love in Modern Russian Theology: The Love Paradigm and the Retrieval of Western Medieval Love Mysticism in Modern Russian Trinitarian Thought (from Solovyov to Bulgakov)* (Quincy, Ill.: Franciscan, 1998).

16. On the centrality of *theosis* for Orthodoxy, see, for instance, John Meyendorff's discussion of the "theocentric anthropology" of the Byzantine tradition—seen most clearly in the doctrine of *theosis*/deification—as that which "distinguishes Byzantine theology, taken as a whole, from the post-Augustinian and Scholastic West." (John Meyendorff, *Byzantine Theology: Historical Trends and Doctrinal Themes* [New York: Fordham University Press, 1983], 4.) In an article addressing Solovyov's philosophy and legacy, Richard Gustafson also describes this emphasis on *theosis* across differing strains of Orthodoxy, and how Solovyov innovated his own version of it, in "Soloviev's Doctrine of Salvation," in Kornblatt and Gustafson, *Russian Religious Thought*, 31–48. Sergey Horujy argues that this doctrine and the practice of Hesychasm "constitute the core components of Eastern Christian spiritual discourse" ("Slavophiles, Westernizers, and the Birth of Russian Philosophical Humanism," trans. Patrick Lally Michelson,

in Hamburg and Poole, *A History of Russian Philosophy, 1830–1930: Faith, Reason, and the Defense of Human Dignity*, 27–51.)

17. Valerie A. Kivelson and Robert H. Greene, *Orthodox Russia: Belief and Practice under the Tsars* (University Park: Penn State University Press, 2003), 10.

18. Blok introduces this phrase into the earliest entries of his *Notebooks* ("September 26, 1901," *Zapisnye knizhki: 1901–1920*, ed. V. N. Orlov [Moscow: Khudozhestvennaia literatura, 1965], 21–22). See Efim Etkind's article "Dvoemirie Bloka," in *Tam, vnutri: O russkoi poezii XX veka. Ocherki* (St. Petersburg: Maksima, 1997) for a discussion of Blok's continued faith, to the end of his life, in a "Beautiful Essence" ("*Prekrasnaia Sushchnost*'") (59).

19. John Baggley describes the Feast of the Transfiguration as "a focal point for many important strands of Orthodox theology," including the "revelation of the divine nature in the God-man, Christ, as well as an eschatological vision showing the future transformation of man and the world" (John Baggley, "The Timeless Light and Brightness of the Father: The Transfiguration of Our Lord and God and Saviour Jesus Christ (6th August)," in *Festival Icons for the Christian Year* [Crestwood, N.Y.: St. Vladimir's Seminary, 2000], 58–71; here, 59).

20. In "Ty daleka, kak prezhde, tak i nyne . . ." Blok echoes representations of the Mosaic theophany at the "Burning Bush" (*ABPSS*, 1:71). In Blok's poem the poet speaks of the Lady's "*svyiatina*" and "*sviatye mesta*" (synonymous expressions for holy places). Here, as depicted in iconic traditions (as in the formative Transfiguration mosaic in St. Catherine's on Mt. Sinai) Moses takes off his sandals because he has unwittingly approached "holy ground" (Exodus 3:5). In this poem Blok clearly connects the Lady with the theophanic presence not only in his reference to her as a "*luchezarnyi khram*" (radiant temple), but also in the title of the cycle in which the poem was originally published in 1914, "Pod znakom Devy" ("Beneath the Sign of the Maiden") (*ABPSS*, 1:487).

21. The poem Blok quotes from is Solovyov's "Zachem slova? V bezbrezhnosti lazurnoi . . ." (*SSVSS*, 12:19). He quotes the last two lines of the poem, and this image of "*nezdeshnyii svet*" immediately precedes these lines. Blok's reference stands as epigraph to his famous poem "Predchuvstvuiu Tebia. Goda prokhodiat mimo . . ." (*ABSS*, 1:94).

22. For detailed and precise accounts of the Transfiguration tradition in Eastern Christianity, see especially John Anthony McGuckin, *The Transfiguration of Christ in Scripture and Tradition* (Lewiston, N.Y.: Edwin Mellen, 1986); and Solrunn Nes, *The Uncreated Light: An Iconographical Study of the Transfiguration in the Eastern Church* (Grand Rapids, Mich.: Wm. B. Eerdmans, 2007).

23. John Baggley explains that

> in Orthodox iconography, the mandorla representing the divine presence is usually darker at the centre and increasingly lighter in color in the outer

circles—holding together the concept of the unknowable essence of God and the reality of God's knowability through the divine energies. (John Baggley, *Festival Icons for the Christian Year*, 64.)

24. "Dnes' khristos" na gorě favōrstěĭ adamovo preměniv" ōcherněvshee ēstestvo, prosvětiv" bogosoděla. . . . Ōblistavshesę světom" nepristūpnȳę slavȳ, na favōrstěĭ gorě, apostoli, khristū vopiękhū: otēts" nashikh" bozhe, blagosloven" ēsi" (*M* August, 71, 78).

25. John Anthony McGuckin outlines the development in Eastern theology of the nature of revelation in the Transfiguration. He points to the tradition of "special election" of the disciples who witnessed the Transfiguration, as described especially by Clement and Origen. He also points to Gregory Nanzianzen's discussion of the radiant light as a "symbolic revelation of Christ's deity" but, as McGuckin paraphrases, "only partly revelatory since its power blinded the eyes of the beholders." (McGuckin, *The Transfiguration of Christ*, 104, 101.)

26. Meyendorff comments on the development of the theology of essence and energies in the Eastern tradition, noting that it received its fullest expression in the work of Gregory Palamas in the fourteenth century (*Byzantine Theology*, 164). This tradition (even as early as the fourth century in the work of Saint Basil) distinguishes between God's unknowable "essence" and the "energies" by which he manifests himself to man. In deification, human nature becomes "penetrated with divine energy" so that he can participate in the divine life (188). In his commentary on the genre of the icon of the Transfiguration, Baggley comments that "the apostles have been overshadowed by the cloud, been touched by the divine glory and have to some degree experienced a transfiguration, though it is beyond their human comprehension" (Baggley, *Festival Icons*, 69).

27. Blok's connection of his Beautiful Lady with the Burning Bush image offers, in essence, a clear blending of Sophia and Mary. As the notes on "Vesna v reke . . ." point out, Blok's use of this image echoes Solovyov's own use of it in his poem "Neopalimaia Kupina" (1891) (*ABPSS*, 1:525). But as the notes also point out, Solovyov is drawing on Russian tradition, found even in folk poetry.

28. Ivanov, "On the Crisis of Humanism," 166; "O krizise gumanizma," 105.

29. See, for instance, Steven Cassedy's discussion of a literary "critique" of language in "Mathematics, Relationalism, and the Rise of Modern Literary Aesthetics," *Journal of the History of Ideas* 49, no. 1 (1988): 109–32.

30. Andrei Bely, "Magiia slov," in *Simvolizm* (Moscow: Musaget, 1910), 433–34.

31. Seifrid, *The Word Made Self*, 111–15. For a thorough account of the *imiaslavie* debates, see Ilarion Alfeev, *Spory ob imeni Bozhiem: Arkhivnye dokumenty 1912–1938 godov* (St. Petersburg: Oleg Abyshko, 2007). For a briefer discussion of *imiaslavie* and a response to Alfeev and others and their account of the theological implications of the *imiaslavie* debates, see Scott Kenworthy,

"Archbishop Nikon (Rozhdestvenskii) and Pavel Florenskii on Spiritual Experience, Theology, and the Name-Glorifiers Dispute," in Patrick Lally Michelson and Judith Deutsch Kornblatt, eds., *Thinking Orthodox in Modern Russia: Culture, History, Context* (Madison: University of Wisconsin Press, 2014), 85–107.

32. Irina Paperno, "On the Nature of the Word: Theological Sources of Mandel'stam's Dialogue with the Symbolists," in Boris Gasparov et al., eds., *Christianity and the Eastern Slavs*, vol. 2, *Russian Culture in Modern Times* (Berkeley: University of California Press, 1994), 287–310.

33. Although there has been little scholarly attention to sound in Blok's poetry, one article in the *Blokovskii sbornik* series explores the use of "anagrams" in Blok's early poetry, specifically in *Ante Lucem* and the first two sections of *Verses on the Beautiful Lady*. In "Poetika Bloka: Anagrammy" V. S. Baevskii and A. D. Koshelev describe how Blok uses key words to create a poetic space dominated by a central idea (in Zara Mints, ed., *Tvorchestvo A. A. Bloka i russkaia kul'tura XX veka: Blokovskii Sbornik III* [Tartu: Tartuskii gosudarstvennyi universitet, 1979]: 50–75). They show in particular how the poet not only repeats the word itself but also repeats parts of it (a syllable or sometimes just one letter) or echoes it throughout a poem or cycle.

34. I am indebted to Sibelan Forrester for this last observation.

35. McGuckin points to the "penetration of the human body of Jesus with divine light" (*The Transfiguration of Christ*, 132). He cites John of Damascus on the transfiguration of the fleshly body: "Now are things seen that are beyond the eyes of man—an earthly body radiating the divine splendour, a mortal body pouring forth the glory of the godhead" (118).

36. I count eight occurrences in the first stanza, ten in the second, and fourteen in the final stanza, taking into account "ы" (which is also considered as the "i" phoneme) and reduced "e." I exclude "e" not immediately preceding the stress and also "i" immediately following the stress. In counting reduced vowels I take my cue from Barry Scherr (*Russian Poetry: Meter, Rhythm, and Rhyme* [Berkeley: University of California Press, 1986], 268). Even, however, if one counts only stressed "i" sounds, we find a striking number—seven occurrences—in the final stanza, the stanza upon which my argument about sound in the poem ultimately rests.

37. I am grateful to my anonymous reviewer for pointing out to me the striking parallel between these two lines.

38. This is a principle Solovyov discusses at length in "The Meaning of Love" ("Smysl' liubvi") (*SSVSS*, 7:1–60; here, 24).

39. In "Smysl' liubvi" ("The Meaning of Love") Solovyov writes, "In order to be filled with absolute content [*absoliutnym soderzhaniem*] (which in religious language is called eternal life or the kingdom of God), human form itself must be restored in its wholeness (integrated)" (*SSVSS*, 7:1–60; here, 24). Compare this description of the spiritual transformation of the world affect-

ing even the physical with Solovyov's analogical description of the suffusion of material by light, such as in "Krasota v prirode" ("Beauty in Nature") (*SSVSS*, 6:33–74): "Matter is inertness and impermeability of existence—a direct contrast to Idea, as positive total permeability or total unity. Only in *light* does matter free itself from its inertness and impermeability" (*SSVSS*, 6:46). (In this last sentence I have used the translation from "Beauty in Nature," in *The Heart of Reality: Essays on Beauty, Love, and Ethics*, ed. and trans. Vladimir Wozniuk [Notre Dame, Ind.: University of Notre Dame Press, 2003], 41). For Solovyov the "beam of eternal Divine femininity" (*luch vechnoi Bozhestvennoi zhenstvennosti*) will manifest the return of the world to harmony and humanity's access to its ideal state. See Solovyov's "Obshchii smysl' iskusstva," from which this cited phrase is taken (*SSVSS*, 6:76). See also "Smysl' liubvi" (*SSVSS*, 7:46).

40. Blok not only flattens out the historical trajectory of Solovyov's conception. Mints notes that the poet also personalizes Solovyov's symbolic and metaphysical scheme in his poetic renditions of the Beautiful Lady ("Lirika 'pervogo toma' (1898–1904)," in *Poetika Aleksandra Bloka*, 24).

41. McGuckin, *The Transfiguration of Christ*, 120–22.

42. Thomas Seifrid, *The Word Made Self*; Steven Cassedy, "Toward a Unified Theory of the Aesthetic Object in Andrej Belyj," *Slavic and East European Journal* 28, no. 2 (1984): 205–22.

43. Seifrid, *The World Made Self*, 60–63.

44. Bely, "Magiia slov," 434.

45. Andrei Bely, "Apokalipsis v russkoi poezii," in *Lug Zelenyi* (Moscow: Al'tsiona, 1910), 243.

46. In particular, the image of "streams" appears in two of the surrounding poems. In "Sgushchalsia mrak tserkovnogo poroga . . ." (January 11) we find the image of streaming light ("I v glubine, nad sumrachnym amvonom, / Osteregaiushchii struilsia svet") (*ABPSS*, 1:90). The poem from January 14, "Tam, v polusumrake sobora . . . ," inverts this image in its lines, "V rechakh o mudrosti nebesnoi / Zemnye chuiutsia strui" (*ABPSS*, 1:90). This poem offers a sinister mirroring of the Epiphany liturgy, hinting at a diabolic meeting in its final double image of a dove and a snake. The dove reminds us of the Epiphany image of the Holy Spirit. Indeed, in its lines "Glubokii zhar sluchainoi vstrechi / Dokhnul s tserkovnoi vysoty," the poem presents a disturbingly similar picture of divine descent as we find in "My preklonilis' u zaveta."

47. In the "Blessing of the Waters" that takes place on this feast the priest asks that the waters be made "a source of incorruption" (*netlěnīę istochnik*") and of "sanctification, blessing, cleansing and health" (*ōsvęshtenīe, zdravīe, ōchishtenīe i blagoslovenīe*) (*FM*, 357; *M* January, 83v). In *The Deification of Man*, John Mantzaridis affirms the renewal of the body by the baptismal sacrament (*The Deification of Man: St. Gregory Palamas and the Orthodox Tradition* [Crestwood, N.Y.: St. Vladimir's Seminary, 1984], 48). The point is not that

Christ is deified through baptism here, but that the sacrament affirms the union of the baptized with God, through Christ, enacted through the divine energies and Holy Spirit pictured in this theophanic event.

48. Although the Feast of Epiphany can also be referred to as the Feast of Theophany, in order to avoid confusion I use the term "Epiphany" to refer to the liturgical celebration. I use the uncapitalized term "theophany" to refer to the scriptural tradition (adapted by Blok) of God's manifestations of himself to man.

49. "Iz Marīi Gospod', vseĭ vselennĕĭ vozsīęvaet" lūchi, Solntse Pravdȳ" (Matins, Ikos, *M* January, 90v).

50. "Dnes' vod" ōsvęshtaetsę ēstestvo" (Today the nature of the waters is sanctified) (Blessing of the Waters, *M* January, 80r).

51. "Zemlę ōsvętisę rozhdestvom" tvoim" svętȳm", Slove, povĕdaiushtȳm" nebesēm" żvĕzdoiu slavū tvoiu. . . . Da radūetsę zemlę vsę, nebo da veselitsę, mir" da igraet". . . . Neizglagolannoe Devȳ tainstvo: ibo bo Sīę, i Prestol" kherūvīmskīĭ, i svĕtonosnȳĭ Chertog" pokazasę Khrista Boga Vsederzhitelę. . . . Pūstȳnnaę Iordanskaę da prosvĕtūt"" (Compline, Second troparion, Ninth Ode of the Canon, *M* January, 49r; Matins, Irmos, Ninth Ode of the Canon, *M* January, 55v).

52. See, for instance, the Matins for the Feast of the Annunciation, where we hear Mary describe herself as made into a "Temple that contains God, a Tabernacle divinely adorned, a living Sanctuary" (*Tserkov' . . . vmĕstitel'nū Boga, Skinīiu bogoūkrashenū, ōdūshevlen" Khram"*) (Matins, Third Troparion, Ode Nine of the Canon, *M* March, 128r).

53. For a discussion of this image in the Orthodox liturgical context (including icons), see Solrunn Nes, *The Uncreated Light: An Iconographical Study of the Transfiguration in the Eastern Church* (Grand Rapids, Mich., 2007). The image of the Burning Bush occurs particularly in the famous Akathist of the Theotokos, to which an entire Saturday of Lent (the fifth Saturday) is dedicated.

54. In her article on the evaluation of Blok's poetry by religious thinkers, Avril Pyman affirms the link between the Most Beautiful Lady of Blok's first volume and the liturgy's presentation of the Mother of God (Avril Pyman, "Tvorchestvo Aleksandra Bloka v otsenke russkikh religioznykh myslitelei 20–30-kh godov," *Blokovskii sbornik*, vol. 12 [Tartu: Kafedra russkoi literatury Tartuskogo universiteta, 1993]: 63).

Other scholars have written about the place of the Mother of God in Blok's work, though largely in relation to works later than *Verses*. See, for instance, S. L. Konstantinova, "'Bogorodichnye motivy' v *Ital'ianskikh stikhakh* A. Bloka," in *Aleksandr Blok i mirovaia kul'tura: Materialy nauchnoi konferentsii 14–17 marta 2000 goda* (Velikii Novgorod, 2000), 62–68. See also N. V. Guzhieva, "Tserkovnyi kalendar' v structure liricheskoi trilogii A. Bloka," *Russkaia literatura* 2 (2005): 81–93.

55. This theme is especially emphasized in services for the Forefeast of the Epiphany (or Theophany). The canon of the Forefeast declares,

> At Thine appearing in the body, the earth was sanctified, the waters blessed, the heaven enlightened, and mankind was set loose from the bitter tyranny of the enemy. . . . Thou hast come forth from a womb that suffered no pangs of childbirth, O Thou who wast begotten of the Father before the ages; Thou goest to him who was born of a barren mother. . . . Thou, O Saviour, by water and through the Spirit hast mystically made the Church, that before was barren, Mother of many children. (*FM*, 298–99)
>
> Iavl'shūsę tebě tělom", ōsvętisę zemlę, vodȳ blagoslovishasę, nebo prosvětisę, rod" zhe chelověkōv" gor'kagō mūchitel'stva vrazhīę izbavisę [. . . .] Ōt chistȳę proshed" rozhdeĭšę iz Otsa prezhde věkōv", k" sūshtemū iz neplodnȳę prishel" ēsi, prosę iakō chelověk" kreshtenīę: no ōt vodȳ tainstvennō Dūkhom" sodělal" ēsi, Spase, mnogochadnū Tserkov', pervěe bezchadnūiu. (Compline, First Troparion, Ode Four, *M* January, 47v; Third Troparion, Ode Five, *M* January, 48r)

56. *Novyi put'* (March 1903): 48–59.

57. See my discussion of the "sophianic" task in the introduction. As I mention there, I draw on Paul Valliere's discussion of sophiology in "Sophiology as the Dialogue of Orthodoxy with Modern Civilization," in Kornblatt and Gustafson, eds., *Russian Religious Thought*, 176–92.

58. The poem is dated in Lent (March 1902), but it is "Paschal-themed" in its evocation of spring, as well as in its reference to the central Passion image in the line, "Why should I grieve before the cross . . . ?" (*Chto sokrushat'sia u kresta?*). Here Blok opposes a Paschal-like spirit of celebration to Lenten mourning.

59. John Bowlt, "Here and There: The Question of Space in Blok's Poetry," in *Aleksandr Blok Centennial Conference*, ed. Walter N. Vickery (Columbus, Ohio: Slavica, 1982), 63.

60. Peter Brown, "The Rise and Function of the Holy Man in Late Antiquity," in *Society and the Holy in Late Antiquity* (Berkeley: University of California Press, 1982), 176.

61. Brown, "The Rise and Function of the Holy Man," 182–83.

62. Ibid., 183.

63. Ibid.

64. Thomas F. Torrance, *Space, Time and Incarnation* (New York: Oxford University Press, 1969), 25.

65. Ibid., 25. Brown speaks at greater length about the "institutionalization" of holiness in regard to the treatment of relics in Eastern and Western churches in his essay "Relics and Social Status in the Age of Gregory of Tours" (in *Society and the Holy in Late Antiquity*, 222–50). In particular he discusses how the relic in the Western Church had to go through a very strict and formalized series of inquiries or proofs by the central hierarchy before it was canonized, whereas in

the Eastern Church, local churches had more autonomy in the relics they chose to view as "holy," and a formalized system of canonization such as is found in the Catholic Church was never developed.

66. Torrance, *Space, Time and Incarnation*, 18. Emphasis in the original.

67. Bely, "Formy iskusstva," in *Simvolizm*, 147–74; "Magiia slov," 431, 432.

68. Blok, *Sobranie sochinenii v vos'mi tomakh* (Leningrad, 1962), 2:433, cited in Igosheva, "Materialy i soobshcheniia: Religioznoe preobrazhenie v kontekste *Stikhov o prekrasnoi dame* A Bloka," 57.

69. Torrance, *Space, Time and Incarnation*, 4.

70. Brown, "The Rise and Function of the Holy Man," 136.

71. Blok notably conflates two parts of the Orpheus myths—the journey to the underworld to rescue Eurydice and Orpheus's death. Ovid tells these stories in *Metamorphoses*, books 10 and 11.

72. Bowlt, "Here and There: The Question of Space in Blok's Poetry," 63.

73. Ibid., 63.

74. Florensky, *Iconostasis*; Florenskii, *Ikonostas*.

75. Immanuel Kant, *Critique of Pure Reason* (New York: Cambridge University Press, 2000), 339.

76. Viacheslav Ivanov, "Ellinskaia religiia stradaiushchego boga," *Novyi put'* 1 (1904): 110–24.

77. Edith Clowes, "The Mystical Symbolists: The Making of Dionysian-Christian Culture," in *The Revolution of Moral Consciousness: Nietzsche in Russian Literature, 1890–1914* (De Kalb: Northern Illinois University Press, 1988), 115–74.

78. Clowes, "The Mystical Symbolists," 142.

79. Kornblatt, *Divine Sophia*, 104.

EXCURSUS

1. Marina Tsvetaeva, *Sobranie sochinenii v semi tomakh* (Moscow: Ellis Lak, 1994), 1:288–99.

2. Alyssa Dinega has notably described the tension between flesh and spirit in Tsvetaeva's life and work as a tightrope act (Alyssa Dinega, *A Russian Psyche: The Poetic Mind of Marina Tsvetaeva* [Madison: University of Wisconsin Press, 2001]). Olga Peters Hasty and Dinega do more than any other scholar to detail how Tsevaeva's creative "psyche" rests on this tension between flesh and spirit (Olga Peters Hasty, *Tsvetaeva's Orphic Journeys in the Worlds of the Word* [Evanston, Ill.: Northwestern University Press, 1996]). Their compelling analyses view Tsvetaeva's poetics, respectively, primarily through classical-mythological modes and psychological concepts. As both scholars show, Tsvetaeva builds her poetics (and her own poetic myth) on the notion of her inability

to be at once a poet (spirit) and a woman (flesh). Discussions of the relationship between flesh and spirit feature prominently in many works on Tsvetaeva. These works include Irina Shevelenko, *Literaturny put' Tsvetaevoi: Ideologiia—poetika—identichnost': Avtor v kontekste epokhi* (Moscow: Novoe literaturnoe obozrenie, 2002); Catherine Ciepiela, *The Same Solitude: Boris Pasternak and Marina Tsvetaeva* (Ithaca, N.Y.: Cornell University Press, 2006); Anya M. Kroth, "Androgyny as an Exemplary Feature of Marina Tsvetaeva's Dichotomous Poetic Vision," *Slavic Review* 38 (1979): 563–82; Sibelan Forrester, "Bells and Cupolas: The Formative Role of the Female Body in Marina Tsvetaeva's Poetry," *Slavic Review* 51, no. 2 (1992): 232–46; and Stephanie Sandler, "Embodied Words: Gender in Cvetaeva's Reading of Puškin," *Slavic and East European Journal* 34, no. 2 (1990): 139–57.

3. Tsvetaeva's Annunciation poems are "V den' Blagoveshchen'ia . . ." and "Kanun Blagoveshchen'ia . . ." (*Sobranie sochinenii*, 1:261, and 1:262–63, respectively).

4. "Tserkov' sotvori mę vmĕstitel'nū Boga, Skinīiu bogoūkrashenū, ōdūshevlen" Khram" naitīem" Presvętagō Dūkha, i Zhizni chistūiu Mater'" (Matins, Third Troparion, Ode Seven of the Canon, *M* March, 128r).

5. "Grade ōdūshevlennȳĭ Tsarę i Boga, v nemzhe Khristos" pozhiv"" (Matins, Third Stikhiron of the Praises, *M* December, 258r).

6. Liza Knapp shows how Tsvetaeva rewrites the Genesis creation story in the "Podruga" cycle to place Eve at front and center (Liza Knapp, "Marina Tsvetaeva's Poetics of Ironic Delight: The 'Podruga' Cycle as Evist Manifesto," *Slavic and East European Review* 41, no. 1 [1997]: 94–113). Sara Pankenier Weld offers a rich exploration of the poem "Po nagoriiam," from Tsvetaeva's 1923 collection *Craft* (*Remeslo*), finding in it an affirmation of the womb as a powerful feminine creative symbol (Sara Pankenier, "Reborn in a Reappropriation of Creation: Marina Tsvetaeva's 'Po nagoriiam,'" *Slavic and East European Journal* 48, no. 4 [2004]: 607–26). Stephanie Sandler, too, shows how, in her Pushkin writings, the poet "merges the female body," including the pregnant body, "with the act of creating poetry," therefore undermining the "opposition between mothering and writing" often noted in Western women's writing (Sandler, "Embodied Words," see especially 149–50). Catherine Ciepiela argues that in Tsvetaeva's work, "writing and mothering, far from being contradictory impulses, can hardly be distinguished" (Ciepiela, "The Demanding Woman Poet: On Resisting Marina Tsvetaeva," *PMLA* 111, no. 3 [1996]: 421–34; here, 422).

7. Sibelan Forrester, "Bells and Cupolas: The Formative Role of the Female Body in Marina Tsvetaeva's Poetry," *Slavic Review* 51, no. 2 (1992): 232–46.

8. Shevelenko, *Literaturny put' Tsvetaevoi*, 118–19.

9. Ibid., 118.

10. The first three titles appear in the third poem, "Ty prokhodish' na Zapad

Solntsa . . ." (*SS*, 1:290). The final two titles appear in the sixth poem, "Dumali—chelovek! . ." (*SS*, 1:291–92).

11. Michael Makin, *Marina Tsvetaeva: Poetics of Appropriation* (Oxford: Clarendon, 1993), 31–32; Ol'ga Sedakova, "Tserkovnoslavianskii iazyk v russkoi kul'ture," in *Perevody* (Moscow: Universitet Dmitriia Pozharskogo, 2010), 125–41; here, 127.

CHAPTER TWO

1. Paul Valliere, "Sophiology as the Dialogue of Orthodoxy with Modern Civilization," in Kornblatt and Gustafson, eds., *Russian Religious Thought*, 176–92; here, 176.

2. All translations of Kuzmin's poems in the chapter are my own.

3. In their commentary in *MKSS*, Malmstad and Bogomolov note at once the closeness of the myth presented here to Gnostic myths, but they also note how difficult it is to discern what exactly Kuzmin takes in any of his Gnostic-themed verse from Gnosticism itself, given his tendency not to distinguish Gnosticism from early Christianity (*MKSS*, 3:667.)

Lada Panova has written most extensively on Kuzmin's interest in and adaptations of Gnosticism. She notes that the modern engagement with Gnostic thought arose after the publication in 1851 in France of *Pistis Sophia* and *Philosophoumena*. Kuzmin included *Pistis Sophia* in his reading lists (L. G. Panova, *Russkii Egipet: Aleksandriiskaia poetika Mikhaila Kuzmina* [Moscow: Volodei, 2006], 125, 346). Malmstad and Bogomolov emphasize multiple times in their extensive work on Kuzmin how fundamental were the poet's early readings of Gnostic writings (*MBMK*, 77). These scholars all point out that Kuzmin's renditions of Gnostic themes cannot be separated from a fundamentally Christian outlook (even though, as I will discuss in this chapter, his expressions of Christianity were quite individualized and often unorthodox). (Panova, *Russkii Egipet*, 480; *MBMK*, 77.)

4. This point is a guiding argument in Kornblatt's book on Solovyov's Sophia writings. See Kornblatt, *Divine Sophia*.

5. Panova connects this image of Sophia in flames on a throne with one found in *Pistis Sophia*, the "Sophia gorniaia" (lit. "Sophia of the hill"), which has its counterpart in the "Sophia dolniaia" ("Sophia of the vale") (Panova, *Russkii Egipet*, 474).

6. Solovyov notes in "Smysl' liubvi" ("The Meaning of Love")—one of his most famous and widely read works in Russia at the turn of the twentieth century (and since)—the incongruence of love's productive idealizations with the mortality of its object (*SSVSS*, 7:3–60; here, 24).

7. Kornblatt mentions these details in her discussion of key elements of Solovyov's poetry. (Kornblatt, "Early Sophianic Poems," in *Divine Sophia*, 101–8).

8. Valliere, "Sophiology as the Dialogue of Orthodoxy with Modern Civilization," 176.

9. For a substantial discussion of the ongoing conversation on sexuality and religion in the Religious-Philosophical meetings and in the period more generally, see Matich, *Erotic Utopia: The Decadent Imagination in Russia's Fin de Siècle*. Matich's sixth chapter, "Religious-Philosophical Meetings: Celibacy contra Marriage," focuses especially on these meetings (212–35). Commenting on the significance of the meetings, Matich writes, "Where else between 1901 and 1903 did people of such different ideological convictions and social origins have free public discussions regarding religion, sex, and politics?" (215).

10. Merezhkovsky coined this term in a paper he gave in one of the Religious-Philosophical gatherings. See note 59 of the introduction.

11. "Zapiski religiozno-filosofskikh sobranii," *Novyi put'* (May 1903): 230. The meeting took place on April 18, 1903.

12. "Religiozno-filosofskaia khronika: Dal'she nekuda!," *Novyi put'* (June 1903): 262–63.

13. The most prominent controversy over sophiology emerged in what came to be known as the "Sophia affair" of 1935, which eventually resulted in the declaration, by the Moscow Patriarchate and the Russian Orthodox Church Outside Russia, of Sergei Bulgakov's writings on Sophia as heretical. For a summary of the affair, see "Theology in the 19th and 20th Centuries," in Erwin Fahlbusch, ed., *The Encyclopedia of Christianity*, vol. 5 (Grand Rapids, Mich.: Wm. B. Eerdmans, 2008), 416. A well-known, point-by-point critique of Bulgakov's thought from the period—defending the charge of heresy—is Archbishop Serafim (Sobolev), *Zashchita Sofianskoi eresi protoiereem Sergiem Bulgakovym, pred litsom Archiereiskogo Sobora Russkoi Zarubezhnoi Tserkvi* (Sofia, 1937). One of the chapters deals specifically with the idea that Bulgakov's thought represents in Sophia "another god" (54).

14. Florensky, *Stolp i utverzhdenie istiny*. Robert Slesinski sees the interpersonal aspect as undergirding all of Florensky's thought. In his monograph on Florensky's thought, *Pavel Florensky: A Metaphysics of Love* (Crestwood, N.Y.: St. Vladimir's Seminary, 1984), Slesinski writes that love is "the key and hallmark to Florensky's metaphysics of consubstantiality in which all reality, both divine and creatural, is bound together by dynamic interrelationships of love" (212). Stephen Cassedy addresses this and other aspects of *The Pillar and Ground of Truth*, and Florensky's thought more generally, in "Pavel Florenskii's Trinitarian Humanism," in Hamburg and Poole, eds., *A History of Russian Philosophy*, 190–201. On the personalist aspect of Florenskii's thought, see 193–94.

15. On the consistency of certain fundamental ideas that Kuzmin held and developed over the course of his writing career, see *MBMK*, 62. See also Satho Tchimichkian-Jennergren, "L'Art en tant que resurrection dans la poésie de M. Kuzmin," in John E. Malmstad, ed., *Studies in the Life and Works of Mixail Kuz-*

min, *Wiener Slawistischer Almanach*, special volume 24 (Vienna, 1989), 47–56. See also Irina Paperno, "Dvoinichestvo i liubovnyi treugol'nik: Poeticheskii mif Kuzmina i ego pushkinskaia proektsiia," in Malmstad, ed., *Studies in the Life and Works of Mixail Kuzmin*, 51–82.

16. This is a point made in multiple ways by Vladimir Markov (see "Poeziia Mikhaila Kuzmina," in *MKSS*, 3:321–426), John Malmstad and Nikolay Bogomolov (see *MBMK*), and Lada Panova (see *Russkii Egipet*).

17. "September 29, 1905," in Kuzmin, *Dnevnik 1905–1907*, 49.

18. In a chapter on Kuzmin's play *The Death of Nero*, Kalb notes that in his 1897 trip to Italy, "Kuzmin rediscovered in Rome's pagan roots the culture that had attracted him in Alexandria and simultaneously found a new, more appealing vision of Christianity in its earliest stages" (Judith E. Kalb, "Emperors in Red: The Poet and the Court in Mikhail Kuzmin's *Death of Nero*," in *Russia's Rome: Imperial Visions, Messianic Dreams, 1890–1940* [Madison: University of Wisconsin Press, 2008], 162–84). See also Panova, *Russkii Egipet*.

19. Mikhail Kuzmin, "October 10, 1934," in *Dnevnik 1934 goda*, ed. G. Morev (St. Petersburg: Ivan Limbakha, 1998), 118.

20. He includes this document in his diary of 1906. See Kuzmin, *Dnevnik 1905–1907*, 267–73.

21. Kuzmin's protagonist in *Wings*, Smurov, spends a summer on the Volga with an Old Believer family, much of whose conversation consists in trying to understand contemporary questions through the lens of their religious tradition. Kuzmin creates in the young woman Mar'ia Dmitrievna a new generation of Old Belief who embraces the body and pleasure, all the while continuing in her pious practices, and seeing no tension between these things.

Nikolay Bogomolov and John Malmstad offer a rich account of Kuzmin's engagement with Old Belief in "U istokov tvorchestva Mikhaila Kuzmina" (*Voprosy literatury* 3 [1993]: 64–121). In this article they cite a number of effusive letters Kuzmin writes about Old Belief and why it attracts him. He places special emphasis on its preservation and observation of traditional ritual in a way that seems very much of a piece with everyday life. He writes of a "happiness" that he connects with a "mystical connection of ritual and custom [*obriada i obychaia*]" and that exists for him in the "everyday life [*byt i zhizn'*] of the Old Believers" (113).

22. In his well-known work Kuzmin depicts a household of Old Believers, and icons seem to dominate the space. In his brief autobiography and also in his diaries he frequently mentions his dealings and relations with an Old Believer, Kazakhov, who sold icons and church books.

23. "Histoire édifiante de mes commencements," in Kuzmin, *Dnevnik 1905–1907*, 267–73; here, 272.

24. See especially Kuzmin's *Dnevnik 1905–1907*. Here he mentions reading the *Spiritual Meadow* (*Limonar'*—a collection of lives of the saints compiled by

John Moschus [550–619]) (29), canons (*kanony*—liturgical songs) (89), the Typicon (*Ustav*—the order of services in the liturgical calendar) (103), and the Prologue (*Prolog*—a work containing saints' lives, sermons, and hymns) (273).

25. Panova, *Russkii Egipet*, 346.

26. He includes a long list of Italian painters in *RGALI-MK* 47:107v–125r, 136v–182r.

27. He lists Whitman's *Leaves of Grass* (49:118r) and Hoffmann's "Meister Floh" (49:137r). In another notebook he lists Flaubert's *La Tentation de St. Antoine* (*RGALI-MK* 46:140v). We find listed several works of Pater and Huysmans (including *La Cathédrale*) listed in *RGALI-MK* 47:525r, 452r.

28. *RGALI-MK*, 47:32r (Vera pravoslavno-vostochnoi tserkvi), 47:31r (Bogoslovnonravouchitel'noe). Kuzmin lists more of Ephrem's works than that of any other Church Father (Efrem Sirin pouchenie [47:35v], Efrema Sirina i Avvy Dorofeia [47:36r], Efrem Sirim [47:457r]). He lists works from the Greek Church Fathers, including Basil the Great (on fasting) (47:33r); Athanasius of Alexandria (47:492r); an 1889 edition of Gregory the Theologian (47:457r); and an 1871 edition of Gregory of Nyssa (47:457r).

29. Kuzmin seems to take these passages from the *Azbuka znamennago peniia*, first published by the Elder Aleskandr Mezenets in 1668, and republished in Kazan' in 1886 (47:345v).

30. Evgenii Bershtein, "An Englishman in the Russian Bathhouse: Kuzmin's *Wings* and the Russian Tradition of Homoerotic Writing," in *The Many Facets of Mikhail Kuzmin: A Miscellany*, ed. Lada Panova and Sarah Pratt (Bloomington, Ind.: Slavica, 2011), 75–88; here, 76.

31. Kuzmin, *Kryl'ia*, in *MKP*, 1:223.

32. In his notebooks Kuzmin notes down numerous works on the icon, including Nikodim Kondakov's *Sovremennoe polozhenie russkoi narodnoi ikonopisi* (1901) (which Kuzmin lists as "*Sovrem. polozhenie rus. ikony*") (*RGALI-MK*, 47:9r) and M. I. and V. I. Uspenskii's *Zametki o drevnerusskoi ikonopisi* (St. Petersburg, 1901) (*RGALI-MK*, 47:9r). He includes a list of icon types in this same notebook (47:520r).

33. Mikhail Kuzmin and Marina Rakhmanova, "O tserkovnom ustave i o tserkovnom penii," *Muzykal'naia akademiia* (1992): 37–44.

34. Malmstad and Bogomolov dismiss the notion that Kuzmin was "in any way [Ivanov's] 'pupil'" (*MBMK*, 126). That said, it is difficult not to see in these two figures at least a strong mutual influence.

35. Robert Bird, *The Russian Prospero: The Creative Universe of Viacheslav Ivanov* (Madison: University of Wisconsin Press, 2006). Other important monographs on Ivanov include James West, *Russian Symbolism: A Study of Vyacheslav Ivanov and the Russian Symbolist Aesthetic* (London: Methuen, 1970); Gennadii Obatnin, *Ivanov-Mistik: Okkul'tnye motivy v poezii i proze Viacheslava Ivanova* (Moscow: Novoe Literaturnoe Obozrenie, 2000); and Pamela Davidson,

The Poetic Imagination of Vyacheslav Ivanov: A Russian Symbolist's Perception of Dante (Cambridge, Eng.: Cambridge University Press, 2009).

36. Clowes, "The Mystical Symbolists, 115–74.

37. See Robert Bird, *The Russian Prospero*. For a detailed discussion of Ivanov's vision of ritual, catharsis, and renewal, see pp. 48–49.

38. Viacheslav Ivanov, "Two Elements in Contemporary Symbolism," in *Selected Essays*, trans. Robert Bird, ed. Michael Wachtel (Evanston, Ill.: Northwestern University Press, 2003), 13–35; here, 33. In the original, Viacheslav Ivanov, "Dve stikhii v sovremennom simbolizme," in *Rodnoe i vselenskoe* (Moscow: Izdatel'stvo "Respublika," 1994), 143–69; here, 160.

39. Florensky, *Stolp i utverzhdenie istiny*, 355. On Florensky's ponderings over "the sophianic mystery, that is Mary, the God-bearer," see Slesinski, *Pavel Florensky: A Metaphysics of Love*, 183–85.

40. I am indebted to my anonymous reviewer for pointing out the use of terza rima here.

41. See, for instance, "Otri glaza i slez ne lei . . . ," (Kuzmin, *Sobranie sochinenii*, 1:289) and "Golyi otrok v pole rzhi . . ." (*Sobranie sochinenii*, 1:309).

42. For discussions of Plato in Kuzmin's work, see John E. Malmstad, "'You Must Remember This': Memory's Shorthand in a Late Poem of Kuzmin," in John E. Malmstad, ed., *Studies in the Life and Works of Mikhail Kuzmin*, 115–40; and Donald C. Gillis, "The Platonic Theme in Kuzmin's *Wings*," *Slavic and East European Journal*, 22, no. 3 (1978): 336–47.

43. These poems are scattered across Kuzmin's work, from *Nets* to *Paraboles* (*Paraboly*). See "Kartonnyi domik" (*MKSS*, 1:70), "Volkhvy" (1:552–53), "Iosif" (2:91–93), "Elka" (2:101–4), and "Rozhdestvo" (2:375).

44. F. M. Dostoevskii, *Polnoe sobranie sochinenii v tridsati tomakh* (Leningrad: Izdatelstvo "Nauka," 1972–90), 14:328.

45. Vladimir Markov, "Poeziia Mikhaila Kuzmina," in *MKSS*, 3:321–426; here, 329.

46. In a letter to G. V. Chicherin dated July 16, 1901, for instance, Kuzmin describes himself as a person "of flesh and ritual" (*ploti i obriada*) (cited in V. Zakharov, "*Sinaiskii paterik* v *Kryl'iakh* M. Kuzmina," in *Evangel'skii tekst v russkoi literature XVIII–XX vekov: Tsitata, reministsentsiia, motiv, siuzhet, zhanr*, ed. V. Zakharov (Petrozavodsk: Petrozavodsk University Press, 1994), 303). In another, undated letter to Chicherin, Kuzmin describes his "main character trait" as a "'striving toward a harmony of everyday life' [*stremleniia k stroinosti byta*], a demand for plastic, outward, symbolic manifestations of inward insights—hence everyday life [*byt*], hence ritual [*obriad*]" (cited in Bogomolov and Malmstad, "U istokov tvorchestva Mikhaila Kuzmina," 110). Later in this same letter he writes, "A firm faith, an unchanging rite, harmony of everyday life—and amidst all this a dynamic, earthly work [*zhivoe zemnoe delo*]—that is the tangible ideal of life and happiness" (112).

47. The idea of "total unity"—*vseedinstvo*—is a fundamental one for Solovyov, representing the ideal state of being—individual and cosmic—toward which man should creatively strive. He especially develops this notion in his *Lectures on Godmanhood* (*Chteniia o Bogochelovechestve*), first published in 1878 (*SSVSS*, 3:3–181). See especially Lecture 5 (3:59–78). On this term and idea see Kornblatt, *Divine Sophia*, 32–33; and Paul Valliere, *Modern Russian Theology*, 121–27. Valliere translates *vseedinstvo* as "the whole of things."

48. Bissera V. Pentcheva, *The Sensual Icon: Space, Ritual, and the Senses in Byzantium* (University Park: Penn State University Press, 2010), 19.

49. Arnold Eisen, *Rethinking Modern Judaism: Ritual, Commandment, Community* (Chicago: University of Chicago Press, 1998).

50. Catherine Bell, *Ritual: Perspectives and Dimensions* (New York: Oxford University Press, 1997), 212.

51. Bell, *Ritual*, 74.

52. Tellingly, Florensky offers his discursus on the value of the liturgy when he is discussing the Christian tradition's embrace of the body—which by extension he seems to affirm in speaking of the liturgy in organic terms, an embodiment of its own kind. I will include the full passage here because of the light it sheds on both his and, I would argue, Kuzmin's projects:

> One might write a whole book on the idea of the body in Church service books [*v bogosluzhebnoi pis'mennosti*] as an absolutely invaluable source. We still have no liturgical theology, i.e., a systematization of the theological ideas in our liturgy [*bogosluzheniia*]. And yet it is precisely here that we find the living self-consciousness of the Church, because the liturgy is the *flower* of church life and, moreover, her root and seed. What a wealth of ideas and new understandings in the realm of dogmatics, what an abundance of the most profound psychological observations and moral directives that even a not particularly diligent researcher could glean here! Yes, liturgical theology awaits someone who will cultivate it [*zhdet sebe vozdelyvatel'ia*]. (Florensky, *Stolp i utverzhdenie istiny*, 298–99)

Both Florensky and Kuzmin view the liturgy as an extremely significant means of embodying faith, of praxis that reflects and honors the realities of its practitioners. From that point, though, they do move in somewhat different directions. As a theologian Florensky desires a theological, "systematic" working out of theological ideas found in the liturgy—whereas Kuzmin desires to create a new kind of poetic liturgy on the basis of the old.

53. Alexander Schmemann, *Introduction to Liturgical Theology* (Bangor, Maine: American Orthodox, 1966).

54. Richard F. Gustafson, "Soloviev's Doctrine of Salvation," in Kornblatt and Gustafson, eds., *Russian Religious Thought*, 31–48.

55. Scott M. Kenworthy, *The Heart of Russia: Trinity-Sergius, Monasticism and Society after 1825* (New York: Oxford University Press, 2010).

56. Kenworthy, *The Heart of Russia*, 6.

57. This theme arises with some frequency in the meetings, but see in particular Dmitri Filosofov's opening remarks for the second meeting ("Zapiski religiozno-filosofskikh sobranii," *Novyi put'* 1 [1903]: 39–42).

58. Bogomolov and Malmstad indicate the extent of Kuzmin's interest in ascetic traditions, speaking of his

> reading and study of religious literature. . . . He was particularly interested in the "lives" of the great ascetics and with mystical writings, especially by the Italian mystics of the fourteenth to the beginning of the fifteenth century.

And here they cite a letter in which Kuzmin discusses Catherine of Siena as well as Thomas à Kempis and Saint Francis. (Bogomolov and Malmstad, "U istokov tvorchestva Mikhaila Kuzmina," 99).

Indeed, Saint Francis in particular was an influential monastic figure for Kuzmin. Several scholars have written about this connection, pointing out in particular Kuzmin's preference for Francis's commendation of and love for the earthly and temporal. See I. G. Vishnevetskii, "Mikhail Kuzmin i Sv. Frantsisk: Zametki k teme," in *Mikhail Kuzmin i russkaia kul'tura XX veka: Tezisy i materialy konferentsii 15–17 maia 1990 g.*, ed. G. Morev (Leningrad, 1990), 25–27. Or, for one of the earliest articulations of this influence by a scholar, see G. Shmakov, in his article "Blok i Kuzmin," *Blokovskii Sbornik* 2 (1972): 341–63. Here Shmakov relates the "seraphimic aspect of Kuzmin's worldview," or the "joyous sense of being," to the Franciscan influence (341–42).

Without diminishing the importance of the Franciscan, and more broadly Catholic, model for Kuzmin, I focus here on a somewhat different, if not unrelated aspect of Kuzmin's presentation of asceticism—that is, on the specifically Orthodox understanding of *theosis* over time.

59. In terms of poems about ascetic figures, see in particular Kuzmin's "Snova uvidel ia gorod, gde ia rodilsia . . ." (*MKSS*, 1:216–17) and "Maria Egipetskaia" (1:567–68). As mentioned above, Kuzmin makes specific reference in his diaries to reading numerous hagiographic works and collections. V. Zakharov notes that the first translation of the *Limonar'* from Greek into Old Russian took place in Kiev in 1628, was used especially in the Old Belief tradition, and appeared in Russian translation in the nineteenth century ("*Sinaiskii paterik* v *Kryl'iakh* M. Kuzmina," 304).

60. Kuzmin, *Dnevnik 1905–1907*, 124–25.

61. See Florensky, *Iconostasis*, or Florenskii, *Ikonostas* for a full discussion of this concept.

62. "Missionerstvo i missionery," in Vasilii Rozanov, *Okolo tserkovnykh sten* (Moscow: Respublika, 1995), 99–107; here, 105.

63. Rozanov, "Optina Pustyn'," in *Okolo tserkovnykh sten*, 285–301; here, 293.

64. Rozanov, "Optina Pustyn'," 301.

65. Kuzmin, "Fish-Scales in the Net (for Myself Alone)," in Mikhail Kuzmin, *Selected Prose and Poetry*, ed. and trans. Michael Green (Ann Arbor, Mich.: Ardis, 1980). This collection of quotes and remarks was originally published in the almanac *Strelets*, vol. 3 (Petrograd, 1922) (*MKSS*, 3:667n.).

66. Kuzmin, "Fish Scales," 274

67. Kenworthy describes two particular works that offered guidelines to the monastic life, including *A Good Word to a Beginner Novice* (*Dobroe slovo novnachal'nomu poslushniki*) by Archimandrite Antonii of Trinity-Sergius Lavra. The work of Ephrem the Syrian constitutes one of the most important sources of this work. Kenworthy speaks of this and *Monastic Life*, by Iuvenalii, prior of the Kievan Caves Lavra, as being "regarded as standard and universally accepted" prescriptions of the "fundamentals of monastic life" (Kenworthy, *The Heart of Russia*, 142–45).

68. Kuzmin, "Fish Scales," 278.

69. Kenworthy, *The Heart of Russia*, 9.

70. Kuzmin, "Fish Scales," 274.

71. Ibid., 277. See also other such entries on pp. 259 and 277.

72. John Climacus, *Lestvitsa* (St. Petersburg: Sviatoslov, 1996), 3. See *RGALI-MK*, 47:41v.

73. See, for instance, André Neher and Renée Neher, *Histoire biblique du peuple d'Israel* (Paris: Jean Maisonnneuve, 1998), 336; Gregory of Nyssa's "Commentary on the Canticle," in Gregory of Nyssa, *From Glory to Glory: Texts from Gregory of Nyssa's Mystical Writings*, trans. and ed. Herbert Musurillo (New York: Charles Scribner's Sons, 1961), for example, 152; or Origen's "Commentary" on the Song of Songs, in Origen, *The Song of Songs: Commentary and Homilies*, trans. R. P. Lawson (London: Longmans, Green, 1957), for example, 58.

74. Jean Danielou, *The Bible and the Liturgy* (Notre Dame, Ind.: Notre Dame University Press, 1956), 193.

75. Andrei Bely, *Nachalo veka* (Moscow: Khudozhestvennaia literatura, 1990), 25.

76. Mikhail Kuzmin, "Predislovie," in *Pesn' pesnei*, trans. Lev Iaroshevskii (Vienna, 1921) 5–6.

77. Mikhail Kuzmin, "Predislovie," in *Pesn' pesnei*, 5.

78. Florensky, *Stolp i utverzhdenie istiny*, 275.

79. The list mentions, simply "Dionis Areopagit," twice. It does not specify which works.

80. Pseudo-Dionysius, *The Celestial Hierarchy*, in *The Complete Works*, trans. Colm Luibheid (New York: Paulist, 1987), 143–91. On the legacy of Pseudo-Dionysius, see in this same volume Jaroslav Pelikan, "The Odyssey of Dionysian Spirituality," 11–24, especially 24.

81. Pseudo-Dionysius, *The Celestial Hierarchy*, 157.

82. Lindsay F. Watton, "Constructs of Sin and Sodom in Russian Modernism, 1906–1909," *Journal of the History of Sexuality* 4, no. 3 (1994): 369–94.

83. The first issue of *Novyi put'* places an article, "On the Freedom of Religious Conscience," by Nikolai Minskii (Vilenkin), second only to the introduction that launches the journal's endeavor (*Novyi put'* [January 1903]: 10–27). The article responds to the first two Religious-Philosophical meetings, transcriptions of which appeared in this issue. In the article Minskii speaks of this freedom as "the nerve center of our spiritual life," referring particularly to the intelligentsia, and he notes how controversial this topic has been in the press and in the meetings thus far (10). This theme is raised multiple times in meetings that follow, with predictably distinct points of view from the intelligentsia and the representatives of the Church.

84. Here I am drawing primarily on Peter Zouboff's translation, with some adjustments (Vladimir Solovyev, *Lectures on Godmanhood*, trans. Peter Zouboff [London: Dennis Dobson, 1948], 113).

85. Florensky, "Druzhba," in *Stolp i utverzhdenie istiny*, 393–463; here 438.

86. Florensky, *Stolp i utverzhdenie istiny*, 439.

87. Ibid., 444–45.

88. Avril Pyman describes Florensky's intense and often anguished approach to friendship in his personal life—the way he would become nearly obsessed with fostering particular male friendships—in her recent biography, *Pavel Florensky: A Quiet Genius; The Tragic and Extraordinary Life of Russia's Unknown Da Vinci* (New York: Continuum, 2010).

89. Bernice Glatzer Rosenthal's monograph on Merezhkovsky offers a far-reaching discussion of Merezhkovsky's thought and epoch-shaping activities (*Dmitri Sergeevich Merezhkovsky and the Silver Age: The Development of a Revolutionary Mentality* [The Hague: Martinus Nijhoff, 1975]). See especially 93–95.

90. Michael Aksionov Meerson, *The Trinity of Love in Modern Russian Theology: The Love Paradigm and the Retrieval of Western Medieval Love Mysticism in Modern Russian Trinitarian Thought (from Solovyov to Bulgakov)* (Quincy, Ill.: Franciscan, 1998).

91. Meerson, *The Trinity of Love in Modern Russian Theology*, 47.

92. Ibid., xv.

93. Laura Engelstein has discussed the significance of publications of the Church Fathers in Russia for the Slavophiles. Paisii Velikhkovskii's translations into Slavonic of the *Philokalia*, collections of writings from the Eastern Church Fathers, played an important role in the monastic revival. But perhaps more central for Slavophile thinkers were the translations of Church Fathers into Russian, on which Ivan Kireevsky collaborated with great passion (Laura Engelstein, *Slavophile Empire: Imperial Russia's Illiberal Path* [Ithaca, N.Y.: Cornell

University Press, 2009], 110, 133). In his article on Slavophile thought, Patrick Lally Michelson describes how Slavophile thinkers "innovatively located" some of their key ideas in Eastern Christian tradition (Patrick Lally Michelson, "Slavophile Religious Thought and the Dilemma of Russian Modernity, 1830–1860," *Modern Intellectual History* 7, no. 2 [2010]: 246).

94. Langen writes, "The searchings of Bely and his characters, Dudkin and Nikolai Apollonovich, are related to the resurgence in the late nineteenth and early twentieth centuries of apophatic theology, 'associated with such Byzantine thinkers as Gregory of Nyssa [on Dudkin's reading list], Maximus the Confessor and Gregory Palamas,' according to Charles Lock" (Timothy Langen, *The Stony Dance: Unity and Gesture in Andrey Bely's Petersburg* [Evanston, Ill.: Northwestern University Press, 2005], 19). Langen quotes here from Charles Lock, "The Bakhtin Scandal/L'Affaire Bakhtine," *Literary Research/Recherche Littéraire* 31 (1999): 13–19.

95. See pp. 75–76 in this chapter for Kuzmin's lists of theological and other Church volumes. Though Kuzmin does not list all the bibliographical information, he gives the year of the Gregory of Nazianzus and Gregory of Nyssa volumes. These editions are Grigorii Nisskii, *Tvoreniia*, 8 vols. (Moscow, 1861–71); and Grigorii Bogoslov, *Tvoreniia*, 4 vols. [?] (Moscow, 1889).

96. Augustine Casiday, "Church Fathers and the Shaping of Orthodox Theology," in *The Cambridge Companion to Orthodox Christian Theology*, ed. Mary B. Cunningham and Elizabeth Theokritoff (New York: Cambridge University Press, 2008), 167–87; here, 171.

97. Florensky's citations of the Cappadocian Fathers even just in *The Pillar and Ground of Truth* are too numerous to list, but it is telling that he takes the epigraph to his work from Gregory of Nyssa: "*ή δε γνωσις ἀγάπη γίνεται*," that is, "But knowledge becomes love" (Florensky, *Stolp i utverzhdenie istiny*). In "Soloviev's Doctrine of Salvation" Gustafson describes how Solovyov remakes key elements of Eastern patristic thought—including that of the Cappadocian Fathers—in his work. Michael Meerson shows how Solovyov incorporates his own brief history of the progressive formulation of the being of God, culminating in the doctrine of the Trinity, by the Alexandrian Fathers (including Athanasius) in his *Chteniia o bogochelovechestve* (*The Trinity of Love in Modern Russian Theology*, 29). Incidentally, Solovyov also includes the Cappadocian Gregory the Theologian (Nazianzus) in this passage (*SSVSS*, 3:83).

98. Kuzmin, "Fish Scales," 275.

CHAPTER THREE

1. This poem was published only relatively recently, in Vadim Chernykh, ed., *Anna Akhmatova: Ia—golos vash . . .* (Moscow: Knizhnaia palata, 1989), 300.

2. David J. Melling, "Andrew of Crete," in *The Blackwell Dictionary of Eastern Christianity*, ed. Ken Parry et al. (Malden, Mass.: Blackwell, 2004), 28.

3. All translations are my own.

4. See, for instance, Susan Amert, "Akhmatova's 'Song of the Motherland': Rereading the Opening Texts of *Rekviem*," *Slavic Review* 49 (1990): 374–89.

5. Nancy K. Anderson, "Biographical and Historical Background," in Anna Akhmatova, *The Word That Causes Death's Defeat: Poems of Memory*, trans. Nancy K. Anderson (New Haven, Conn.: Yale University Press, 2004), 125–26.

6. Cavanagh presents Akhmatova's continual revision of the poem and the poem's confusing form as a way of complicating the poet's status as a voice for her people—a certain avoidance or disavowal of "the choral 'we'" (128) (Cavanagh, "Akhmatova and the Forms of Responsibility," in *Lyric Poetry and Modern Politics* [New Haven, Conn.: Yale University Press, 2009], 120–48).

7. Cavanagh discusses Akhmatova's polemic with *zhiznetvorchestvo* in "Akhmatova and the Forms of Responsibility" (139). For a seminal critical account of *zhiznetvorchestvo*, see Irina Paperno and Joan Delaney Grossman, eds., *Creating Life: The Aesthetic Utopia of Russian Modernism* (Stanford, Calif.: Stanford University Press, 1994). On the motif of the masquerade—and particularly *sviatki*—mummers in Silver Age culture and in *Poem without a Hero* more specifically, see McQuillen, *The Modernist Masquerade*, especially 154–58.

8. See McQuillen, *The Modernist Masquerade*, 39–42.

9. McQuillen has written briefly about *sviatki* and other holiday mumming traditions in this vein, as well as literary genres associated with these practices, in ibid., 40–48.

10. All translations of passages from *Poem without a Hero* are mine unless otherwise noted.

11. For a well-known account of Orthodox Lent, its themes and rituals, see Alexander Schmemann, *Great Lent* (Crestwood, N.Y.: St. Vladimir's Seminary, 1996). For a much briefer account, see the appendix in the present study.

12. Edith Clowes discusses the rivalry between Akhmatova and Pasternak to sustain elements of the "Orthodox legacy," as she describes it, in their Soviet-period works (Clowes, "Seeking Miracles in the Rubble: Anna Akhmatova, Boris Pasternak, and the Orthodox Legacy in Stalin's Time," *Modern Greek Studies Yearbook* 26/27 [2010]: 1–23).

13. The narrator proclaims in her "Instead of a Foreword," "I often hear rumors of wrong and absurd interpretations of *Poem without a Hero*. Someone even suggested that I make the Poem more understandable. I'll refrain from that" (Akhmatova, *PBG*, 871). She includes lists of such interpretations in her notebooks that cover some of the period when she was writing the poem (see Anna Akhmatova, *Zapisnye knizhki Anny Akhmatovoi (1958–1966)*, ed. Giulio Einaudfi [Moscow: 1996], 450–51). Many of the most influential early readings of this work came from the Tartu school, with its emphasis on analyzing and de-

coding units of meaning. A fuller list of these works is included in Kraineva's volume (which contains the version of *PBG* referenced here), in a bibliography of critical literature on *Poem without a Hero* (Akhmatova, *PBG*, 478–86). T. V. Tsiv'ian, R. D. Timenchik, and V. N. Toporov offered several foundational articles, including T. V. Tsiv'ian's representative "Zametki k deshifrovke *Poemy bez geroia*" [Notes toward Deciphering *Poem without a Hero*], in the seminal journal *Trudy po znakovym sistemam* 5: *Mif, fol'klor, religiia kak modeliruiushchie sistemy* (Tartu, 1971): 255–77. For a more contemporary, English-language example—and one that both provides important background and comments on the poem's larger concerns—see Susan Amert, "The Poet's Lot in *Poem without a Hero*," in *In a Shattered Mirror: The Later Poetry of Anna Akhmatova* (Stanford, Calif.: Stanford University Press, 1992), 93–130.

14. Much of the existing scholarship on the *Poem* tries to untangle its massive intertextual web; I will mention some of the most important works here, also primarily from the semiotic school. See Tsiv'ian's article cited above, "Zametki k deshifrovke *Poemy bez geroia*." In this early, important article, Tsiv'ian includes an abbreviated list of citations within the poem both to Akhmatova's own, earlier works and to the poetry of her contemporaries, as well as to that of Pushkin and Zhukovskii. For the poem's Khlebnikov subtext, see R. D. Timenchik, "Neskol'ko primechanii k stat'e T. Tsiv'ian," in *Trudy po znakovym sistemam, V: Mif, fol'klor, religiia kak modeliruiushchie sistemy*, 278–80. There are two major articles on Akhmatova's use of Blok's poetry and myth, with some reference to *Poem without a Hero*, namely, V. M. Zhirmunskii's "Anna Akhmatova i Aleksandr Blok," *Russkaia literatura* 3 (1970): 57–82; and V. N. Toporov's "Akhmatova i Blok (k probleme postroeniia poeticheskogo dialoga: 'Blokovskii' tekst Akhmatovoi)," in *Peterburgskii tekst russkoi literatury* (St. Petersburg, 2003), 372–452. For Akhmatova's engagement with the work of Mikhail Kuzmin, see R. D. Timenchik, V. N. Toporov, and T. V. Tsiv'ian, "Akhmatova i Kuzmin," *Russian Literature* 6, no. 3 (1978): 213–305.

15. Galina Rylkova, *The Archaeology of Anxiety: The Russian Silver Age and Its Legacy* (Pittsburgh, Pa.: University of Pittsburgh Press, 2007). Rylkova notes that "even in Akhmatova's lifetime, the *Poem* was generally considered to be a carefully encoded message about the past that required a similarly careful deciphering on the part of the reader" (17).

16. Representative examples include Barbara Lönnqvist, "Rol' maski v russkom modernizme: Riazhenye v *Poeme bez geroiia* Akhmatovoi," *Studia Slavic Finlandensia* 15, ed. Jyrki Papinniemi et al. (Helsinki, 1998): 104–13, which describes the work as a vehicle for reconstituting selfhood; Clare Cavanagh, "Akhmatova and the Forms of Responsibility," which describes the poem's "endless construction" as a "way of deferring indefinitely . . . questions of personal and poetic responsibility" (133); and Alexandra Harrington, "Worlds within Worlds—*Poem without a Hero*," in *The Poetry of Anna Akhmatova: Living in*

Different Mirrors (New York: Anthem, 2006), which makes a convincing argument for the *Poem* as a postmodernist text.

17. Bissera Pentcheva, *The Sensual Icon: Space, Ritual, and the Senses in Byzantium* (University Park: Penn State University Press, 2010).

18. Wendy Rosslyn, *The Prince, the Fool and the Nunnery: The Religious Themes in the Early Poetry of Anna Akhmatova* (Amersham, Eng.: Avebury, 1984).

19. Roberta Reeder, *Anna Akhmatova: Poet and Prophet* (New York: St. Martin's, 1994).

20. In her Akhmatova diaries Chukovskaia recounts visiting churches in May 1953 with Akhmatova and witnessing the poet kneel down before a Mother and Child (*Bozh'aia Mater'*) icon (Lidiia Chukovskaia, *Zapiski ob Anne Akhmatovoi, Tom 2 (1952–1962)* [Paris: YMCA, 1980], 17).

21. N. Punin, "Vystavka drevnerusskogo iskusstva (ustroennaia Moskovskim Arkheologicheskim Institutom imeni Imp. Nikolaia II)," *Apollon* 5 (1913): 38. This review is cited and discussed in Jefferson A. Gatrall, "Introduction," in Gatrall and Greenfield, eds., *Alter Icons: The Russian Icon and Modernity*, 1–25; here, 13.

22. Camilla Gray discusses at length the importance of the rediscovery of the Russian icon for Russian modernist artists, focusing especially on the groundbreaking work of the Abramtsevo circle, but also on the impact their discoveries had on later painters (Camilla Gray, *The Russian Experiment in Art, 1863–1922* (London: Thames and Hudson, 1971). A recent set of fascinating new accounts of this resurgence can be found in Gatrall and Greenfield, eds., *Alter Icons*. See especially Gatrall's "Introduction," 1–25.

23. In the epigraph to the tenth numbered section of *Requiem*, "Crucifixion," Akhmatova quotes a line from a canon in the Holy Saturday Matins: "Weep not for Me, Mother, seeing in the tomb" (*Ne rydai Mene, Mati, vo grobe zriashchi*) (*AASS*, 3:28). The whole prayer reads,

> Ne rȳdaĭ mene Mati, zręshti vo grobě, ēgozhe vo chrevě sěmene zachala ēsi Sȳna: vostanū bo i proslavliusę i voznesū so slavoiu, neprestannō iakō Bog", věroiu i liubovīiu tę velichaiushtȳę. (Irmos, Tone Six, Ode Nine, *TP*, 484v)

> Weep not for me, O Mother, beholding in the sepulchre the Son whom thou hast conceived without seed in thy womb. For I shall rise and shall be glorified, and as God I shall exalt in everlasting glory those who magnify thee with faith and love. ("Holy Saturday: Matins," *LT*, 651)

24. Clowes, "Seeking Miracles in the Rubble," 13.

25. "Vozsīęl" ēsi Khriste ōt Děvȳ razūmnoe Solntse Pravdȳ: i zvězda pokaza v" vertepě vměshtaiushtasę Nevměstimago. . . . Nȳně Děva nebes" shirshi" (Christmas Eve, Troparion, Tone Six, *M* December, 249r; Lity, Third Stikhiron, 251r).

26. "Ognem" bozhestva neveshtestvennȳm", v plot' veshtestvennū odě̜vsę, ı̄ordanskoiu ōblagaetsę vodoiu, voploshteĭsę ōt Děvȳ Gospod', iakō proslavisę" (Matins, Second Troparion, Ode One of the First Canon, *M* January, 88r).

27. "Beznachal'ne strūęm" spogrebshasę Tebě, Slove" (Matins, Second Troparion, Ode One of the Second Canon, *M* January, 88v).

28. Valliere, *Modern Russian Theology*, 14.

29. Florensky writes that "the I, in this 'emptying out' or '*kenosis*—χένωσις' of itself, undergoes a reverse restoration of the I in its natural mode of being [*v svoistvennoi emu norme bytiia*]" (Pavel Florenskii, *Stolp i utverzhdenie istiny: Opyt pravoslavnoi teoditsei v dvenadtsati pis'makh* [Moscow: Lepta, 2002], 92).

30. In her chapter on *Poem without a Hero*, Clare Cavanagh begins by comparing the poem itself to the Winchester Mystery House in California's Santa Clara Valley—a house which the owner kept adding on to in order to escape and confuse sinister spirits she believed were pursuing her ("Akhmatova and the Forms of Responsibility," 120). Cavanagh speaks of the poem's "endless construction" as part of the poet's strategy to defer troubling questions about her role as a poet (133).

31. Ol'ga Sedakova, "Shkatulka s zerkalom: Ob odnom glubinnom motive A. A. Akhmatovoi," *Trudy po znakovym sistemam* 17 (1984): 93–108; here, 94.

32. Sedakova, "Shkatulka s zerkalom," 96–102.

33. Akhmatova herself described this figure as Blok, a "Poet with a capital 'P'"—see an account by V. Vilenkin, *V sto pervom zerkale* (Moscow: Sovetskii pisatel', 1987), 227–28. Others have argued that this figure is strongly associated with Kuzmin, as part of Akhmatova's competing with him to write a long poem that would define the legacy of the Silver Age. See Timenchik, Toporov, and Tsiv'ian, "Akhmatova i Kuzmin," 213–305.

34. Galina Rylkova, *The Archaeology of Anxiety*; Irina Paperno, "Lidiia Chukovskaia's Diary of Anna Akhmatova's Life: 'Intimacy and Terror,'" in *Stories of the Soviet Experience: Memoirs, Diaries, Dreams* (Ithaca, N.Y.: Cornell University Press, 2009), 57–117.

35. Paperno, *Stories of the Soviet Experience*, 52.

36. Ibid., 83.

37. Robert Bird, "Envoicing History: On the Narrative Poem in Russian Modernism," *Slavic and East European Journal* 51, no. 1 (Spring, 2007): 53–73.

38. Cavanagh, "Akhmatova and the Forms of Responsibility."

39. One classic discussion of this difference—if given more from a confessional than scholarly standpoint—is that found in Florensky's *Iconostasis*, where the Russian theologian writes that "in the Renaissance, the Roman Church survived a very grave illness wherein it gained certain immunities but suffered immense losses, for the price it paid for the few immunities it gained was the distortion of the whole of spiritual life" (101) (Florenskii, *Ikonostas*, 97). He discusses

elements of Renaissance versus icon perspective in various places in the work. See especially 105, 144–45, and 148–51 in *Iconostasis* (Florenskii, *Ikonostas*, 100–101, 135–36, 138–41). Another important and somewhat updated discussion of this aspect of iconography from a semiotic approach can be found in Boris Uspensky, *The Semiotics of the Russian Icon* (Lisse: Peter de Ridder, 1976), especially chapter 2, "Principles of Spatial Organization in Ancient Painting," 30–47. In the original, B. A. Uspenskii, "Semiotika ikony," in *Semiotika iskusstva* (Moscow: Shkola "Iazyki russkoi kul'tury," 1995), 221–94.

40. Zholkovsky sees across Akhmatova's biography an "imperial" impulse that morphs into a "totalitarian" impulse—ways the poet self-presents in response to an absolutist setting ("The Obverse of Stalinism: Akhmatova's Self-Serving Charisma of Selflessness," in *Self and Story in Russian History*, ed. Laura Engelstein and Stephanie Sandler [Ithaca, N.Y.: Cornell University Press, 2000], 46–68). Rylkova sees such an impulse manifesting itself only in the last decade of Akhmatova's life (*The Archaeology of Anxiety*, 158).

41. Many scholars have written about intertextuality in this poem. See T. V. Tsiv'ian, "Zametki k deshifrovke *Poemy bez geroia*." In this early, important article, Tsiv'ian examines layers of references and semantic structure in *Poem without a Hero*. The article includes an abbreviated list of citations within the poem both to Akhmatova's own, earlier works and to the poetry of her contemporaries, as well as to that of Pushkin and Zhukovskii. For the poem's Khlebnikov subtext, see R. D. Timenchik, "Neskol'ko primechanii k stat'e T. Tsiv'ian," in *Trudy po znakovym sistemam, V: Mif, fol'klor, religiia kak modeliruiushchie sistemy* (Tartu, 1971): 278–80. There are two major articles on Akhmatova's use of Blok's poetry and myth, with some reference to *Poem without a Hero*, namely, V. M. Zhirmunskii's "Anna Akhmatova i Aleksandr Blok," *Russkaia literatura* 3 (1970): 57–82; and V. N. Toporov's "Akhmatova i Blok (k probleme postroeniia poeticheskogo dialoga: 'Bblokovskii' tekst Akhmatovoi)," in *Peterburgskii tekst russkoi literatury* (St. Petersburg, 2003), 372–452. See also Anna Lisa Crone, "Blok as Don Juan in Akhmatova's *Poema bez geroia*," *Russian Language Journal* 35, nos. 121–22 (1981): 145–62. For Akhmatova's engagement with the work of Mikhail Kuzmin, see Timenchik, Toporov, and Tsiv'ian, "Akhmatova i Kuzmin." For the work's Gumilevian subtext, see Michael Basker, "Symbolist Devils and Acmeist Transformation: Gumilev, Demonism, and the Absent Hero in Akhmatova's *Poem without a Hero*," in *Russian Literature and Its Demons*, ed. Pamela Davidson (New York: Berghahn, 2000), 401–39.

42. I am grateful to Gregory Freidin for pointing this out to me.

43. Matich, *Erotic Utopia*; Presto, *Beyond the Flesh*.

44. Johann Wolfgang von Goethe, *Faust*, in *Sämtliche Werke: Briefe, Tagebücher und Gespräche*, vol. 7.1 (Frankfurt am Main: Deutscher Klassiker Verlag, 1994), 179. Johann Wolfgang von Goethe, *Faust: A Tragedy*, trans. Walter Arndt (New York: W. W. Norton, 1976), 104.

45. Goethe, *Faust*, trans. Arndt, 98.

46. Goethe, *Faust*, in *Sämtliche Werke*, 171.

47. The image of Jesus's passion as a cup is found in all four Gospels (Matthew 26:39, Mark 14:36, Luke 22:42, John 18:11). In Matthew 26:39 we read, for instance, "And going a little farther, he threw himself on the ground and prayed, 'My Father, if it is possible, let this cup pass from me; yet not what I want but what you want'" (New Revised Standard Version). The key phrase ("let this cup pass from me") reads in Russian, "Da minuet menia chasha siia"—using the same verb—*minovat'*—which Akhmatova employs.

48. "Sĕdit"" (Matins, Nativity of Christ, First Stikhiron of The Praises, Tone Four, *M* 12, 257v); "Grade Ōdūshevlennȳĭ" (Matins, Nativity of Christ, Third Stikhiron of The Praises, Tone Four, *M* 12, 258r); "Kivōt" (Matins, Annunciation, Irmos, Ninth Ode of the Canon, *M* 3, 228v).

49. "The Akathistos Hymn," *LT*, 419–46; here, 424, 425, 427, 428, 432, 433, 429, 424, 424, 424, 429. In the Slavonic texts, "ploda bezsmertnagō stęzhanīe" (Third Ikos, *TP*, 324v), "dvore slovesnȳkh ovet"" (Fourth Ikos of the Akathist, *TP*, 324v), "Khristov[a] knig[a] ōdūshevlenn[aę]" (Matins, Canon, First Troparion, Ode One, *TP*, 325v), "istochniche" (Matins, Canon, First Troparion, Ode Three, *TP*, 326r), "sosūde, bozhestvennȳĭ biser" proizvedshaę" (Matins, Canon, Fifth Troparion, Ode Nine, *TP*, 328r), "chertozhe" (Matins, Canon, First Troparion, Ode Six, *TP*, 328r), "Boga nevmĕstimagō vmĕstilishte" (Eight Ikos of the Akathist, *TP*, 326v), "lĕstvitse" (Second Ikos of the Akathist, *TP*, 324r), "moste" (Second Ikos of the Akathist, *TP*, 324r), "otrasli neūvędaemȳę rozgo (Third Ikos of the Akathist, *TP*, 324v), "dveri" (Eighth Ikos of the Akathist, *TP*, 326v).

50. Prominent folklorist of Petersburg culture Naum Sindalovskii includes this saying in his work *Petersburgskii folk'lor* (St. Petersburg: Maksima, 1994), 261. He sources the saying in a collection of folk sayings published in Petersburg in 1900—which indicates the strong possibility that Akhmatova could have known this version.

51. Paperno, *Stories of the Soviet Experience: Memoirs, Diaries, Dreams*, 11.

52. Ibid., xii.

53. Ibid., 8.

54. Stuart Finkel, "Nikolai Berdiaev and the Philosophical Tasks of the Emigration," in Hamburg and Poole, eds., *A History of Russian Philosophy, 1830–1930*, 346–62; here, 347.

55. Nicolas Berdyaev, *Dream and Reality: An Essay in Autobiography*, trans. Katharine Lampert (London: Geoffrey Bles, 1950); Nikolai Berdiaev, *Samopoznanie: Opyt filosofskoi avtobiografii* (Paris: YMCA, 1949). It is not clear how Akhmatova obtained a copy of Berdiaev's work, but Edith Clowes notes that they were accessible to the bold even in Stalinist Russia, "in private collections and secondhand bookstores" (Edith Clowes, *Fiction's Overcoat: Russian Liter-*

ary Culture and the Question of Philosophy [Ithaca, N.Y.: Cornell University Press, 2004], 207).

56. This collection of essays reconsidering the role of the intelligentsia in contemporary Russia was first published in 1909 and sold widely. See A. A. Iakovleva, ed., *Vekhi: Iz glubiny* (Moscow: Pravda, 1991). Boris Shragin and Albert Todd, eds., *Landmarks: A Collection of Essays on the Russian Intelligentsia*, trans. Marian Schwartz (New York: Karz Howard, 1977); Berdiaev's essay comes first in this important volume. In "Philosophic Truth and the Moral Truth of the Intelligentsia" ("Filosofskaia istina i intelligentskaia pravda") he offers a classic argument against positivistic and rationalistic philosophies borrowed from the West and in favor of a more "creative" and even mystical approach to knowledge (*Vekhi*, 11–30; *Landmarks*, 3–22).

57. In this quote and the quotes that follow from Berdiaev's autobiography I have worked with the available translation (*NBDR*), adapting where needed to make the quotes more accurate to the original. Indeed, the *NBDR* translation is a rather liberal one with not a few added poetic touches.

58. Akhmatova, *Zapisnye knizhki*, 152.

59. Roberta Reeder, *Anna Akhmatova: Poet and Prophet* (New York: St. Martin's, 1994), 33.

60. Akhmatova is recalling here lines that her husband Gumilev wrote about her, in his poem "Sviashchennye plyvut i taiut nochi . . ." (in Nikolai Gumilev, *Polnoe sobranie sochinenii* [Moscow: Voskresen'e, 1999], 56).

61. Martin Jay, *Downcast Eyes: The Denigration of Sight in Twentieth-Century French Thought* (Berkeley: University of California Press, 1993). Jay introduces this phrase on p. 69.

62. Jay, *Downcast Eyes*, 69–81; quote from 81.

63. See Rylkova, *The Archaeology of Anxiety*, 91. Laura Engelstein notes that Freud was first translated into Russian in 1911, although professional journals discussed his work before that time (Laura Engelstein, *The Keys to Happiness: Sex and the Search for Modernity in Fin-de-Siècle Russia* [Ithaca, N.Y.: Cornell University Press, 1992], 132n).

64. Paperno, *Stories of the Soviet Experience*, xiii.

65. Sigmund Freud, *The Interpretation of Dreams*, trans. Joyce Crick (New York: Oxford University Press, 1999).

66. Sigmund Freud, "The Medusa's Head," in *Writings on Art and Literature* (Stanford, Calif.: Stanford University Press, 1997), 264–65.

67. Vyacheslav Ivanov, "The Precepts of Symbolism," in *Russian Silver Age Poetry: Texts and Contexts*, ed. Sibelan E. S. Forrester and Martha M. F. Kelly (Boston: Academic Studies, 2015), 304–20; here, 315–16.

68. See Matich, "Blok's Femme Fatale: History as Palimpsest," in *Erotic Utopia*, 126–61.

69. She writes, "The invisible similitude that haunts the visible image does

not concern any category of material signs. Rather, it is the gaze that constitutes an index" (*MIIE*, 96).

70. Jay, *Downcast Eyes*, 220.

71. In his 1918 "The Intelligentsia and the Revolution," Blok refers to the music of revolution as "the music which he who has ears should hear" ("Intelligentsiia i revoliutsiia," *ABSS*, 6:9–21; here, 13). He describes this same "gul" a decade earlier in "The People and the Intelligentsia" ("Narod i intelligentsiia," *ABSS*, 5:318–28).

72. Some have suggested that Akhmatova refers here to the seventh elegy in her *Northern Elegies*, which Susan Amert links with Akhmatova's enforced silence after the 1946 resolution by the Central Committee of the Communist Party against her and Zoshchenko (Susan Amert, *In a Shattered Mirror: The Later Poetry of Anna Akhmatova* [Stanford, Calif.: Stanford University Press, 1992], 112). On the other hand, in an alternate ending for *Poem without a Hero* Akhmatova describes her verse creation "calling itself 'The Seventh'" and in her own footnotes links the reference to Shostakovich's famous Seventh *Leningrad Symphony*, which he finished in December of 1941 and dedicated to the city, which was under siege (*PBG*, 896, n.897).

73. Akhmatova underlines the lines relating to Anna on the saint's day for Simeon, Receiver of God (*Bogopriimtsa*), February 3.

74. Akhmatova, *Zapisnye knizhki*; see, for example, p. 473.

75. Cited in Reeder, *Anna Akhmatova*, 170.

76. These comments by Akhmatova, recalled by Chukovskaia in her diaries, are cited in *MBMK*, 222, 223.

77. David Bentley Hart, *The Beauty of the Infinite: The Aesthetics of Christian Truth* (Grand Rapids, Mich.: Wm. B. Eerdmans, 2003). It is important to note that in his capacity as a theologian, Hart does not engage in the kind of critique that lies at the heart of Mondzain's project. That is, Hart's project is to justify religion's use of rhetoric to "declare God's glory." His work embodies the kind of religious imperialism that Mondzain critiques.

It is also instructive to note that both Berdiaev and Hart seem to be drawing on the same theological tradition in their discussion of art and the infinite. Hart openly sets the thought of the fourth-century theologian Gregory of Nyssa at the center of his project. In the *Life of Moses*, a central work of Gregory's, the theologian sets himself the task of explaining how Moses could see God, given the radical holiness that separates God from man. Gregory explains Moses's encounters with God and his vision of the edge of God's garment as a pursuit of God who ever verges just beyond sight. Hart uses this notion to affirm art's capacity for conveying truth. Berdiaev seems as though he, too, may be drawing on Gregory of Nyssa, but interpreting him very differently. Berdiaev refers to Gregory in *Self-Knowing* as the lone patristic thinker who attracted him, while the others "did not on the whole excite [his] enthusiasm" (*NBDR*, 165; *NBSP*, 172). If Berdiaev takes anything from Gregory, it is the incommensurability Gregory sees between the human and eternal, finite and infinite.

78. Hart, *The Beauty of the Infinite*; see, for instance, 144–48, 206–8.

79. A number of scholars have read *Poem without a Hero* as a ritual. For example, in "*Poema bez geroia* v ritual'nom aspekte," in *Anna Akhmatova i russkaia kul'tura nachala XX veka: Tezisy konferentsii* (Moscow, 1989), 15–21, V. N. Toporov speaks in anthropological terms about *Poem without a Hero* as a ritual that marks the crossing of a threshold between old and new (epitomized in New Year's rituals). In "'Not a Whiff of a Roman Carnival': Akhmatova's *Poema bez geroia*," in *Russian and Yugoslav Culture in the Age of Modernism*, ed. Cynthia Marsh and Wendy Rosslyn (Nottingham, Eng.: Astra, 1991), 69–87, Wendy Rosslyn speaks of the work as "a secular rite" that helps "achieve self-knowledge and integration, a kind of spiritual healing" (82).

80. See, for instance, the sixth ode in the canon in the Matins for the Feast of the Nativity of Christ, in which we hear, "The sea monster spat forth Jonah as it had received him, like a babe from the womb: while the Word, having dwelt in the Virgin and taken flesh, came forth from her" (*FM*, 276) (*Iz outrobȳ Īōnū mladentsa izbleva morskīĭ zvěr', iakova prīęt": v" Děvū zhe vsel'sheesę Slovo, i plot' prīemshee, proĭde* [Matins, Irmos, Ode Six of the First Canon, *M* December, 255r]). The Easter service explicitly presents Jonah's time in the whale as a prefiguration of Christ's time in the tomb, also in the sixth ode of its canon: "On the third day, like Jonas from the sea monster, Thou didst arise from the grave" (*The Pentecostarion* [Boston: Holy Transfiguration Monastery, 1990], 30), (*Tridneven" iako ōt kita Īōna, voskresl" ĕsi ōt groba* [Paschal Canon, Irmos, Tone One, Ode Six, *TTs*, 3v]). (A note on this translation of the Pentecostarion: although this particular volume is translated from the Greek, the selected passage corresponds precisely to the Slavonic texts.)

81. David J. Melling and Archimandrite Ephrem, "Cherubikon," in *The Blackwell Dictionary of Eastern Christianity*, 117. The authors note in particular the hymn's Lenten exclusion from services on Holy Thursday and Holy Saturday.

82. Amert and others have seen this image as a picture of religious repression in the Soviet period (Amert, "The Poet's Lot in *Poem without a Hero*," 109). In the context of *Poem without a Hero* we might see the image instead as one of latent strength.

EXCURSUS

1. This connection to Mandelstam has been made by many commentators on the poem. Susan Amert, for one, discusses the Mandelstam subtext of the poem especially as regards this quote, in "The Poet's Lot in *Poem without a Hero*," in *In a Shattered Mirror: The Later Poetry of Anna Akhmatova*, 93–130; here, 101–4.

2. One of Mandelstam's poems, from 1909, begins with this line—in Russian, "Dano mne telo—chto mne delat' s nim . . ." (Osip Mandel'shtam, *Sochinenii v dvukh tomakh* [Moscow: Khudozhestvennaia literatura, 1990], 1:68–69).

3. Ibid., 1:300.

4. I first encountered the term "pyx" as the corresponding term to *daronositsa* in Stuart Goldberg's discussion of this poem. As Goldberg notes, Mandelstam actually uses—wittingly or unwittingly—an incorrect term. The vessel that would be used for the Eucharist in the church itself would be the *darokhranitel'nitsa*. (Stuart Goldberg, *Mandelstam, Blok, and the Boundaries of Mythopoetic Symbolism* [Columbus: Ohio State University Press, 2011], 123–25).

5. For a brief discussion of time in this poem, see Gregory Freidin, *A Coat of Many Colors: Osip Mandelstam and His Mythologies of Self-Presentation*, 121–22.

6. For a full discussion of ancient Christian conceptions of time, see Oscar Cullmann's work *Christ and Time* (Philadelphia: Westminster, 1950).

7. Ibid., 39, 49.

8. Ibid., 40.

9. Mandel'shtam, *Sochineniia*, 2:176.

10. See, for instance, Freidin, *A Coat of Many Colors*, especially the third and fourth chapters, "Le Nouvel Hippolyte and Phaedra-Russia: 1915–1916" and "Setting the Stage: Prolepsis in *Tristia*, 1915–1917" (56–123); or Clarence Brown, *Mandelstam* (New York: Cambridge University Press, 1973), especially his thirteenth chapter, "Transparent Sadness: The Classical in *Tristia*" (253–75).

11. Mandel'shtam, *Sochineniia*, 1:70–71.

12. See Freidin, *A Coat of Many Colors*, especially 58, where Freidin finds in Mandelstam a revolt against the symbolist presumption to see into the mysteries of the universe, or 185, where Freidin notes how Mandelstam at once takes on the symbolist and Solovyovian theurgic mantle while at the same time bringing art down to earth and retaining "the principle of existential uncertainty." In *Osip Mandelstam and the Modernist Creation of Tradition* (Princeton, N.J.: Princeton University Press, 1995), Clare Cavanagh addresses Mandelstam's relations to symbolism in numerous places, but see in particular her discussion of the poem "Hagia Sophia" (80–81). See also Stuart Goldberg, *Mandelstam, Blok, and the Boundaries of Mythopoetic Symbolism*, especially "Struggling with the Faith," 56–81.

CHAPTER FOUR

1. Christopher Barnes describes Akhmatova's reactions to drafts of the novel, and he even notes that she transported drafts to other readers in Petersburg. (*BBP*, 243, 255.)

2. Clowes, "Seeking Miracles in the Rubble," 1–23.

3. Jerome Spencer, "'Soaked in *The Meaning of Love* and *The Kreutzer Sonata*': The Nature of Love in *Doctor Zhivago*," in *Doctor Zhivago: A Critical Companion*, ed. Edith Clowes (Evanston, Ill.: Northwestern University Press, 1995), 76–88. See also my article "What Is Beauty? Pasternak's Adaptations of Russian Religious Thought," in *Thinking Orthodox in Modern Russia: Culture, History, Context*, ed. Patrick Lally Michelson and Judith Deutsch Kornblatt (Madison: University of Wisconsin Press, 2014), 253–74.

4. In a brief section on Sophia in Pasternak's work, Bodin presents Pasternak's whole body of work as "an expression of this special Russian idea of Sophia—a conviction of a higher unity and wholeness in existence, of a world full of interconnections and linkages uniting humans with nature and the universe." He argues that Sophia was, for Pasternak, "an existing reality," whereas for the symbolists it was "a distant hope" (Bodin, "Boris Pasternak and the Christian Tradition," in *Eternity and Time: Studies in Russian Literature and the Orthodox Tradition* [Stockholm: Almqvist & Wiksell International, 2007], 182–204; here, 197).

5. Pasternak's letter of November 10, 1945, to I. S. Postupal'sky, in *Sobranie sochinenii v piati tomakh* (Moscow: 1989–92), 5:436. Cited in *BBP*, 222.

6. Clowes, "Seeking Miracles in the Rubble," 13.

7. For a discussion of Tsvetaeva's self-association with Mary Magdalene, see Sibelan Forrester's article "Not Quite in the Name of the Lord: A Biblical Subtext in Marina Cvetaeva's Opus," *Slavic and East European Journal* 40, no. 2 (1996): 278–96; see especially 288–90. See also Liza Knapp's article "Tsvetaeva's Marine Mary Magdalene," *Slavic and East European Journal* 43, no. 4 (1999): 597–620. In her book-length study of the poetic and personal relations between Tsvetaeva and Pasternak (*The Same Solitude: Boris Pasternak and Marina Tsvetaeva* [Ithaca, N.Y.: Cornell University Press, 2006]), Ciepiela discusses at length the conversation that unfolded between Pasternak and Tsvetaeva around the issue and place of femininity. In this context she describes Pasternak's incorporation of Mary Magdalene into *Doctor Zhivago* as the incorporation of Tsvetaeva's poetic myth into his novel and its poems (see especially 244–45).

8. Susanna Witt, *Creating Creation: Readings of Pasternak's Doctor Živago* (Stockholm: Almqvist & Wiksell International, 2000); see especially 16, 20–21, although as Witt points out in her introductory chapter, images of textual distortion can serve as emblems for the process of creation that Pasternak depicts in his work as a whole. Lazar Fleishman also discusses textual distortion in *Doctor Zhivago* in "Boris Pasternak i khristianstvo," in *Christianity and the Eastern Slavs*, vol. 3, *Russian Literature in Modern Times*, ed. Boris Gasparov et al. (Berkeley: University of California Press, 1995), 288–300.

9. See Olga Raevsky-Hughes, "Liturgicheskoe vremia i evkharistiia v romane Pasternaka *Doktor Zhivago*," in *Christianity and the Eastern Slavs*, vol. 3, *Russian Literature in Modern Times*, ed. Boris Gasparov et al. (Berkeley: Uni-

versity of California Press, 1995), 302–24; Per-Arne Bodin, "Boris Pasternak and the Christian Tradition"; Mary Catherine Gannon, "The Threshold of Transfiguration and the Elusive 'Other' in the Poetics of Boris Pasternak" (Ph.D. diss., Cornell University, 1997); and Witt, *Creating Creation*.

More than these other works, Witt's study touches on a number of the points I will raise in this chapter, but she presents them in a manner that is somewhat distinct from my own. Witt takes as a starting point for her study Pasternak's reference to his novel as a "dopisyvanie" or a work that continues the writing of the biblical book of Revelation (13–15). In connection with this idea she convincingly shows how Pasternak sets before him (and represents) art's task as that of restoring wholeness to things—to unfinished texts, to the self, to the world. She also points out how this task connects Pasternak's project to that of Solovyov's (114–21). As a whole, though, her book does not explore the larger religious aims of Pasternak's work—aims that necessarily define his approach to art, his search for a new religious aesthetic. Our distinct approaches to images of Transfiguration in *Doctor Zhivago* is indicative: whereas Witt refers to such images at various points to support her interpretation of the novel as "dopisyvanie," I take these images as emblems of the novel's unorthodox religious project.

10. Boris Gasparov, "Temporal Counterpoint as a Principle of Formation in *Doctor Zhivago*," in *Intersections and Transpositions: Russian Music, Literature and Society*, ed. Andrew Wachtel (Evanston, Ill.: Northwestern University Press, 1998), 165–84; here, 171; David Bethea, "*Doctor Zhivago*: The Revolution and the Red Crosse Knight," in *The Shape of Apocalypse in Modern Russian Fiction* (Princeton, N.J.: Princeton University Press, 1989), 230–68; here, 251.

11. Bodin, "Boris Pasternak and the Christian Tradition," 185–87.

12. Gannon, "The Threshold of Transfiguration and the Elusive 'Other' in the Poetics of Boris Pasternak," 7.

13. Per-Arne Bodin and others have noted Yurii's association with this prominent holy fool. (See, for instance, Bodin, "Boris Pasternak and the Christian Tradition," 198. See also Witt, *Creating Creation*, 60.) This association appears most obviously in Yurii's name—Yurii Andreievich, a practical reversal of "Andrei Iurodivyi." But it also emerges in the shape of Yurii's character as a whole. As the novel progresses, Yurii comes increasingly to resemble the wandering "holy fool" in his neglect of social conventions and rules and in the poetic-visionary capacities with which Pasternak endows him. At moments, the novelist sets this resemblance in relief, such as when Yurii returns to Yuriatin, having escaped the partisans (*DZh*, 371–72). The narrator describes Yurii here as "emaciated and dark with the dirt that had accumulated from not bathing," wild-looking and with long, unkempt hair and beard. He wears ragged, ill-fitting clothes and receives food as alms. Such a description strongly recalls iconic depictions of Andrew the Holy Fool (and other saints in the holy fool tradition), with his bare and emaciated chest and legs, his long hair and ragged clothing, all indicating

both his freedom from the body's desires and from usual social demands. Yurii appears in similar eccentric guise in his return to Moscow at the novel's conclusion. To clinch the importance of this saint as a kind of model for his protagonist, Pasternak inspires a key scene in the novel with the Orthodox Feast of the "Virgin's Protection" or the "Virgin's Veil" (*Pokrov*), in which Andrew the Holy Fool plays a central role.

14. Per-Arne Bodin has explored this topic most fully. Bodin has shown conclusively and in detail how in *Doctor Zhivago* Pasternak adapts liturgical texts—twenty pages of which he had transcribed and apparently carried around with him. Bodin's key work on this topic is his *Nine Poems from Doctor Živago: A Study of Christian Motifs in Boris Pasternak's Poetry* (Stockholm: Almqvist & Wiksell International, 1976). In this book Bodin offers close readings of poems from the Zhivago cycle, and he convincingly links each with excerpts from the liturgical passages Pasternak had transcribed, as well as with details from the Orthodox calendar and from particular services. While Bodin is not concerned here with Pasternak's metaliterary figurations, as I am, nevertheless his conclusions support my basic argument here. That is, he returns repeatedly to Pasternak's presentation of an active, self-sacrificing Christ; this focus on an active kenosis along with his final description of "Pasternak's syncretistic approach to the cultural inheritance of Christianity" certainly point to a sophianic trajectory, even though Bodin nowhere in his book refers to Solovyov or sophiology (114). Olga Raevsky-Hughes also brings to light the strong presence of liturgical texts and structures that Pasternak uses in his novel to underscore the notion of defeating death (Raevsky-Hughes, "Liturgicheskoe vremia i evkharistiia v romane Pasternaka *Doktor Zhivago*"). I. A. Esaulov points out crucial correspondences between Pasternak's novel and Paschal liturgy, connecting elements of the work's structure with the liturgical calendar and the Paschal narrative—what he terms the "Paschal archetype." (See Esaulov, "The Paschal Archetype of Russian Literature and the Structure of Boris Pasternak's Novel *Doctor Zhivago*," *Literature and Theology* 20, no. 1 [2006]: 63–78.) Ultimately, though, Esaulov's study reductively frames the novel as an extended allegory. In *Doctor Zhivago* we find nothing as straightforward as this. Here, every transfiguration proceeds through a *dis*figuration—no Easter resurrection that does not proceed through death.

15. "Ouvȳ mně ōkaęnnaę dūshe, chto oupodobilasę ēsi pervěĭ Ēvě; viděla bo ēsi zlě, i ouęzvilasę ēsi gortsě. . . . Pogūbikh" pervozdannūiu dobrotū, i blagolěpīe moe" (Great Canon, Fourth Troparion, Ode One, *TP*, 295; Eleventh Troparion, Ode Two, *TP*, 296v).

16. "Fairer in His beauty than all mortal men, He appears now as a corpse without form or comeliness, He who has made beautiful the nature of all things" (*Krasnȳĭ dobrotoiu pache vsěkh" chelověk", iakō bezzrachen" mertv" iavlęetsę, ēstestvo oukrasivȳĭ vsěkh"*) ("Holy Saturday: Matins," *LT*, 624; Matins, First Stasis, Ninth Troparion of The Praises, *TP*, 478).

17. "Pogrebokh" ōbraz" Tvoĭ, i rastlikh" zapověd' Tvoiu, vsę pomrachisę dobrota, i strast'mi ougasisę, Spase, svěshta." (Great Canon, Eighteenth Troparion, Ode Seven, *TP*, 308v.) John Anthony McGuckin notes that the notion of the deification (*theosis*) of the flesh was articulated even by the Alexandrian Fathers, but only with Andrew of Crete, in the seventh century, did this theme appear in commentaries on the Transfiguration (John Anthony McGuckin, *The Transfiguration of Christ in Scripture and Tradition* [Lewiston, N.Y.: Edwin Mellen, 1986], 117).

18. Bodin, "Boris Pasternak and the Christian Tradition," esp. 191–95.

19. Sima herself notes the debate over whether this figure is "Mary Magdalene or another Mary," but, in subsequently drawing on a passage more surely identified with Magdalene, she manages at least to associate the diverse liturgical passages with Mary Magdalene.

20. "I have fallen into the destruction of the passions and into the corruption of material things" (*Vpadokh" v" strastnūiu pagūbū, i v" veshtestvennūiu tliu . . .*) ("Thursday of the Great Canon," *LT*, 382; Sixteenth Troparion, Ode Two, *TP*, 297).

21. Karen Evans-Romaine, *Boris Pasternak and the Tradition of German Romanticism* (Munich: Verlag Otto Sagner, 1997), 136.

22. Gustafson, "Soloviev's Doctrine of Salvation," in Kornblatt and Gustafson, eds., *Russian Religious Thought*, 31–48; here, 33, 47.

23. Ibid., 33.

24. See notes 22–26 in chapter 1.

25. "Izobrazhenīe pervoōbraznagō: seĭ ēst' . . . Spas" nash"" (Matins, Third Troparion, Ode Nine of the First Canon, *M* August, 79r).

26. See McGuckin, *The Transfiguration of Christ*, 131, for a discussion of this notion.

27. Bodin, "Boris Pasternak and the Christian Tradition," 195–97.

28. Dimitri Brady, "Andrew the Scythian," in *The Blackwell Dictionary of Eastern Christianity* (Malden, Mass.: Blackwell, 2001), 29.

29. The canon for the Akathist service addresses Mary as "dwelling-place of the Light" (*Světa zhilishte*) and names her the "spacious tabernacle of the word" (*prostrannoe selenīe Slova*), the "spotless bridal chamber of the Word" (*Chertozhe Slova neskvernȳĭ*), and tells how the angels saw in her "the living Book of Christ, sealed by the Spirit" (*Khristovū Knigū ōdūshevlennūiu*). ("Saturday of the Akathistos," *LT*, 428, 432, 433, 427; Matins, Third Troparion, Ode Three, *TP*, 326v; Fifth Troparion, Ode Five, *TP*, 328r; First Troparion, Ode One, *TP*, 325v.)

30. Sima notes, "Adam wanted to become God and failed, but now God becomes man in order to make Adam God." She offers the second clause as a direct quote (though in modern Russian) of the liturgy, which she also cites: "chelovek byvaet Bog, da Boga Adama sodelaet" (*DZh*, 407). Sima is quoting from the Vespers leading up to the main service of the Akathist to the Theotokos on the fifth

Saturday of Lent: "Chelověk" bȳvaet" Bog", da Boga Adama sodělaet"" (Vespers, Doxasticon on "Lord, I have cried . . . ," Tone Two, *TP*, 321v).

31. Bodin, *Nine Poems from Doctor Zhivago*, 97–98.

32. Galina Rylkova, "The Silver Age in Translation: Boris Pasternak's *Doctor Zhivago*," in *The Archaeology of Anxiety: The Russian Silver Age and Its Legacy*, 127–53.

33. This is a driving point in Clowes, "Seeking Miracles in the Rubble."

34. In Bodin's reading of this poem he points out its liturgical connections, and he also argues that Pasternak adapts the scene in part from the Russo-Byzantine tradition—as well as from a Breughel painting (Bodin, *Nine Poems*, 67–78).

35. Timothy D. Sergay, "'Blizhe k suti, k miru Bloka'": The *Mise-en-Scène* of Boris Pasternak's 'Hamlet' and Pasternak's Blokian-Christological Ideal," *Russian Review* 64 (2005): 401–21.

36. Pasternak Trust, "Unpublished Pasternak Letters and Photographs," *Quarto: Film, Drama, Books, Reportage, Poetry*, no. 6 (London, 1980). Cited in Sergay, "'Blizhe k suti, k miru Bloka,'" 411.

37. "In my beginning is my end" (*PBG*, 888). In earlier drafts Akhmatova listed Eliot's work as the source of this quote. Later, however, she changed the ascription to "Motto of Mary Queen of Scots" (*Deviz Marii Shotlandskoi*). As Kraineva's notes explain, Akhmatova found out that Eliot had taken this line from a phrase the Scottish queen was embroidering while in prison (*PBG*, 925). In this detail, too, then, we find yet another of Akhmatova's dungeon/hell spaces, another of the spaces into which she can make her poetic doubles descend.

EPILOGUE

1. Irina Paperno and Joan Delaney Grossman, eds., *Creating Life: The Aesthetic Utopia of Russian Modernism* (Stanford, Calif.: Stanford University Press, 1994).

2. See Ivanov, "Dve stikhii v sovremennom simvolizme," 156.

3. Space does not allow a full bibliography, but representative works include S. J. Barnett, *Enlightenment and Religion: The Myths of Modernity* (Manchester, 2003); Steve Bruce, ed., *Religion and Modernization: Sociologists and Historians Debate the Secularization Thesis* (New York: Oxford University Press, 1992); Leigh Eric Schmidt, *Hearing Things: Religion, Illusion, and the American Enlightenment* (Cambridge, Mass.: Harvard University Press, 2000); Jonathan Sheehan, "Enlightenment, Religion and the Enigma of Secularization: A Review Essay," *American Historical Review* 108, no. 3 (2003): 1061–80; Charles Taylor, *A Secular Age* (Cambridge, Mass.: Belknap, 2007).

4. Mark D. Steinberg and Heather J. Coleman, "Introduction: Rethinking Religion in Modern Russian Culture," in *Sacred Stories: Religion and Spirituality in Modern Russia*, ed. Mark D. Steinberg and Heather J. Coleman (Bloomington: Indiana University Press, 2007), 1–21; here, 9.

5. Ol'ga Sedakova, "Tserkovnoslavianskii iazyk v russkoi kul'ture," in *Perevody* (Moscow: Universitet Dmitriia Pozharskogo, 2010), 125–41; here, 126.

6. Sedakova, "Tserkovnoslavianskii iazyk v russkoi kul'ture," 127.

7. Gregory of Nyssa, *From Glory to Glory: Texts from Gregory of Nyssa's Mystical Writings*, ed. and trans. Herbert Musurillo (New York: Charles Scribner's Sons, 1961), 227–28.

8. Ol'ga Sedakova, *Stikhi* (Moscow: Universitet Dmitriia Pozharskogo, 2010), 27.

9. Ol'ga Sedakova, *Moralia: Esse, lektsii, zametki, interv'iu* (Moscow: Universitet Dmitriia Pozharskogo, 2010), 799–811; here, 807–8.

10. Ol'ga Sedakova, "Dikii shipovnik," in *Stikhi*, 59.

11. Ol'ga Sedakova, "Nemnogo o poezii: O ee kontse, nachale i prodolzhenii," in *Poetica* (Moscow: Universitet Dmitriia Pozharskogo, 2010), 141–46. This speech is available in English translation in Olga Sedakova, *Freedom to Believe: Philosophical and Cultural Essays* (Lewiston, Pa.: Bucknell University Press, 2010), 219–27.

12. Sedakova, *Stikhi*, 325–45.

13. Ibid., 328.

14. Ibid., 335.

15. Benjamin Paloff, "The God Function in Joseph Brodsky and Olga Sedakova," *Slavic and East European Journal* 51, no. 4 (2007): 716–36.

16. Ol'ga Sedakova, "'Ne smertnye, tainstvennye chuvstva' (O khristianstve Pushkina)," *Kontinent* 115 (2003): 364–75; here, 373.

17. Andrew Louth, "The Theology of the *Philokalia*," in *Abba: The Tradition of Orthodoxy in the West: Festschrift for Bishop Kallistos (Ware) of Diokleia*, ed. John Behr et al. (Crestwood, N.Y.: St. Vladimir's Seminary, 2003), 351–62; here, 358.

18. Sedakova, "Iz liturgicheskoi poezii," in *Perevody*, 123–52.

19. See, for instance, "Srednevekovaia slovesnost'" ("Iz 'Poslanii Sv. Antoniia Velikogo,'" "Iz 'Sinaiskogo Paterika,'" "'Vse vo vsekh veshchakh': O Frantsiske Assizskom," "Iz 'Vtorogo zhitiia Sviatogo Frantsiska Assizskogo,'" "Sostavlennogo Fomoi Chelanskim," "Iz 'Slov Brata Egidiia'") in *Perevody*, 47–121.

20. Ol'ga Sedakova, *Poetika obriada: Pogrebal'naia obriadnost' vostochnykh i iuzhnykh slavian* (Moscow: Izdatel'stvo Indrik, 2004).

21. Ol'ga Sedakova, *Slovar' trudnykh slov iz bogosluzheniia: Tserkovnoslaviano-russkie paronimy* (Moscow: Greko-latinskii kabinet IU. A. Shichalina, 2008).

APPENDIX

1. Alexander Schmemann, *Introduction to Liturgical Theology*, trans. Asheleigh E. Moorhouse (Crestwood, N.Y.: St. Vladimir's Seminary, 1986), 14.

2. See "The Orthodox Services and Their Structure," *FM*, 38–80. I have

drawn on this account of liturgical structure, but also on a number of others, as reflected in the bibliography that I have included. The names of the feasts are translated variously. I have drawn on several translations in my rendition of them, to reflect both their meaning and their distinction from corresponding Western feasts.

3. Hugh Wybrew, *The Orthodox Liturgy: The Development of the Eucharistic Liturgy in the Byzantine Rite* (Crestwood, N.Y.: St. Vladimir's Seminary, 1990), 130, 145.

4. For a discussion of the canon form, see "Kanon," in Johann von Gardner, *Russian Church Singing*, vol. 1, *Orthodox Worship and Hymnography*, trans. Vladimir Morosan (Crestwood, N.Y.: St. Vladimir's Seminary, 1980), 40–44.

5. See the entries on the canon and the ode in *The Blackwell Dictionary of Eastern Christianity* (Archimandrite Ephrem, "Canon," and David J. Melling, "Ode," in *The Blackwell Dictionary of Eastern Christianity*, 110–11 and 351).

6. "Světa Chertog" i Kniga Slova Zhivotnagō . . . i iazhe k vostokōm Dver'" (Vespers, Second Stikhiron on "Lord, I have cried . . . ," Tone Six, *M* September, 75r); "zlatаę kadil'nitsa" (Matins, Theotokion, Ode Six of the Second Canon, *M* September, 81v); "Gor[a] i dver' nebesn[aę], i mȳslenn[aę] tę Lěstvits[a]" (Second Troparion, Ode Seven of the First Canon, *M* September, 82r).

7. For a brief discussion of the history of this feast, see "The Presentation of the Holy Virgin in the Temple" and, for comparison, "The Protection of the Mother of God," in Leonid Ouspensky and Vladimir Lossky, *The Meaning of Icons*, trans. G. E. H. Palmer and E. Kadloubovsky (Crestwood, N.Y.: St. Vladimir's Seminary, 1999), 153–56 and 151–52, respectively.

8. A classic, twentieth-century account of this theology and its development can be found in Vladimir Lossky, *The Mystical Theology of the Eastern Church* (Crestwood, N.Y.: St. Vladimir's Seminary, 1976).

Works Cited

Akhmatova, Anna. *Anna Akhmatova: Ia—golos vash . . .* Ed. Vadim Chernykh. Moscow: Knizhnaia palata, 1989.

———. *"Ia ne takoi tebia kogda-to znala . . .": Anna Akhmatova: Poema bez Geroia. Proza o Poeme. Nabroski baletnogo libretto: Materialy k tvorcheskoi istorii*, 679–798. Ed. N. I. Kraineva. St. Petersburg: Mir, 2009.

———. *Sobranie sochinenii v shesti tomakh*. Moscow: Ellis Lak, 1998.

———. *Sochinenii v dvukh tomakh*. Moscow: Pravda, 1990.

———. *Zapisnye knizhki Anny Akhmatovoi (1958–1966)*. Ed. Giulio Einaudfi. Moscow: 1996.

Alfeev, Ilarion. *Spory ob imeni Bozhiem: Arkhivnye dokumenty 1912-1938 godov*. St. Petersburg: Oleg Abyshko, 2007.

Amert, Susan. "Akhmatova's 'Song of the Motherland': Rereading the Opening Texts of *Rekviem*." *Slavic Review* 49 (1990): 374–89.

———. *In a Shattered Mirror: The Later Poetry of Anna Akhmatova*. Stanford, Calif.: Stanford University Press, 1992.

Anderson, Nancy K. "Biographical and Historical Background." In Anna Akhmatova, *The Word That Causes Death's Defeat: Poems of Memory*, 3–131. Trans. Nancy K. Anderson. New Haven, Conn.: Yale University Press, 2004.

Averintsev, Sergei. *Poetika rannevizantiiskoi literatury*. Moscow: Coda, 1997.

Baevskii, V. S., and A. D. Koshelev. "Poetika Bloka: Anagrammy." In *Tvorchestvo A. A. Bloka i russkaia kul'tura XX veka: Blokovskii Sbornik III*, 50–75. Ed. Zara Mints. Tartu: Tartuskii gosudarstvennyi universitet, 1979.

Baggley, John. *Festival Icons for the Christian Year*. London: Society for Promoting Christian Knowledge, 2000.

Banerjee, Maria Nemcova. *Dostoevsky: The Scandal of Reason*. Great Barrington, Mass.: Lindisfarne Books, 2006.

Barnes, Christopher. *Boris Pasternak: A Literary Biography*. Vol. 2, *1928–1960*. New York: Cambridge University Press, 1998.

Barnett, S. J. *Enlightenment and Religion: The Myths of Modernity*. Manchester, Eng.: Manchester University Press, 2003.

Barta, Peter, and Ulrich Goebel. *The European Foundations of Russian Modernism*. Lewiston, N.Y.: Edwin Mellen, 1991.

Basker, Michael. "Symbolist Devils and Acmeist Transformation: Gumilev, Demonism, and the Absent Hero in Akhmatova's *Poem without a Hero*." In *Russian Literature and Its Demons*, 401–39. Ed. Pamela Davidson. New York: Berghahn, 2000.

Baudelaire, Charles. *Selected Poems from "Les Fleurs du mal": A Bilingual Edition*. Chicago: University of Chicago Press, 1998.

Bell, Catherine. *Ritual: Perspectives and Dimensions*. New York: Oxford University Press, 1997.

———. *Ritual Theory, Ritual Practice*. New York: Oxford University Press, 1992.

Bely, Andrei. "Apokalipsis v russkoi poezii." In *Lug Zelenyi*. Moscow: Al'tsiona, 1910.

———. "Magiia slov." In *Simvolizm*, 433–34. Moscow: Musaget, 1910.

———. *Nachalo veka*. Moscow: Khudozhestvennaia literatura, 1990.

Benua, Aleksandr, ed. "Patriarshaia riznitsa v Moskve: 53 snimka s predmetov (tserkovnye oblacheniia i utvar'), khraniashchikhsia v riznitse." *Mir iskusstva* 12 (1904): 203–36.

Berdiaev, Nikolai. *Dream and Reality: An Essay in Autobiography*. Trans. Katharine Lampert. London: Geoffrey Bles, 1950.

———. *The Russian Idea*. Hudson, N.Y.: Lindisfarne, 1992.

———. *Samopoznanie: Opyt filosofskoi avtobiografii*. Paris: YMCA, 1949.

———. *Sobranie sochinenii*. Paris: YMCA, 1989.

Bershtein, Evgenii. "An Englishman in the Russian Bathhouse: Kuzmin's *Wings* and the Russian Tradition of Homoerotic Writing." In *The Many Facets of Mikhail Kuzmin: A Miscellany*, 75–88. Ed. Lada Panova and Sarah Pratt. Bloomington, Ind.: Slavica, 2011.

Bethea, David. *The Shape of Apocalypse in Modern Russian Fiction*. Princeton, N.J.: Princeton University Press, 1989.

Bird, Robert. "Envoicing History: On the Narrative Poem in Russian Modernism." *Slavic and East European Journal* 51, no. 1 (2007): 53–73.

———. *The Russian Prospero: The Creative Universe of Viacheslav Ivanov*. Madison: University of Wisconsin Press, 2006.

Blok, Aleksandr. *Polnoe sobranie sochinenii i pisem v dvadtsati tomakh*. Moscow: Nauka, 1997.

———. *Sobranie sochineniia v vos'mi tomakh*. Moscow: Gosudarstvennoe izdatel'stvo khudozhestvennoi literatury, 1962.

———. *Sochineniia*. 2 vols. Moscow: Gosudarstvennaia izdatel'stvo khudozhestvennoi literatury, 1955.

———. *Zapisnye knizhki: 1901–1920*. Ed. V. N. Orlov. Moscow: Khudozhestvennaia literatura, 1965.

Bodin, Per-Arne. *Eternity and Time: Studies in Russian Literature and the Orthodox Tradition*. Stockholm: Almqvist & Wiksell International, 2007.

———. *Nine Poems from "Doktor Zhivago": A Study of Christian Motifs in Boris Pasternak's Poetry*. Stockholm: Almqvist & Wiksell International, 1976.

Bogomolov, Nikolai. *Russkaia literatura nachala XX veka i okkul'tizm: Issledovaniia i materialy*. Moscow: Novoe literaturnoe obozrenie, 1999.

Bogomolov, Nikolay, and John E. Malmstad. "U istokov tvorchestva Mikhaila Kuzmina." *Voprosy literatury* 3 (1993): 64–121.

Bowlt, John. "Here and There: The Question of Space in Blok's Poetry." In *Aleksandr Blok Centennial Conference*. Ed. Walter N. Vickery. Columbus, Ohio: Slavica, 1982.

Brodsky, Patricia. *Russia in the Works of Rainer Maria Rilke*. Detroit, Mich.: Wayne State University Press, 1994.

Brown, Clarence. *Mandelstam*. New York: Cambridge University Press, 1973.

Brown, Peter. *Society and the Holy in Late Antiquity*. Berkeley: University of California Press, 1982.

Bruce, Steve, ed. *Religion and Modernization: Sociologists and Historians Debate the Secularization Thesis*. New York: Oxford University Press, 1992.

Burchardi, Kristiane. *Die Moskauer "Religiös-philosophische Vladimir-Solov'ev Gesellschaft" (1905–1918)*. Wiesbaden: Harrassowitz, 1998.

Carlson, Maria. *"No Religion Higher than Truth": A History of the Theosophical Movement in Russia, 1875–1922*. Princeton, N.J.: Princeton University Press, 1993.

Cassedy, Steven. "Bely the Thinker." In *Andrey Bely: Spirit of Symbolism*, 313–35. Ed. John E. Malmstad. Ithaca, N.Y.: Cornell University Press, 1987.

———. *Dostoevsky's Religion*. Stanford, Calif.: Stanford University Press, 2005.

———. *Flight from Eden: The Origins of Modern Literary Criticism and Theory*. Berkeley: University of California Press, 1990.

———. "Mathematics, Relationalism, and the Rise of Modern Literary Aesthetics." *Journal of the History of Ideas* 49, no. 1 (1988): 109–32.

———. "Pavel Florenskij's Philosophy of Language: Its Contextuality and Its Context." *Slavic and East European Journal* 35, no. 4 (1991): 537–52.

———. "Toward a Unified Theory of the Aesthetic Object in Andrej Belyj." *Slavic and East European Journal* 28, no. 2 (1984): 205–22.

Casiday, Augustine. "Church Fathers and the Shaping of Orthodox Theology." In *The Cambridge Companion to Orthodox Christian Theology*, 167–87. Ed. Mary B. Cunningham and Elizabeth Theokritoff. New York: Cambridge University Press, 2008.

Cavanagh, Claire. "Akhmatova and the Forms of Responsibility." In *Lyric Poetry and Modern Politics: Russia, Poland, and the West*. New Haven, Conn.: Yale University Press, 2009.

———. *Osip Mandelstam and the Modernist Creation of Tradition*. Princeton, N.J.: Princeton University Press, 1995.

Chukovskaia, Lidiia. *Zapiski ob Anne Akhmatovoi*. Vol. 2, *1952–1962*. Paris: YMCA, 1980.

Chulos, Chris. *Converging Worlds: Religion and Community in Peasant Russia, 1861–1917*. De Kalb: Northern Illinois University Press, 2003.

Ciepiela, Catherine. "The Demanding Woman Poet: On Resisting Marina Tsvetaeva." *PMLA* 111, no. 3 (1996): 421–34.

———. *The Same Solitude: Boris Pasternak and Marina Tsvetaeva*. Ithaca, N.Y.: Cornell University Press, 2006.

Cioran, Samuel. *The Apocalyptic Symbolism of Andrej Belyj*. The Hague: Mouton, 1973.

Clowes, Edith. *Fiction's Overcoat: Russian Literary Culture and the Question of Philosophy*. Ithaca, N.Y.: Cornell University Press, 2004.

———. *The Revolution of Moral Consciousness: Nietzsche in Russian Literature, 1890–1914*. De Kalb: Northern Illinois University Press, 1988.

———. "Seeking Miracles in the Rubble: Anna Akhmatova, Boris Pasternak, and the Orthodox Legacy in Stalin's Time." *Modern Greek Studies Yearbook* 26/27 (2010): 1–23.

Coates, Ruth. "Religious Writing in Post-Petrine Russia." In *The Routledge Companion to Russian Literature*, 49–63. Ed. Neil Cornwell. London: Routledge, 2001.

Coleman, Heather. *Russian Baptists and Spiritual Revolution, 1905–1929*. Bloomington: Indiana University Press, 2005.

Cullmann, Oscar. *Christ and Time*. Philadelphia: Westminster, 1950.

Danielou, Jean. *The Bible and the Liturgy*. Notre Dame, Ind.: University of Notre Dame Press, 1956.

Davidson, Pamela. "The Moral Dimension of the Prophetic Ideal: Pushkin and His Readers." *Slavic Review* 61, no. 3 (2002): 490–518.

———. *The Poetic Imagination of Vyacheslav Ivanov: A Russian Symbolist's Perception of Dante*. New York: Cambridge University Press, 1989.

Derzhavin, G. R. *Stikhotvoreniia*. Leningrad: Sovetskii Pisatel', 1957.

Dinega, Alyssa. *A Russian Psyche: The Poetic Mind of Marina Tsvetaeva*. Madison: University of Wisconsin Press, 2001.

Dix, Gregory. *The Shape of the Liturgy*. London: Dacre, 1945.

Dobrenko, Evgeny. "Socialist Realism." In *The Cambrige Companion to Twentieth-Century Russian Literature*, 97–114. Ed. Evgeny Dobrenko and Marina Balina. New York: Cambridge University Press, 2011.

Dostoevsky, Fyodor. *Polnoe sobranie sochenenii v tridsati tomakh*. Leningrad: Nauka, 1973.

Dunaev, M. M. *Pravoslavie i russkaia literatura*. 6 vols. Moscow, 2001–4.

———. *Vera v gornile somnenii: Pravoslavie i russkaia literatura v XVII–XX vv*. Moscow: Izdatel'skii sovet russkoi pravoxlavnoi tserkvi, 2002.

Eisen, Arnold. *Rethinking Modern Judaism: Ritual, Commandment, Community*. Chicago: University of Chicago Press, 1998.

Engelstein, Laura. *Castration and the Heavenly Kingdom: A Russian Folktale*. Ithaca, N.Y.: Cornell University Press, 1999.

———. *Slavophile Empire: Imperial Russia's Illiberal Path*. Ithaca, N.Y.: Cornell University Press, 2009.

Ephrem, Archimandrite. "Canon." In *The Blackwell Dictionary of Eastern Christianity*, 110–11. Ed. Ken Perry, David J. Melling, et al. Malden, Mass.: Blackwell, 2001.

Esaulov, I. A. *Kategoriia sobornosti v russkoi literature*. Petrozavodsk: Izdatel'stvo Petrozavodskogo universiteta, 1995.

———. "The Paschal Archetype of Russian Literature and the Structure of Boris Pasternak's Novel *Doctor Zhivago*." *Literature and Theology* 20, no. 1 (2006): 63–78.

Etkind, Aleksandr. *Khlyst: Sekty, literatura i revoliutsiia*. Moscow, 1998.

Etkind, Efim. "Dvoemirie Bloka." In *Tam, vnutri: o russkoi poezii XX veka: Ocherki*. St. Petersburg, 1997.

Evans-Romaine, Karen. *Boris Pasternak and the Tradition of German Romanticism*. Munich: Verlag Otto Sagner, 1997.

Eysteinsson, Astradur. *The Concept of Modernism*. Ithaca, N.Y.: Cornell University Press, 1990.

Festal Menaion. Trans. Mother Mary and Archimandrite Kallistos Ware. London: Faber and Faber, 1977.

Finkel, Stuart. "Nikolai Berdiaev and the Philosophical Tasks of the Emigration." In *A History of Russian Philosophy, 1830–1930: Faith, Reason, and the Defense of Human Dignity*, 346–62. Ed. G. M. Hamburg and Randall A. Poole. New York: Cambridge University Press, 2010.

Fleishman, Lazar. *Boris Pasternak: The Poet and His Politics*. Cambridge, Mass.: Harvard University Press, 1990.

———. "Boris Pasternak i khristianstvo." In *Christianity and the Eastern Slavs*, vol. 3, *Russian Literature in Modern Times*, 288–300. Ed. Boris Gasparov et al. Berkeley: University of California Press, 1995.

Florensky, Pavel. *Iconostasis*. Crestwood, N.Y.: St. Vladimir's Seminary, 1996.

———. *Ikonostas*. Moscow: Iskusstvo, 1994.

———. *Stolp i utverzhdenie istiny: Opyt pravoslavnoi teoditsei v dvenadtsati pis'makh*. Moscow: Lepta, 2002.

Florovsky, Georges. *Ways of Russian Theology: Part Two*. Vaduz: Büchervertriebsanstalt, 1987.

Forrester, Sibelan. "Bells and Cupolas: The Formative Role of the Female Body in Marina Tsvetaeva's Poetry." *Slavic Review* 51, no. 2 (1992): 232–46.

———. "Not Quite in the Name of the Lord: A Biblical Subtext in Marina Cvetaeva's Opus." *Slavic and East European Journal* 40, no. 2 (1996): 278–96.

Forrester, Sibelan E. S., and Martha M. F. Kelly, eds. *Russian Silver Age Poetry: Texts and Contexts*. Boston: Academic Studies, 2015.

Frank, Joseph. *Dostoevsky: The Miraculous Years, 1865–1871*. Princeton, N.J.: Princeton University Press, 1997.

Freidin, Gregory. *A Coat of Many Colors: Osip Mandelstam and His Mythologies of Self-Presentation*. Berkeley: University of California Press, 1987.

Freud, Sigmund. *The Interpretation of Dreams*. Trans. Joyce Crick. New York: Oxford University Press, 1999.

———. "The Medusa's Head." In *Writings on Art and Literature*, 264–65. Stanford, Calif.: Stanford University Press, 1997.

Gannon, Mary Catherine. "The Threshold of Transfiguration and the Elusive 'Other' in the Poetics of Boris Pasternak." Ph.D. diss. Cornell University, 1997.

Gaonkar, Dilip Parameshwar, ed. *Alternative Modernities*. Durham, N.C.: Duke University Press, 2001.

Gasparov, Boris. "Temporal Counterpoint as a Principle of Formation in *Doctor Zhivago*." In *Intersections and Transpositions: Russian Music, Literature and Society*, 165–84. Ed. Andrew Wachtel. Evanston, Ill.: Northwestern University Press, 1998.

Gasparov, Boris, Robert P. Hughes, Irina Paperno, and Olga Raevsky-Hughes, eds. *Christianity and the Eastern Slavs*. Vol. 3, *Russian Culture in Modern Times*. Berkeley: University of California Press, 1995.

Gatrall, Jefferson J. A., and Douglas Greenfield, eds. *Alter Icons: The Russian Icon and Modernity*. University Park: Penn State University Press, 2010.

Gillis, Donald C. "The Platonic Theme in Kuzmin's *Wings*." *Slavic and East European Journal* 22, no. 3 (1978): 336–47.

Goethe, Johann Wolfgang von. *Faust*. In *Sämtliche Werke. Briefe, Tagebücher und Gespräche*, vol. 7.1. Frankfurt am Main: Deutscher Klassiker Verlag, 1994.

———. *Faust: A Tragedy*. Trans. Walter Arndt. New York: W. W. Norton, 1976.

Goldberg, Stuart. *Mandelstam, Blok, and the Boundaries of Mythopoetic Symbolism*. Columbus: Ohio State University Press, 2011.

Goncharova, O. M. "*Vozvrashchenie k sebe* kak natsional'no-religioznoe vozrozhdenie v russkoi masonskoi mistike XVIII veka." In *Vlast' traditsii i "Novaia Rossiia" v literaturnom soznanii vtoroi poloviny XVIII veka*, 52–95. St. Petersburg: Izdatel'stvo Khristianskogo Gumanitarnogo Instituta, 2004.

Grabar', Igor'. *O Drevnerusskom iskusstve*. Moscow: Nauka, 1966.

Gray, Camilla. *The Russian Experiment in Art, 1863–1922*. London: Thames and Hudson, 1971.

Greene, Thomas M. *Poetry, Signs, and Magic*. Newark: University of Delaware Press, 2005.

Gregory of Nyssa. *From Glory to Glory: Texts from Gregory of Nyssa's Mystical Writings*. Trans. and ed. Herbert Musurillo. New York: Charles Scribner's Sons, 1961.

———. *The Life of Moses*. Trans. Abraham J. Malherbe and Everett Ferguson. New York: Paulist, 1978.

Grossman, Joan Delaney. "Alternate Beliefs: Spiritualism and Pantheism among the Early Modernists." In *Christianity and the Eastern Slavs*, vol. 3, *Russian Literature in Modern Times*, 113–33. Ed. Boris Gasparov et al. Berkeley: University of California Press, 1995.

Gumilev, Nikolai. *Polnoe sobranie sochinenii*. Moscow: Voskresen'e, 1999.

Gustafson, Richard. *Leo Tolstoy, Resident and Stranger: A Study in Fiction and Theology*. Princeton, N.J.: Princeton University Press, 1986.

———. "Soloviev's Doctrine of Salvation." In *Russian Religious Thought*, by Judith Deutsch Kornblatt and Richard F. Gustafson, 31–48. Madison: University of Wisconsin Press, 1996.

Guzhieva, N. V. "Tserkovnyi kalendar' v structure liricheskoi trilogii A. Bloka." *Russkaia literatura* 2 (2005): 81–93.

Harrington, Alexandra. *The Poetry of Anna Akhmatova: Living in Different Mirrors*. London: Anthem, 2006.

Hart, David Bentley. *The Beauty of the Infinite: The Aesthetics of Christian Truth*. Grand Rapids, Mich.: Wm. B. Eerdmans, 2003.

Hasty, Olga Peters. *Tsvetaeva's Orphic Journeys in the Worlds of the Word*. Evanston, Ill.: Northwestern University Press, 1996.

Heretz, Leonid. *Russia on the Eve of Modernity: Popular Religion and Traditional Culture under the Last Tsars*. Cambridge, Eng.: Cambridge University Press, 2008.

Hervieu-Léger, Danièle. *Religion as a Chain of Memory*. New Brunswick, N.J.: Rutgers University Press, 2000.

Hopko, Thomas. "The Daily Cycles of Prayer." In *The Orthodox Faith*, vol. 2, *Worship*, 59–68. Syosset, N.Y.: Orthodox Church in America, 1997.

Horujy, Sergey. "Slavophiles, Westernizers, and the Birth of Russian Philosophical Humanism." Trans. Patrick Lally Michelson. In *A History of Russian Philosophy, 1830–1930: Faith, Reason, and the Defense of Human Dignity*, 27–51. Ed. G. M. Hamburg and Randall A. Poole. New York: Cambridge University Press, 2010.

Hughes, Robert P., and Irina Paperno, eds. *Christianity and the Eastern Slavs*. Vol. 2, *Russian Culture in Modern Times*. Berkeley: University of California Press, 1994.

Hutchings, Stephen. *Russian Modernism: The Transfiguration of the Everyday*. New York: Cambridge University Press, 1997.

Iakovleva, A. A., ed. *Vekhi: Iz glubiny*. Moscow: Pravda, 1991.

Igosheva, T. V. "Materialy i soobshcheniia: Religioznoe preobrazhenie v kontekste *Stikhov o prekrasnoi dame* A Bloka." *Izvestiia RAN: Seriia literatury i iazyka* 63, no. 4 (2004): 54–62.

Iur'eva, I. *Pushkin i khristianstvo*. Moscow: Muravei, 1998.

Ivanov, Viacheslav. "O russkoi idee." In *Russkaia ideia*. Ed. M. A. Maslin. Moscow: Respublika, 1992.

———. *Rodnoe i vselenskoe*. Moscow: Respublika, 1994.

———. *Selected Essays*. Trans. Robert Bird. Ed. Michael Wachtel. Evanston, Ill.: Northwestern University Press, 2003.

Jay, Martin. *Downcast Eyes: The Denigration of Sight in Twentieth-Century French Thought*. Berkeley: University of California Press, 1993.

John Climacus (Saint). *Lestvitsa*. St. Petersburg: Sviatoslov, 1996.

Kalb, Judith. *Russia's Rome: Imperial Visions, Messianic Dreams, 1890–1940*. Madison: University of Wisconsin Press, 2008.

Kant, Immanuel. *Critique of Pure Reason*. New York: Cambridge University Press, 2000.

Kelly, Martha M. F. "What Is Beauty? Pasternak's Adaptations of Russian Religious Thought." In *Thinking Orthodox in Modern Russia: Culture, History, Context*, 253–74. Ed. Patrick Lally Michelson and Judith Deutsch Kornblatt. Madison: University of Wisconsin Press, 2014.

Kenworthy, Scott. "Archbishop Nikon (Rozhdestvenskii) and Pavel Florenskii on Spiritual Experience, Theology, and the Name-Glorifiers Dispute." In *Thinking Orthodox in Modern Russia: Culture, History, Context*. 85–107. Ed. Patrick Lally Michelson and Judith Deutsch Kornblatt. Madison: University of Wisconsin Press, 2014.

———. *The Heart of Russia: Trinity-Sergius Monasticism and Society after 1825*. New York: Oxford University Press, 2010.

Khomiakov, Aleksei. "Some Remarks by an Orthodox Christian Concerning the Western Communions, on the Occasion of a Letter Published by the Archbishop of Paris." In *On Spiritual Unity: A Slavophile Reader*, 63–116. Ed. Boris Jakim and Robert Bird. Hudson, N.Y.: Lindisfarne Books, 1998.

———. *Stikhotvoreniia i dramy*. Leningrad: Sovetskii pisatel', 1969.

Kivelson, Valerie A., and Robert H. Greene. *Orthodox Russia: Belief and Practice under the Tsars*. University Park: Penn State University Press, 2003.

Kizenko, Nadieszda. *A Prodigal Saint: Father John of Kronstadt and the Russian People*. University Park: Penn State University Press, 2000.

Knapp, Liza. "Marina Tsvetaeva's Poetics of Ironic Delight: The 'Podruga' Cycle as Evist Manifesto." *Slavic and East European Review* 41, no. 1 (1997): 94–113.

Konstantinova, S. L. "'Bogorodichnye motivy' v *Ital'ianskikh stikhakh* A. Bloka." In *Aleksandr Blok i mirovaia kul'tura: Materialy nauchnoi konferentsii 14–17 marta 2000 goda*, 62–68. Velikii Novgorod, 2000.

Kornblatt, Judith Deutsch. *Divine Sophia: The Wisdom Writings of Vladimir Solovyov*. Ithaca, N.Y.: Cornell University Press, 2009.

———. "The Truth of the Word: Solovyov's 'Three Conversations' Speaks on Tolstoy's *Resurrection*." *Slavic and East European Journal* 45, no. 2 (2001): 301–21.

Kornblatt, Judith Deutsch, and Richard F. Gustafson. *Russian Religious Thought*. Madison: University of Wisconsin Press, 1996.

Koshchemchuk, Tatiana. *Russkaia poeziia v kontekste pravoslavnoi kul'tury*. St. Petersburg: Nauka, 2006.

Kostalevsky, Marina. *Dostoevsky and Soloviev: The Art of Integral Vision*. New Haven, Conn.: Yale University Press, 1997.

Kotel'nikov, V. A., ed. *Dukhovnyi truzhenik: A. S. Pushkin v kontekste russkoi kul'tury*. St. Peteresburg: Nauka, 1999.

———, ed. *Khristianstvo i russkaia literatura*. Vols. 1–4. St. Petersburg: Nauka, 1994–2002.

Kraineva, N. I., I. V. Tamontseva, and O. D. Filatova. "Istoriia izdaniia i problemy publikatsii *Poemy bez geroia*." In Anna Akhmatova. *"Ia ne takoi tebia kogda-to znala . . .": Anna Akhmatova. Poema bez Geroia. Proza o Poeme. Nabroski baletnogo libretto: materialy k tvorcheskoi istorii*, 679–798. Ed. N. I. Kraineva. St. Petersburg: Mir, 2009.

Kroth, Anya M. "Androgyny as an Exemplary Feature of Marina Tsvetaeva's Dichotomous Poetic Vision." *Slavic Review* 38 (1979): 563–82.

Kurbanovsky, Alexei. "Malevich's Mystic Signs: From Iconoclasm to New Theology." In *Sacred Stories: Religion and Spirituality in Modern Russia*, 358–76. Ed. Mark D. Steinberg and Heather J. Coleman. Bloomington: Indiana University Press, 2007.

Kuzmin, Mikhail. *Dnevnik 1905–1907*. Ed. N. A. Bogomolov and S. V. Shumikhina. St. Petersburg, 2000.

———. *Dnevnik 1934 goda*. Ed. G. Morev. St. Petersburg: Ivan Limbakha, 1998.

———. "Predislovie." In *Pesn' pesnei*, 5–6. Trans. Lev Iaroshevskii. Vienna, 1921.

———. *Proza*. 3 vols. Ed. Vladimir Markov. Berkeley, Calif.: Berkeley Slavic Specialties, 1984.

———. *Sobranie stikhov*. 3 vols. Ed. John E. Malmstad and Vladimir Markov. Munich: Wilhelm Fink Verlag, 1977–78.

Kuzmin, Mikhail, and Marina Rakhmanova. "O tserkovnom ustave i o tserkovnom penii." In *Muzykal'naia akademiia*, 37–44. 1992.

Langen, Timothy. *The Stony Dance: Unity and Gesture in Andrey Bely's "Petersburg."* Evanston, Ill.: Northwestern University Press, 2005.

The Lenten Triodion. Trans. Mother Mary and Archimandrite Kallistos Ware. Boston: Faber and Faber, 1978.

Levitt, Marcus. *Early Modern Russian Letters: Texts and Contexts*. Boston: Academic Studies, 2009.

Lönnqvist, Barbara. "Rol' maski v russkom modernizme: riazhenye v *Poeme bez geroiia* Akhmatovoi." In *Studia Slavic Finlandensia*. Vol. 15: 104–13. Ed. Jyrki Papinniemi et al. Helsinki, 1998.

Lossky, Vladimir. *The Mystical Theology of the Eastern Church*. Crestwood, N.Y.: St. Vladimir's Seminary, 1976.

Louth, Andrew. "The Theology of the *Philokalia*." In *Abba: The Tradition of Orthodoxy in the West; Festschrift for Bishop Kallistos (Ware) of Diokleia*, 351–62. Ed. John Behr et al. Crestwood, N.Y.: St. Vladimir's Seminary, 2003.

Makin, Michael. *Marina Tsvetaeva: Poetics of Appropriation*. Oxford: Clarendon, 1993.

———. *Nikolai Klyuev: Time and Text, Place and Poet*. Evanston, Ill.: Northwestern University Press, 2009.

Mal'chukova, T. G. *Antichnye i khristianskie traditsii v poezii A. S. Pushkina*. Petrozavodsk: Izdatel'stvo Petrozavodskogo universiteta, 1997.

Mallarmé, Stéphane. "Les Fleurs." In *Collected Poems and Other Verse*. Trans. E. H. Blackmore and A. M. Blackmore. New York: Oxford University Press, 2006.

Malmstad, John E., ed. *Studies in the Life and Works of Mixail Kuzmin*. *Wiener Slawistischer Almanach*, special volume 24. Vienna, 1989.

———. "'You Must Remember This': Memory's Shorthand in a Late Poem of Kuzmin." In *Studies in the Life and Works of Mikhail Kuzmin*, 115–40. Ed. John E. Malmstad. Vienna, 1989.

Malmstad, John, and Nikolay Bogomolov. *Mikhail Kuzmin: A Life in Art*. Cambridge, Mass.: Harvard University Press, 1999.

Mandel'shtam, Osip. *Sochinenii v dvukh tomakh*. Moscow: Khudozhestvennaia literatura, 1990.

Mantzaridis, John. *The Deification of Man: St. Gregory Palamas and the Orthodox Tradition*. Crestwood, N.Y.: St. Vladimir's Seminary, 1984.

Masing-Delic, Irene. *Abolishing Death: A Salvation Myth in Russian Twentieth Century Literature*. Stanford, Calif.: Stanford University Press, 1992.

Matich, Olga. *Erotic Utopia: The Decadent Imagination in Russia's Fin de Siècle*. Madison: University of Wisconsin Press, 2005.

———. *Paradox in the Religious Poetry of Zinaida Gippius*. Munich: Wilhelm Fink Verlag, 1972.

McGuckin, John Anthony. *The Transfiguration of Christ in Scripture and Tradition*. Lewiston, N.Y.: Edwin Mellen, 1986.

McQuillen, Colleen. *The Modernist Masquerade: Stylizing Life, Literature and Costumes in Russia*. Madison: University of Wisconsin Press, 2013.

Medzhibovskaya, Inessa. *Tolstoy and the Religious Culture of His Time: A Biography of a Long Conversion, 1845–1887*. Lanham, Md.: Lexington Books, 2008.

Meerson, Michael Aksionov. *The Trinity of Love in Modern Russian Theology: The Love Paradigm and the Retrieval of Western Medieval Love Mysticism in Modern Russian Trinitarian Thought (from Solovyov to Bulgakov)*. Quincy, Ill.: Franciscan, 1998.

Meerson, Ol'ga. *Personalizm kak poetika: Literaturnyi mir glazami ego obitatelei*. St. Petersburg: Izdatel'stvo 'Pushkinskii Dom,' 2009.

Melling, David J. "Andrew of Crete." In *The Blackwell Dictionary of Eastern Christianity*, 28. Ed. Ken Parry et al. Malden, Mass.: Blackwell, 2001.

________. "Ode." In *The Blackwell Dictionary of Eastern Christianity*, 351. Ed. Ken Parry et al. Malden, Mass.: Blackwell, 2001.

Melling, David J., and Archimandrite Ephrem. "Cherubikon." In *The Blackwell Dictionary of Eastern Christianity*, 117. Ed. Ken Parry et al. Malden, Mass.: Blackwell, 2001.

Men', Aleksandr. *Tainstvo, slovo i obraz*. Leningrad: Ferro-Logas, 1991.

Merezhkovskii, Dmitrii. *Polnoe sobranie sochinenii Dmitriia Sergeevicha Merezhkovskogo*. Moscow: Tipographiia I. D. Sytina, 1914.

Meyendorff, John. *Byzantine Theology: Historical Trends and Doctrinal Themes*. New York: Fordham University Press, 1983.

Michelson, Patrick Lally. "Slavophile Religious Thought and the Dilemma of Russian Modernity, 1830–1860." *Modern Intellectual History* 7, no. 2 (2010): 239–67.

Michelson, Patrick Lally, and Judith Deutsch Kornblatt, eds. *Thinking Orthodox in Modern Russia: Culture, History, Context*. Madison: University of Wisconsin Press, 2014.

Minię (Menaion). Kiev: Kievan Cave Lavra, 1893. Reprinted Moscow: Pravilo very, 1996. 12 vols.

Mints, Z. G. *Poetika Aleksandra Bloka*. St. Petersburg: Iskusstvo-SPB, 1999.

Mochulsky, Konstantin. *Dostoevsky: His Life and Work*. Princeton, N.J.: Princeton University Press, 1973.

Mondzain, Marie-José. *Image, Icon, Economy: The Byzantine Origins of the Contemporary Imaginary*. Trans. Rico Franses. Stanford, Calif.: Stanford University Press, 2005.

Morrison, Simon. *Russian Opera and the Symbolist Movement*. Berkeley: University of California Press, 2002.

Muckle, James. *Nikolai Leskov and the "Spirit of Protestantism."* Birmingham, Eng.: University of Birmingham Press, 1978.

Neher, André, and Renée Neher. *Histoire biblique du peuple d'Israel*. Paris: Jean Maisonnneuve, 1998.

Nes, Solrunn. *The Uncreated Light: An Iconographical Study of the Transfiguration in the Eastern Church*. Grand Rapids, Mich.: Wm. B. Eerdmans, 2007.

Obatnin, Gennadii. *Ivanov-Mistik: Okkul'tnye motivy v poezii i proze Viacheslava Ivanova*. Moscow: Novoe Literaturnoe Obozrenie, 2000.

Origen. *The Song of Songs: Commentary and Homilies*. Trans. R. P. Lawson. London: Longmans, Green, 1957.

Paloff, Benjamin. "The God Function in Joseph Brodsky and Olga Sedakova." *Slavic and East European Journal* 51, no. 4 (2007): 716–36.

Pankenier, Sara. "Reborn in a Reappropriation of Creation: Marina Tsvetaeva's 'Po nagoriiam.'" *Slavic and East European Journal* 48, no. 4 (2004): 607–26.

Panova, L. G. *Russkii Egipet: Aleksandriiskaia poetika Mikhaila Kuzmina*. Moscow: Volodei, 2006.

Paperno, Irina. "On the Nature of the Word: Theological Sources of Mandel'stam's Dialogue with the Symbolists." In *Christianity and the Eastern Slavs*, vol. 2, *Russian Culture in Modern Times*, 287–310. Ed. Boris Gasparov et al. Berkeley: University of California Press, 1994.

———. *Stories of the Soviet Experience: Memoirs, Diaries, Dreams*. Ithaca, N.Y.: Cornell University Press, 2009.

Paperno, Irina, and Joan Delaney Grossman, eds. *Creating Life: The Aesthetic Utopia of Russian Modernism*. Stanford, Calif.: Stanford University Press, 1994.

Parry, Ken, et al., eds. *The Blackwell Dictionary of Eastern Christianity*. Malden, Mass.: Blackwell, 2004.

Pasternak, Boris. *Doctor Zhivago*. Trans. Max Hayward and Manya Harari. New York: Pantheon Books, 1991.

———. *Sobranie sochinenii v piati tomakh*. Vol. 3. Moscow: Khudozhestvennaia literatura, 1990.

Pattison, George, and Diane Thompson, eds. *Dostoevsky and the Christian Tradition*. Cambridge, Eng.: Cambridge University Press, 2001.

Pentcheva, Bissera V. *The Sensual Icon: Space, Ritual, and the Senses in Byzantium*. University Park: Penn State University Press, 2010.

The Pentecostarion. Boston: Holy Transfiguration Monastery, 1990.

Polonsky, Rachel. *English Literature and the Russian Aesthetic Renaissance*. Cambridge, Eng.: Cambridge University Press, 2006.

Pratt, Sarah. *Nikolai Zabolotsky: Enigma and Cultural Paradigm*. Evanston, Ill.: Northwestern University Press, 2000.

———. *Russian Metaphysical Romanticism: The Poetry of Tiutchev and Boratynskii*. Stanford, Calif.: Stanford University Press, 1984.

Presto, Jenifer. *Beyond the Flesh: Alexander Blok, Zinaida Gippius, and the Symbolist Sublimation of Sex*. Madison: University of Wisconsin Press, 2008.

Pseudo-Dionysius. *The Celestial Hierarchy*. In *The Complete Works*, 143–91. Trans. Colm Luibheid. New York: Paulist, 1987.

Pyman, Avril. "The Church and the Intelligentsia with Special Reference to the Religious-Philosophical Meetings in St. Petersburg, 1901–1903." In *Russian Thought and Society, 1800–1917: Essays in Honor of Eugene Lampert*. Ed. Roger Bartlett. Keele: University of Keele Press, 1984.

———. *The Life of Alexander Blok*. Vol. 1, *The Distant Thunder, 1880–1908*. New York: Oxford University Press, 1979; and Vol. 2, *The Release of Harmony, 1908–1921*. New York: Oxford University Press, 1980.

———. *Pavel Florensky: A Quiet Genius; The Tragic and Extraordinary Life of Russia's Unknown Da Vinci*. New York: Continuum, 2010.

———. "Tvorchestvo Aleksandra Bloka v otsenke russkikh religioznykh myslitelei 20–30-kh godov." In *Blokovskii sbornik 12*, 54–70. Tartu: Its-Garant, 1993.

Raevsky-Hughes, Olga. "Liturgicheskoe vremia i evkharistiia v romane Pasternaka *Doktor Zhivago*." In Boris Gasparov et al., eds., *Christianity and the Eastern Slavs*, vol. 3, *Russian Literature in Modern Times*, 302–24. Berkeley: University of California Press, 1995.

Ram, Harsha. *The Imperial Sublime: A Russian Poetics of Empire*. Madison: University of Wisconsin Press, 2003.

Reeder, Roberta. *Anna Akhmatova: Poet and Prophet*. New York: St. Martin's, 1994.

Rilke, Rainer Maria. *Gedichte*. Frankfurt: Erster Teil Insel Verlag, 1987.

Robson, Roy. *Old Believers in Modern Russia*. De Kalb: Northern Illinois University Press, 1995.

Rosenthal, Bernice Glatzer. *Dmitri Sergeevich Merezhkovsky and the Silver Age: The Development of a Revolutionary Mentality*. The Hague: Martinus Nijhoff, 1975.

———, ed. *The Occult in Russian and Soviet Culture*. Ithaca, N.Y.: Cornell University Press, 1997.

———. "Russian Religious-Philosophical Renaissance." In *Routledge Encyclopedia of Philosophy*, 422–28. Ed. Edward Craig. New York: 1998.

Rosslyn, Wendy. "'Not a Whiff of a Roman Carnival': Akhmatova's *Poema bez geroia*." In *Russian and Yugoslav Culture in the Age of Modernism*, 69–87. Ed. Cynthia Marsh and Wendy Rosslyn. Nottingham, Eng.: Astra, 1991.

———. *The Prince, the Fool and the Nunnery: The Religious Themes in the Early Poetry of Anna Akhmatova*. Amersham, Eng.: Avebury, 1984.

Rozanov, Vasilii. *Okolo tserkovnykh sten*. Moscow: Respublika, 1995.

Rylkova, Galina. *The Archaeology of Anxiety: The Russian Silver Age and Its Legacy*. Pittsburgh, Pa.: University of Pittsburgh Press, 2007.

Safran, Gabriella. *Rewriting the Jew: Assimilation Narratives in the Russian Empire*. Stanford, Calif.: Stanford University Press, 2002.

Sandler, Stephanie. "Embodied Words: Gender in Cvetaeva's Reading of Puškin." *Slavic and East European Journal* 34, no. 2 (1990): 139–57.

Scherr, Barry. *Russian Poetry: Meter, Rhythm, and Rhyme*. Berkeley: University of California Press, 1986.

Scherrer, Jutta. *Die Petersburger religiös-philosophischen Vereinigungen: Die Entwicklung des religiösen Selbstverständnisses ihrer Intelligencija-Mitglieder (1901–1917)*. Wiesbaden: Harrassowitz, 1973.

Schmemann, Alexander. *Great Lent*. Crestwood, N.Y.: St. Vladimir's Seminary, 1969.

———. *Introduction to Liturgical Theology*. Portland, Maine: American Orthodox, 1966.

Schmidt, Leigh Eric. *Hearing Things: Religion, Illusion, and the American Enlightenment*. Cambridge, Mass.: Harvard University Press, 2000.

Sedakova, Ol'ga. *Moralia: Esse, lektsii, zametki, interv'iu*. Moscow: Universitet Dmitriia Pozharskogo, 2010.

———. "'Ne smertnye, tainstvennye chuvstva' (O khristianstve Pushkina)." *Kontinent* 115 (2003): 364–75.

———. "Nemnogo o poezii: O ee kontse, nachale i prodolzhenii." In *Poetica*. Moscow: Universitet Dmitriia Pozharskogo, 2010.

———. *Perevody*. Moscow: Universitet Dmitriia Pozharskogo, 2010.

———. *Poetika obriada: Pogrebal'naia obriadnost' vostochnykh i iuzhnykh slavian*. Moscow: Indrik, 2004.

———. "Shkatulka s zerkalom: Ob odnom glubinnom motive A. A. Akhmatovoi." *Trudy po znakovym sistemam* 17 (1984): 93–108.

———. *Slovar' trudnykh slov iz bogosluzheniia: Tserkovnoslaviano-russkie paronimy*. Moscow: Greko-latinskii kabinet IU. A. Shichalina, 2008.

———. *Stikhi*. Moscow: Universitet Dmitriia Pozharskogo, 2010.

Seifrid, Thomas. *The Word Made Self: Russian Writings on Language, 1860–1930*. Ithaca, N.Y.: Cornell University Press, 2005.

Sergay, Timothy D. "'Blizhe k suti, k miru Bloka': The *Mise-en-Scène* of Boris Pasternak's 'Hamlet' and Pasternak's Blokian-Christological Ideal." *Russian Review* 64 (2005): 401–21.

Sheehan, Jonathan, "Enlightenment, Religion and the Enigma of Secularization: A Review Essay." *American Historical Review* 108, no. 3 (2003): 1061–80.

Shevelenko, Irina. *Literaturny put' Tsvetaevoi: Ideologiia—poetika—identichnost': Avtor v kontekste epokhi*. Moscow: Novoe literaturnoe obozrenie, 2002.

Shevzov, Vera. *Russian Orthodoxy on the Eve of Revolution*. New York: Oxford University Press, 2003.

Shragin, Boris, and Albert Todd, eds. *Landmarks: A Collection of Essays on the Russian Intelligentsia*. Trans. Marian Schwartz. New York: Karz Howard, 1977.

Sindalovskii, Naum. *Peterburgskii folk'lor*. St. Petersburg: Maksima, 1994.

Slesinski, Robert. *Pavel Florensky: A Metaphysics of Love*. Crestwood, N.Y.: St. Vladimir's Seminary, 1984.

———. "Postmodernity and the Resources of the Christian East." *Essays in Diakonia: Eastern Catholic Theological Reflections*, 37–51. New York: Peter Lang, 1998.

Smith, Oliver. *Vladimir Soloviev and the Spiritualization of Matter*. Boston: Academic Studies, 2011.

(Sobolev), Archbishop Serafim. *Zashchita Sofianskoi eresi protoiereem Sergiem Bulgakovym, pred litsom Archiereiskogo Sobora Russkoi Zarubezhnoi Tserkvi*. Sofia, 1937.

Solovyov, Vladimir. *The Heart of Reality: Essays on Beauty, Love, and Ethics*.

Ed. and trans. Vladimir Wozniuk. Notre Dame, Ind.: University of Notre Dame Press, 2003.

———. *Lectures on Godmanhood*. Trans. Peter Zouboff. London: Dennis Dobson, 1948.

———. *Sobranie sochinenii V. S. Solov'eva*. 12 vols. Brussels: Foyer Oriental Chrétien, 1966.

Spencer, Jerome. "'Soaked in *The Meaning of Love* and *The Kreutzer Sonata*': The Nature of Love in *Doctor Zhivago*." In *"Doctor Zhivago": A Critical Companion*, 76–88. Ed. Edith Clowes. Evanston, Ill.: Northwestern University Press, 1995.

Sperrie, Irmhild Christina. *The Organic Worldview of Nikolai Leskov*. Evanston, Ill.: Northwestern University Press, 2002.

Spira, Andrew. *The Avant-Garde Icon: Russian Avant-Garde Art and the Icon Painting Tradition*. Burlington, Vt.: Lund Humphries, 2008.

Stanton, Leonard. *Interpreting Nikolai Gogol within Russian Orthodoxy: A Neglected Influence on the First Great Russian Novelist*. Lewiston, N.Y.: Edwin Mellen Press, 2006.

Steinberg, Mark D., and Heather J. Coleman, eds. *Sacred Stories: Religion and Spirituality in Modern Russia*. Bloomington: Indiana University Press, 2007.

Strathausen, Carsten. *The Look of Things: Poetry and Vision around 1900*. Chapel Hill: University of North Carolina Press, 2003.

Taruskin, Richard. *Stravinsky and the Russian Traditions: A Biography of the Works*. Vol. 2, *A Biography of the Works through Mavra*. New York: Oxford University Press, 1996.

Tavis, Anna. *Rilke's Russia: A Cultural Encounter*. Evanston, Ill.: Northwestern University Press, 1994.

Taylor, Charles. *A Secular Age*. Cambridge, Mass.: Belknap, 2007.

Ternavtsev, V. A. "Russkaia tserkov' pred velikoiu zadachei," *Novyi put'* (January 1903): 5–22.

Timenchik, R. D. "Neskol'ko primechanii k stat'e T. Tsiv'ian." *Trudy po znakovym sistemam, V: Mif, fol'klor, religiia kak modeliruiushchie sistemy*, 278–80. Tartu, 1971.

Timenchik, R. D., V. N. Toporov, and T. V. Tsiv'ian. "Akhmatova i Kuzmin." *Russian Literature* 6, no. 3 (1978): 213–305.

Toporov, V. N. "Akhmatova i Blok (k probleme postroeniia poeticheskogo dialoga: 'Blokovskii' tekst Akhmatovoi)." *Peterburgskii tekst russkoi literatury*, 372–452. St. Petersburg, 2003.

———. "*Poema bez geroia* v ritual'nom aspekte." In *Anna Akhmatova i russkaia kul'tura nachala XX veka: Tezisy konferentsii*, 15–21. Moscow, 1989.

Torrance, Thomas F. *Space, Time and Incarnation*. New York, 1969.

Trīōd' postnaę. Moscow: Moscow Patriarch, 1992.

Trīōd' tsvětnaę. Moscow: Moscow Patriarch, 1992.

Tsiv'ian, T. V. *Zametki k deshifrovke "Poemy bez geroia": Trudy po znakovym sistemam, V: Mif, fol'klor, religiia kak modeliruiushchie sistemy*, 255–77. Tartu, 1971.

Tsvetaeva, Marina. *Sobranie sochinenii v semi tomakh*. Moscow: Ellis Lak, 1994.

Valliere, Paul. *Modern Russian Theology: Bukharev, Soloviev, Bulgakov: Orthodox Theology in a New Key*. Grand Rapids, Mich.: Wm. B. Eerdmans, 2000.

———. "Sophiology as the Dialogue of Orthodoxy with Modern Civilization." In *Russian Religious Thought*, 176–92. Ed. Judith Deutsch Kornblatt and Richard F. Gustafson. Madison: University of Wisconsin Press, 1996.

Verheul, Kees. "Public Themes in the Poetry of Anna Axmatova." In *Tale without a Hero and Twenty-Two Poems by Anna Axmatova*, by Anna Akhmatova. Paris: Mouton, 1973.

Vilenkin, V. *V sto pervom zerkale*. Moscow: Sovetskii pisatel', 1987.

Von Balthasar, Hans Urs. *Cosmic Liturgy: The Universe According to Maximus the Confessor*. San Francisco: Ignatius, 1988.

Von Gardner, Johann. *Russian Church Singing*. Vol. 1, *Orthodox Worship and Hymnography*. Trans. Vladimir Morosan. Crestwood, N.Y.: St. Vladimir's Seminary, 1980.

Ware, Timothy. *The Orthodox Church*. New York: Penguin, 1991.

Watton, Lindsay F. "Constructs of Sin and Sodom in Russian Modernism, 1906–1909." *Journal of the History of Sexuality*, 4, no. 3 (1994): 369–94.

West, James. *Russian Symbolism: A Study of Vyacheslav Ivanov and the Russian Symbolist Aesthetic*. London: Methuen, 1970.

Witt, Susanna. *Creating Creation: Readings of Pasternak's "Doctor Živago."* Stockholm: Almqvist and Wiksell International, 2000.

Worobec, Christine. *Possessed: Women, Witches and Demons in Imperial Russia*. De Kalb: Northern Illinois University Press, 2001.

Wybrew, Hugh. *Orthodox Feasts of Jesus Christ and the Virgin Mary: Liturgical Texts with Commentary*. Crestwood, N.Y.: St. Vladimir's Seminary, 2000.

———. *Orthodox Lent, Holy Week and Easter: Liturgical Texts with Commentary*. Crestwood, N.Y.: St. Vladimir's Seminary, 1997.

———. *The Orthodox Liturgy: The Development of the Eucharistic Liturgy in the Byzantine Rite*. Crestwood, N.Y.: St. Vladimir's Seminary, 1990.

———. *Risen with Christ: Eastertide in the Orthodox Church (Commentaries and Translation of Liturgical Texts)*. London: Society for Promoting Christian Knowledge, 2001.

Zakharov, V. N. *Evangel'skii tekst v russkoi literature XVIII–XX vekov: Tsitata, reministsentsiia, motiv, siuzhet, zhanr*. Vols. 1–5. Petrozavodsk: Izdatel'stvo Petrozavodskogo universiteta, 1994–2008.

Zernov, Nikolai. *The Russian Religious Renaissance of the Twentieth Century*. New York: Harper and Row, 1963.

Zhirmunskii, V. M. "Anna Akhmatova i Aleksandr Blok." *Russkaia literatura* 3 (Leningrad, 1970): 57–82.

Zhivov, Viktor. "Tserkovnoslavianskaia literaturnaia traditsiia v russkoi literature XVIII v. i retseptsiia spora 'drevnykh' i 'novykh." In *Istoriia kul'tury i poetika*, 62–82. Ed. L. A. Safronova et al. Moscow: Nauka, 1994.

Zholkovsky, Aleksandr. "The Obverse of Stalinism: Akhmatova's Self-Serving Charisma of Selflessness." In *Self and Story in Russian History*, 46–68. Ed. Laura Engelstein and Stephanie Sandler. Ithaca, N.Y.: Cornell University Press, 2000.

Ziolkowski, Margaret. *Hagiography and Modern Russian Literature*. Princeton, N.J.: Princeton University Press, 1988.

Index

Page numbers in *italic* refer to illustrations.